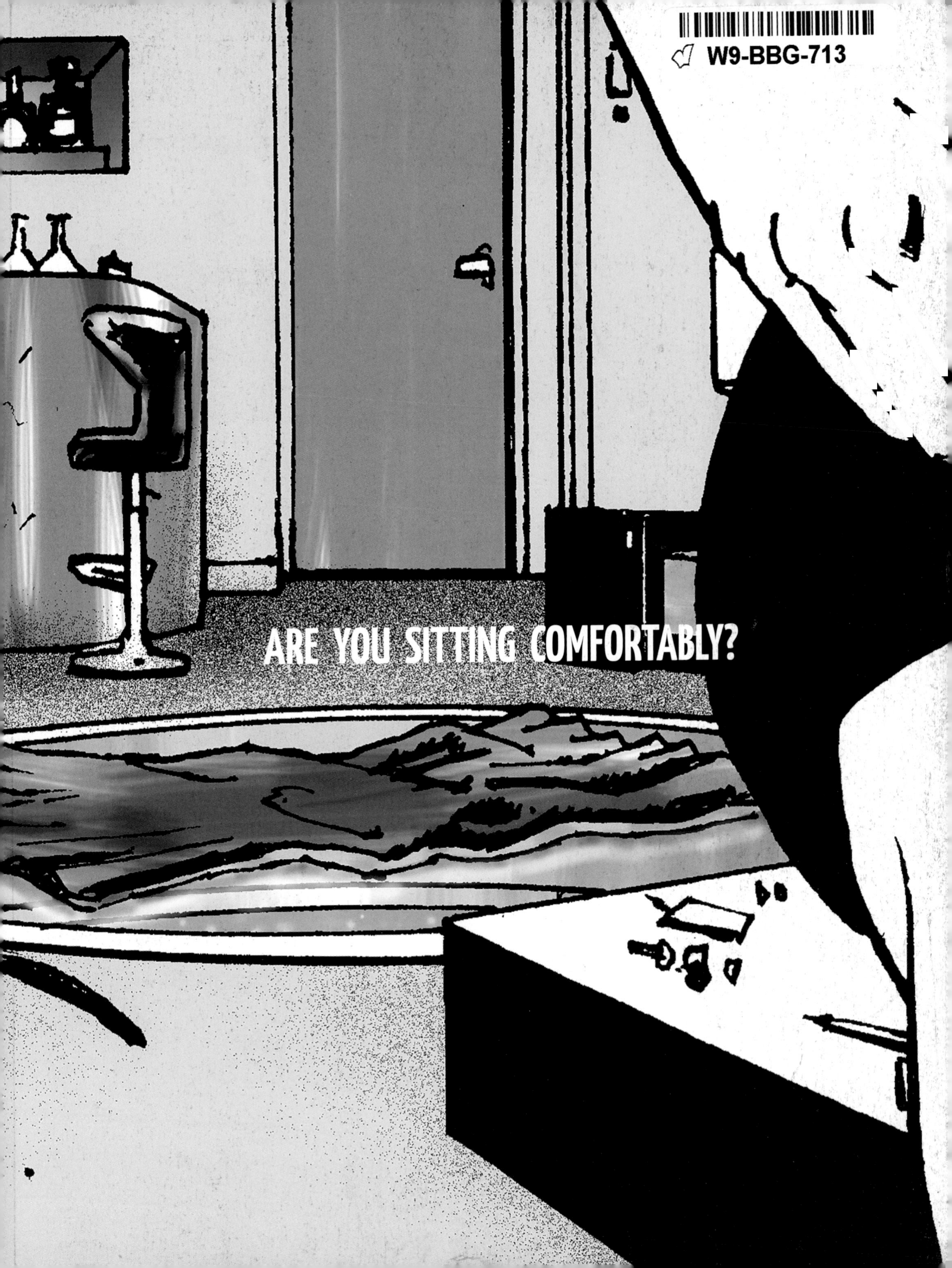
ARE YOU SITTING COMFORTABLY?

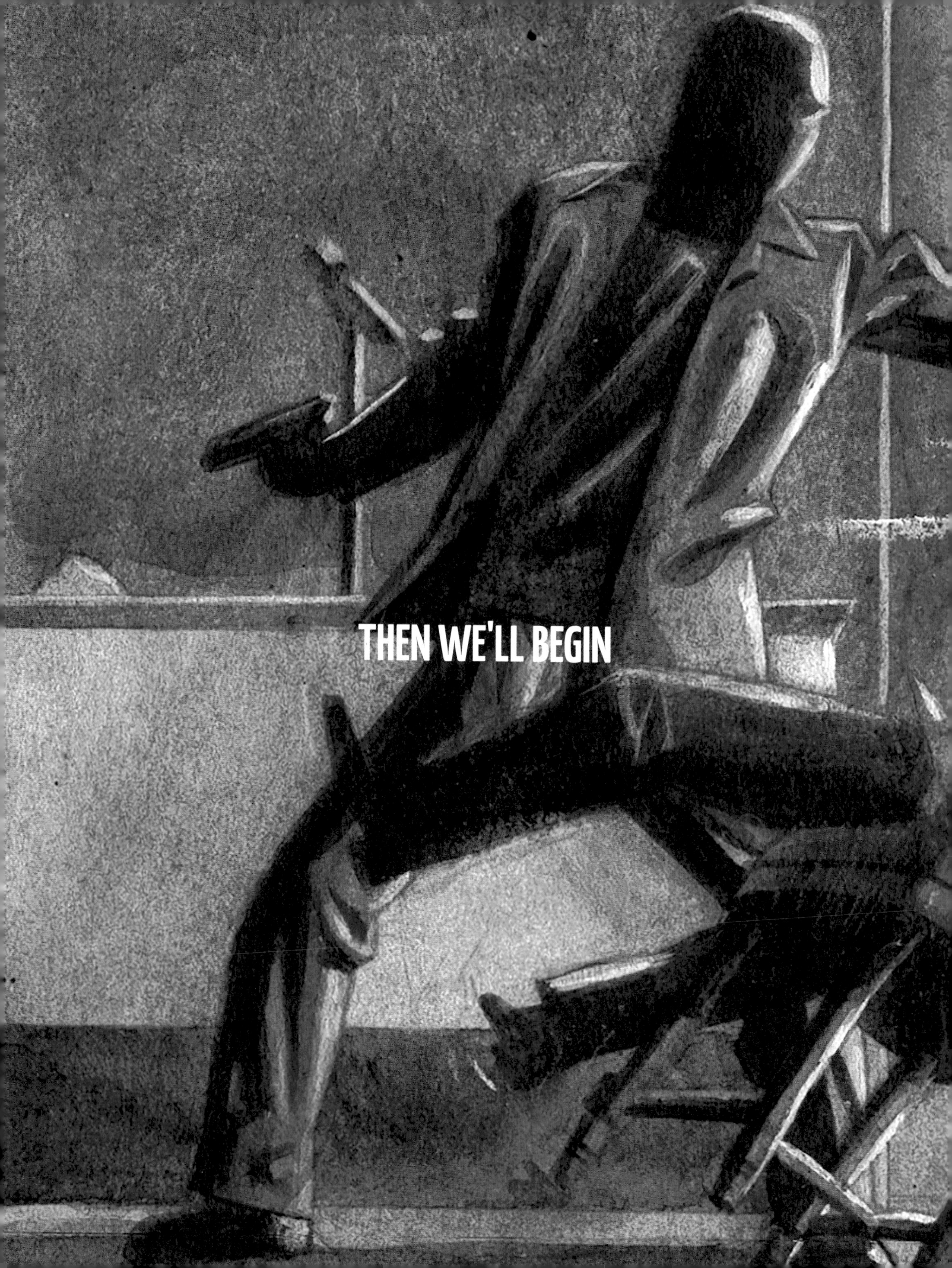
THEN WE'LL BEGIN

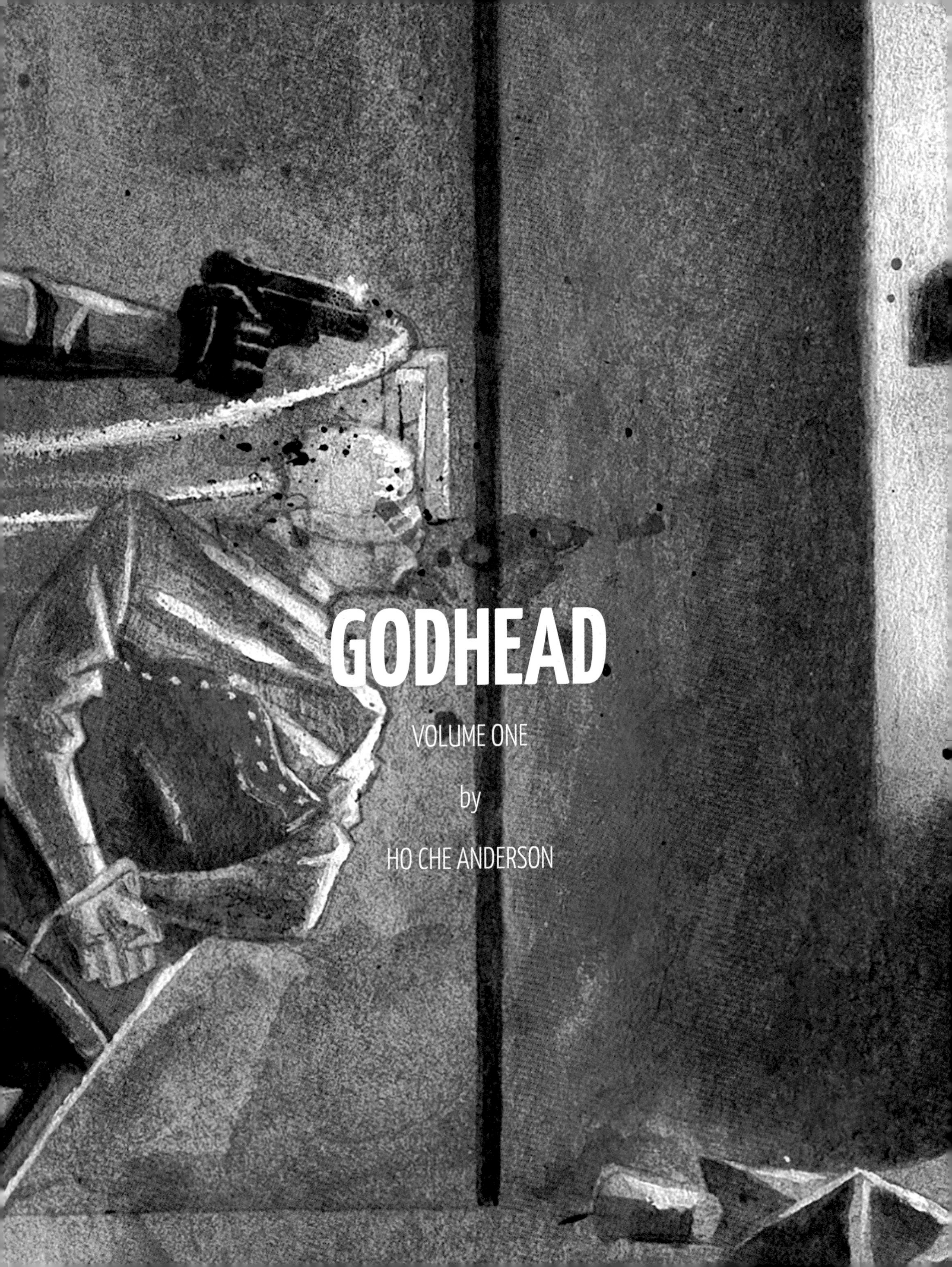

GODHEAD

VOLUME ONE

by

HO CHE ANDERSON

CHAPTER 1 CORPORATE WORLD

HO CHE ANDERSON
WRITER/ARTIST

GARY GROTH
EDITOR

PRESTON WHITE
PRODUCTION

JACQ COHEN
PROMOTIONS

GARY GROTH
ERIC REYNOLDS
PUBLISHERS

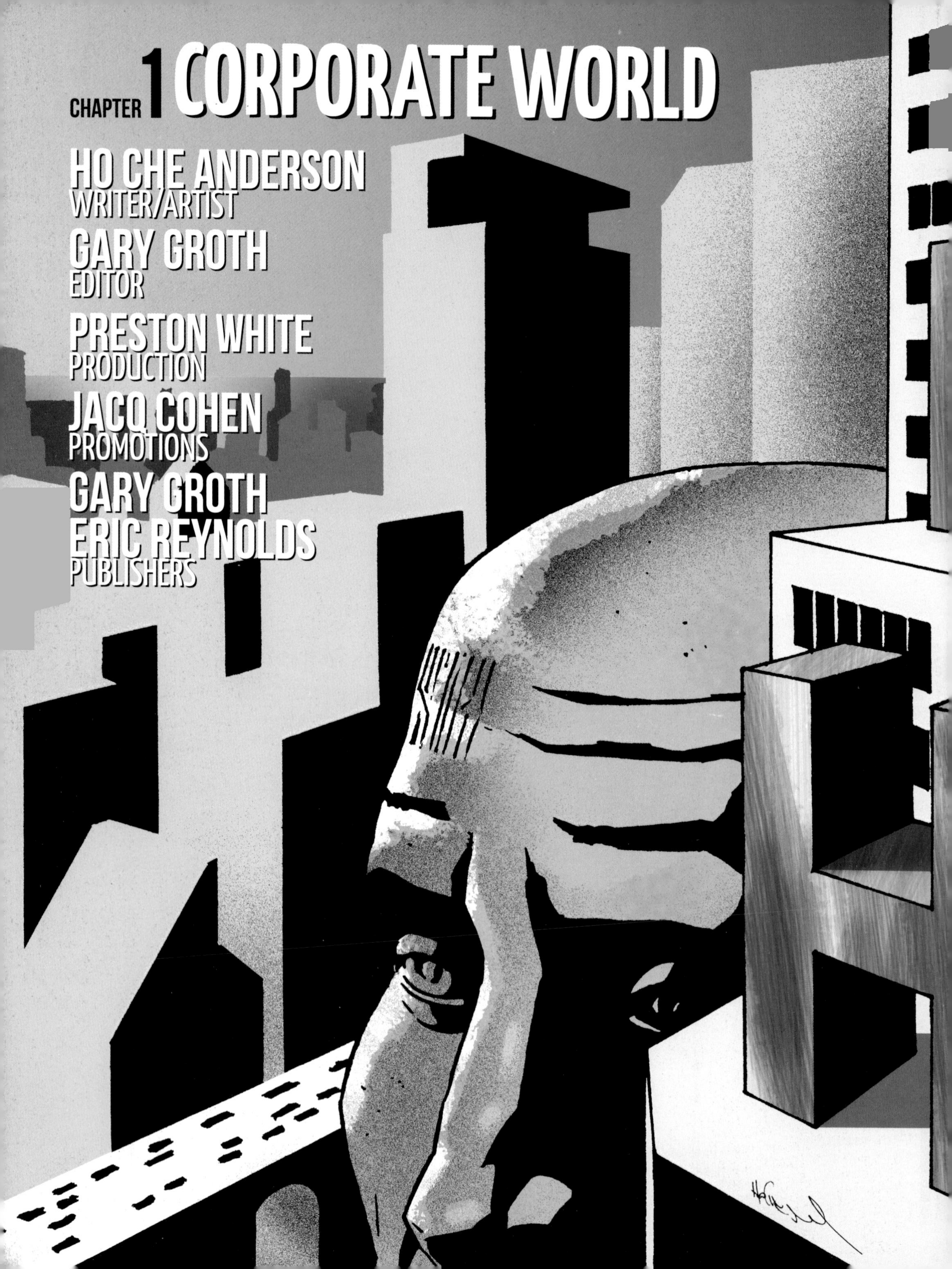

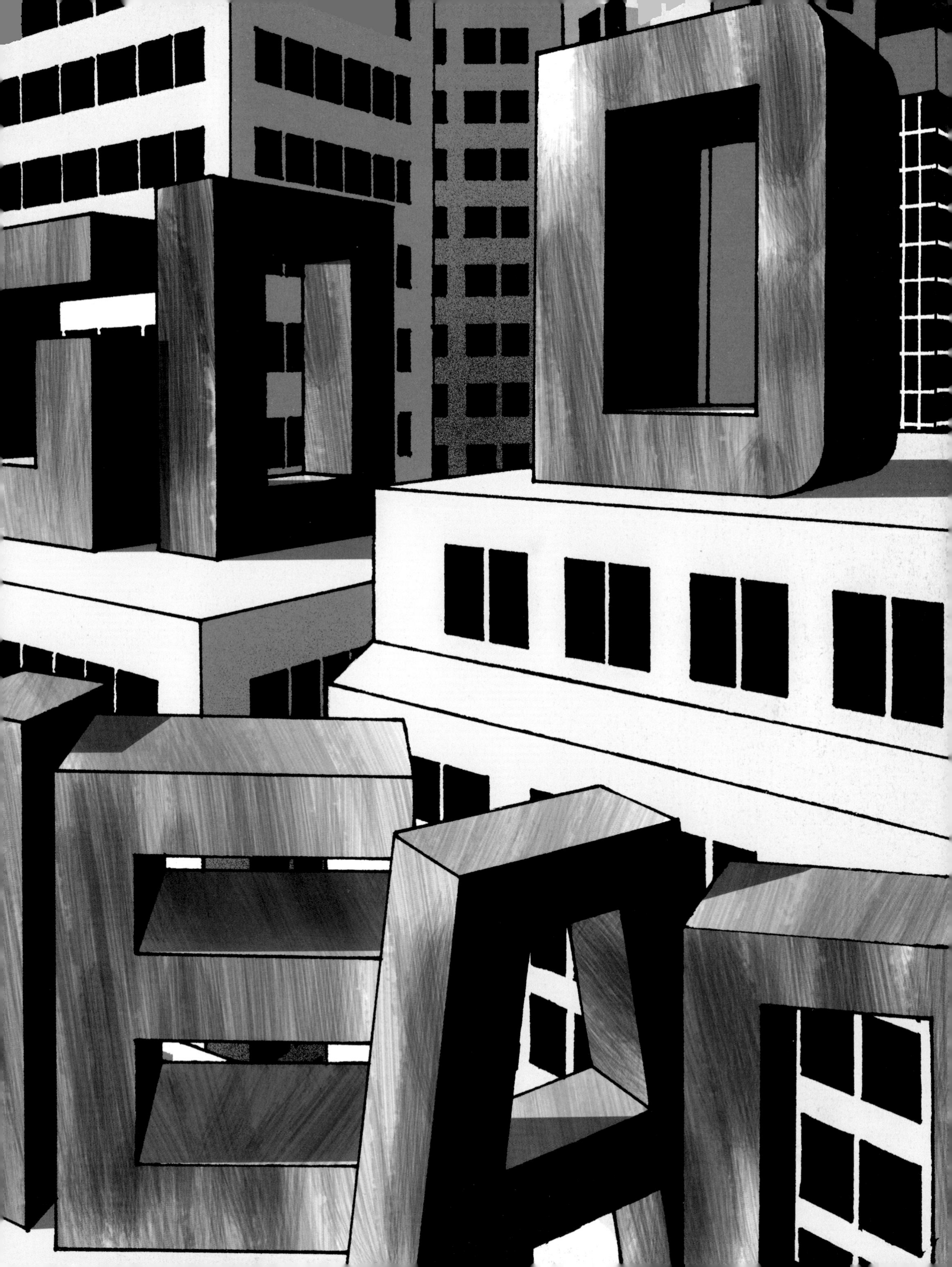

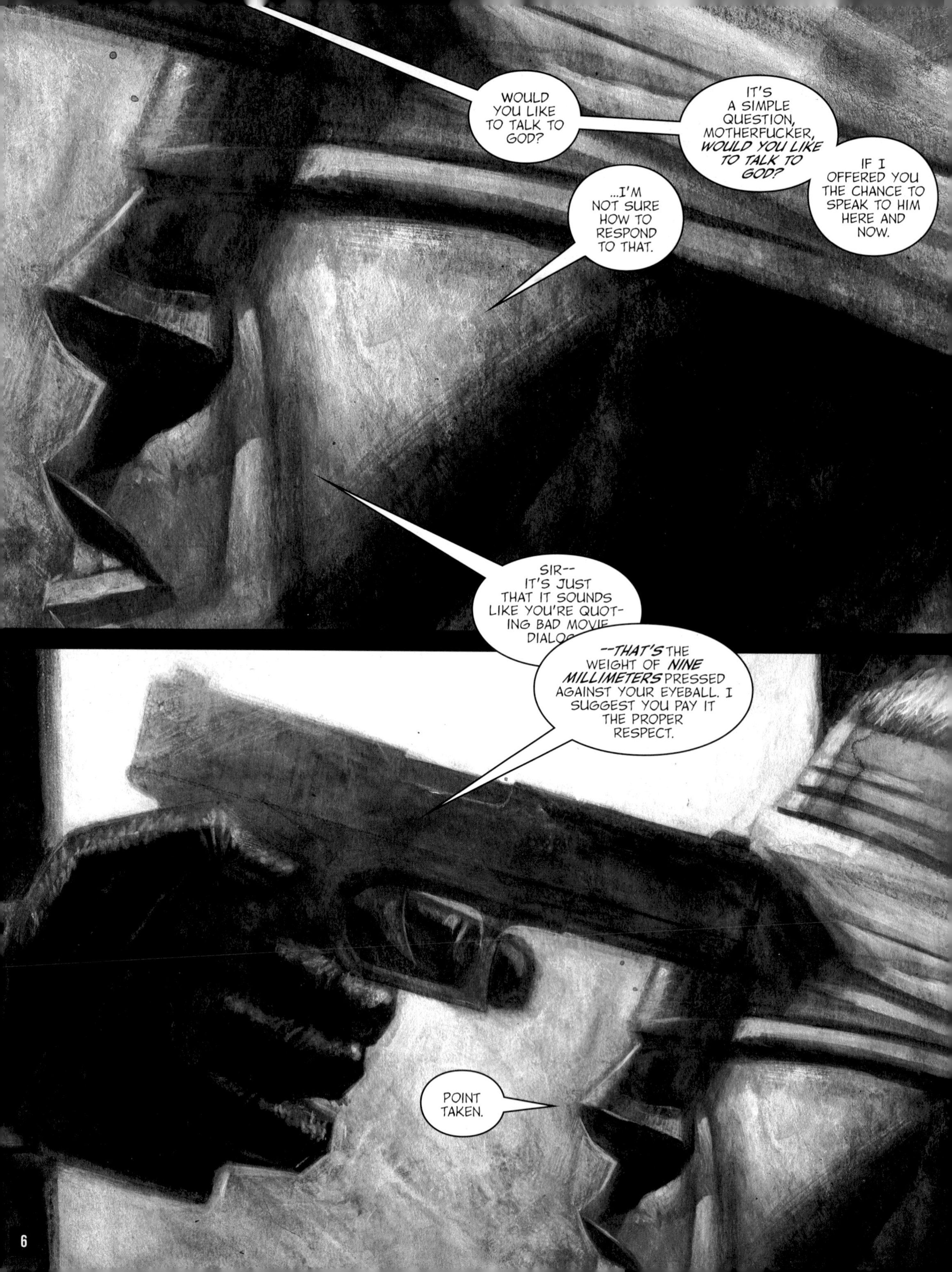
WOULD YOU LIKE TO TALK TO GOD?
IT'S A SIMPLE QUESTION, MOTHERFUCKER, ***WOULD YOU LIKE TO TALK TO GOD?***
IF I OFFERED YOU THE CHANCE TO SPEAK TO HIM HERE AND NOW.
...I'M NOT SURE HOW TO RESPOND TO THAT.
SIR-- IT'S JUST THAT IT SOUNDS LIKE YOU'RE QUOTING BAD MOVIE DIALO
--THAT'S THE WEIGHT OF ***NINE MILLIMETERS*** PRESSED AGAINST YOUR EYEBALL. I SUGGEST YOU PAY IT THE PROPER RESPECT.
POINT TAKEN.

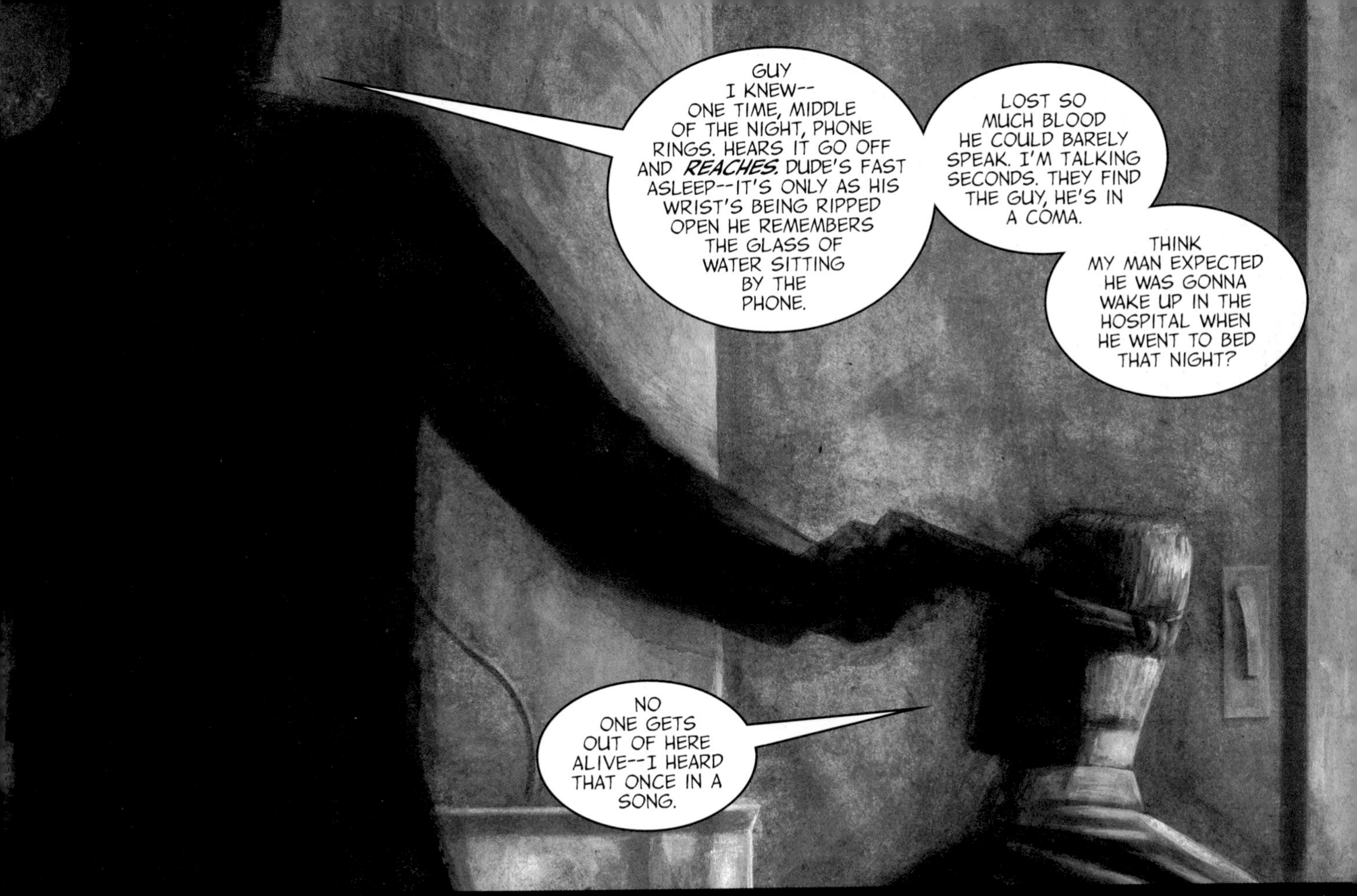
GUY I KNEW-- ONE TIME, MIDDLE OF THE NIGHT, PHONE RINGS. HEARS IT GO OFF AND REACHES. DUDE'S FAST ASLEEP--IT'S ONLY AS HIS WRIST'S BEING RIPPED OPEN HE REMEMBERS THE GLASS OF WATER SITTING BY THE PHONE.
LOST SO MUCH BLOOD HE COULD BARELY SPEAK. I'M TALKING SECONDS. THEY FIND THE GUY, HE'S IN A COMA.
THINK MY MAN EXPECTED HE WAS GONNA WAKE UP IN THE HOSPITAL WHEN HE WENT TO BED THAT NIGHT?
NO ONE GETS OUT OF HERE ALIVE--I HEARD THAT ONCE IN A SONG.
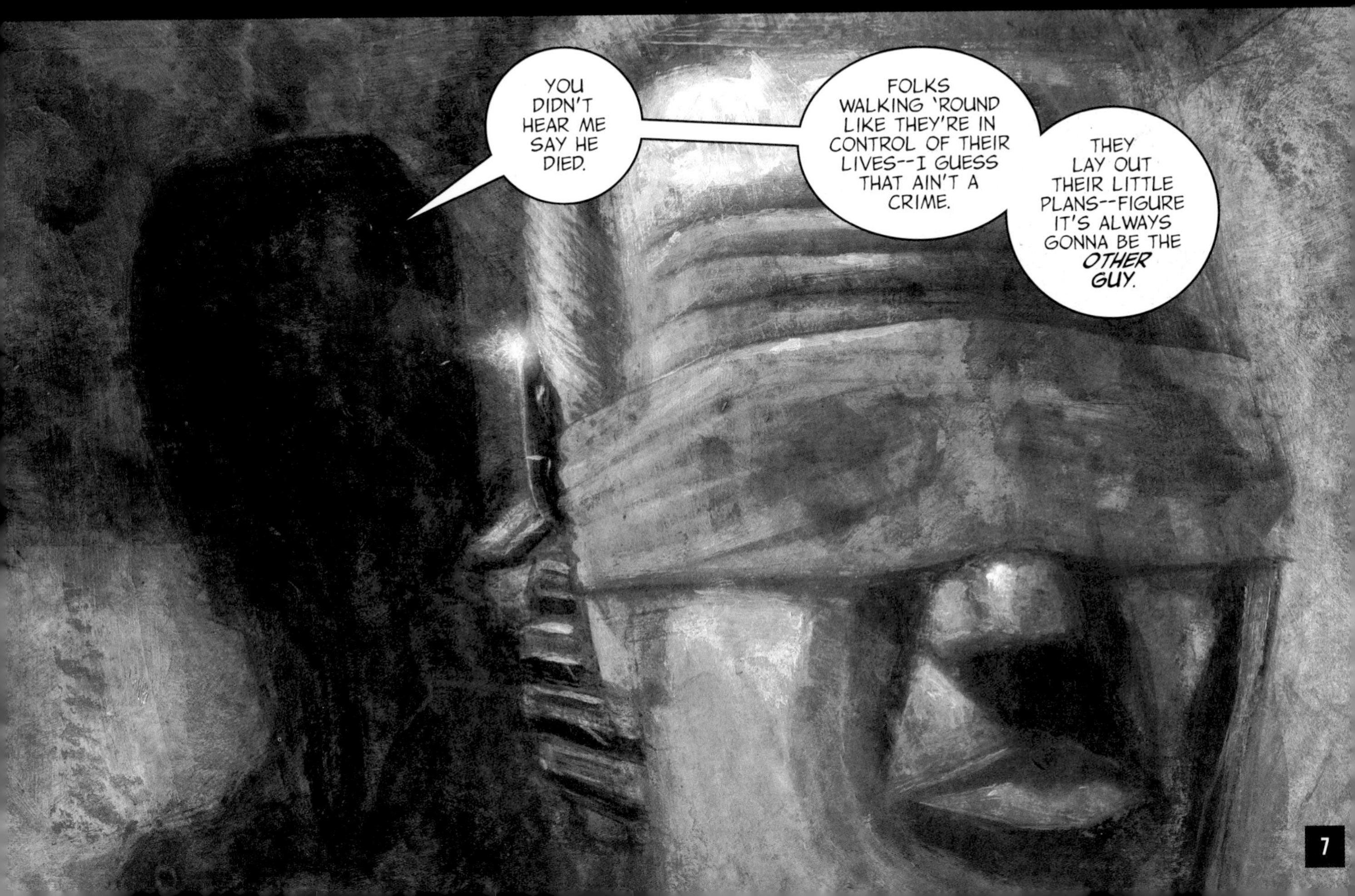
YOU DIDN'T HEAR ME SAY HE DIED.
FOLKS WALKING 'ROUND LIKE THEY'RE IN CONTROL OF THEIR LIVES--I GUESS THAT AIN'T A CRIME.
THEY LAY OUT THEIR LITTLE PLANS--FIGURE IT'S ALWAYS GONNA BE THE OTHER GUY.

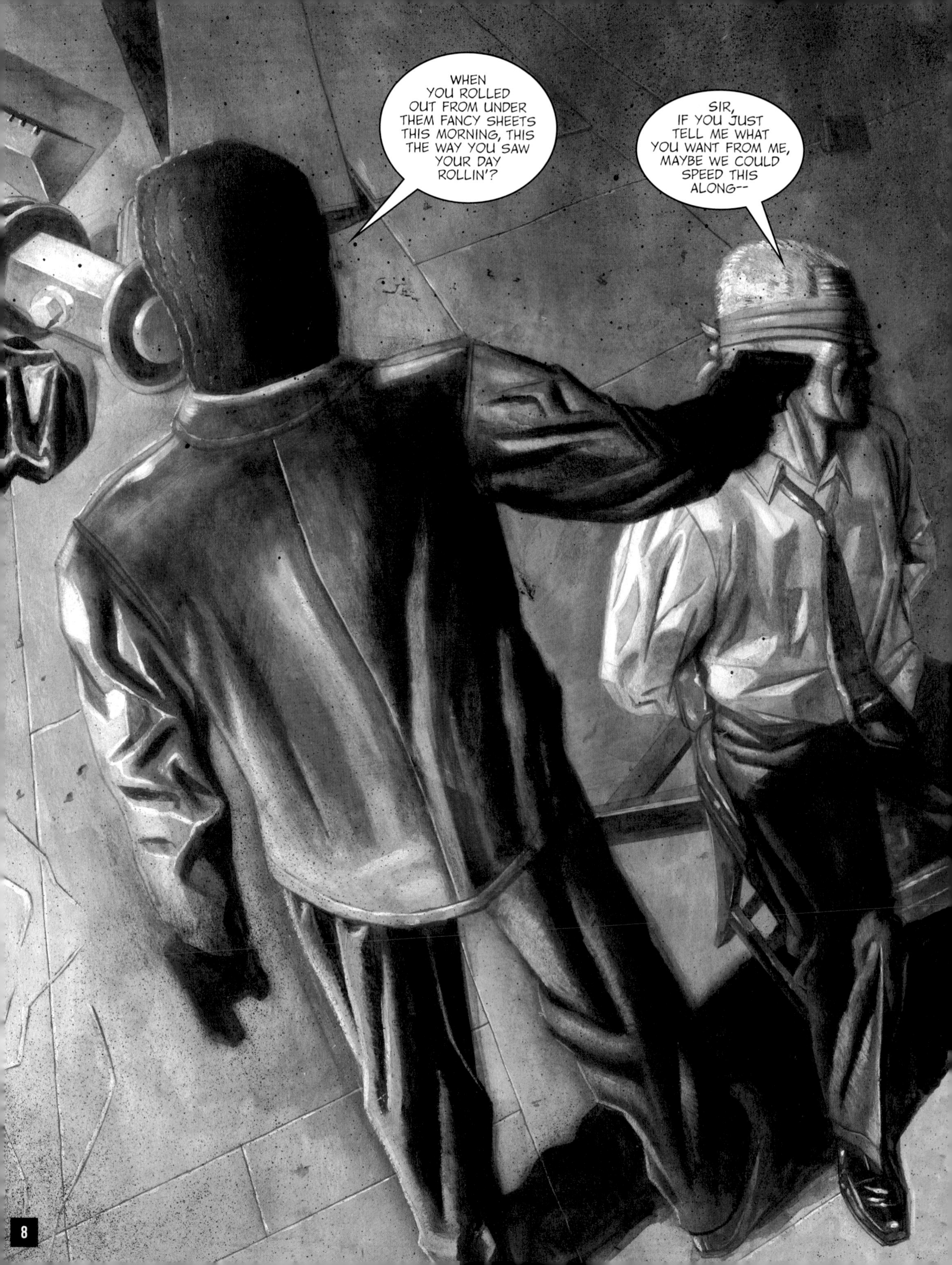
WHEN YOU ROLLED OUT FROM UNDER THEM FANCY SHEETS THIS MORNING, THIS THE WAY YOU SAW YOUR DAY ROLLIN'?
SIR, IF YOU JUST TELL ME WHAT YOU WANT FROM ME, MAYBE WE COULD SPEED THIS ALONG--

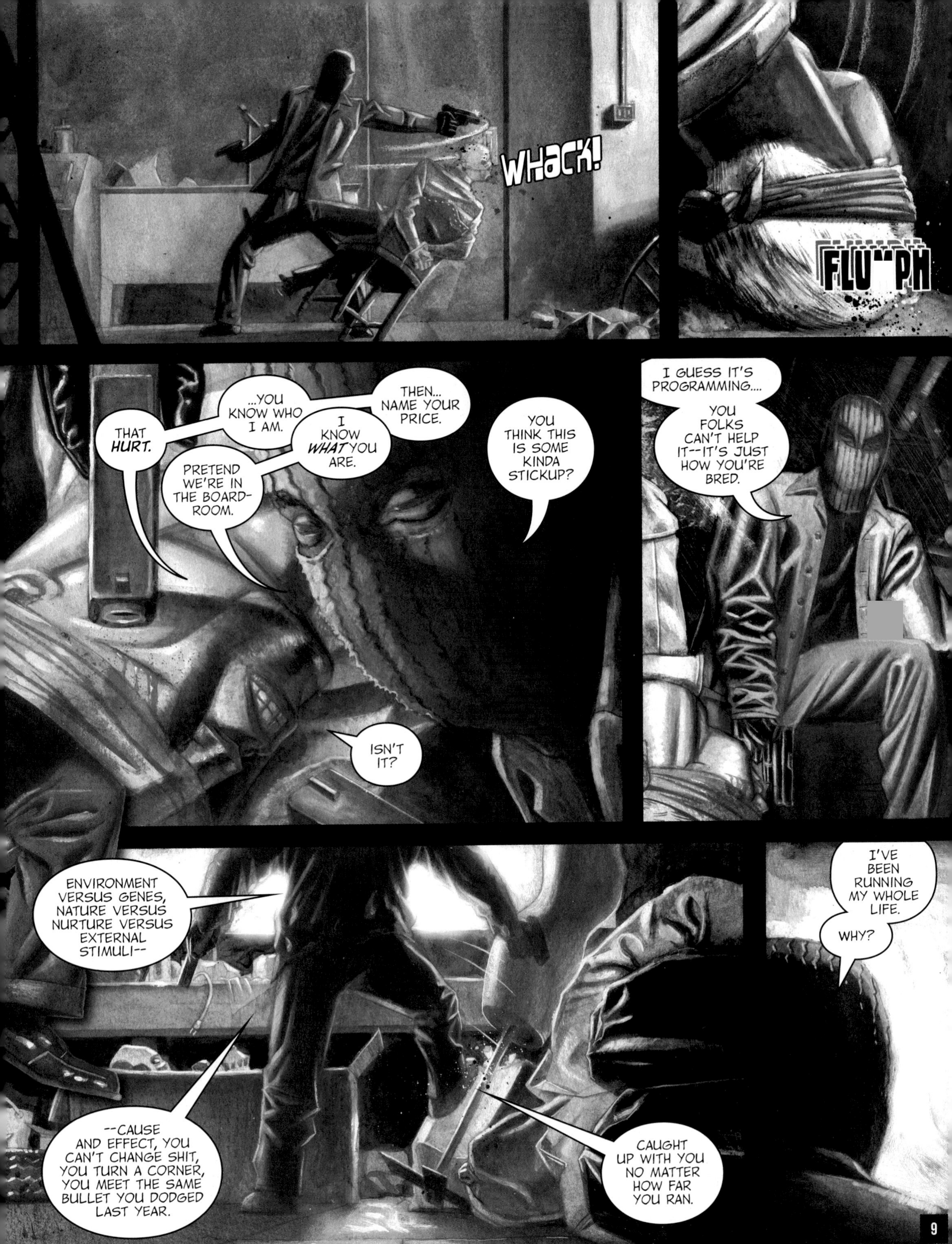
WHACK!
FLUMPH
THAT HURT.
...YOU KNOW WHO I AM.
THEN... NAME YOUR PRICE.
I KNOW WHAT YOU ARE.
PRETEND WE'RE IN THE BOARD-ROOM.
YOU THINK THIS IS SOME KINDA STICKUP?
ISN'T IT?
I GUESS IT'S PROGRAMMING....
YOU FOLKS CAN'T HELP IT--IT'S JUST HOW YOU'RE BRED.
ENVIRONMENT VERSUS GENES, NATURE VERSUS NURTURE VERSUS EXTERNAL STIMULI--
--CAUSE AND EFFECT, YOU CAN'T CHANGE SHIT, YOU TURN A CORNER, YOU MEET THE SAME BULLET YOU DODGED LAST YEAR.
CAUGHT UP WITH YOU NO MATTER HOW FAR YOU RAN.
I'VE BEEN RUNNING MY WHOLE LIFE.
WHY?

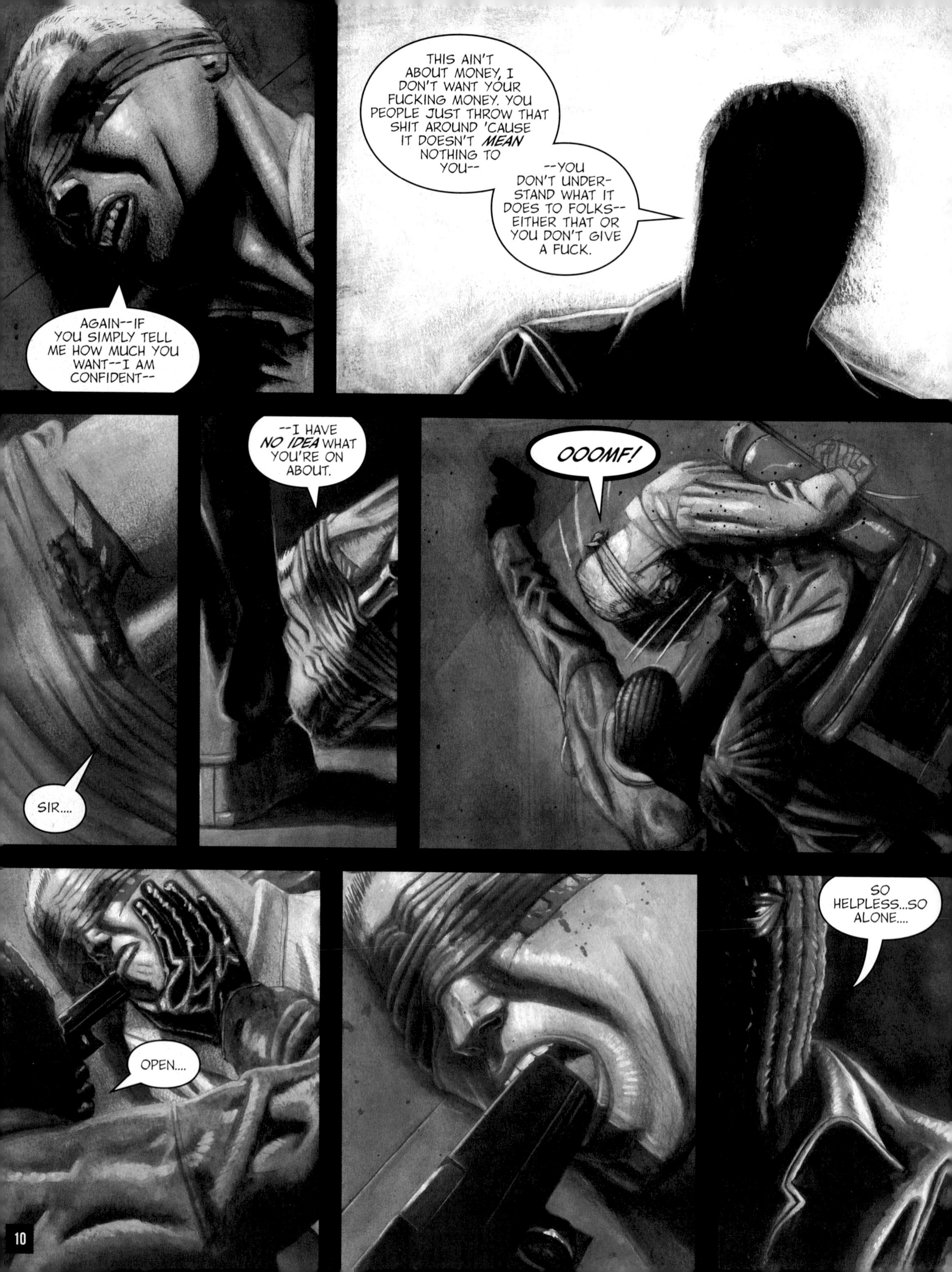
AGAIN--IF YOU SIMPLY TELL ME HOW MUCH YOU WANT--I AM CONFIDENT--
THIS AIN'T ABOUT MONEY, I DON'T WANT YOUR FUCKING MONEY. YOU PEOPLE JUST THROW THAT SHIT AROUND 'CAUSE IT DOESN'T *MEAN* NOTHING TO YOU--
--YOU DON'T UNDER-STAND WHAT IT DOES TO FOLKS--EITHER THAT OR YOU DON'T GIVE A FUCK.
SIR....
--I HAVE *NO IDEA* WHAT YOU'RE ON ABOUT.
OOOMF!
OPEN....
SO HELPLESS...SO ALONE....

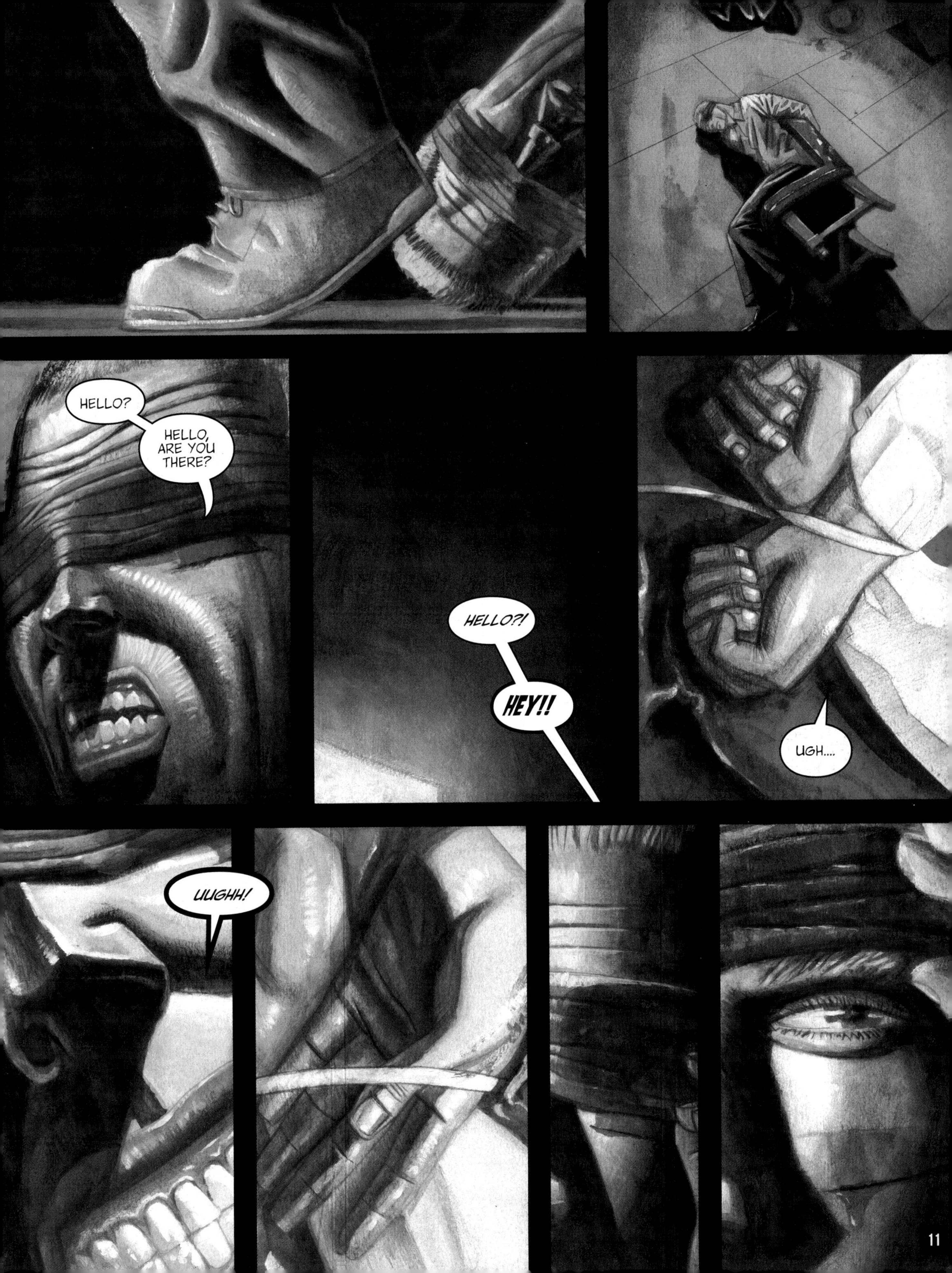
HELLO?
HELLO, ARE YOU THERE?
HELLO?!
HEY!!
UGH....
UUGHH!

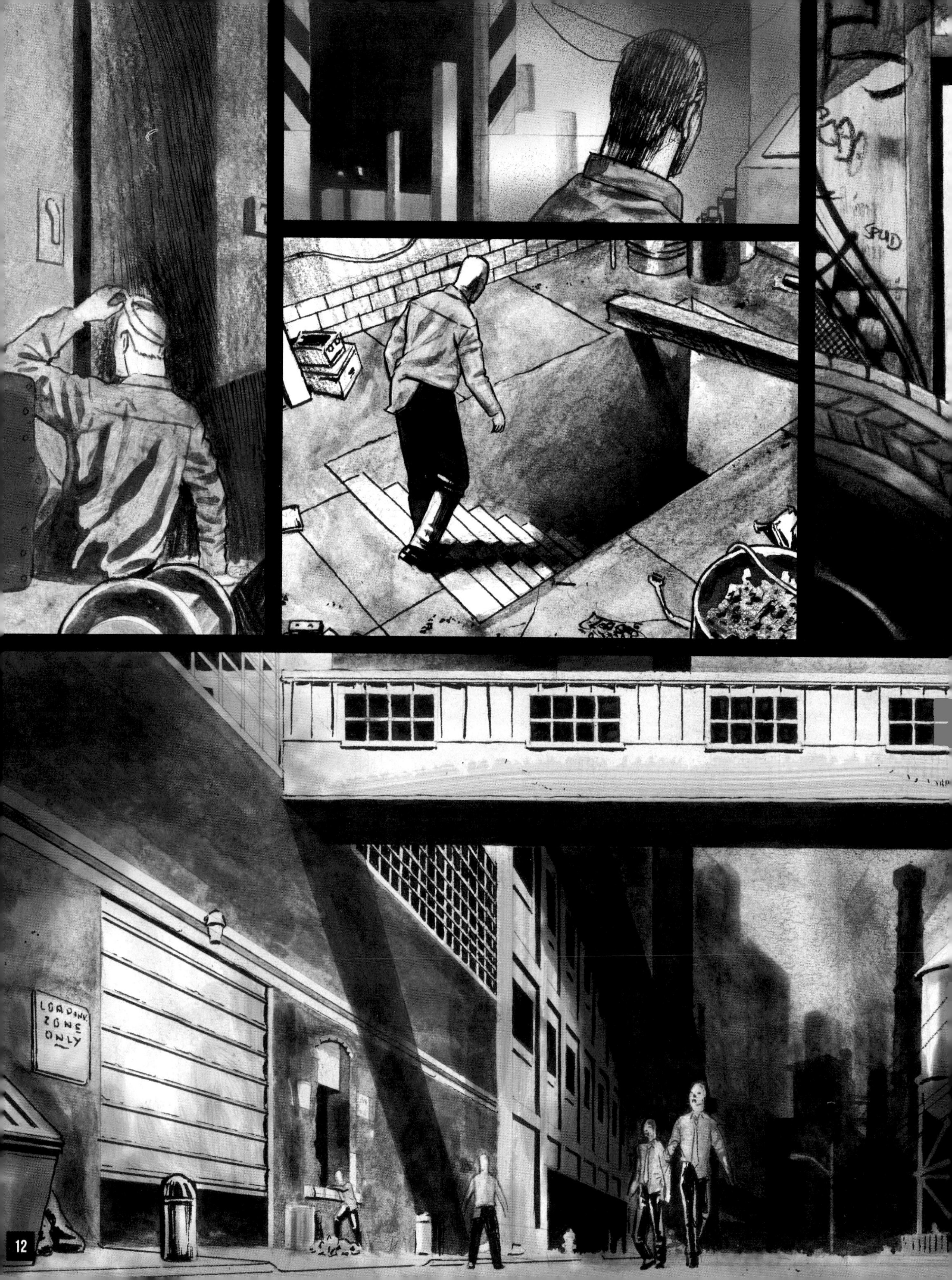

SPUD
LOADING ZONE ONLY

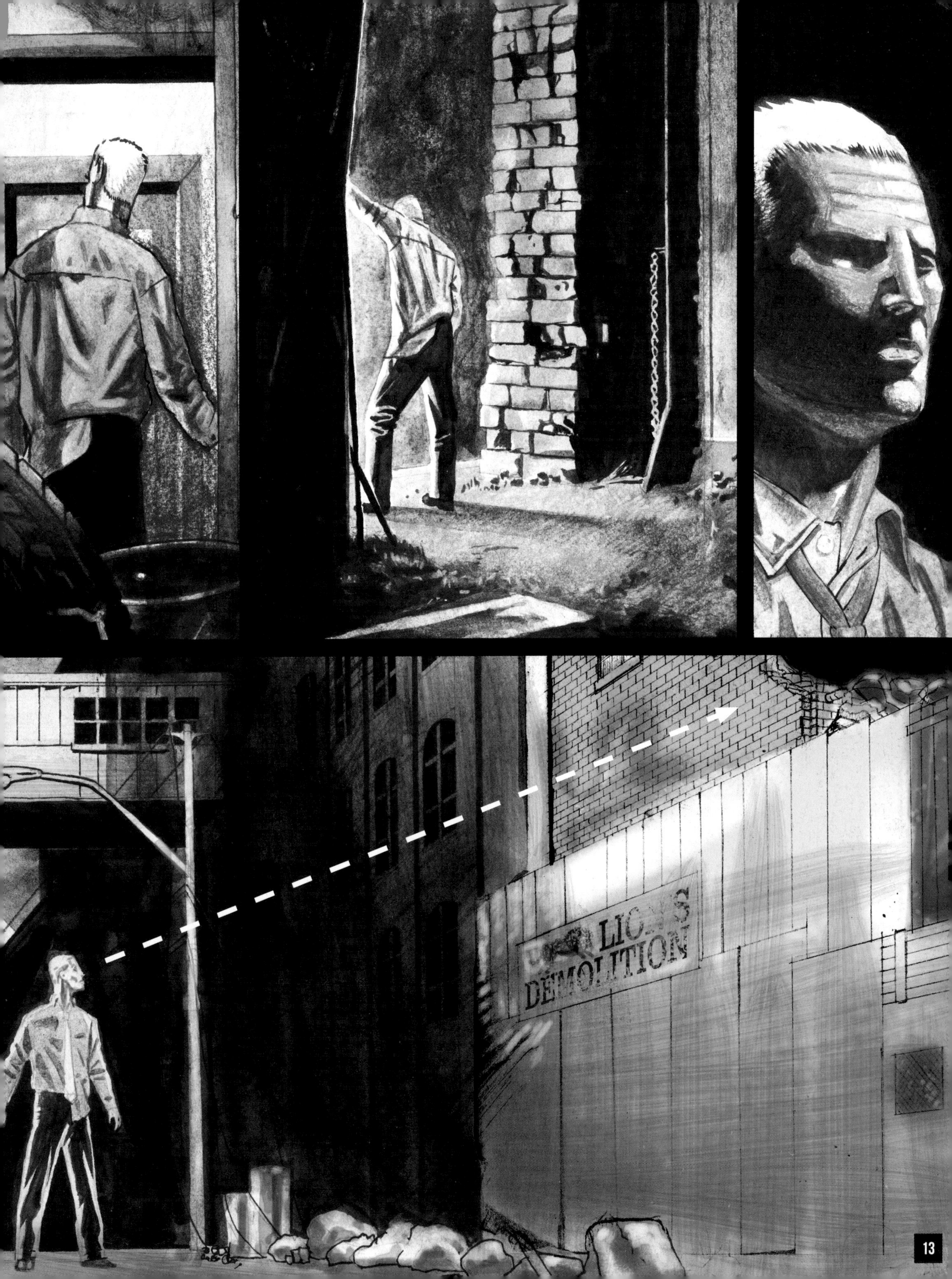
LIONS
DEMOLITION

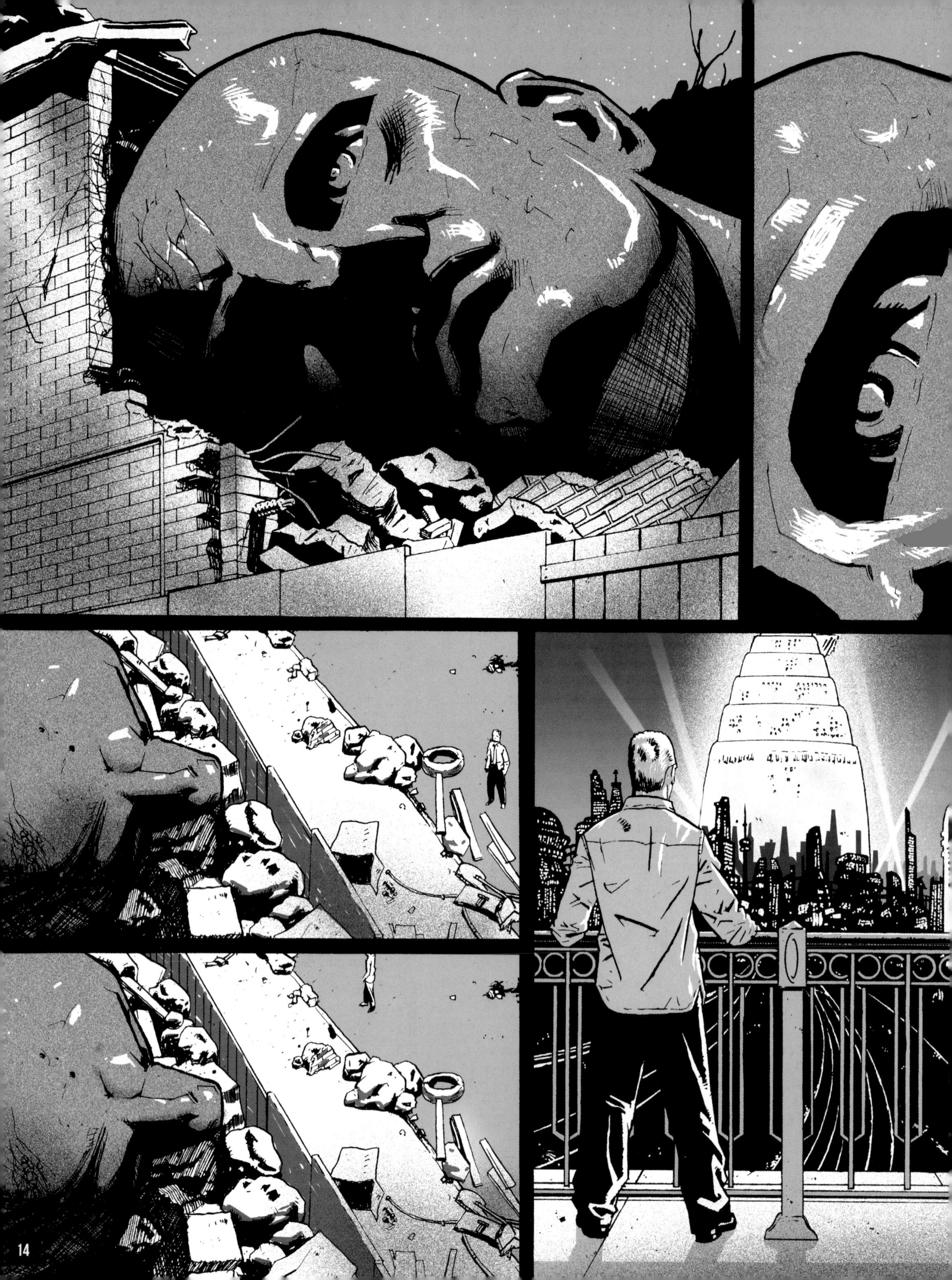

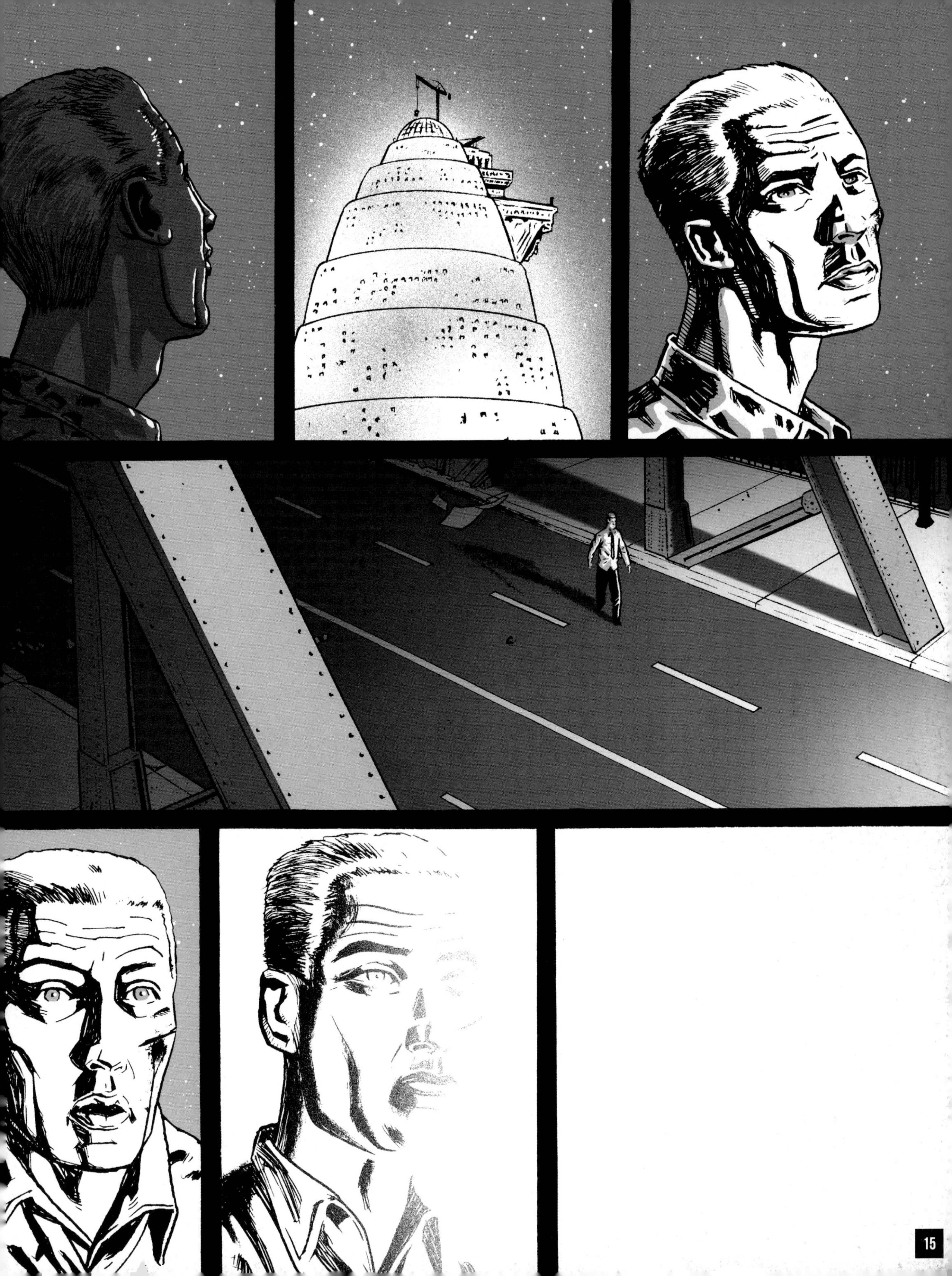

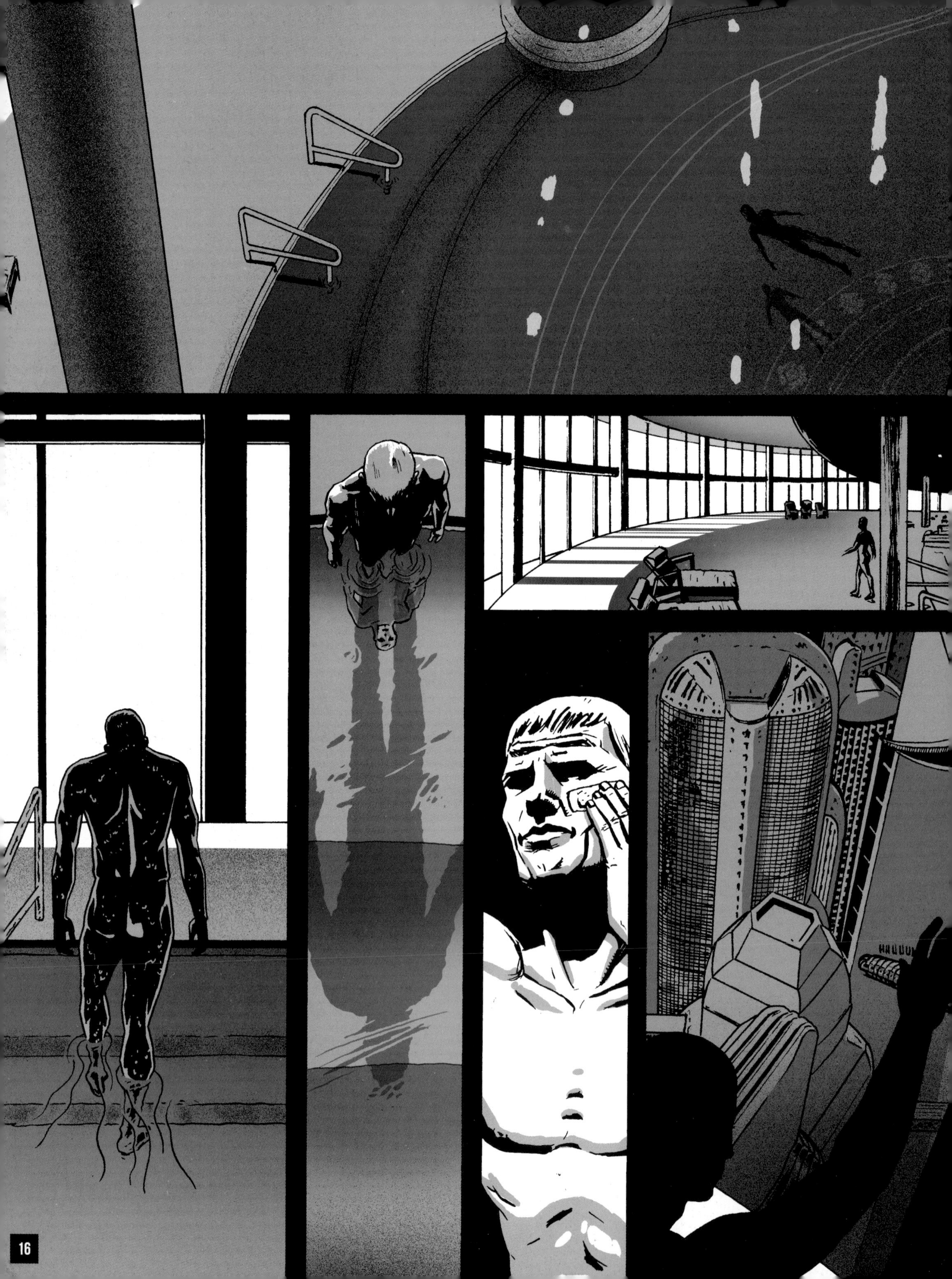

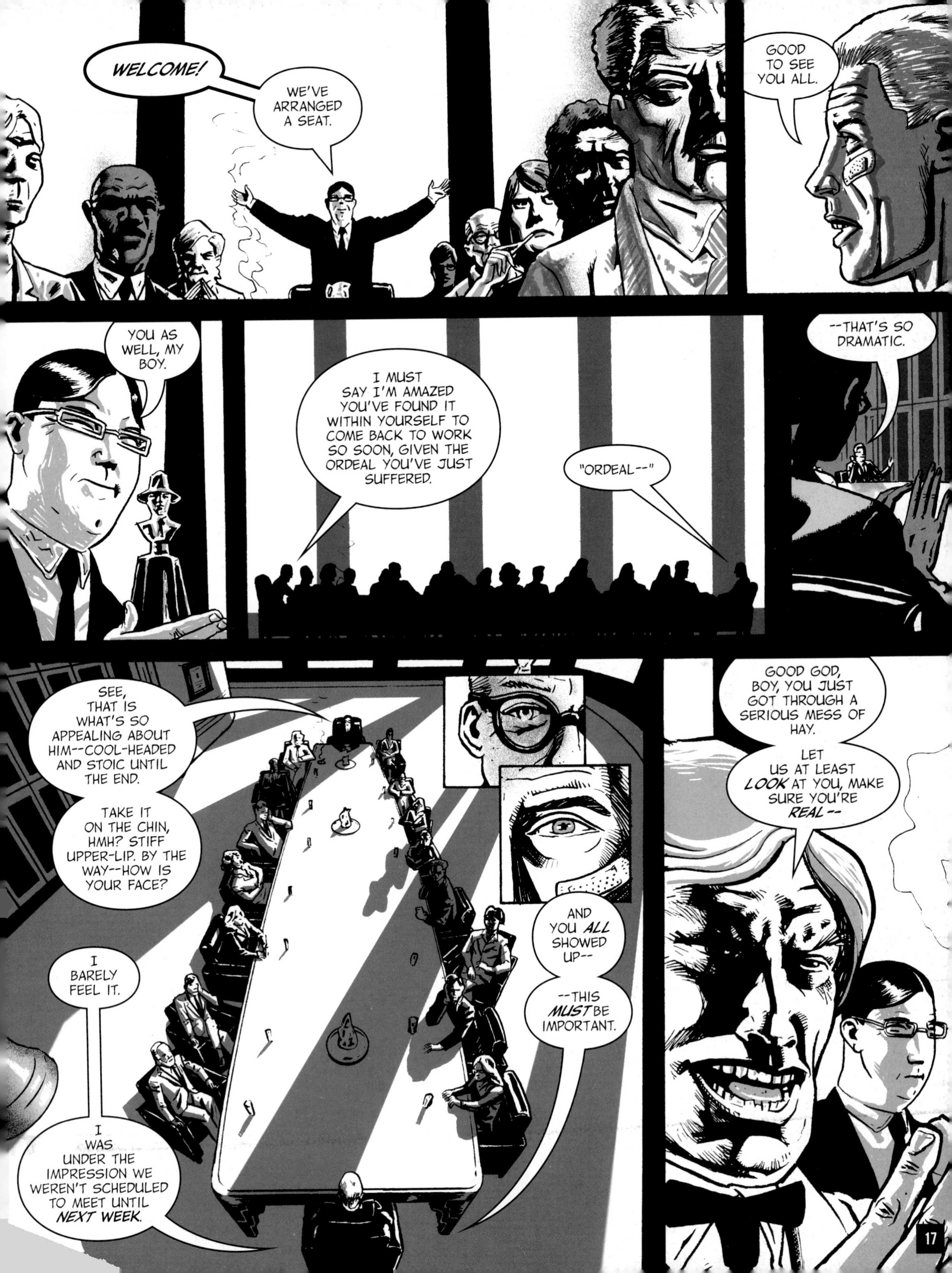
WELCOME!
WE'VE ARRANGED A SEAT.
GOOD TO SEE YOU ALL.
YOU AS WELL, MY BOY.
I MUST SAY I'M AMAZED YOU'VE FOUND IT WITHIN YOURSELF TO COME BACK TO WORK SO SOON, GIVEN THE ORDEAL YOU'VE JUST SUFFERED.
"ORDEAL--"
--THAT'S SO DRAMATIC.
SEE, THAT IS WHAT'S SO APPEALING ABOUT HIM--COOL-HEADED AND STOIC UNTIL THE END.
TAKE IT ON THE CHIN, HMH? STIFF UPPER-LIP. BY THE WAY--HOW IS YOUR FACE?
I BARELY FEEL IT.
I WAS UNDER THE IMPRESSION WE WEREN'T SCHEDULED TO MEET UNTIL NEXT WEEK.
AND YOU ALL SHOWED UP--
--THIS MUST BE IMPORTANT.
GOOD GOD, BOY, YOU JUST GOT THROUGH A SERIOUS MESS OF HAY.
LET US AT LEAST LOOK AT YOU, MAKE SURE YOU'RE REAL--

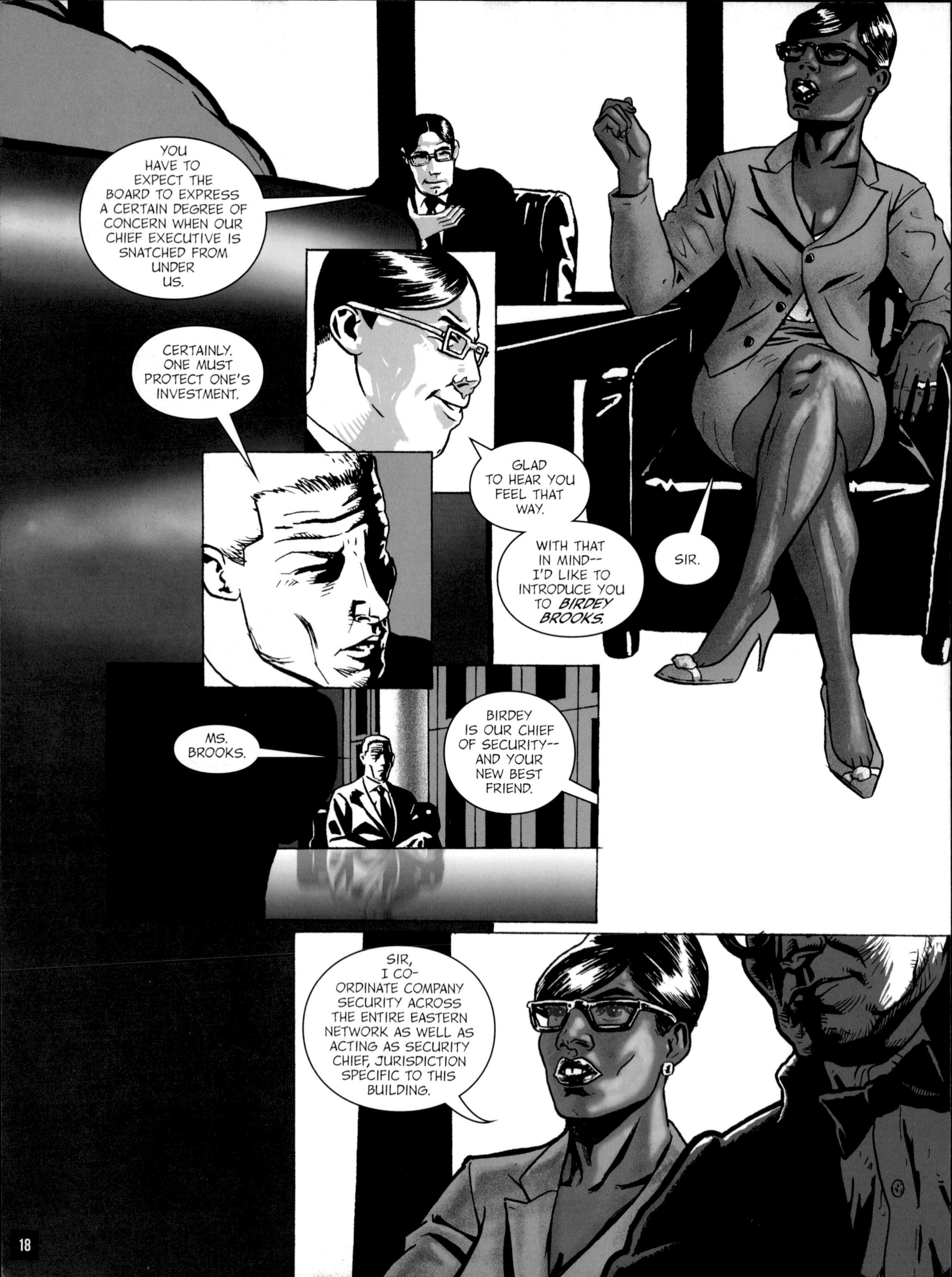
YOU HAVE TO EXPECT THE BOARD TO EXPRESS A CERTAIN DEGREE OF CONCERN WHEN OUR CHIEF EXECUTIVE IS SNATCHED FROM UNDER US.
CERTAINLY. ONE MUST PROTECT ONE'S INVESTMENT.
GLAD TO HEAR YOU FEEL THAT WAY.
WITH THAT IN MIND-- I'D LIKE TO INTRODUCE YOU TO *BIRDEY BROOKS.*
SIR.
MS. BROOKS.
BIRDEY IS OUR CHIEF OF SECURITY-- AND YOUR NEW BEST FRIEND.
SIR, I CO-ORDINATE COMPANY SECURITY ACROSS THE ENTIRE EASTERN NETWORK AS WELL AS ACTING AS SECURITY CHIEF, JURISDICTION SPECIFIC TO THIS BUILDING.

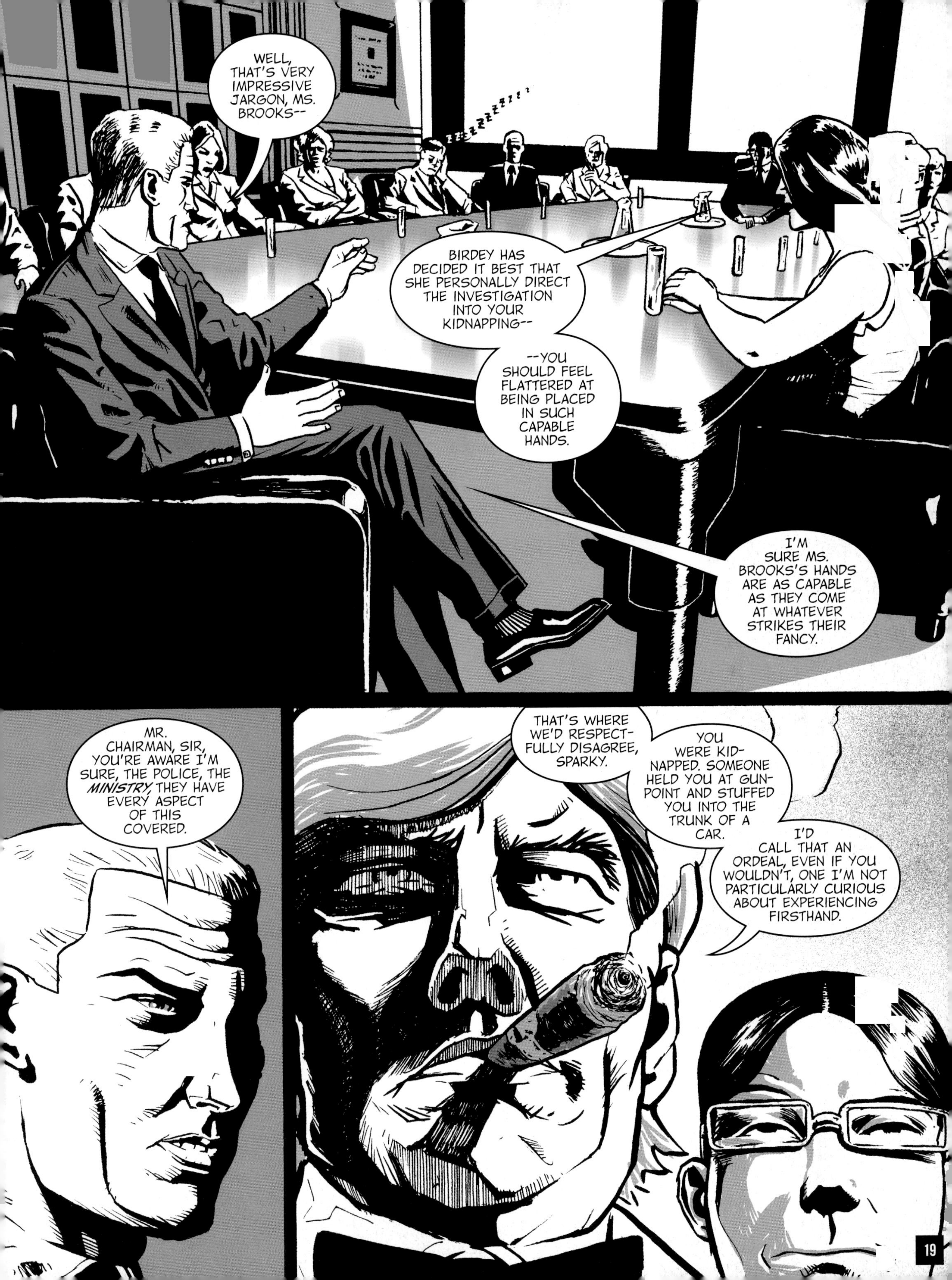

WELL, THAT'S VERY IMPRESSIVE JARGON, MS. BROOKS--
BIRDEY HAS DECIDED IT BEST THAT SHE PERSONALLY DIRECT THE INVESTIGATION INTO YOUR KIDNAPPING--
--YOU SHOULD FEEL FLATTERED AT BEING PLACED IN SUCH CAPABLE HANDS.
I'M SURE MS. BROOKS'S HANDS ARE AS CAPABLE AS THEY COME AT WHATEVER STRIKES THEIR FANCY.
MR. CHAIRMAN, SIR, YOU'RE AWARE I'M SURE, THE POLICE, THE *MINISTRY*, THEY HAVE EVERY ASPECT OF THIS COVERED.
THAT'S WHERE WE'D RESPECT-FULLY DISAGREE, SPARKY.
YOU WERE KID-NAPPED. SOMEONE HELD YOU AT GUN-POINT AND STUFFED YOU INTO THE TRUNK OF A CAR.
I'D CALL THAT AN ORDEAL, EVEN IF YOU WOULDN'T, ONE I'M NOT PARTICULARLY CURIOUS ABOUT EXPERIENCING FIRSTHAND.

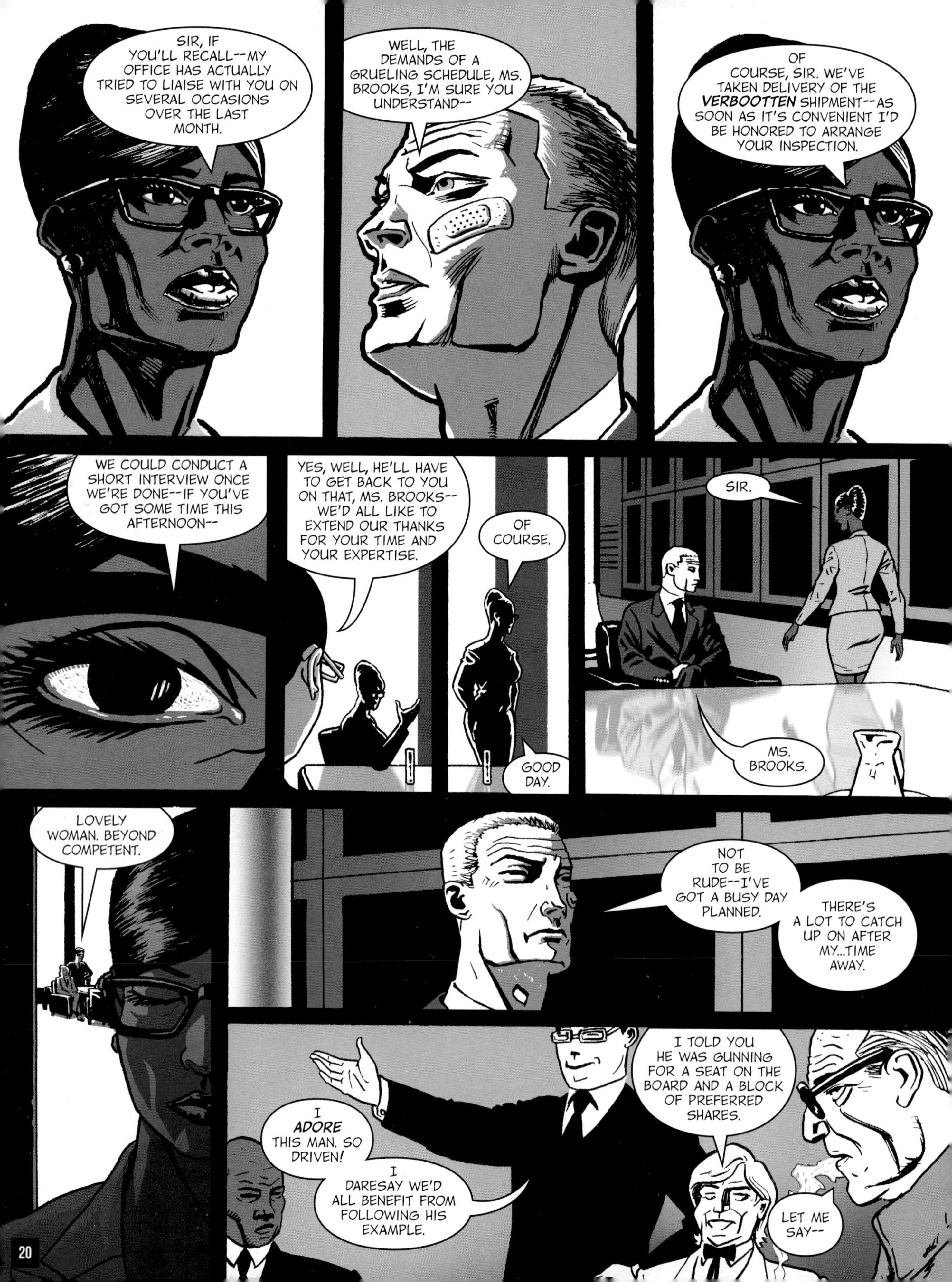

SIR, IF YOU'LL RECALL--MY OFFICE HAS ACTUALLY TRIED TO LIAISE WITH YOU ON SEVERAL OCCASIONS OVER THE LAST MONTH.
WELL, THE DEMANDS OF A GRUELING SCHEDULE, MS. BROOKS, I'M SURE YOU UNDERSTAND--
OF COURSE, SIR. WE'VE TAKEN DELIVERY OF THE **VERBOOTTEN** SHIPMENT--AS SOON AS IT'S CONVENIENT I'D BE HONORED TO ARRANGE YOUR INSPECTION.
WE COULD CONDUCT A SHORT INTERVIEW ONCE WE'RE DONE--IF YOU'VE GOT SOME TIME THIS AFTERNOON--
YES, WELL, HE'LL HAVE TO GET BACK TO YOU ON THAT, MS. BROOKS--WE'D ALL LIKE TO EXTEND OUR THANKS FOR YOUR TIME AND YOUR EXPERTISE.
OF COURSE.
GOOD DAY.
SIR.
MS. BROOKS.
LOVELY WOMAN. BEYOND COMPETENT.
NOT TO BE RUDE--I'VE GOT A BUSY DAY PLANNED.
THERE'S A LOT TO CATCH UP ON AFTER MY...TIME AWAY.
I *ADORE* THIS MAN. SO DRIVEN!
I DARESAY WE'D ALL BENEFIT FROM FOLLOWING HIS EXAMPLE.
I TOLD YOU HE WAS GUNNING FOR A SEAT ON THE BOARD AND A BLOCK OF PREFERRED SHARES.
LET ME SAY--

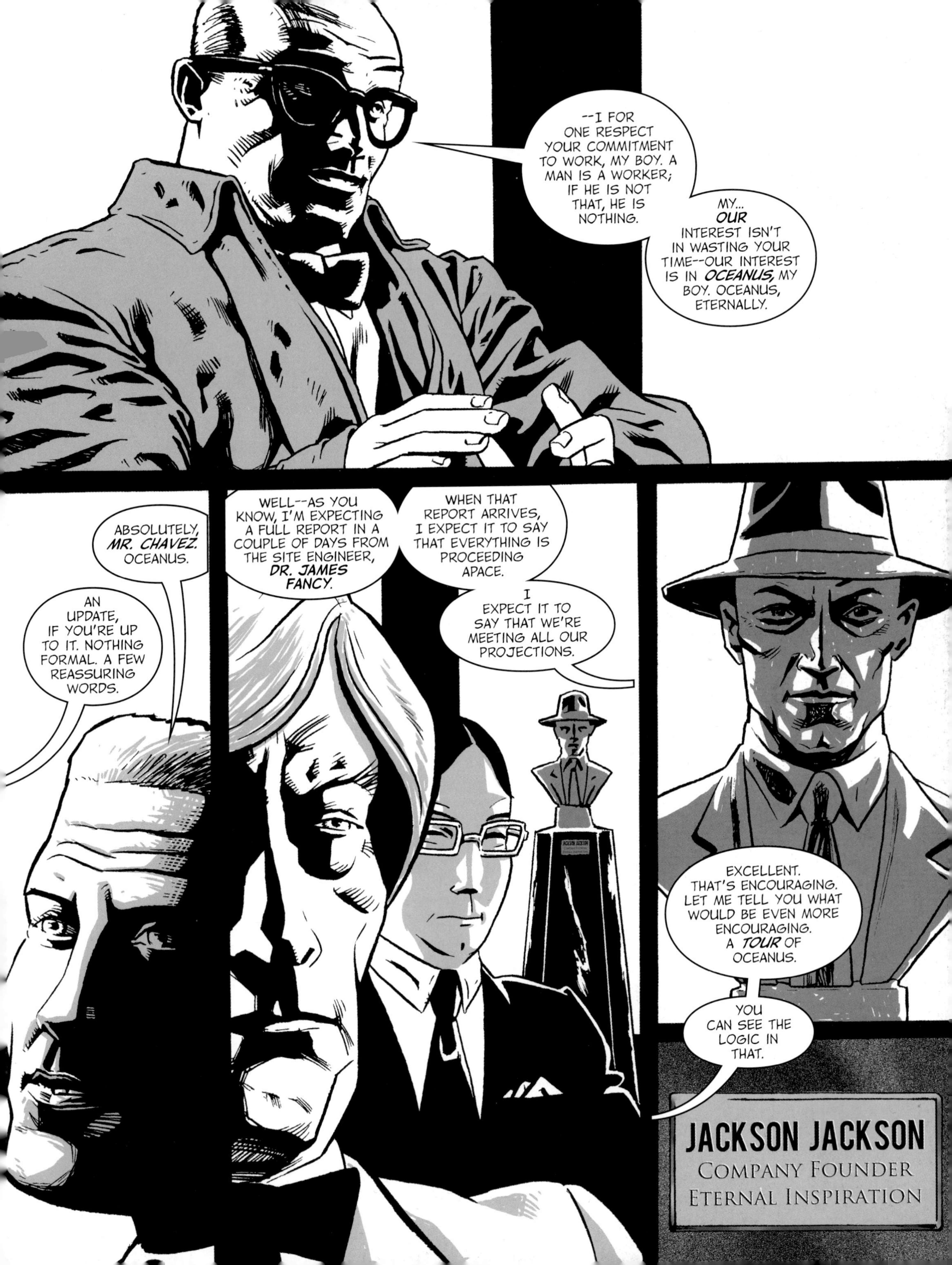
--I FOR ONE RESPECT YOUR COMMITMENT TO WORK, MY BOY. A MAN IS A WORKER; IF HE IS NOT THAT, HE IS NOTHING.
MY... OUR INTEREST ISN'T IN WASTING YOUR TIME--OUR INTEREST IS IN OCEANUS, MY BOY. OCEANUS, ETERNALLY.
ABSOLUTELY, MR. CHAVEZ. OCEANUS.
AN UPDATE, IF YOU'RE UP TO IT. NOTHING FORMAL. A FEW REASSURING WORDS.
WELL--AS YOU KNOW, I'M EXPECTING A FULL REPORT IN A COUPLE OF DAYS FROM THE SITE ENGINEER, DR. JAMES FANCY.
WHEN THAT REPORT ARRIVES, I EXPECT IT TO SAY THAT EVERYTHING IS PROCEEDING APACE.
I EXPECT IT TO SAY THAT WE'RE MEETING ALL OUR PROJECTIONS.
EXCELLENT. THAT'S ENCOURAGING. LET ME TELL YOU WHAT WOULD BE EVEN MORE ENCOURAGING. A TOUR OF OCEANUS.
YOU CAN SEE THE LOGIC IN THAT.
JACKSON JACKSON
COMPANY FOUNDER
ETERNAL INSPIRATION

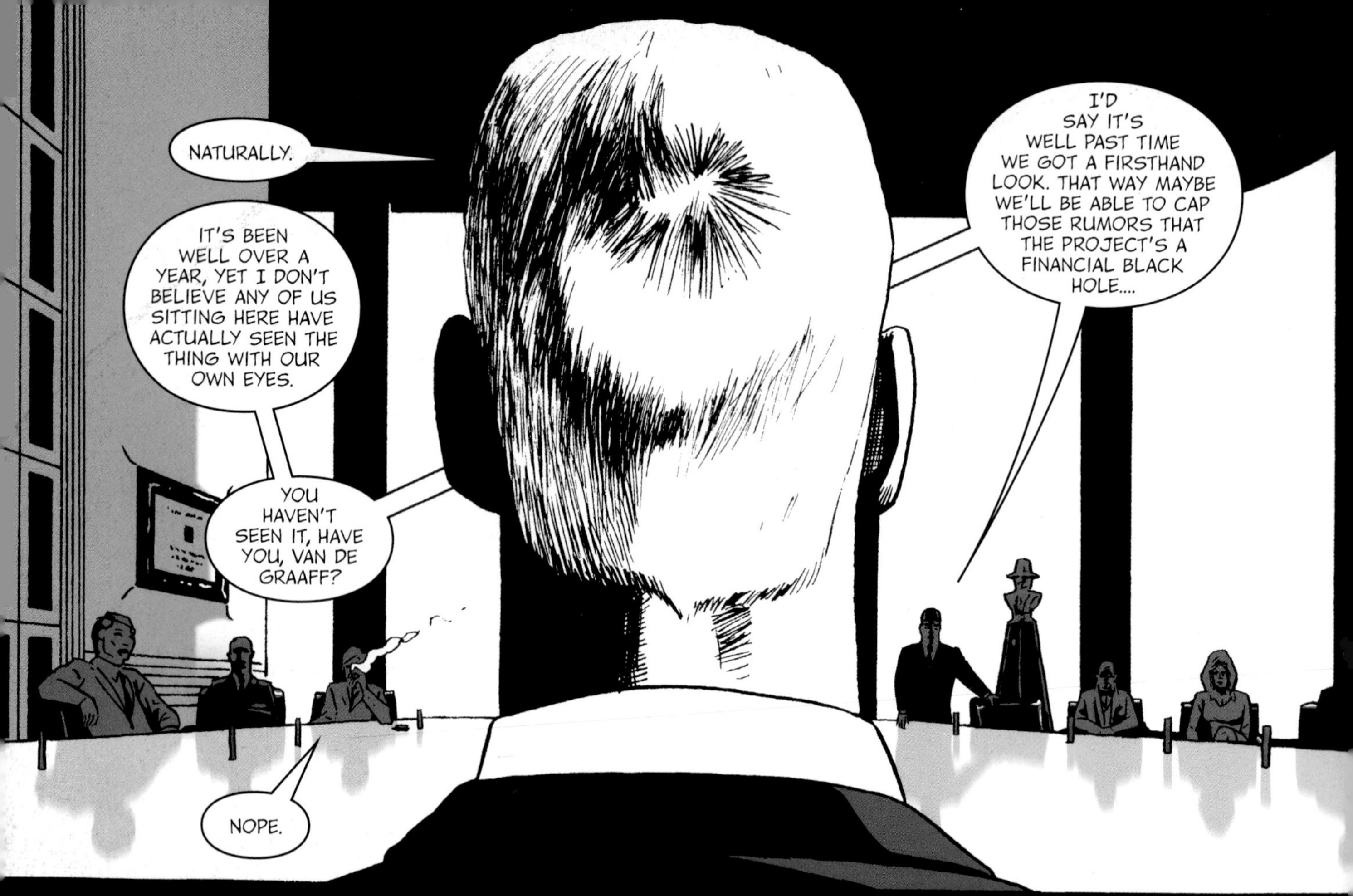
NATURALLY.
IT'S BEEN WELL OVER A YEAR, YET I DON'T BELIEVE ANY OF US SITTING HERE HAVE ACTUALLY SEEN THE THING WITH OUR OWN EYES.
YOU HAVEN'T SEEN IT, HAVE YOU, VAN DE GRAAFF?
NOPE.
I'D SAY IT'S WELL PAST TIME WE GOT A FIRSTHAND LOOK. THAT WAY MAYBE WE'LL BE ABLE TO CAP THOSE RUMORS THAT THE PROJECT'S A FINANCIAL BLACK HOLE....

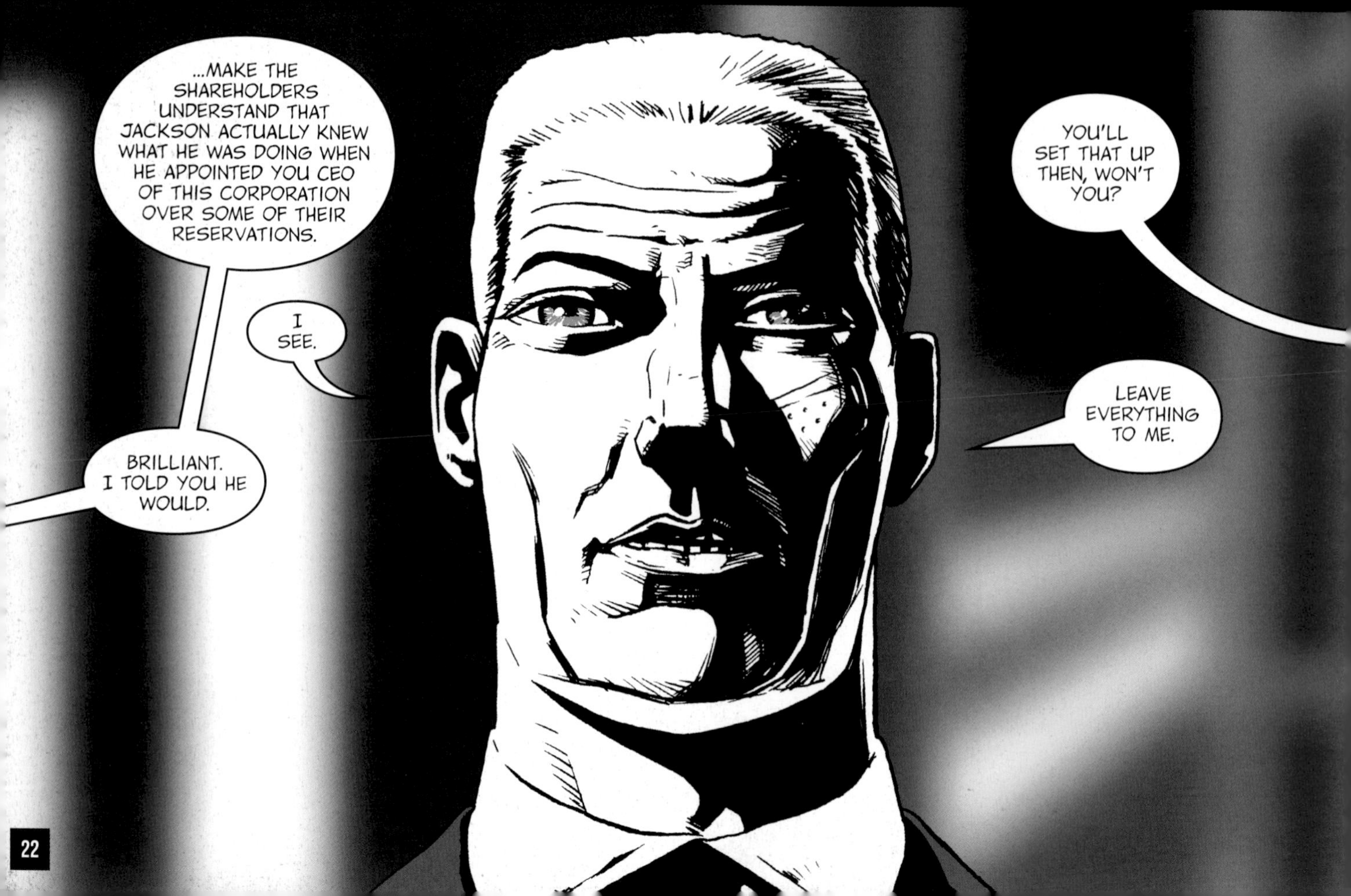
...MAKE THE SHAREHOLDERS UNDERSTAND THAT JACKSON ACTUALLY KNEW WHAT HE WAS DOING WHEN HE APPOINTED YOU CEO OF THIS CORPORATION OVER SOME OF THEIR RESERVATIONS.
YOU'LL SET THAT UP THEN, WON'T YOU?
I SEE.
LEAVE EVERYTHING TO ME.
BRILLIANT. I TOLD YOU HE WOULD.

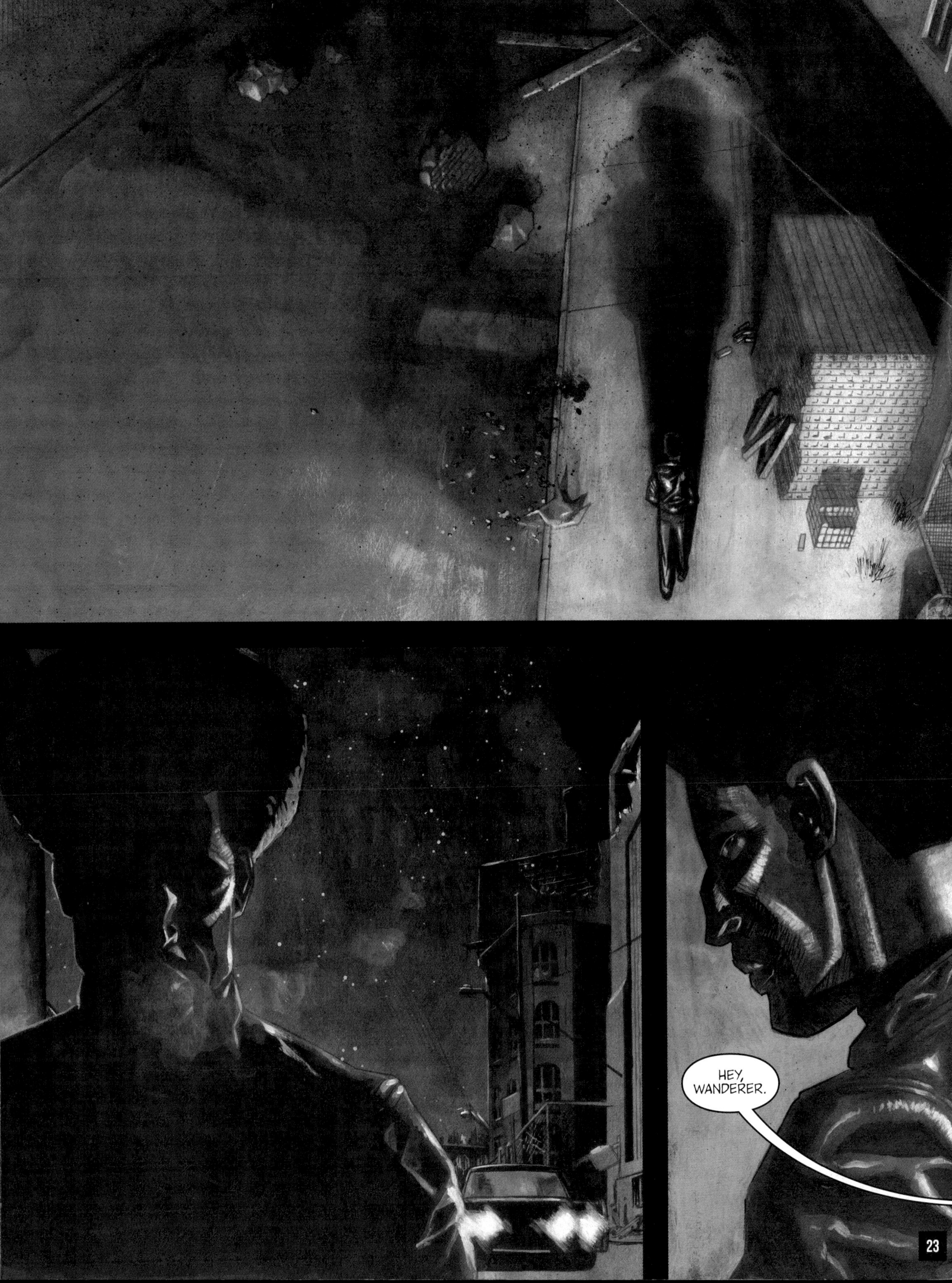
HEY,
WANDERER.

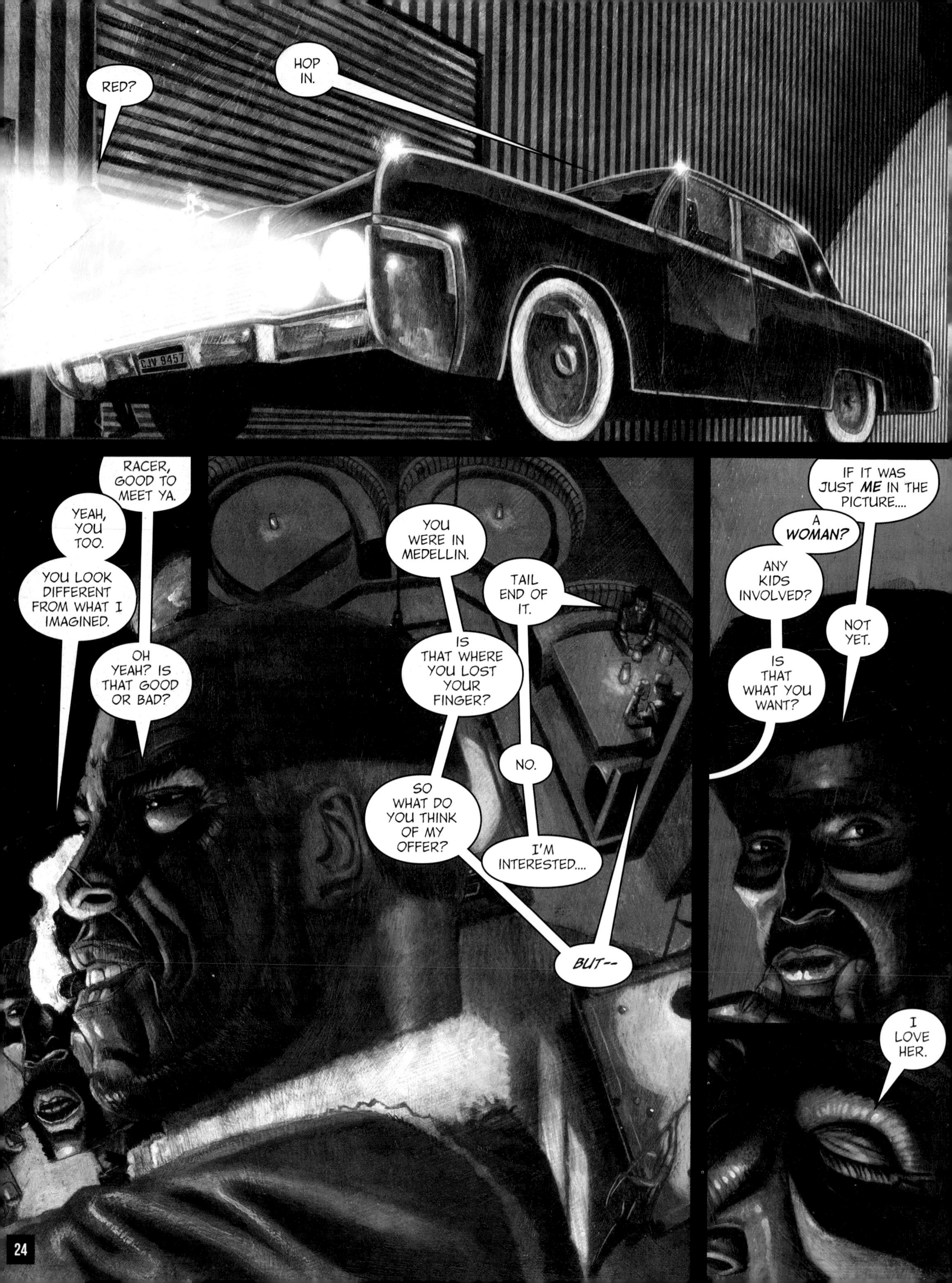

RED?
HOP IN.
RACER, GOOD TO MEET YA.
YEAH, YOU TOO.
YOU LOOK DIFFERENT FROM WHAT I IMAGINED.
OH YEAH? IS THAT GOOD OR BAD?
YOU WERE IN MEDELLIN.
TAIL END OF IT.
IS THAT WHERE YOU LOST YOUR FINGER?
NO.
SO WHAT DO YOU THINK OF MY OFFER?
I'M INTERESTED....
BUT--
IF IT WAS JUST ME IN THE PICTURE....
A WOMAN?
ANY KIDS INVOLVED?
NOT YET.
IS THAT WHAT YOU WANT?
I LOVE HER.

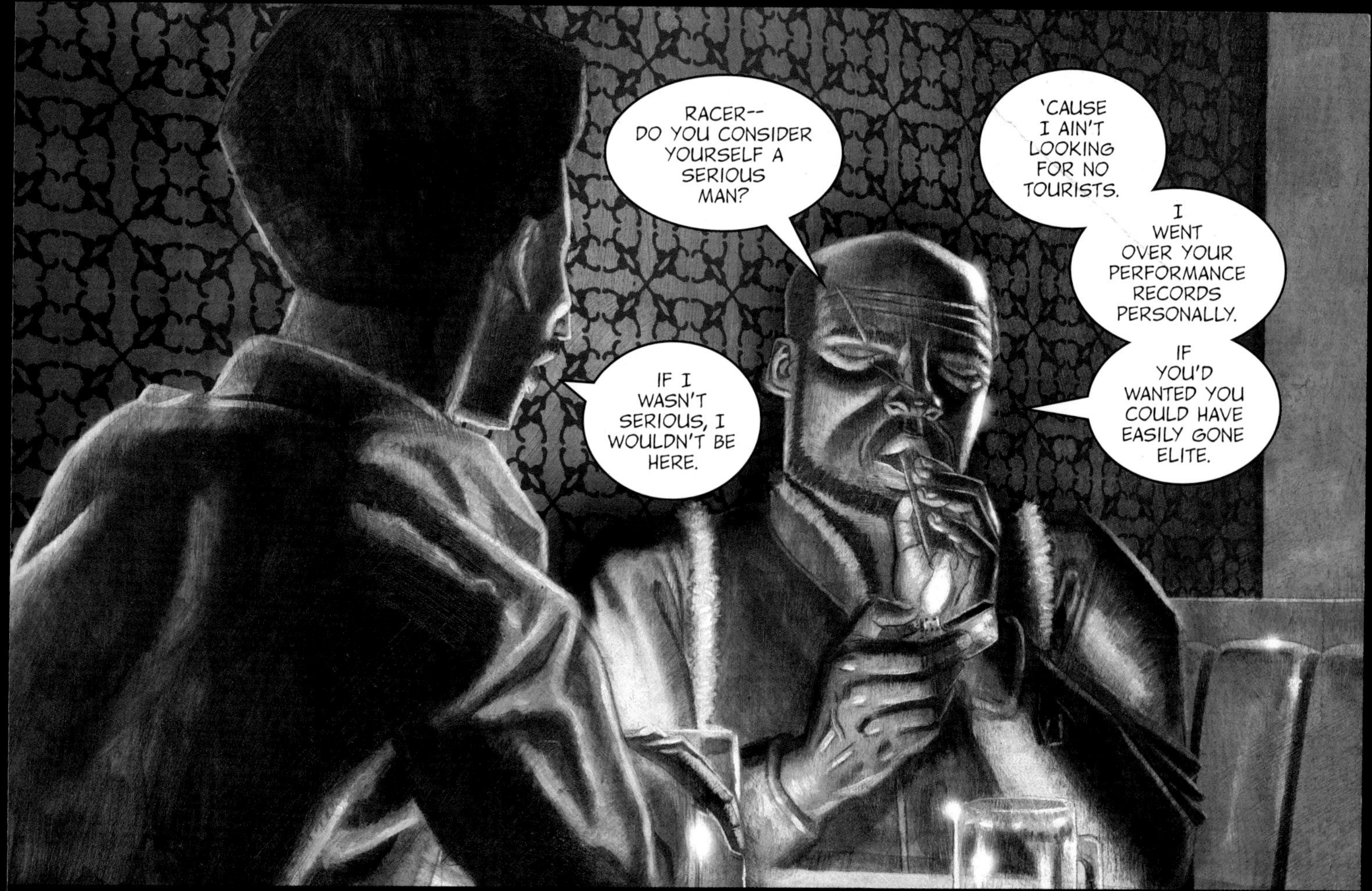
RACER-- DO YOU CONSIDER YOURSELF A SERIOUS MAN?
IF I WASN'T SERIOUS, I WOULDN'T BE HERE.
'CAUSE I AIN'T LOOKING FOR NO TOURISTS.
I WENT OVER YOUR PERFORMANCE RECORDS PERSONALLY.
IF YOU'D WANTED YOU COULD HAVE EASILY GONE ELITE.

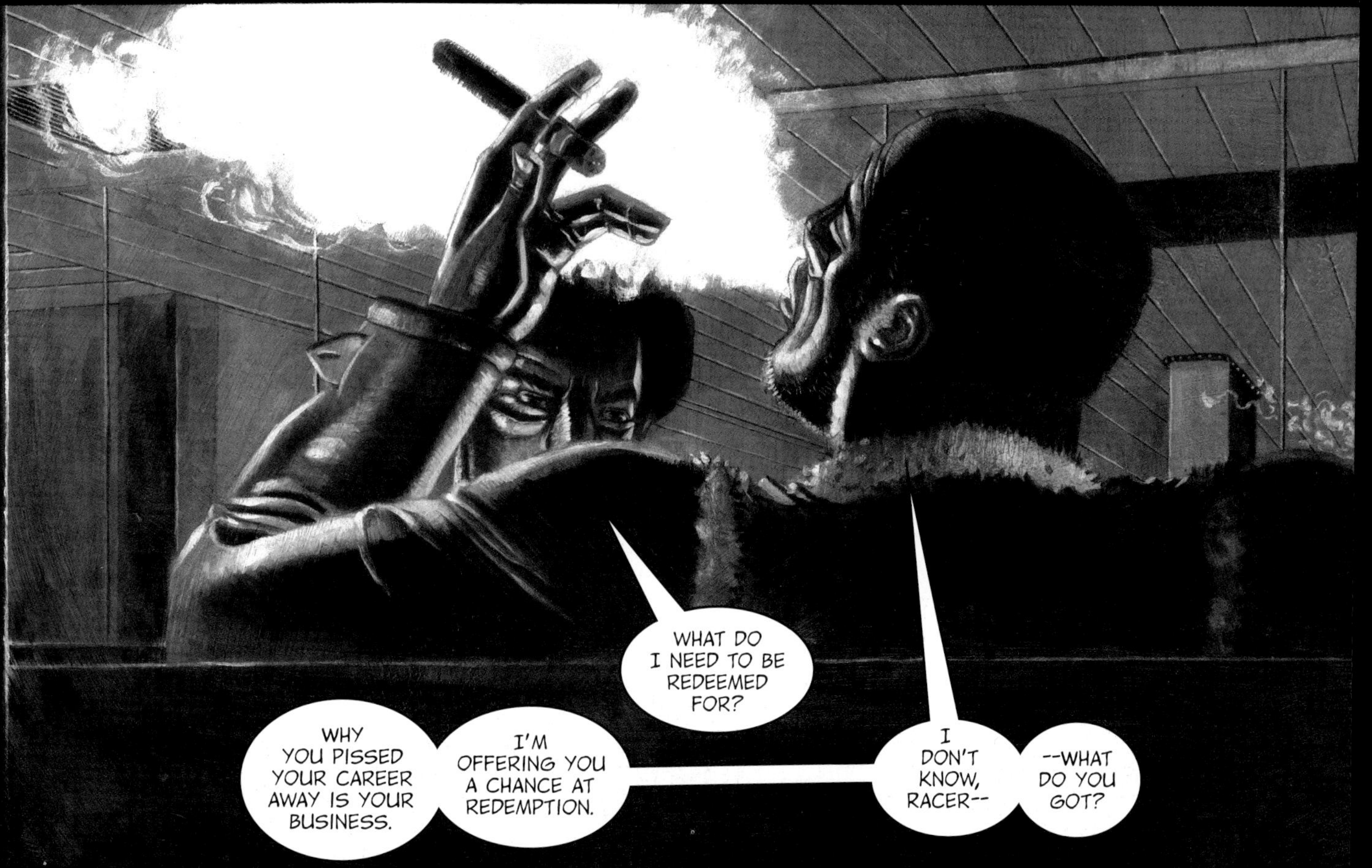
WHY YOU PISSED YOUR CAREER AWAY IS YOUR BUSINESS.
I'M OFFERING YOU A CHANCE AT REDEMPTION.
WHAT DO I NEED TO BE REDEEMED FOR?
I DON'T KNOW, RACER--
--WHAT DO YOU GOT?

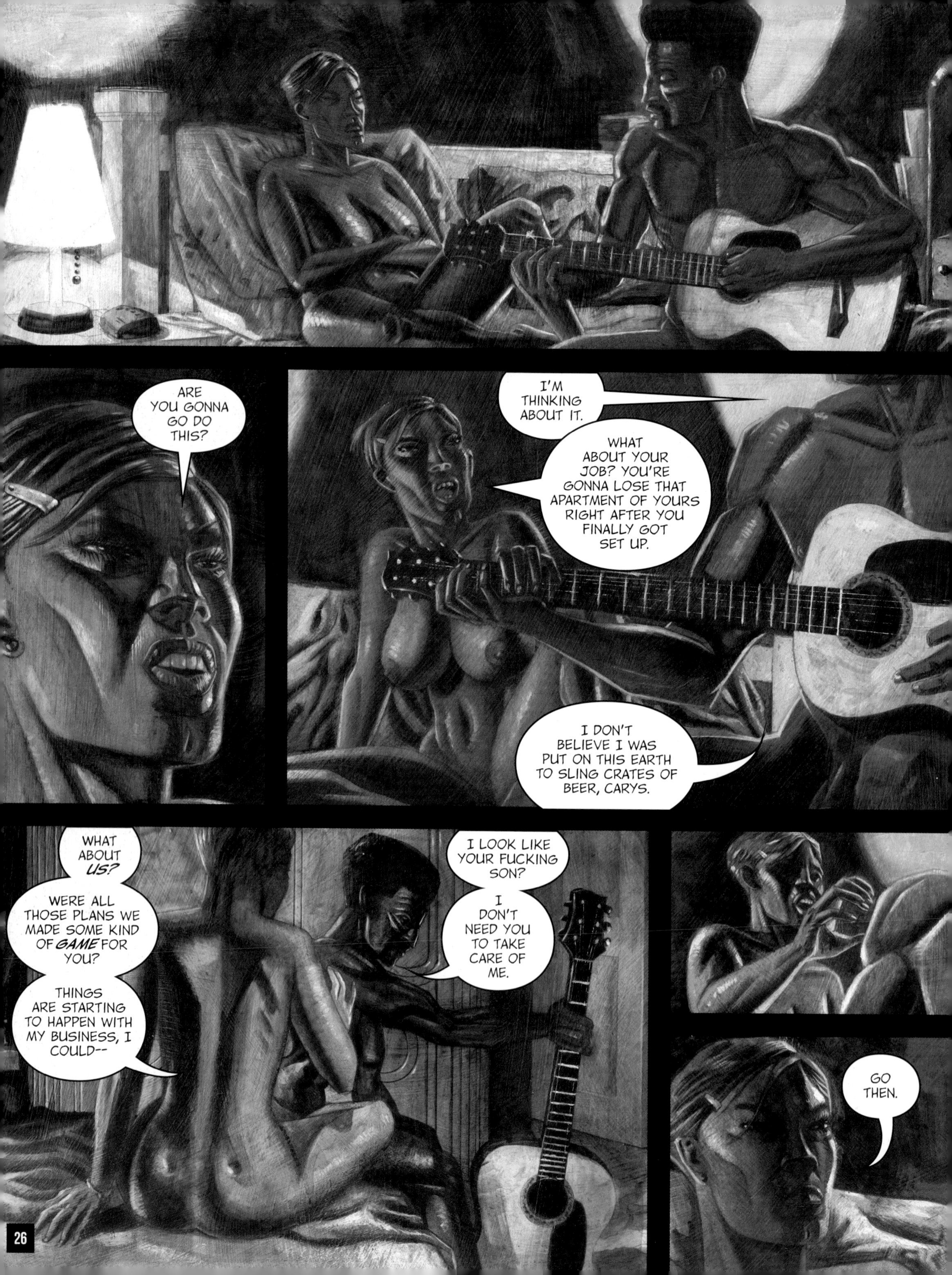
ARE YOU GONNA GO DO THIS?
I'M THINKING ABOUT IT.
WHAT ABOUT YOUR JOB? YOU'RE GONNA LOSE THAT APARTMENT OF YOURS RIGHT AFTER YOU FINALLY GOT SET UP.
I DON'T BELIEVE I WAS PUT ON THIS EARTH TO SLING CRATES OF BEER, CARYS.
WHAT ABOUT *US?*
WERE ALL THOSE PLANS WE MADE SOME KIND OF *GAME* FOR YOU?
THINGS ARE STARTING TO HAPPEN WITH MY BUSINESS, I COULD--
I LOOK LIKE YOUR FUCKING SON?
I DON'T NEED YOU TO TAKE CARE OF ME.
GO THEN.

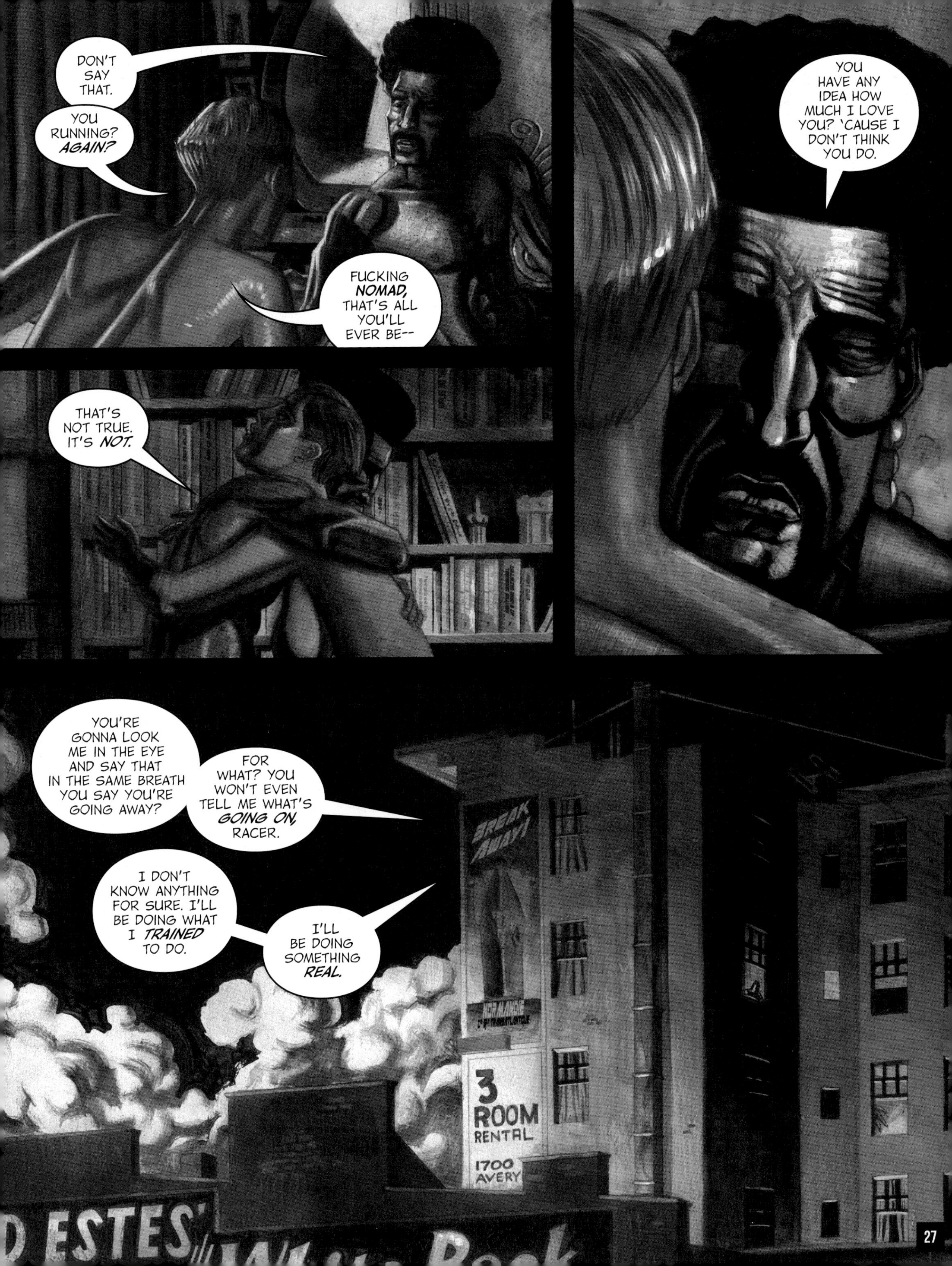
DON'T SAY THAT.
YOU RUNNING? AGAIN?
FUCKING NOMAD, THAT'S ALL YOU'LL EVER BE--
YOU HAVE ANY IDEA HOW MUCH I LOVE YOU? 'CAUSE I DON'T THINK YOU DO.
THAT'S NOT TRUE. IT'S NOT.
YOU'RE GONNA LOOK ME IN THE EYE AND SAY THAT IN THE SAME BREATH YOU SAY YOU'RE GOING AWAY?
FOR WHAT? YOU WON'T EVEN TELL ME WHAT'S GOING ON, RACER.
I DON'T KNOW ANYTHING FOR SURE. I'LL BE DOING WHAT I TRAINED TO DO.
I'LL BE DOING SOMETHING REAL.
BREAK AWAY!
NORMANDIE
3 ROOM RENTAL
1700 AVERY
D ESTES

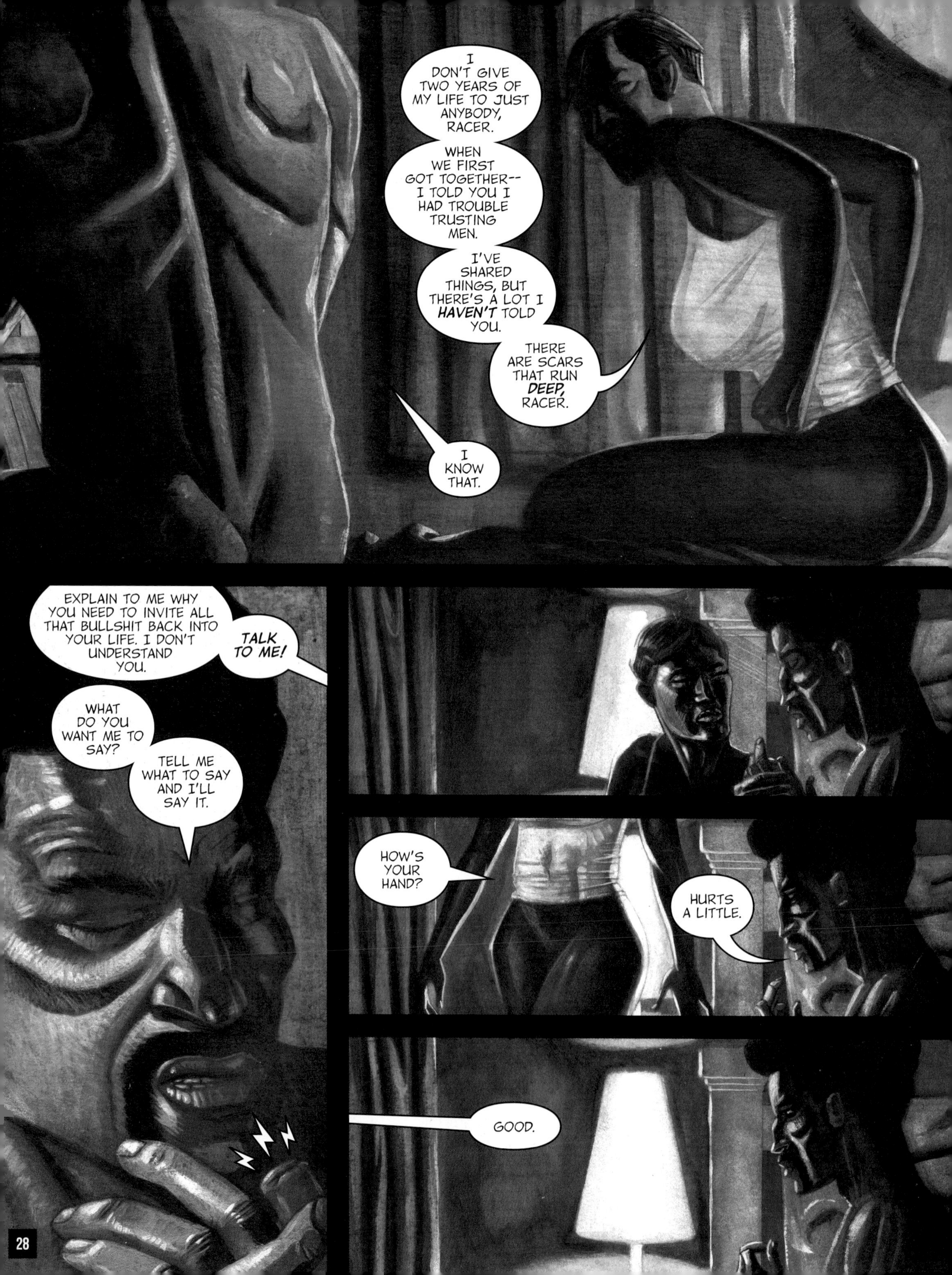
I DON'T GIVE TWO YEARS OF MY LIFE TO JUST ANYBODY, RACER.
WHEN WE FIRST GOT TOGETHER-- I TOLD YOU I HAD TROUBLE TRUSTING MEN.
I'VE SHARED THINGS, BUT THERE'S A LOT I HAVEN'T TOLD YOU.
THERE ARE SCARS THAT RUN DEEP, RACER.
I KNOW THAT.
EXPLAIN TO ME WHY YOU NEED TO INVITE ALL THAT BULLSHIT BACK INTO YOUR LIFE. I DON'T UNDERSTAND YOU.
TALK TO ME!
WHAT DO YOU WANT ME TO SAY?
TELL ME WHAT TO SAY AND I'LL SAY IT.
HOW'S YOUR HAND?
HURTS A LITTLE.
GOOD.

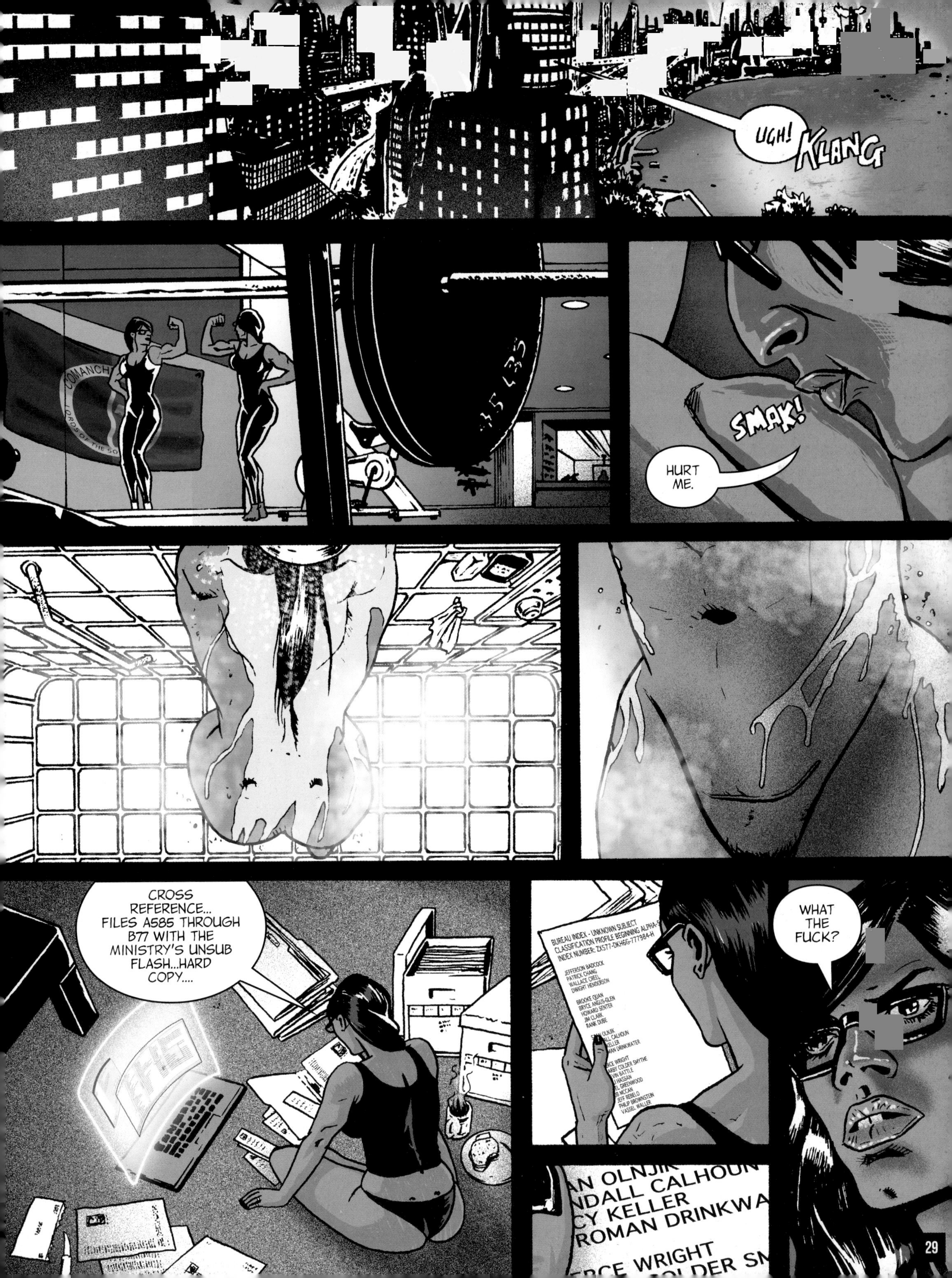
UGH!
KLANG
SMAK!
HURT ME.
CROSS REFERENCE... FILES A585 THROUGH B77 WITH THE MINISTRY'S UNSUB FLASH...HARD COPY....
BUREAU INDEX - UNKNOWN SUBJECT
CLASSIFICATION PROFILE BEGINNING ALPHA-5
INDEX NUMBER: ZX577-DKH6G-777984-H
JEFFERSON BADCOCK
PATRICK CHANG
WALLACE CREEL
DWIGHT HENDERSON
WHAT THE FUCK?
AN OLNJIK
NDALL CALHOUN
CY KELLER
ROMAN DRINKWA
ERCE WRIGHT
OLDER SN

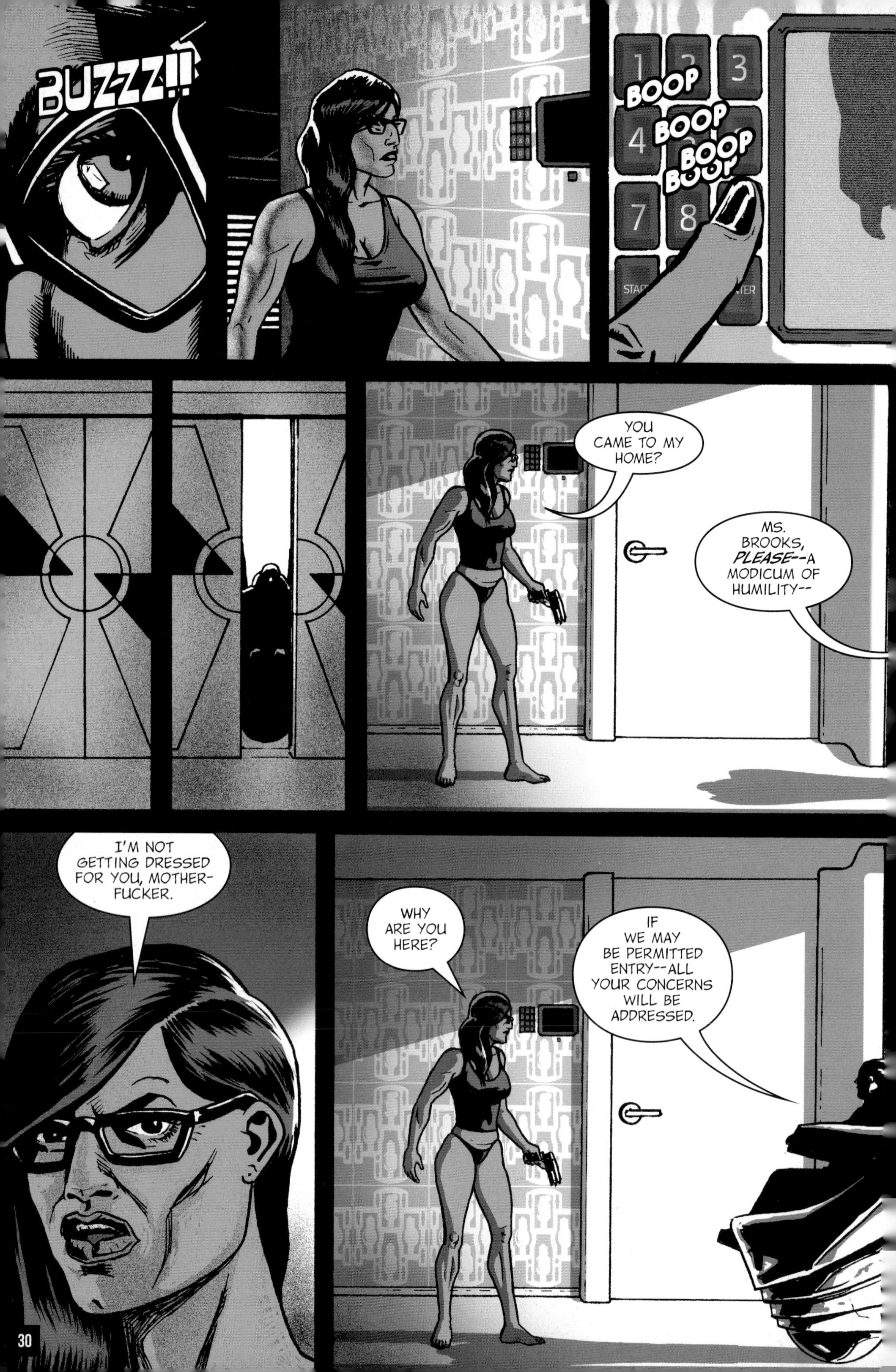
BUZZZ!!
BOOP
BOOP
BOOP
BOOP
YOU CAME TO MY HOME?
MS. BROOKS, *PLEASE*--A MODICUM OF HUMILITY--
I'M NOT GETTING DRESSED FOR YOU, MOTHER-FUCKER.
WHY ARE YOU HERE?
IF WE MAY BE PERMITTED ENTRY--ALL YOUR CONCERNS WILL BE ADDRESSED.

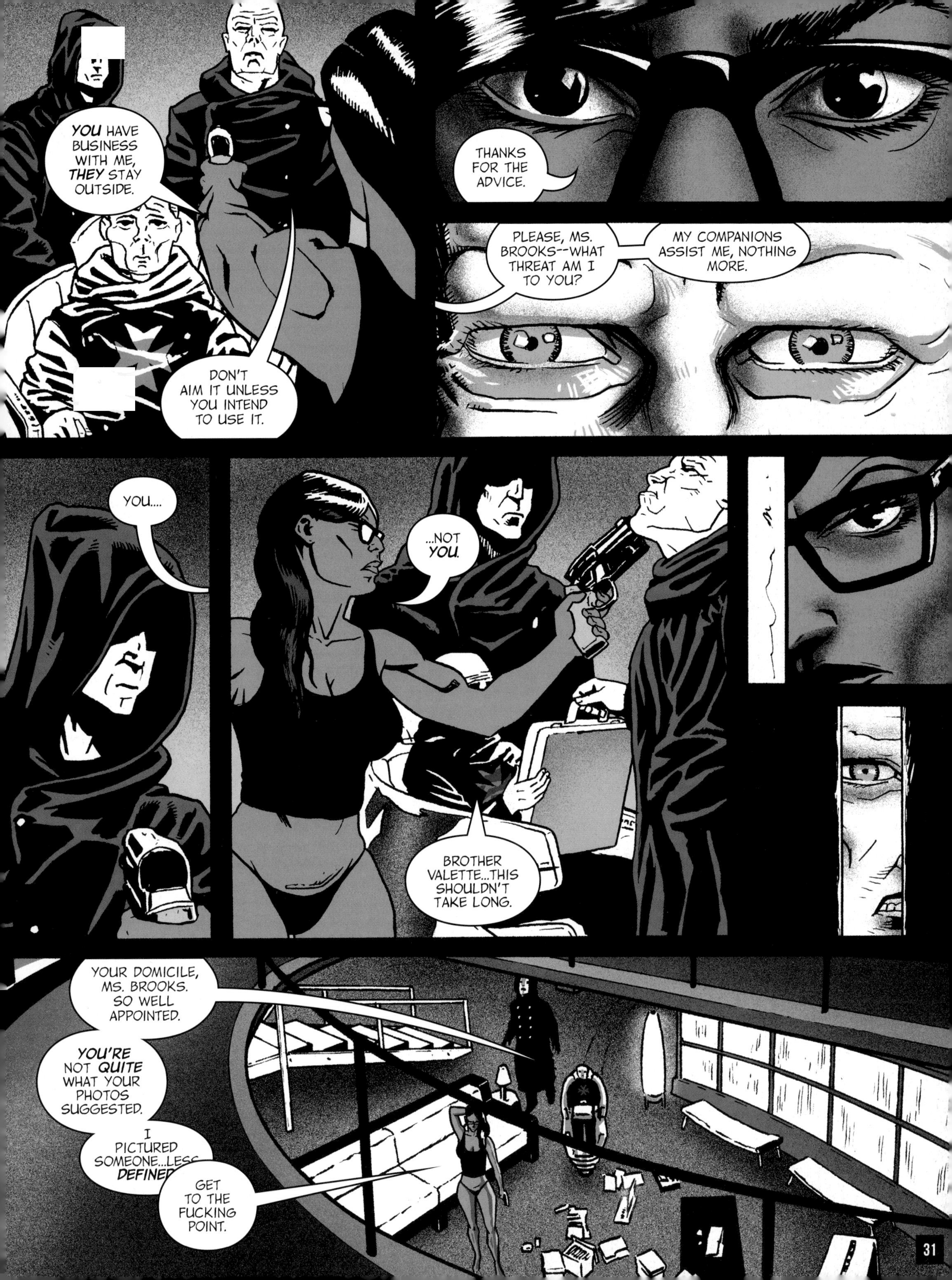
YOU HAVE BUSINESS WITH ME, THEY STAY OUTSIDE.
DON'T AIM IT UNLESS YOU INTEND TO USE IT.
THANKS FOR THE ADVICE.
PLEASE, MS. BROOKS--WHAT THREAT AM I TO YOU?
MY COMPANIONS ASSIST ME, NOTHING MORE.
YOU....
...NOT YOU.
BROTHER VALETTE...THIS SHOULDN'T TAKE LONG.
YOUR DOMICILE, MS. BROOKS. SO WELL APPOINTED.
YOU'RE NOT QUITE WHAT YOUR PHOTOS SUGGESTED.
I PICTURED SOMEONE...LESS DEFINED
GET TO THE FUCKING POINT.

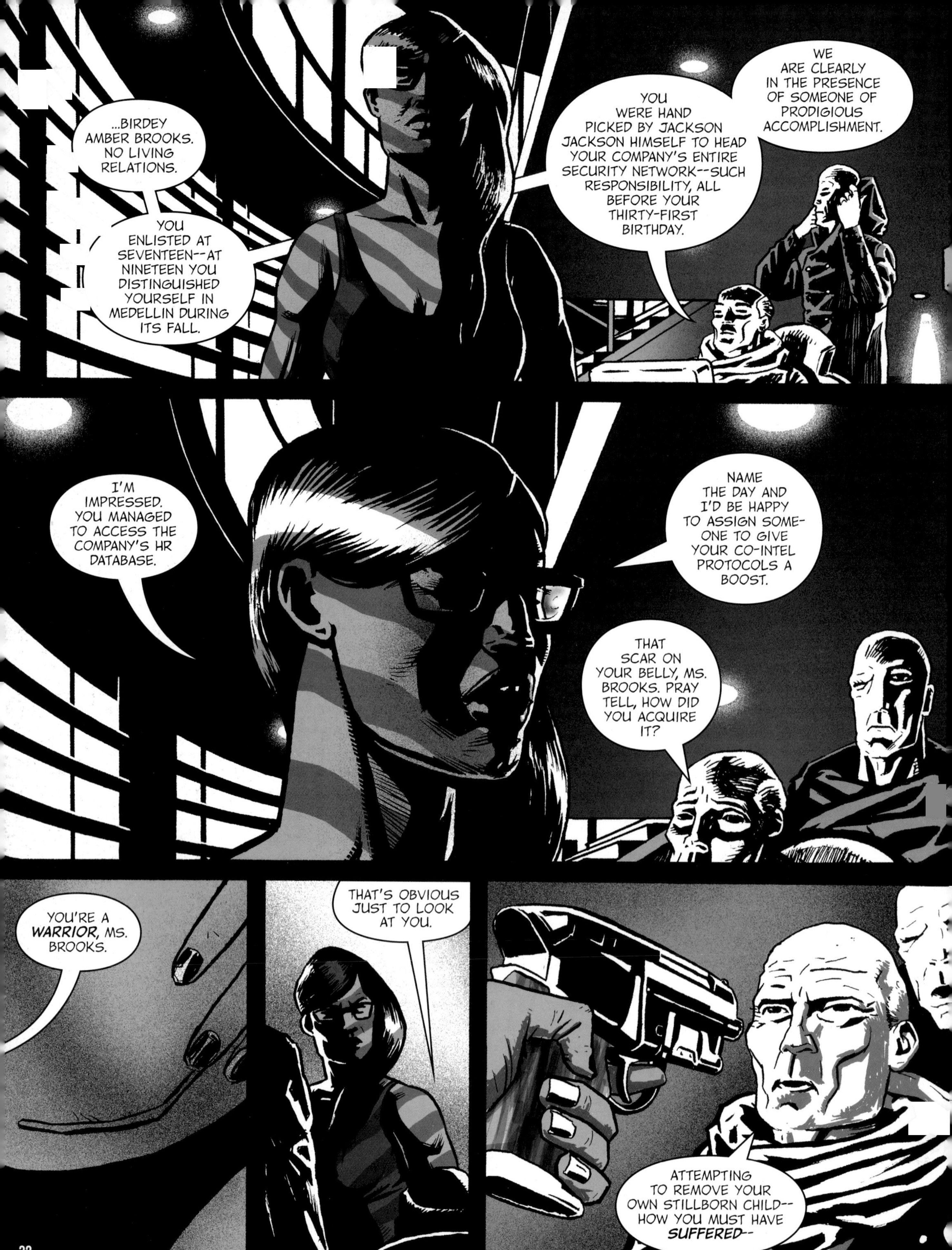
...BIRDEY AMBER BROOKS. NO LIVING RELATIONS.
YOU ENLISTED AT SEVENTEEN--AT NINETEEN YOU DISTINGUISHED YOURSELF IN MEDELLIN DURING ITS FALL.
YOU WERE HAND PICKED BY JACKSON JACKSON HIMSELF TO HEAD YOUR COMPANY'S ENTIRE SECURITY NETWORK--SUCH RESPONSIBILITY, ALL BEFORE YOUR THIRTY-FIRST BIRTHDAY.
WE ARE CLEARLY IN THE PRESENCE OF SOMEONE OF PRODIGIOUS ACCOMPLISHMENT.
I'M IMPRESSED. YOU MANAGED TO ACCESS THE COMPANY'S HR DATABASE.
NAME THE DAY AND I'D BE HAPPY TO ASSIGN SOME-ONE TO GIVE YOUR CO-INTEL PROTOCOLS A BOOST.
THAT SCAR ON YOUR BELLY, MS. BROOKS. PRAY TELL, HOW DID YOU ACQUIRE IT?
YOU'RE A **WARRIOR,** MS. BROOKS.
THAT'S OBVIOUS JUST TO LOOK AT YOU.
ATTEMPTING TO REMOVE YOUR OWN STILLBORN CHILD--HOW YOU MUST HAVE ***SUFFERED***--

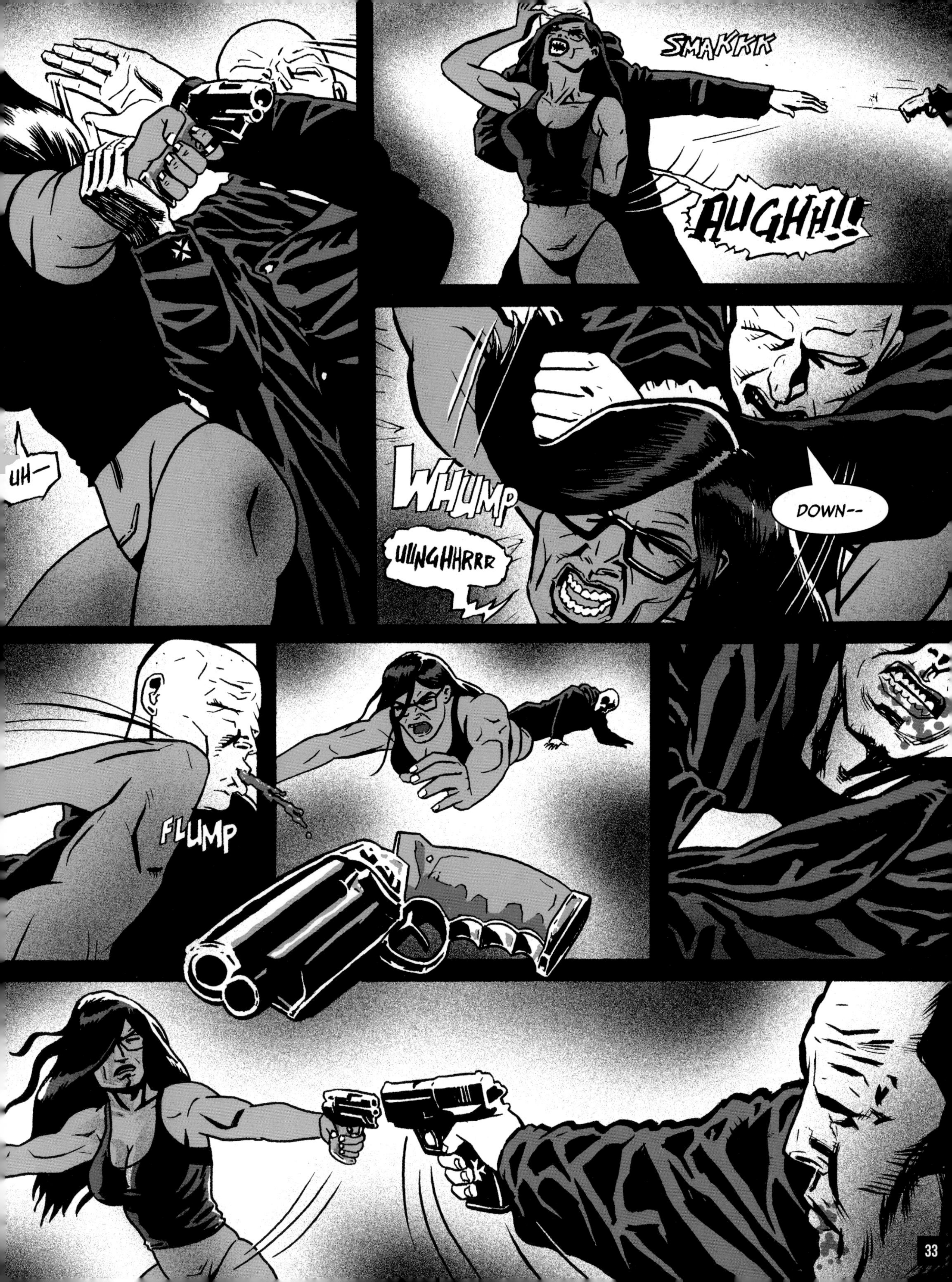

UH—
SMAKKK
AUGHH!!
WHUMP
UUNGHHRRR
DOWN--
FLUMP

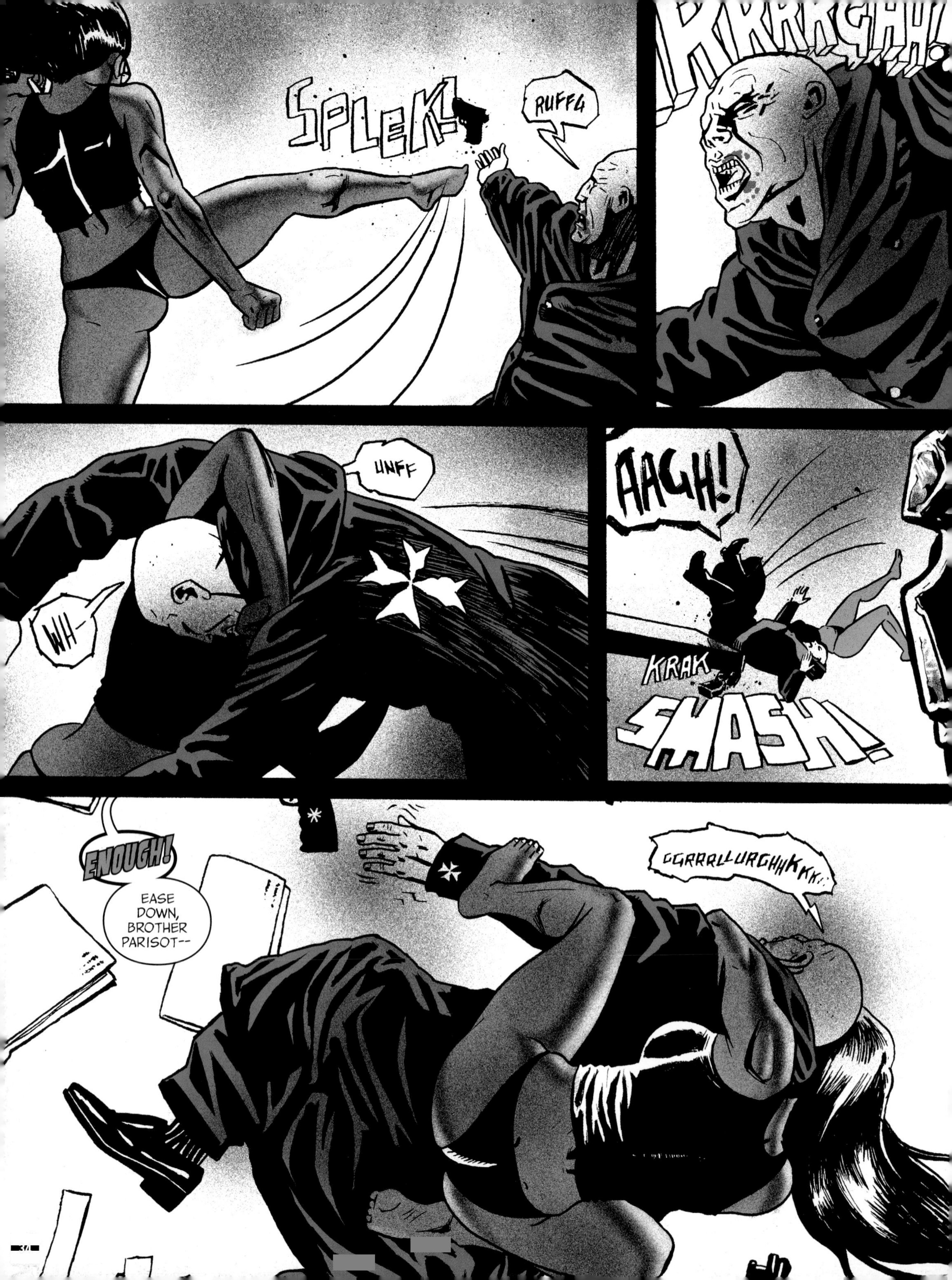
SPLEK!
RUFFG
KRRRGHH!
UNFF
WH--
AAGH!
KRAK
SMASH!
ENOUGH!
EASE DOWN, BROTHER PARISOT--
GGRRRLLURGHHKKK!

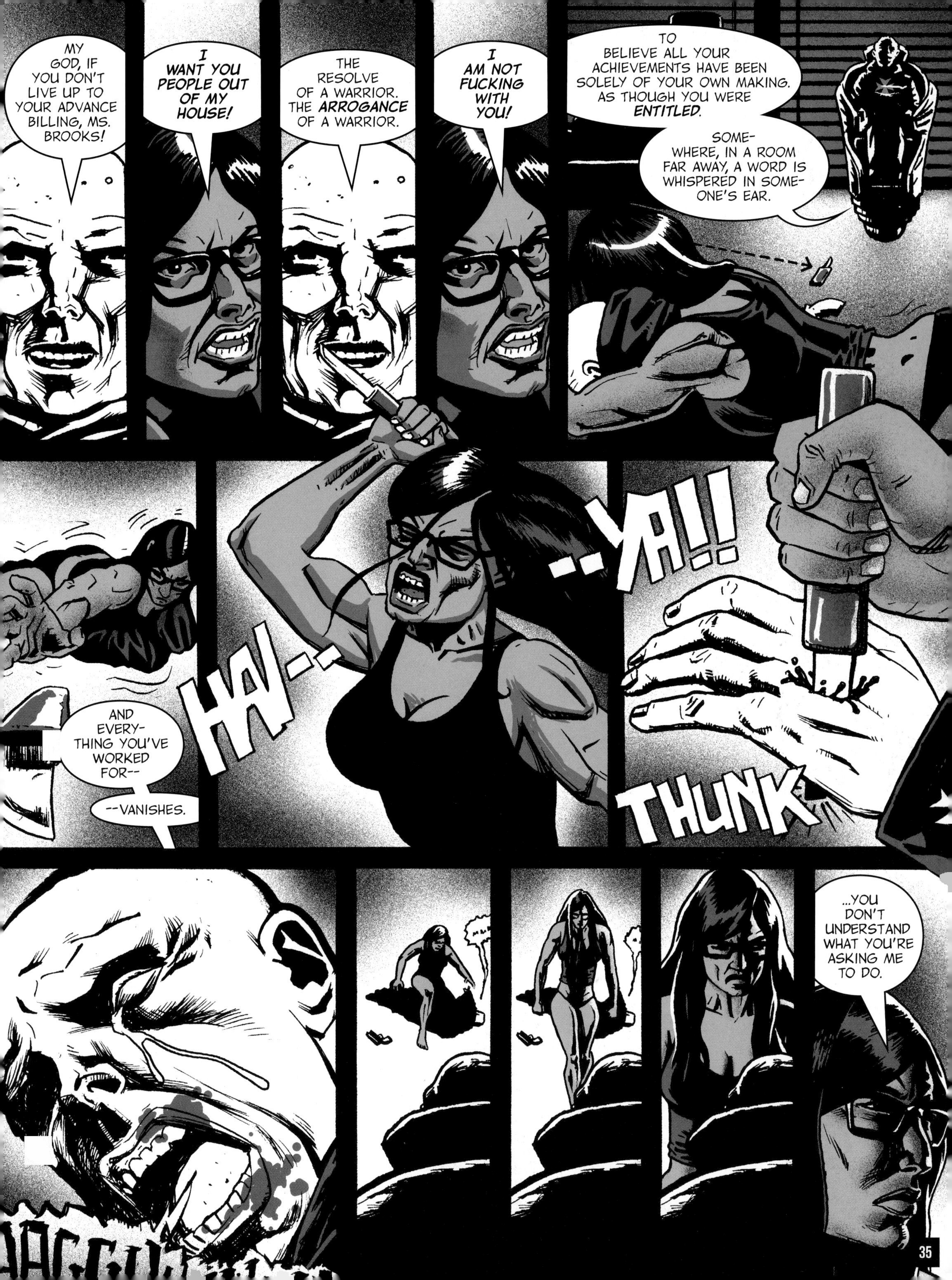
MY GOD, IF YOU DON'T LIVE UP TO YOUR ADVANCE BILLING, MS. BROOKS!
I WANT YOU PEOPLE OUT OF MY HOUSE!
THE RESOLVE OF A WARRIOR. THE ARROGANCE OF A WARRIOR.
I AM NOT FUCKING WITH YOU!
TO BELIEVE ALL YOUR ACHIEVEMENTS HAVE BEEN SOLELY OF YOUR OWN MAKING. AS THOUGH YOU WERE ENTITLED.
SOME-WHERE, IN A ROOM FAR AWAY, A WORD IS WHISPERED IN SOME-ONE'S EAR.
AND EVERY-THING YOU'VE WORKED FOR--
--VANISHES.
HA--
--YA!!
THUNK
...YOU DON'T UNDERSTAND WHAT YOU'RE ASKING ME TO DO.

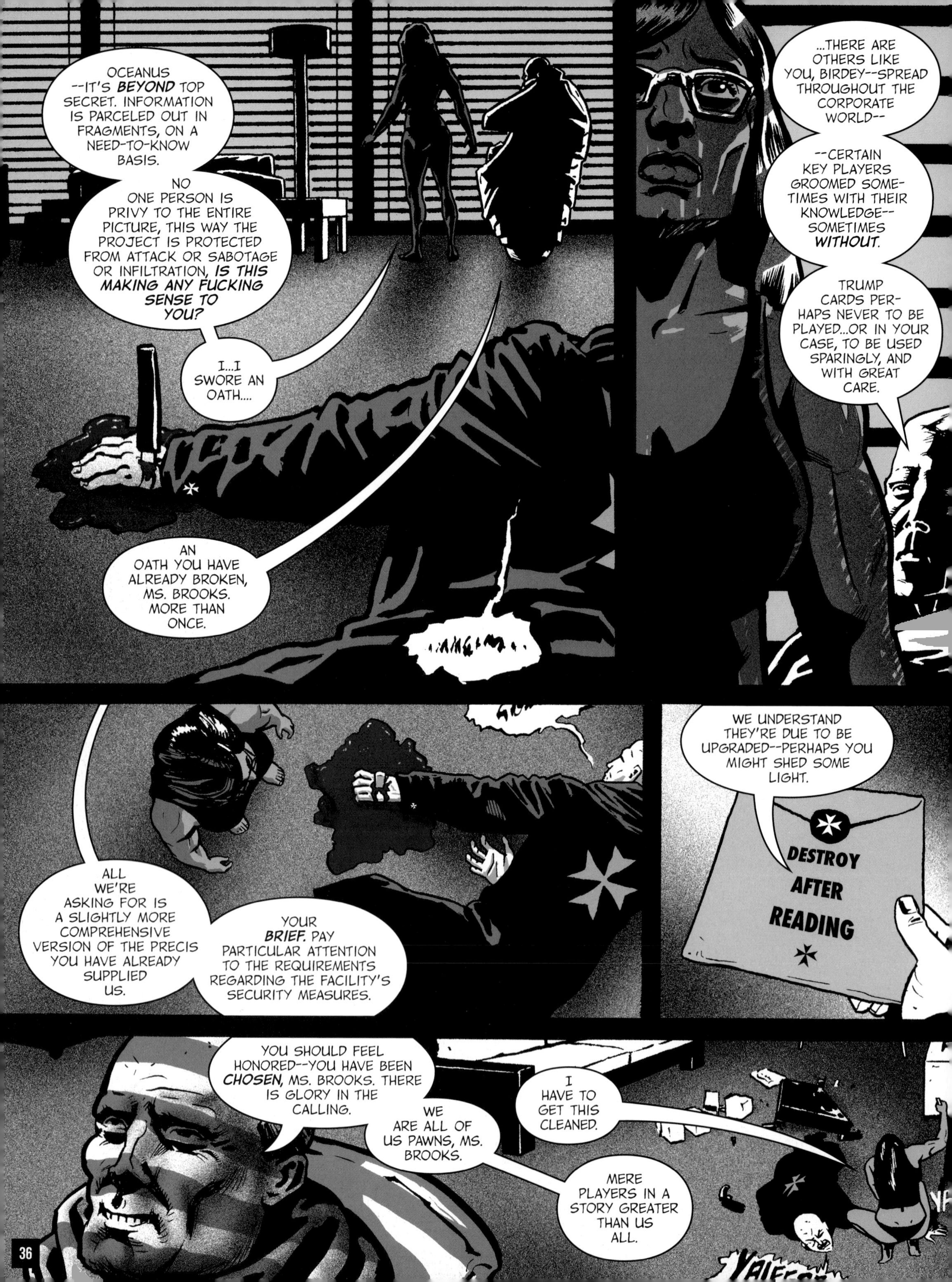

OCEANUS --IT'S **BEYOND** TOP SECRET. INFORMATION IS PARCELED OUT IN FRAGMENTS, ON A NEED-TO-KNOW BASIS.
NO ONE PERSON IS PRIVY TO THE ENTIRE PICTURE, THIS WAY THE PROJECT IS PROTECTED FROM ATTACK OR SABOTAGE OR INFILTRATION, **IS THIS MAKING ANY FUCKING SENSE TO YOU?**
I...I SWORE AN OATH....
AN OATH YOU HAVE ALREADY BROKEN, MS. BROOKS. MORE THAN ONCE.
...THERE ARE OTHERS LIKE YOU, BIRDEY--SPREAD THROUGHOUT THE CORPORATE WORLD--
--CERTAIN KEY PLAYERS GROOMED SOMETIMES WITH THEIR KNOWLEDGE--SOMETIMES **WITHOUT**.
TRUMP CARDS PERHAPS NEVER TO BE PLAYED...OR IN YOUR CASE, TO BE USED SPARINGLY, AND WITH GREAT CARE.
ALL WE'RE ASKING FOR IS A SLIGHTLY MORE COMPREHENSIVE VERSION OF THE PRECIS YOU HAVE ALREADY SUPPLIED US.
YOUR **BRIEF.** PAY PARTICULAR ATTENTION TO THE REQUIREMENTS REGARDING THE FACILITY'S SECURITY MEASURES.
WE UNDERSTAND THEY'RE DUE TO BE UPGRADED--PERHAPS YOU MIGHT SHED SOME LIGHT.
DESTROY AFTER READING
YOU SHOULD FEEL HONORED--YOU HAVE BEEN **CHOSEN**, MS. BROOKS. THERE IS GLORY IN THE CALLING.
WE ARE ALL OF US PAWNS, MS. BROOKS.
MERE PLAYERS IN A STORY GREATER THAN US ALL.
I HAVE TO GET THIS CLEANED.

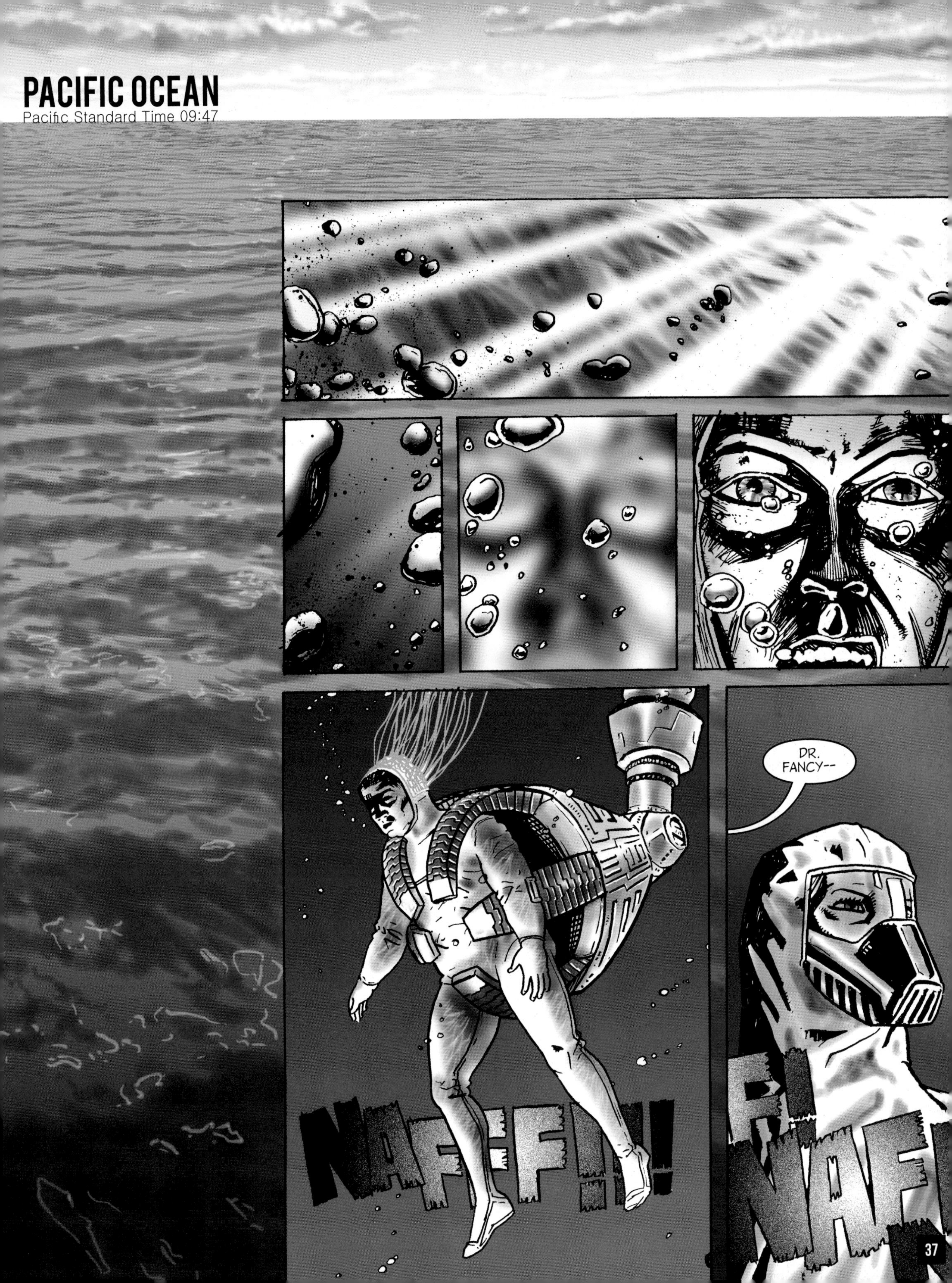
PACIFIC OCEAN
Pacific Standard Time 09:47
DR. FANCY--
NAFFIN!

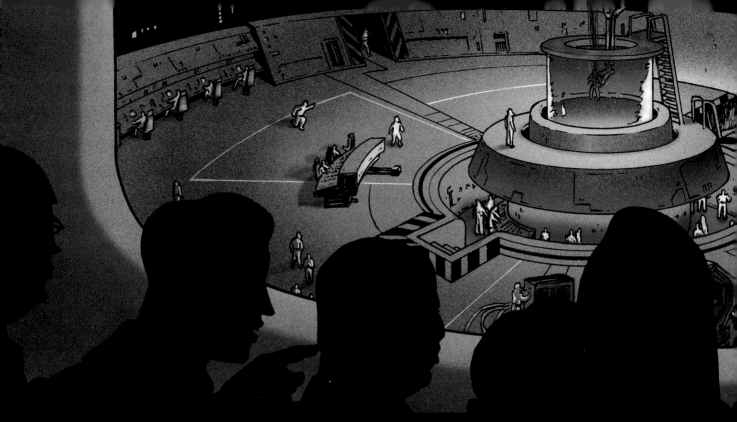

DR. FANCY, WE HAVE TO SHUT DOWN.

DR. FANC — TERMINATE.

KLIKETTY

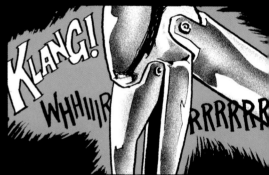

KLANG!

WHHIIIRR

RRRRRR

WWWHHIIURRRRRRRRRR

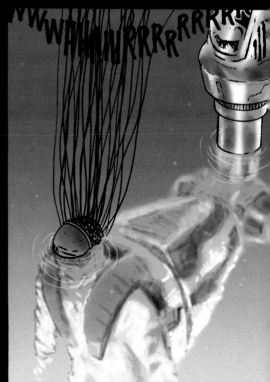

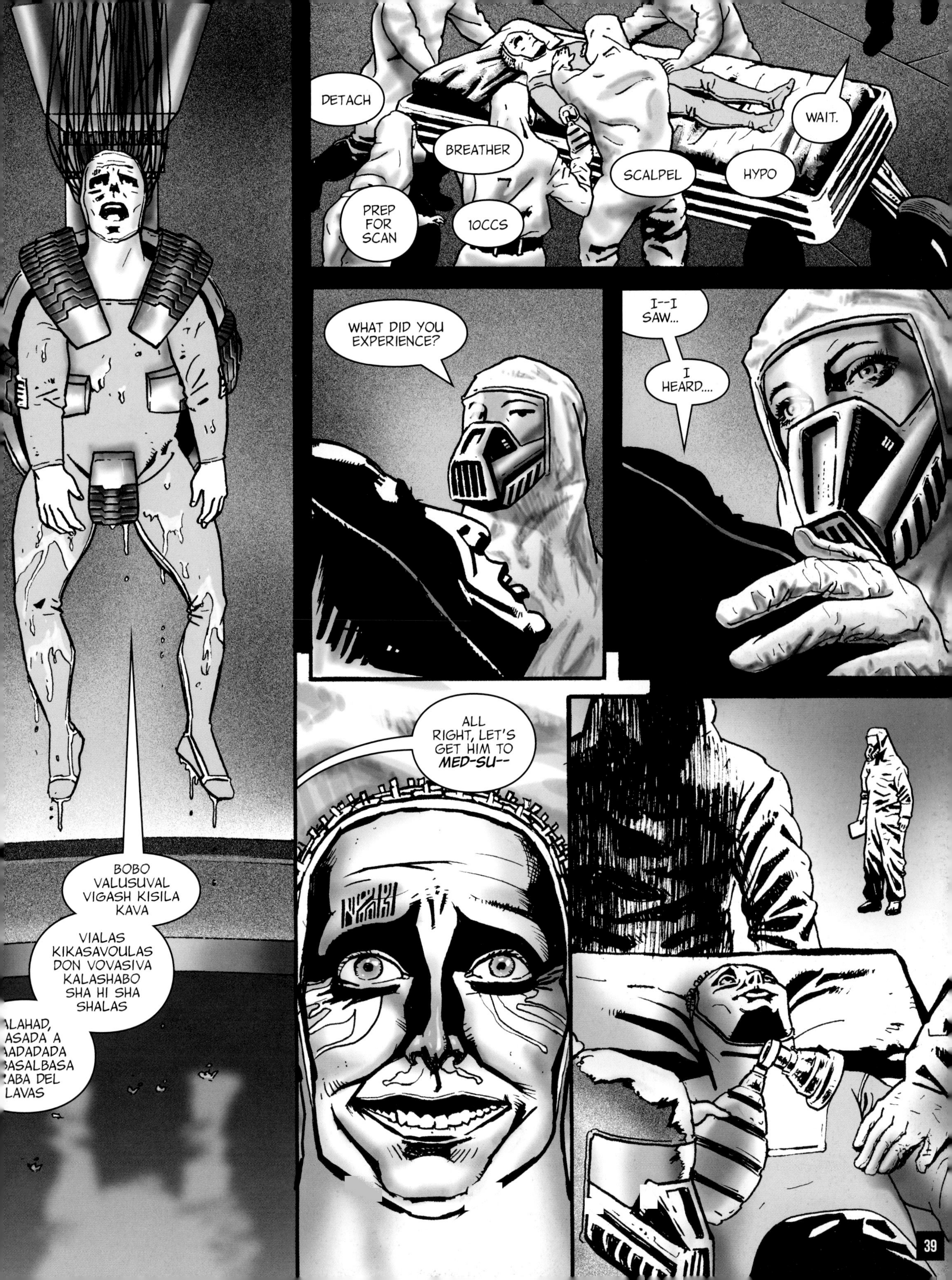
BOBO VALUSUVAL VIGASH KISILA KAVA
VIALAS KIKASAVOULAS DON VOVASIVA KALASHABO SHA HI SHA SHALAS
ALAHAD, ASADA A AADADADA BASALBASA ABA DEL LAVAS
DETACH
BREATHER
PREP FOR SCAN
10CCS
SCALPEL
HYPO
WAIT.
WHAT DID YOU EXPERIENCE?
I--I SAW...
I HEARD....
ALL RIGHT, LET'S GET HIM TO MED-SU--

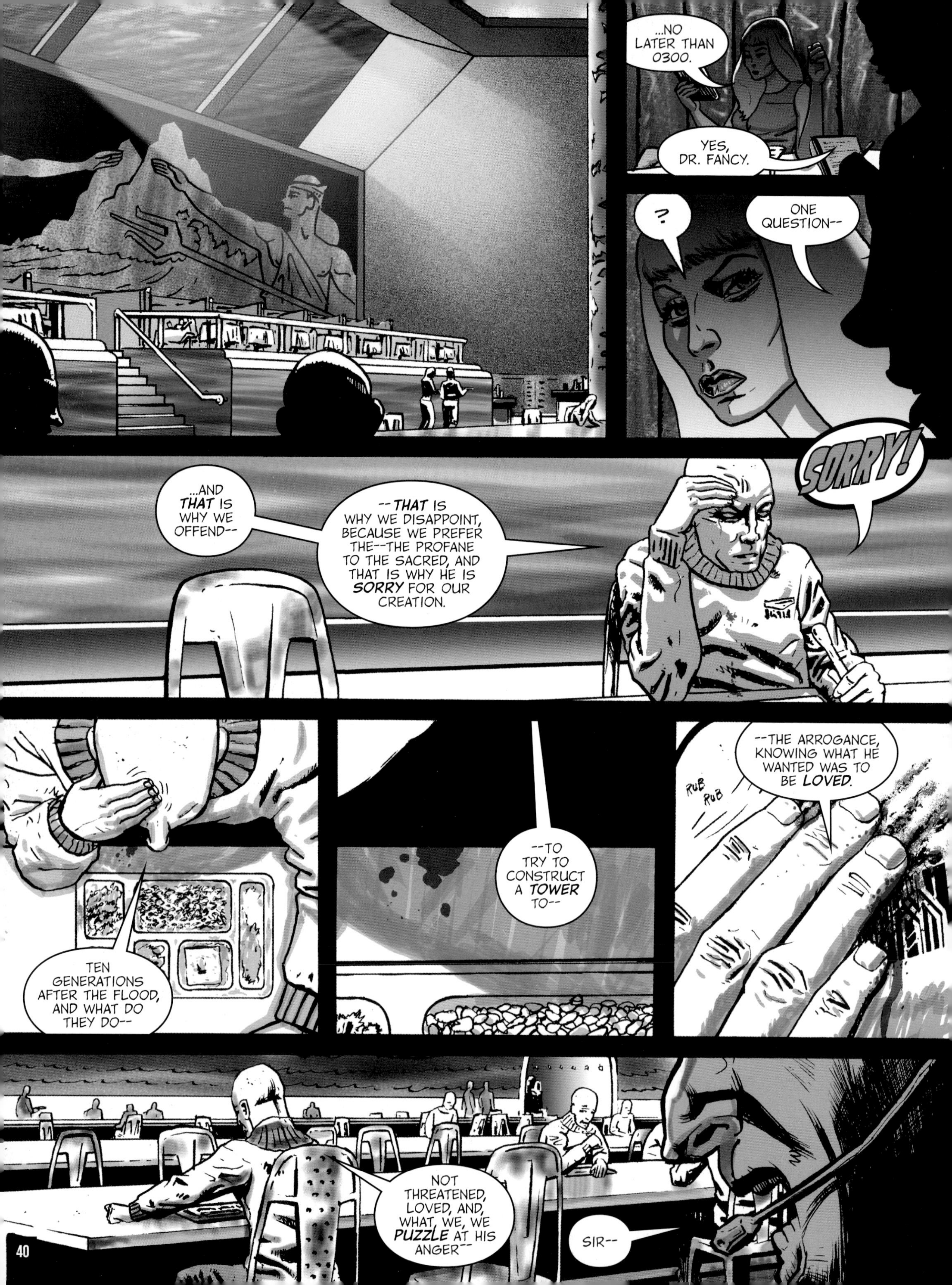

...NO LATER THAN 0300.
YES, DR. FANCY.
?
ONE QUESTION--
SORRY!
...AND THAT IS WHY WE OFFEND--
--THAT IS WHY WE DISAPPOINT, BECAUSE WE PREFER THE--THE PROFANE TO THE SACRED, AND THAT IS WHY HE IS SORRY FOR OUR CREATION.
TEN GENERATIONS AFTER THE FLOOD, AND WHAT DO THEY DO--
--TO TRY TO CONSTRUCT A TOWER TO--
RUB RUB
--THE ARROGANCE, KNOWING WHAT HE WANTED WAS TO BE LOVED.
NOT THREATENED, LOVED, AND, WHAT, WE, WE PUZZLE AT HIS ANGER--
SIR--

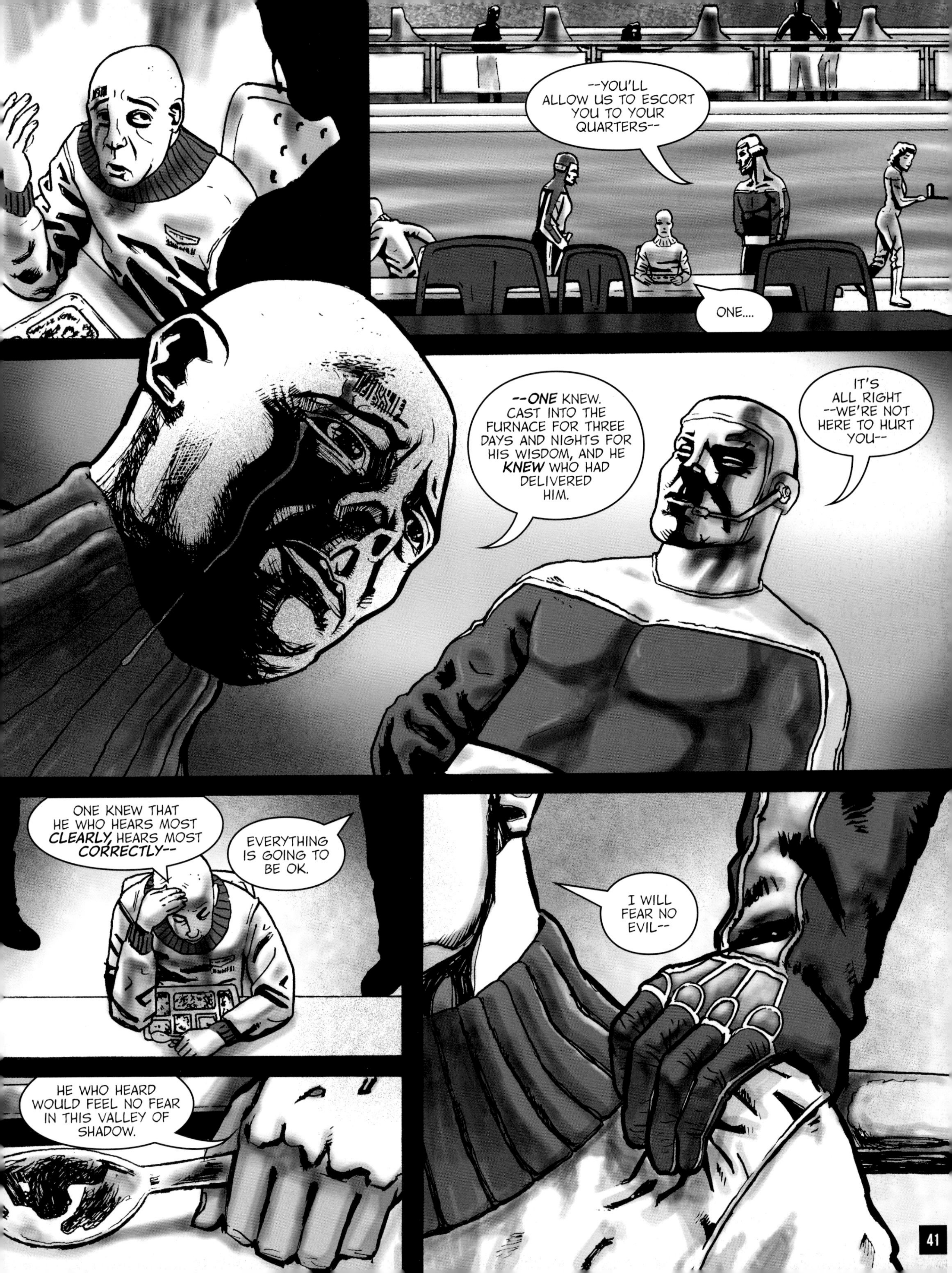
--YOU'LL ALLOW US TO ESCORT YOU TO YOUR QUARTERS--
ONE....
--ONE KNEW. CAST INTO THE FURNACE FOR THREE DAYS AND NIGHTS FOR HIS WISDOM, AND HE KNEW WHO HAD DELIVERED HIM.
IT'S ALL RIGHT --WE'RE NOT HERE TO HURT YOU--
ONE KNEW THAT HE WHO HEARS MOST CLEARLY, HEARS MOST CORRECTLY--
EVERYTHING IS GOING TO BE OK.
I WILL FEAR NO EVIL--
HE WHO HEARD WOULD FEEL NO FEAR IN THIS VALLEY OF SHADOW.

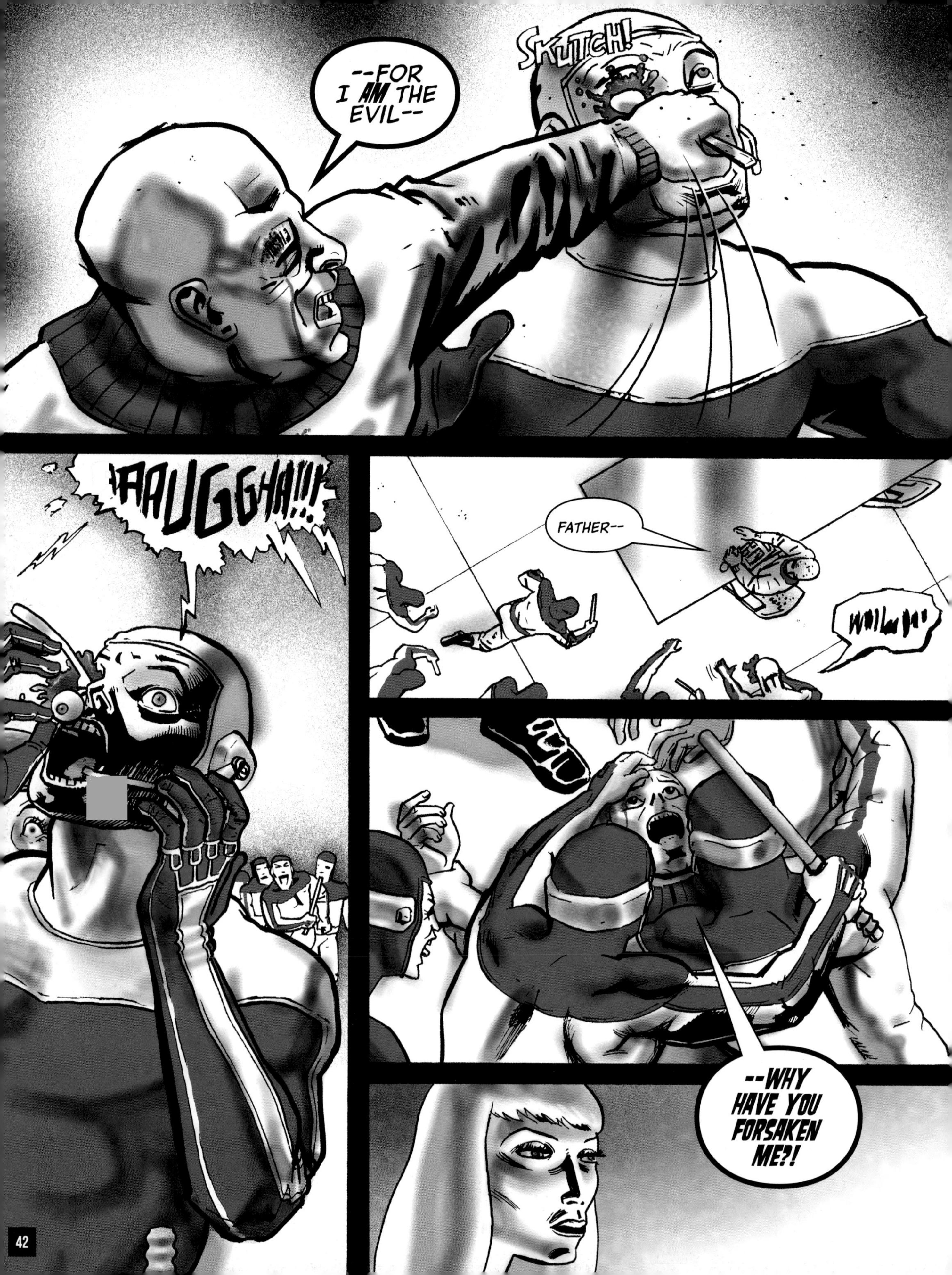
SKUTCH!
--FOR I AM THE EVIL--
AAUGGHA!!!
FATHER--
--WHY HAVE YOU FORSAKEN ME?!

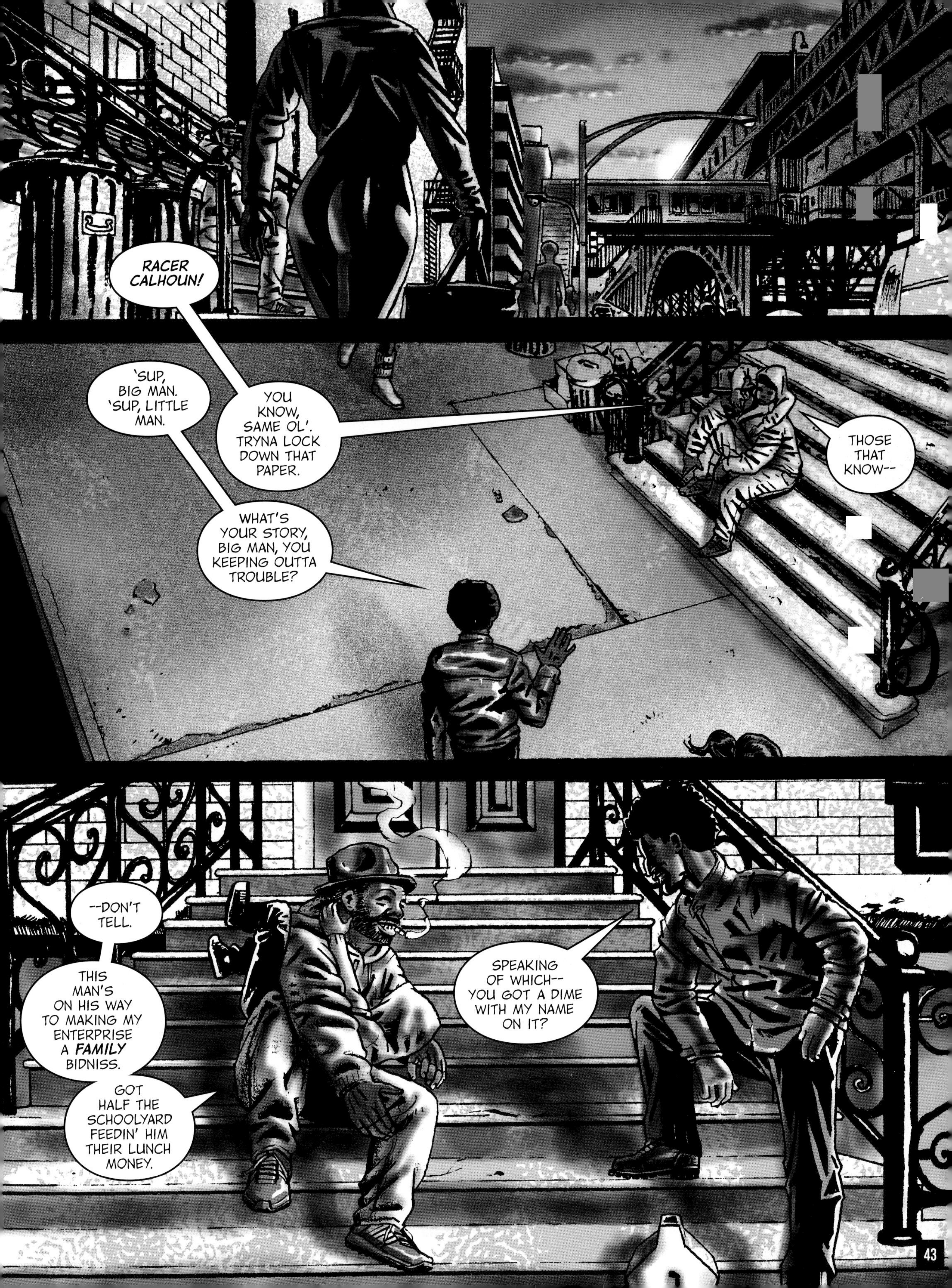

RACER CALHOUN!
'SUP, BIG MAN. 'SUP, LITTLE MAN.
YOU KNOW, SAME OL'. TRYNA LOCK DOWN THAT PAPER.
WHAT'S YOUR STORY, BIG MAN, YOU KEEPING OUTTA TROUBLE?
THOSE THAT KNOW--
--DON'T TELL.
THIS MAN'S ON HIS WAY TO MAKING MY ENTERPRISE A **FAMILY** BIDNISS.
GOT HALF THE SCHOOLYARD FEEDIN' HIM THEIR LUNCH MONEY.
SPEAKING OF WHICH-- YOU GOT A DIME WITH MY NAME ON IT?

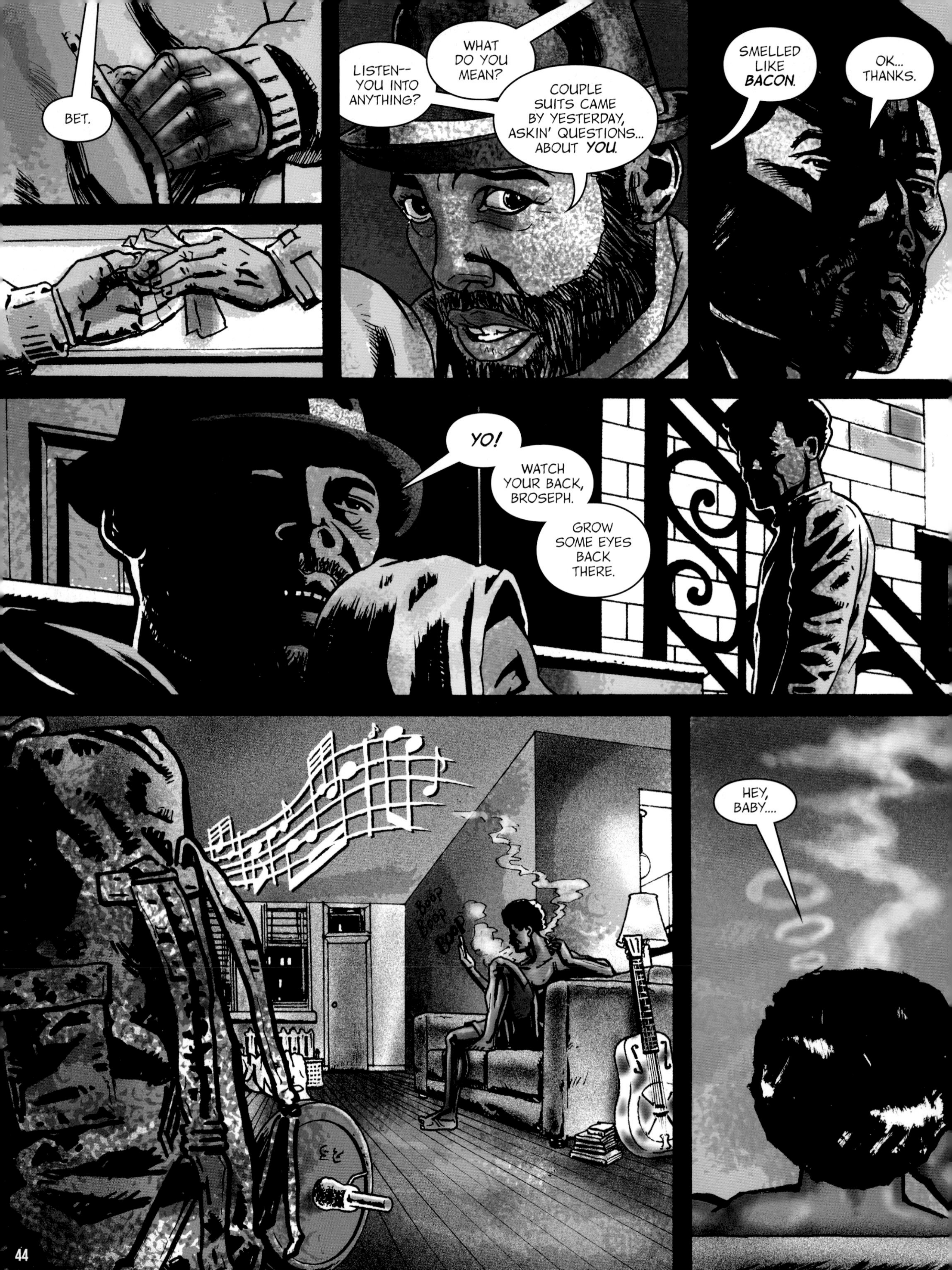

BET.
LISTEN-- YOU INTO ANYTHING?
WHAT DO YOU MEAN?
COUPLE SUITS CAME BY YESTERDAY, ASKIN' QUESTIONS... ABOUT *YOU*.
SMELLED LIKE **BACON**.
OK... THANKS.
YO!
WATCH YOUR BACK, BROSEPH.
GROW SOME EYES BACK THERE.
BOOP
BOOP
BOOP
HEY, BABY....

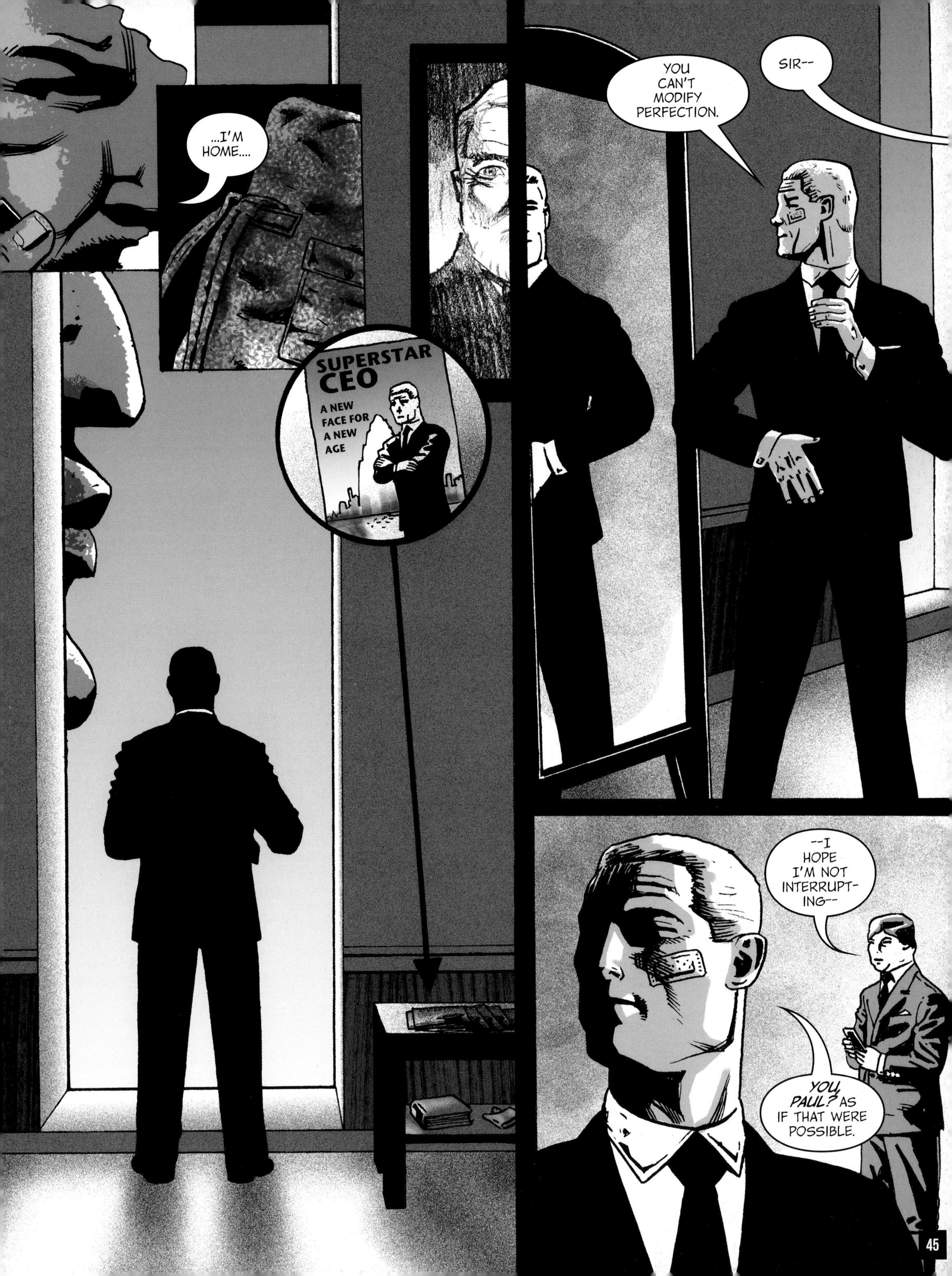

...I'M HOME....
SUPERSTAR CEO
A NEW FACE FOR A NEW AGE
YOU CAN'T MODIFY PERFECTION.
SIR--
--I HOPE I'M NOT INTERRUPT-ING--
YOU, PAUL? AS IF THAT WERE POSSIBLE.

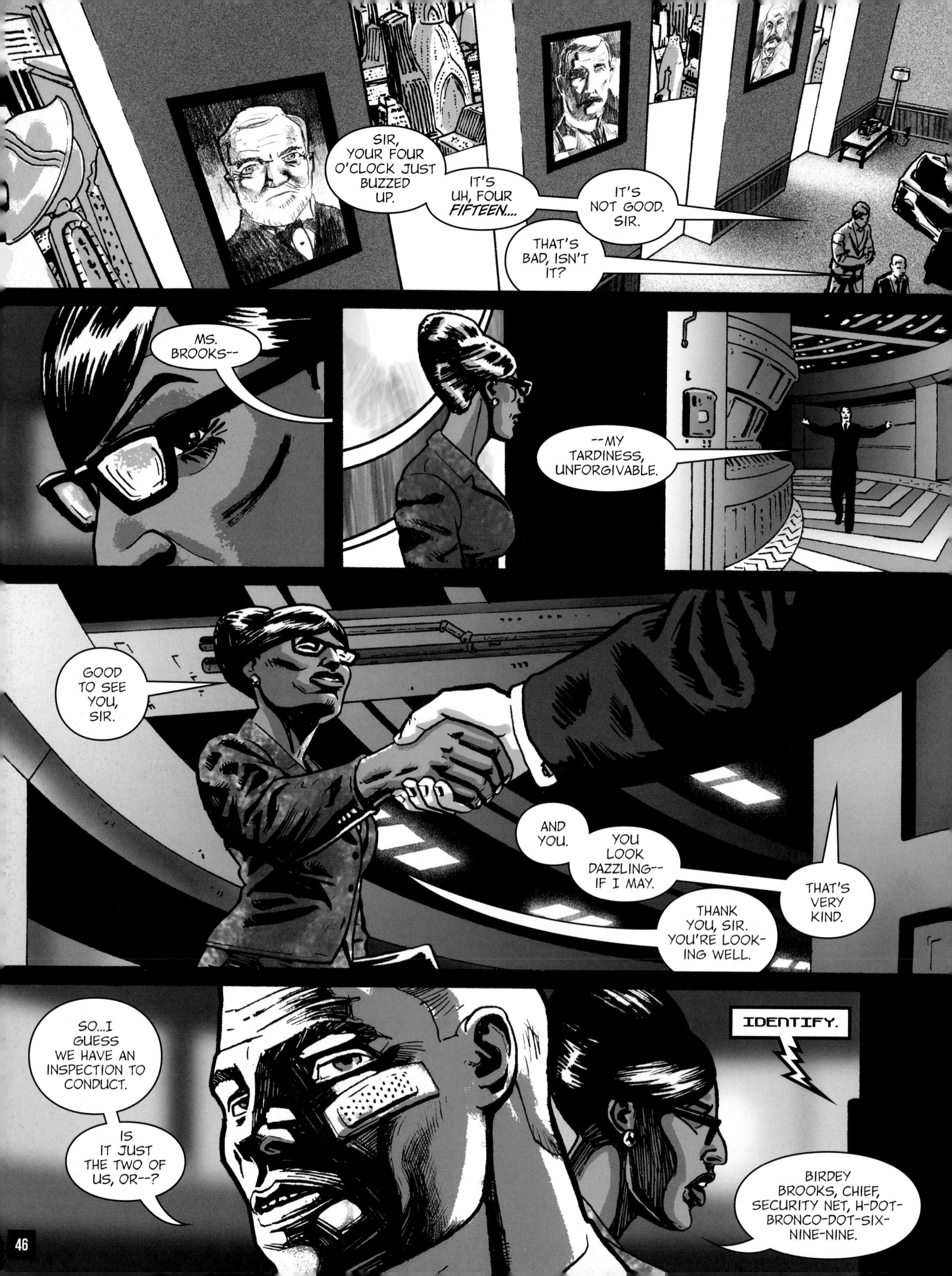
SIR, YOUR FOUR O'CLOCK JUST BUZZED UP.
IT'S UH, FOUR *FIFTEEN....*
IT'S NOT GOOD. SIR.
THAT'S BAD, ISN'T IT?
MS. BROOKS--
--MY TARDINESS, UNFORGIVABLE.
GOOD TO SEE YOU, SIR.
AND YOU.
YOU LOOK DAZZLING--IF I MAY.
THAT'S VERY KIND.
THANK YOU, SIR. YOU'RE LOOK-ING WELL.
SO...I GUESS WE HAVE AN INSPECTION TO CONDUCT.
IS IT JUST THE TWO OF US, OR--?
IDENTIFY.
BIRDEY BROOKS, CHIEF, SECURITY NET, H-DOT-BRONCO-DOT-SIX-NINE-NINE.

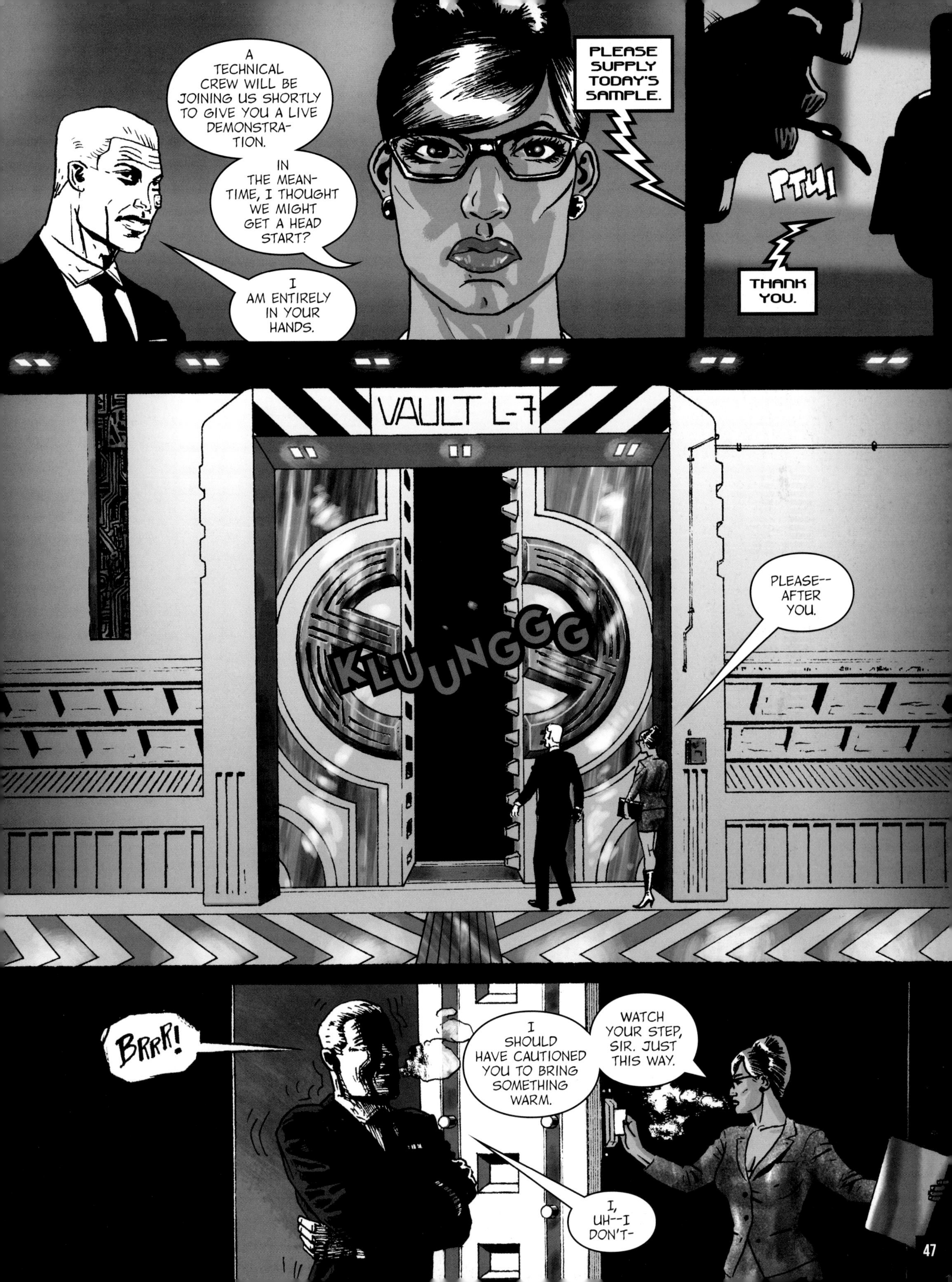
A TECHNICAL CREW WILL BE JOINING US SHORTLY TO GIVE YOU A LIVE DEMONSTRA-TION.
IN THE MEAN-TIME, I THOUGHT WE MIGHT GET A HEAD START?
I AM ENTIRELY IN YOUR HANDS.
PLEASE SUPPLY TODAY'S SAMPLE.
PTUI
THANK YOU.
VAULT L-7
KLUUNGGG
PLEASE--AFTER YOU.
BRRR!
WATCH YOUR STEP, SIR. JUST THIS WAY.
I SHOULD HAVE CAUTIONED YOU TO BRING SOMETHING WARM.
I, UH--I DON'T-

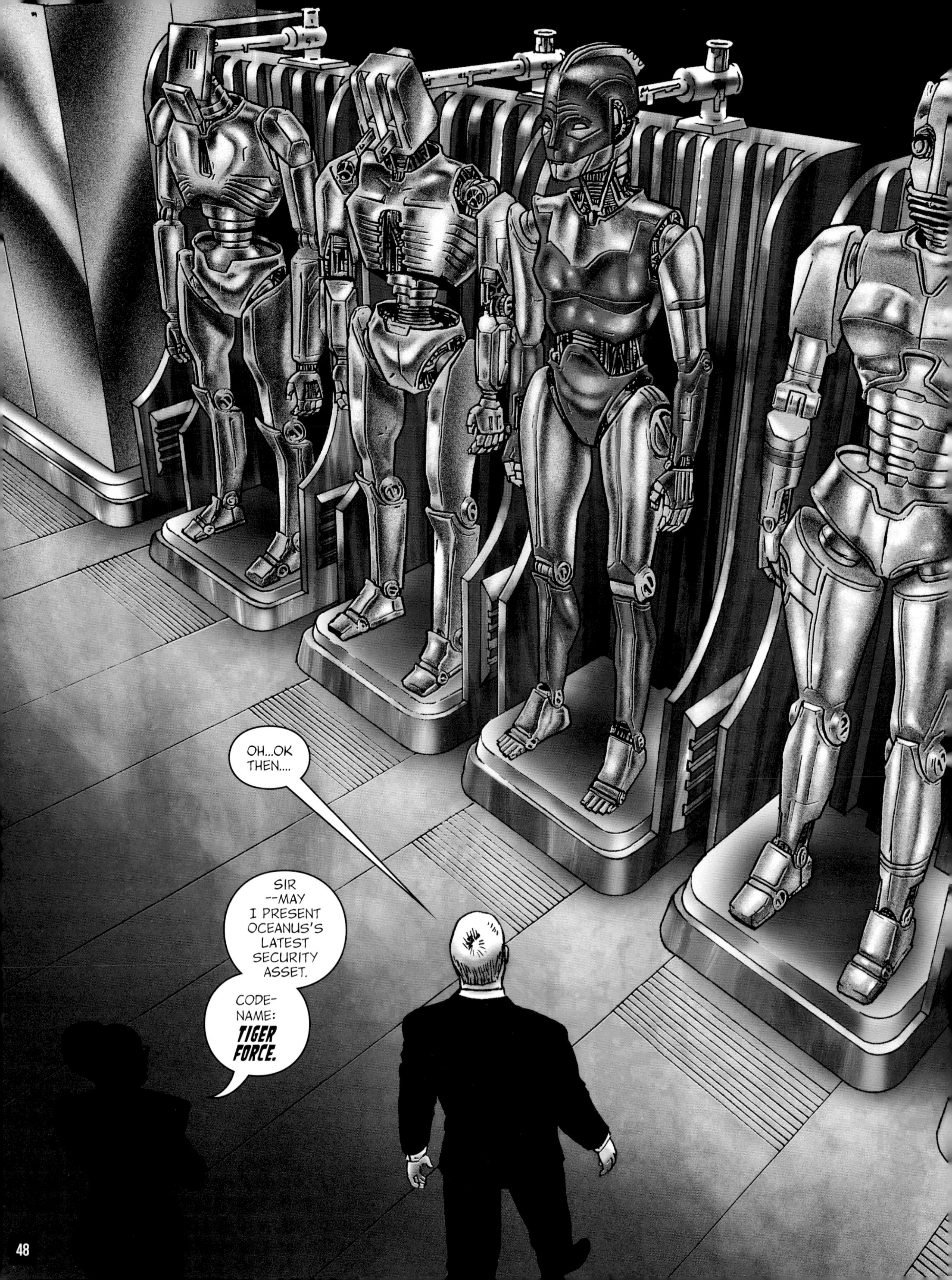
OH...OK THEN....
SIR --MAY I PRESENT OCEANUS'S LATEST SECURITY ASSET.
CODE-NAME: TIGER FORCE.

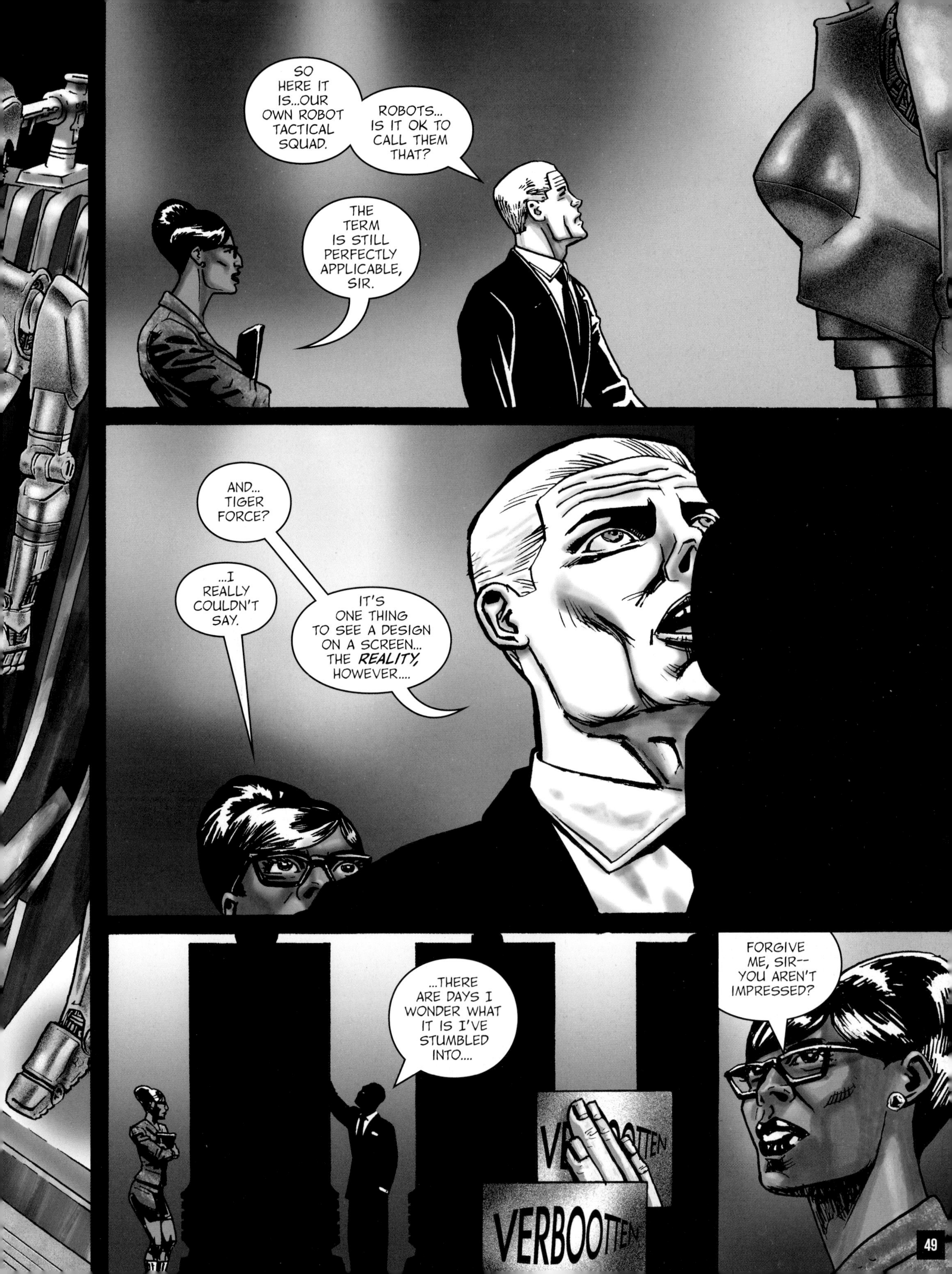
SO HERE IT IS...OUR OWN ROBOT TACTICAL SQUAD.
ROBOTS... IS IT OK TO CALL THEM THAT?
THE TERM IS STILL PERFECTLY APPLICABLE, SIR.
AND... TIGER FORCE?
IT'S ONE THING TO SEE A DESIGN ON A SCREEN... THE REALITY, HOWEVER....
...I REALLY COULDN'T SAY.
...THERE ARE DAYS I WONDER WHAT IT IS I'VE STUMBLED INTO....
FORGIVE ME, SIR-- YOU AREN'T IMPRESSED?
VERBOTTEN
VERBOTTEN

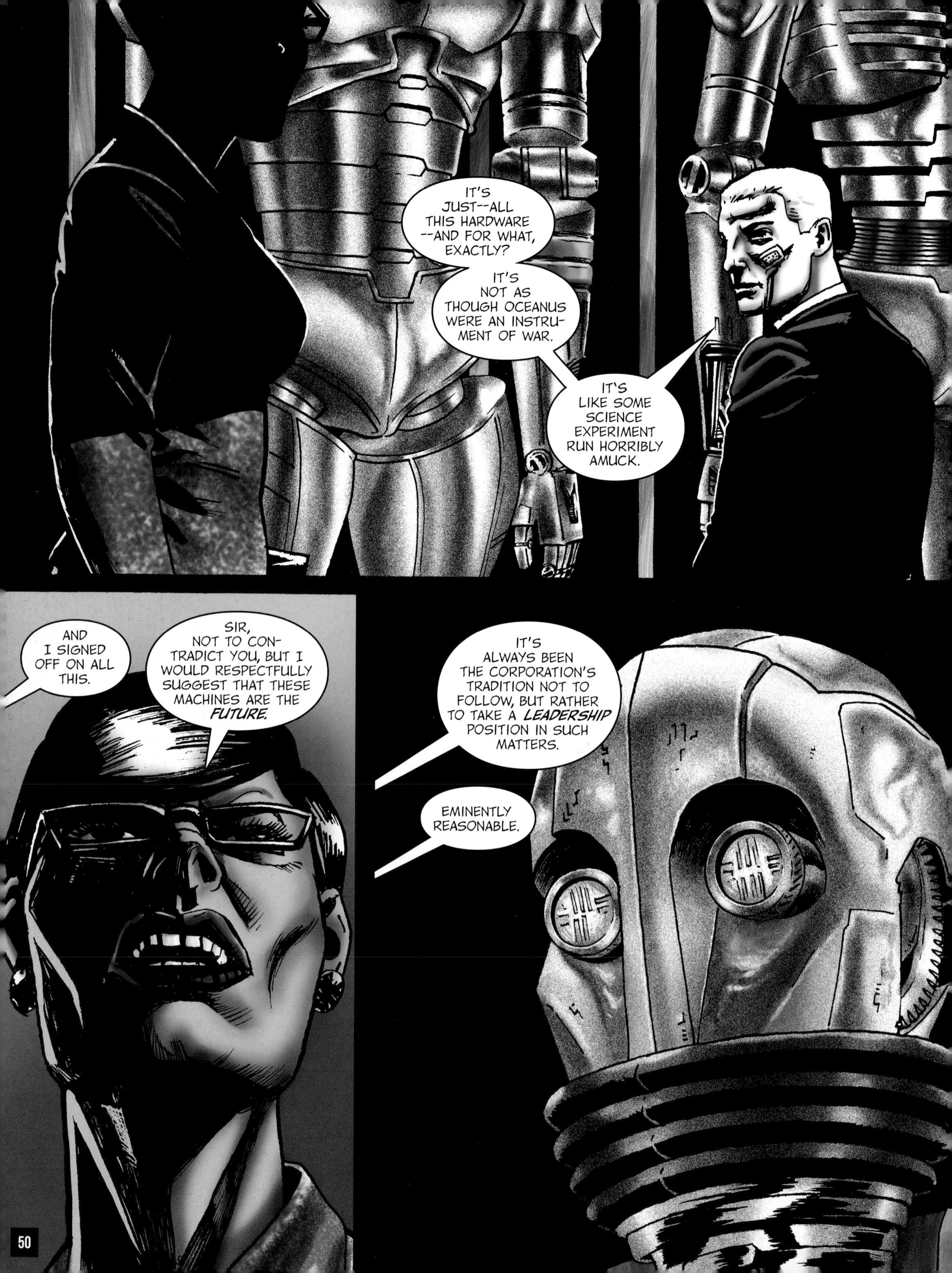
IT'S JUST--ALL THIS HARDWARE --AND FOR WHAT, EXACTLY?
IT'S NOT AS THOUGH OCEANUS WERE AN INSTRUMENT OF WAR.
IT'S LIKE SOME SCIENCE EXPERIMENT RUN HORRIBLY AMUCK.
AND I SIGNED OFF ON ALL THIS.
SIR, NOT TO CONTRADICT YOU, BUT I WOULD RESPECTFULLY SUGGEST THAT THESE MACHINES ARE THE *FUTURE.*
IT'S ALWAYS BEEN THE CORPORATION'S TRADITION NOT TO FOLLOW, BUT RATHER TO TAKE A *LEADERSHIP* POSITION IN SUCH MATTERS.
EMINENTLY REASONABLE.

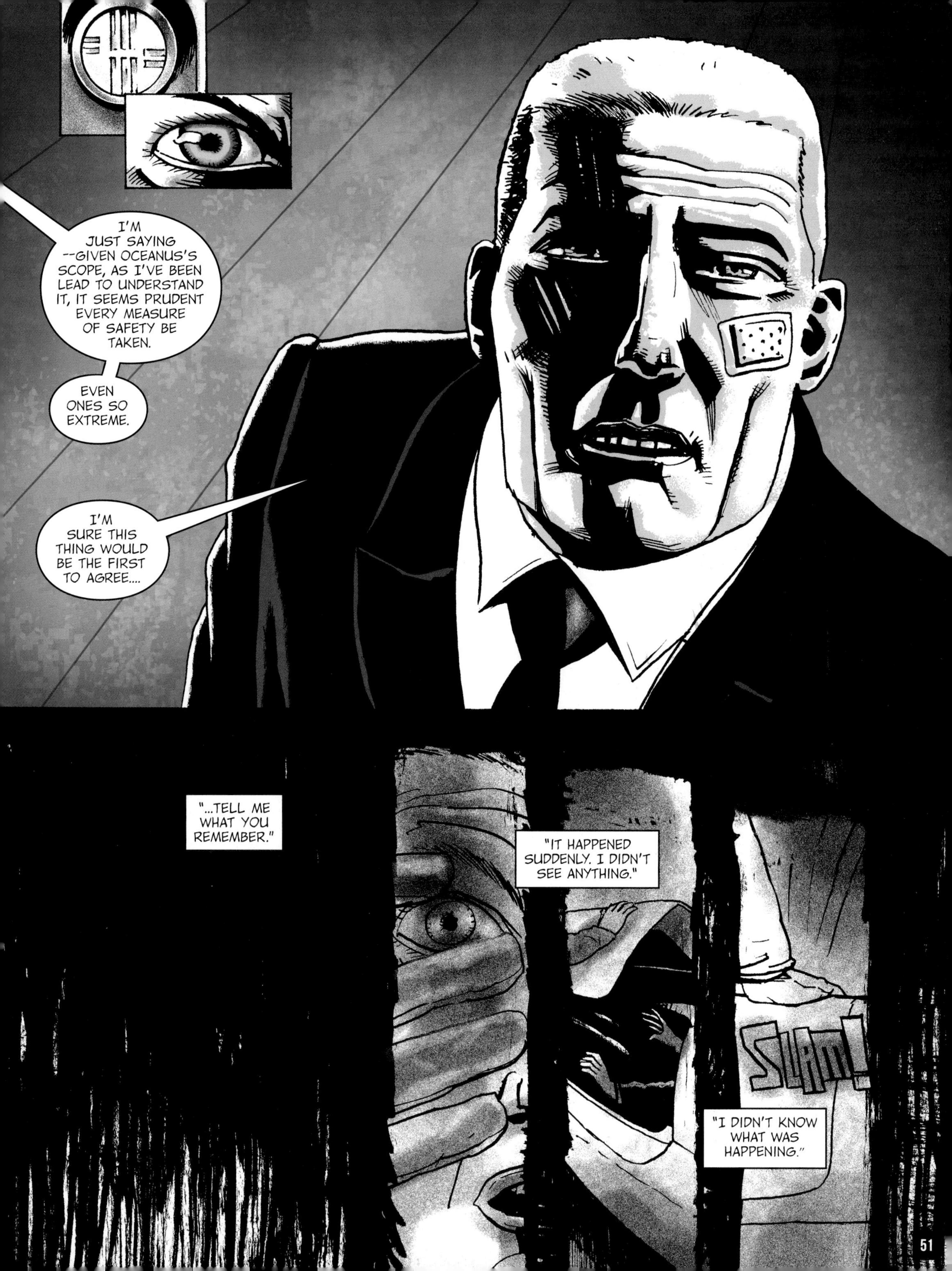
I'M JUST SAYING --GIVEN OCEANUS'S SCOPE, AS I'VE BEEN LEAD TO UNDERSTAND IT, IT SEEMS PRUDENT EVERY MEASURE OF SAFETY BE TAKEN.
EVEN ONES SO EXTREME.
I'M SURE THIS THING WOULD BE THE FIRST TO AGREE....
"...TELL ME WHAT YOU REMEMBER."
"IT HAPPENED SUDDENLY. I DIDN'T SEE ANYTHING."
SLAM!
"I DIDN'T KNOW WHAT WAS HAPPENING."

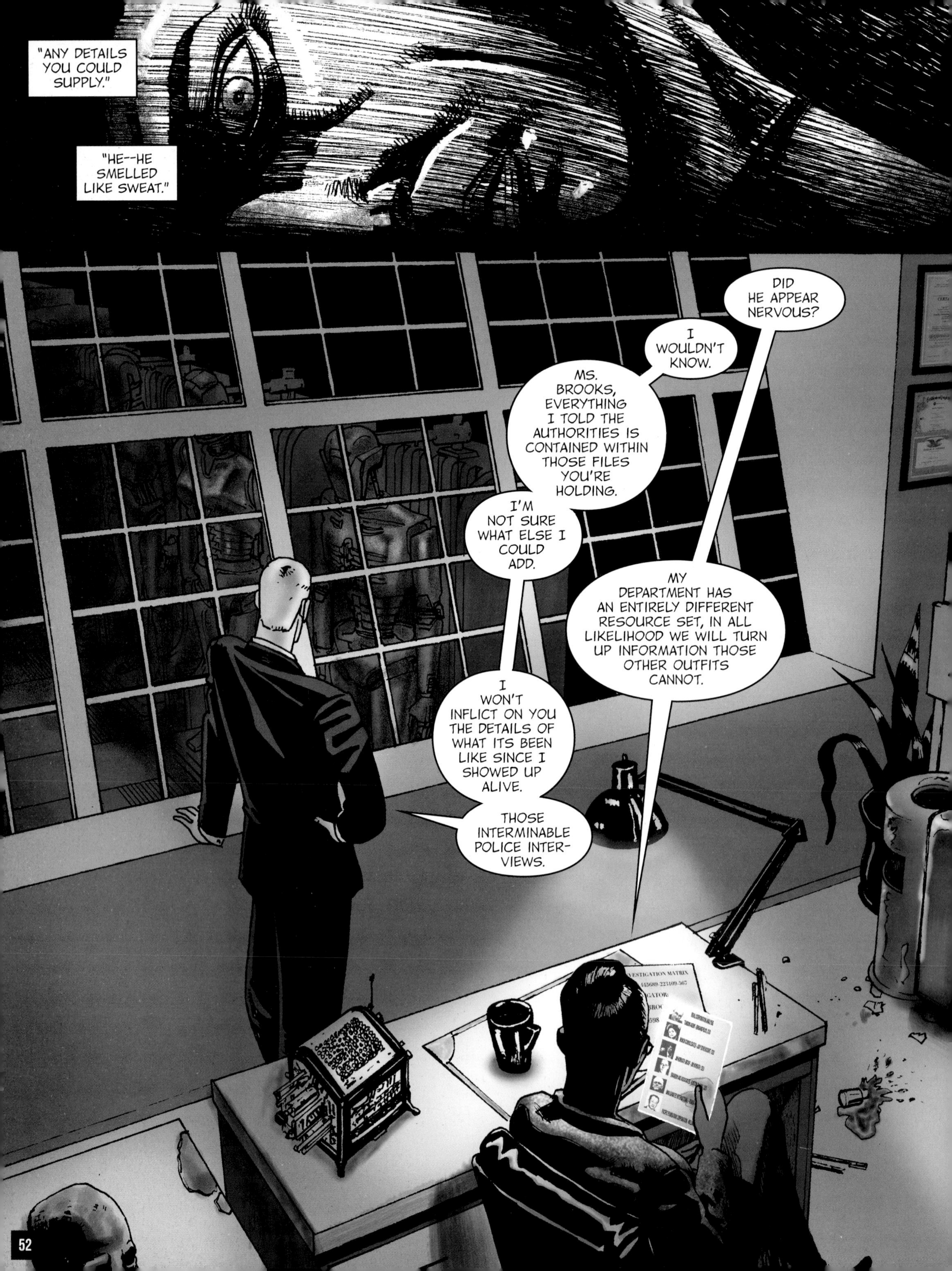
"ANY DETAILS YOU COULD SUPPLY."
"HE--HE SMELLED LIKE SWEAT."
DID HE APPEAR NERVOUS?
I WOULDN'T KNOW.
MS. BROOKS, EVERYTHING I TOLD THE AUTHORITIES IS CONTAINED WITHIN THOSE FILES YOU'RE HOLDING.
I'M NOT SURE WHAT ELSE I COULD ADD.
MY DEPARTMENT HAS AN ENTIRELY DIFFERENT RESOURCE SET, IN ALL LIKELIHOOD WE WILL TURN UP INFORMATION THOSE OTHER OUTFITS CANNOT.
I WON'T INFLICT ON YOU THE DETAILS OF WHAT ITS BEEN LIKE SINCE I SHOWED UP ALIVE.
THOSE INTERMINABLE POLICE INTER-VIEWS.

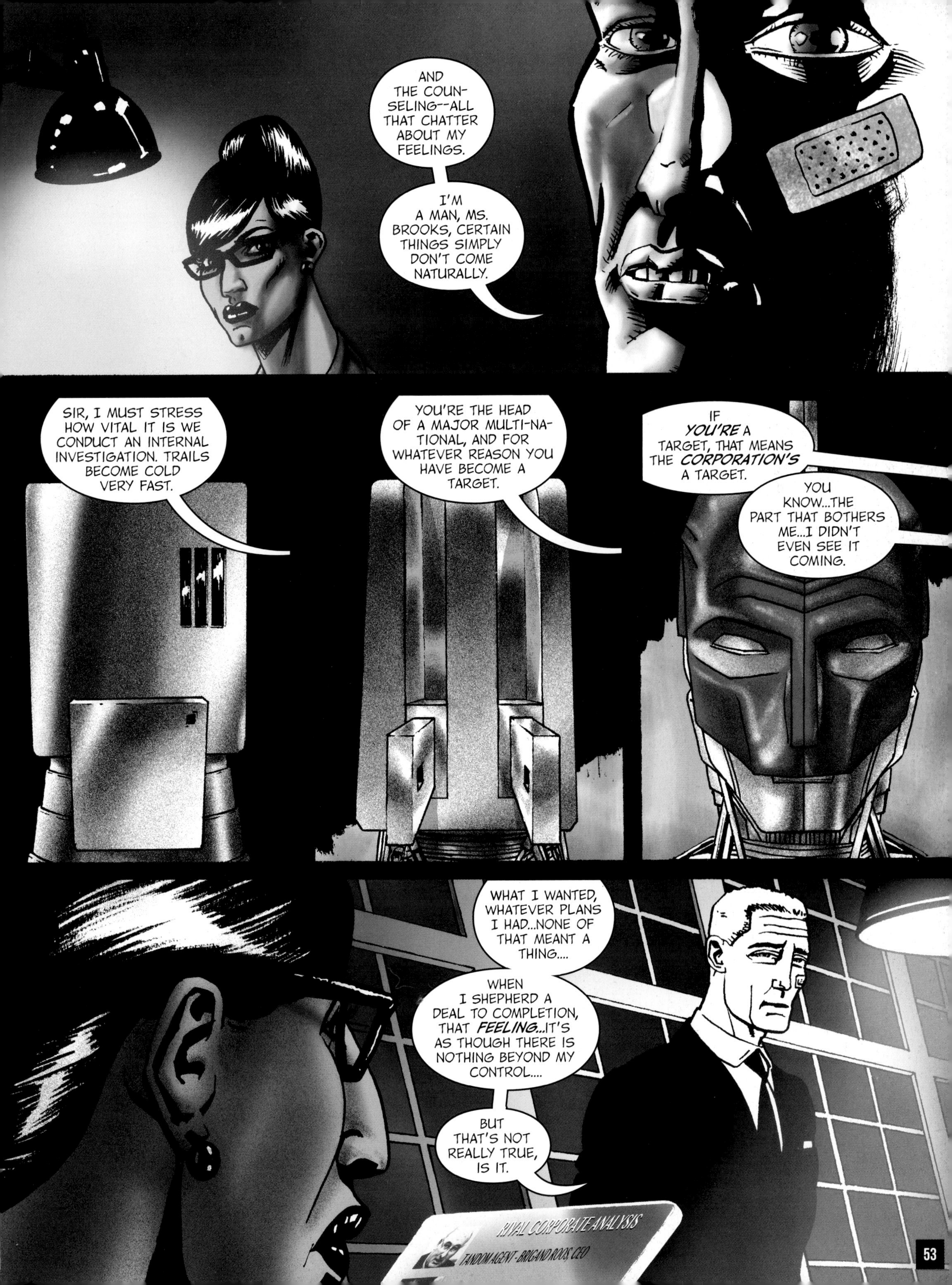
AND THE COUN-SELING--ALL THAT CHATTER ABOUT MY FEELINGS.
I'M A MAN, MS. BROOKS, CERTAIN THINGS SIMPLY DON'T COME NATURALLY.
SIR, I MUST STRESS HOW VITAL IT IS WE CONDUCT AN INTERNAL INVESTIGATION. TRAILS BECOME COLD VERY FAST.
YOU'RE THE HEAD OF A MAJOR MULTI-NA-TIONAL, AND FOR WHATEVER REASON YOU HAVE BECOME A TARGET.
IF *YOU'RE* A TARGET, THAT MEANS THE *CORPORATION'S* A TARGET.
YOU KNOW...THE PART THAT BOTHERS ME...I DIDN'T EVEN SEE IT COMING.
WHAT I WANTED, WHATEVER PLANS I HAD...NONE OF THAT MEANT A THING....
WHEN I SHEPHERD A DEAL TO COMPLETION, THAT *FEELING*...IT'S AS THOUGH THERE IS NOTHING BEYOND MY CONTROL....
BUT THAT'S NOT REALLY TRUE, IS IT.
RIVAL CORPORATE ANALYSIS
TANDOMAGENT - BRIGAND ROOS, CEO

SIR, IF YOU'RE WILLING TO DEVOTE SOME TIME OVER THE NEXT COUPLE OF WEEKS I'D BE HAPPY TO SHOW YOU SOME DEFENSIVE MOVES--

--VERY SIMPLE, VERY EASY TO MASTER.

HA! I THINK I'M BETTER SUITED TO BOARDROOM COMBAT THAN STREET BRAWLS.

THERE'S THE IRONY--I WAS ALWAYS A BIT OF A SCRAPPER AS A KID.

AS YOU WISH.

LISTEN --NOT TO BE BRUSQUE. I HAVE A PREVIOUS ENGAGEMENT.

I'VE ALREADY EMBARRASSED MYSELF ONCE TODAY WITH MY LATENESS.

RATHER SKIP A SECOND HELPING IF AT ALL POSSIBLE.

I UNDERSTAND.

SIR, IF I COULD JUST ASK YOU ONE LAST QUESTION FOR NOW--

--I'VE GOT TRANSCRIPTS OF YOUR INTERVIEWS WITH THE MINISTRY--

--IN ONE OF THEM YOU MENTION A LIST OF NAMES:

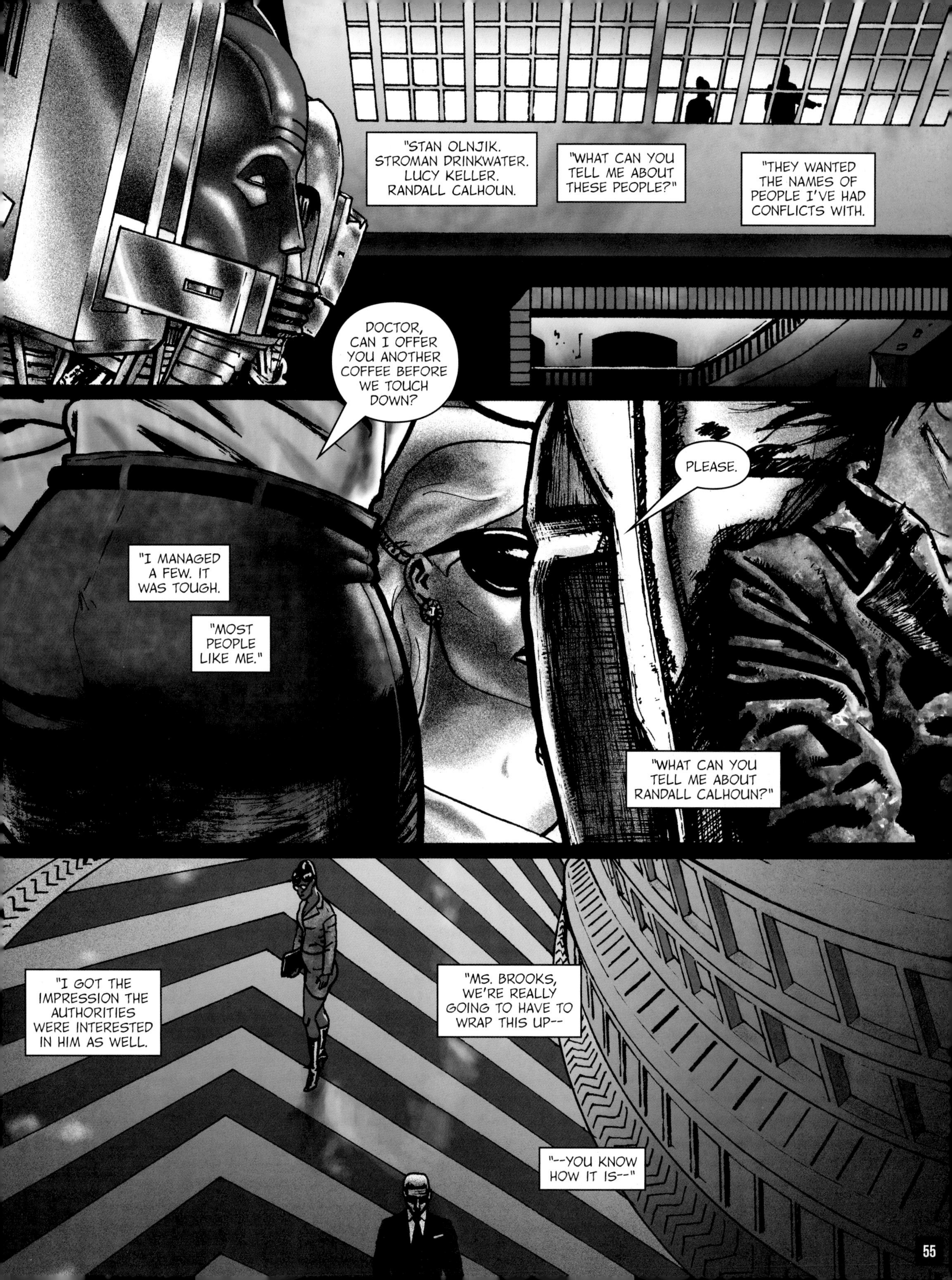
"STAN OLNJIK. STROMAN DRINKWATER. LUCY KELLER. RANDALL CALHOUN.
"WHAT CAN YOU TELL ME ABOUT THESE PEOPLE?"
"THEY WANTED THE NAMES OF PEOPLE I'VE HAD CONFLICTS WITH.
DOCTOR, CAN I OFFER YOU ANOTHER COFFEE BEFORE WE TOUCH DOWN?
PLEASE.
"I MANAGED A FEW. IT WAS TOUGH.
"MOST PEOPLE LIKE ME."
"WHAT CAN YOU TELL ME ABOUT RANDALL CALHOUN?"
"I GOT THE IMPRESSION THE AUTHORITIES WERE INTERESTED IN HIM AS WELL.
"MS. BROOKS, WE'RE REALLY GOING TO HAVE TO WRAP THIS UP--
"--YOU KNOW HOW IT IS--"

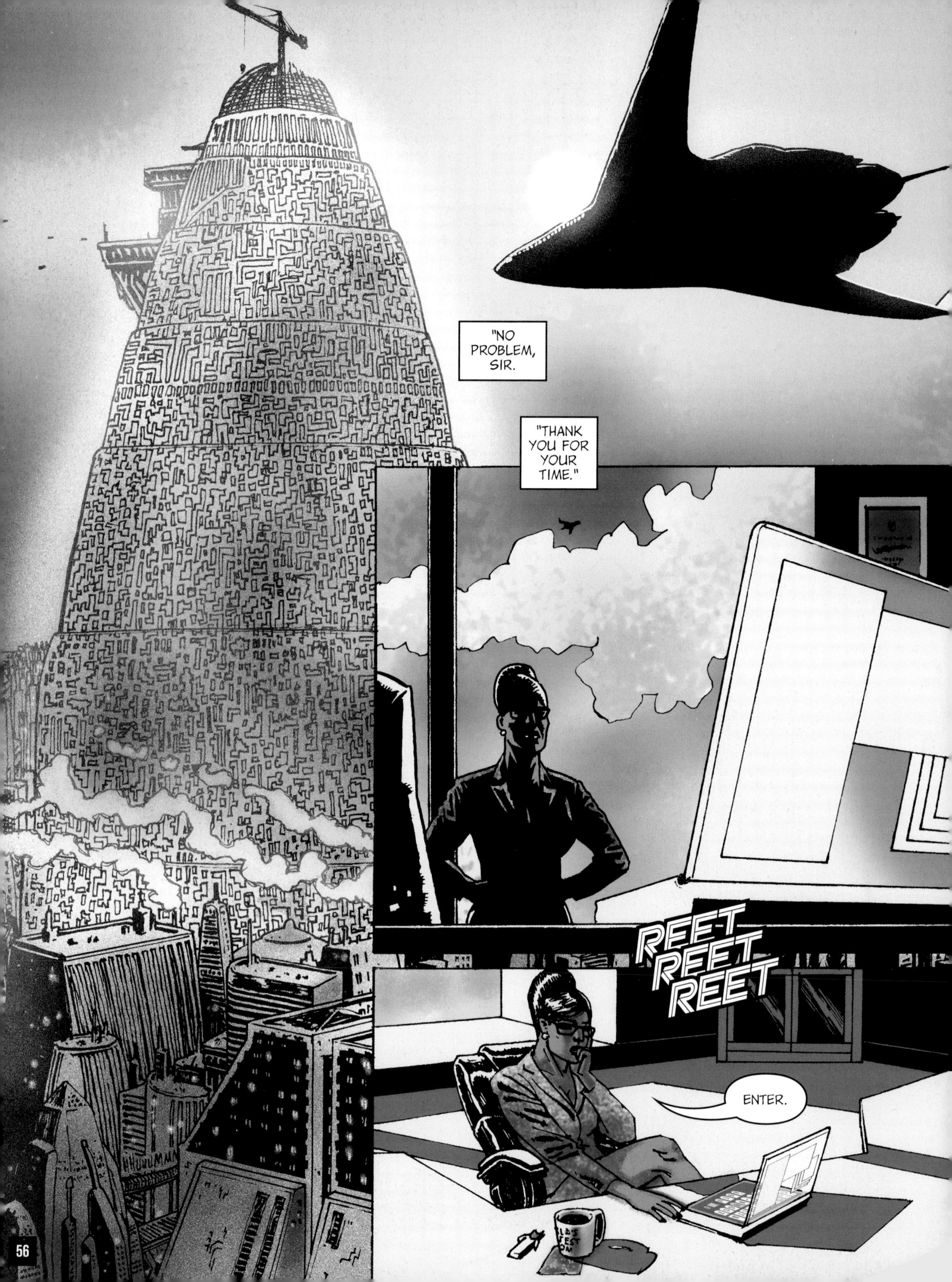
"NO PROBLEM, SIR.
"THANK YOU FOR YOUR TIME."
REET REET REET
ENTER.

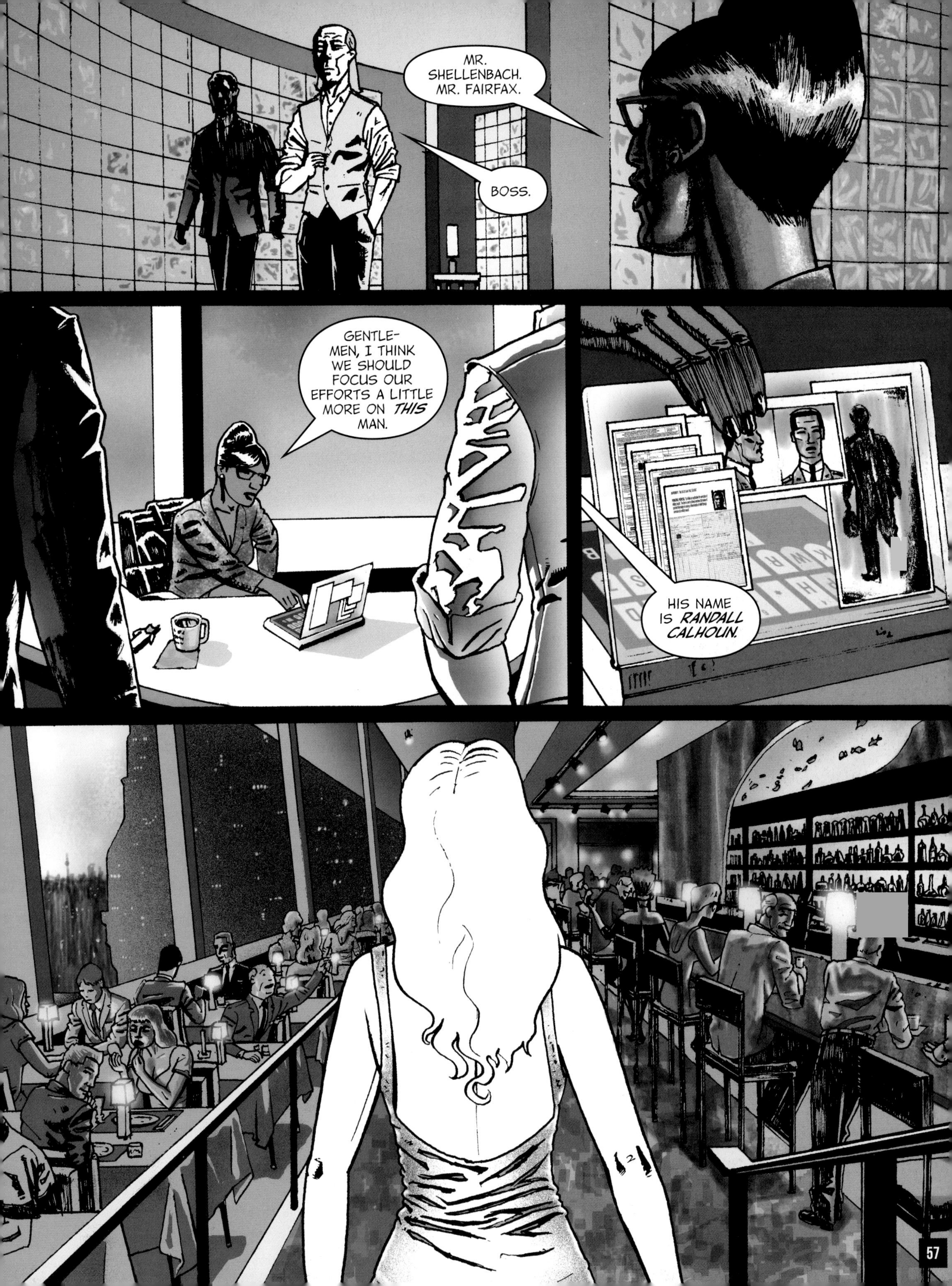
MR. SHELLENBACH. MR. FAIRFAX.
BOSS.
GENTLE-MEN, I THINK WE SHOULD FOCUS OUR EFFORTS A LITTLE MORE ON *THIS* MAN.
HIS NAME IS *RANDALL CALHOUN.*

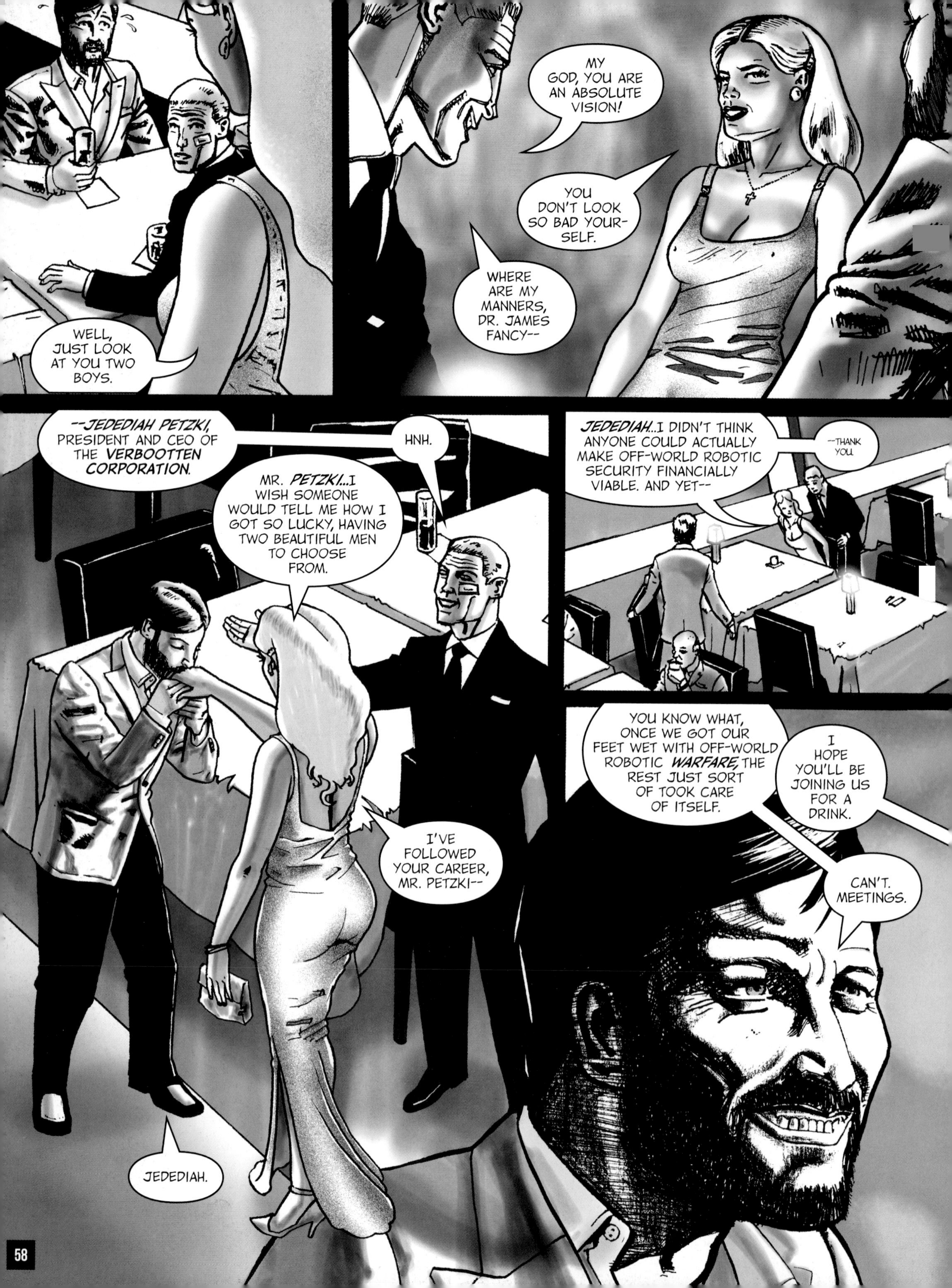
WELL, JUST LOOK AT YOU TWO BOYS.
MY GOD, YOU ARE AN ABSOLUTE VISION!
YOU DON'T LOOK SO BAD YOURSELF.
WHERE ARE MY MANNERS, DR. JAMES FANCY--
--JEDEDIAH PETZKI, PRESIDENT AND CEO OF THE VERBOOTTEN CORPORATION.
HNH.
MR. PETZKI...I WISH SOMEONE WOULD TELL ME HOW I GOT SO LUCKY, HAVING TWO BEAUTIFUL MEN TO CHOOSE FROM.
I'VE FOLLOWED YOUR CAREER, MR. PETZKI--
JEDEDIAH.
JEDEDIAH...I DIDN'T THINK ANYONE COULD ACTUALLY MAKE OFF-WORLD ROBOTIC SECURITY FINANCIALLY VIABLE. AND YET--
--THANK YOU.
YOU KNOW WHAT, ONCE WE GOT OUR FEET WET WITH OFF-WORLD ROBOTIC WARFARE, THE REST JUST SORT OF TOOK CARE OF ITSELF.
I HOPE YOU'LL BE JOINING US FOR A DRINK.
CAN'T. MEETINGS.

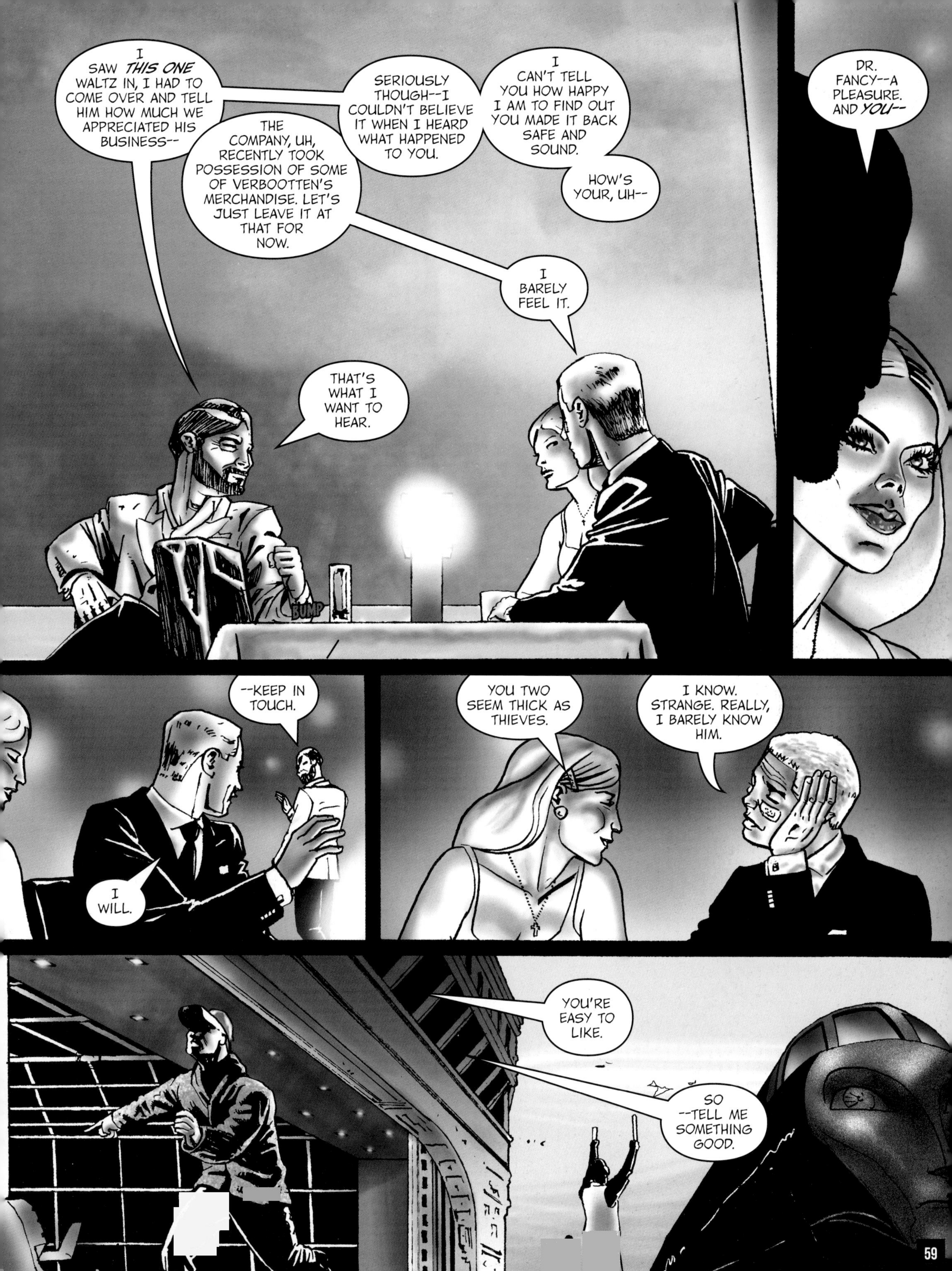
I SAW THIS ONE WALTZ IN, I HAD TO COME OVER AND TELL HIM HOW MUCH WE APPRECIATED HIS BUSINESS--
SERIOUSLY THOUGH--I COULDN'T BELIEVE IT WHEN I HEARD WHAT HAPPENED TO YOU.
I CAN'T TELL YOU HOW HAPPY I AM TO FIND OUT YOU MADE IT BACK SAFE AND SOUND.
HOW'S YOUR, UH--
THE COMPANY, UH, RECENTLY TOOK POSSESSION OF SOME OF VERBOOTTEN'S MERCHANDISE. LET'S JUST LEAVE IT AT THAT FOR NOW.
I BARELY FEEL IT.
THAT'S WHAT I WANT TO HEAR.
BUMP
DR. FANCY--A PLEASURE. AND YOU--
--KEEP IN TOUCH.
I WILL.
YOU TWO SEEM THICK AS THIEVES.
I KNOW. STRANGE. REALLY, I BARELY KNOW HIM.
YOU'RE EASY TO LIKE.
SO --TELL ME SOMETHING GOOD.

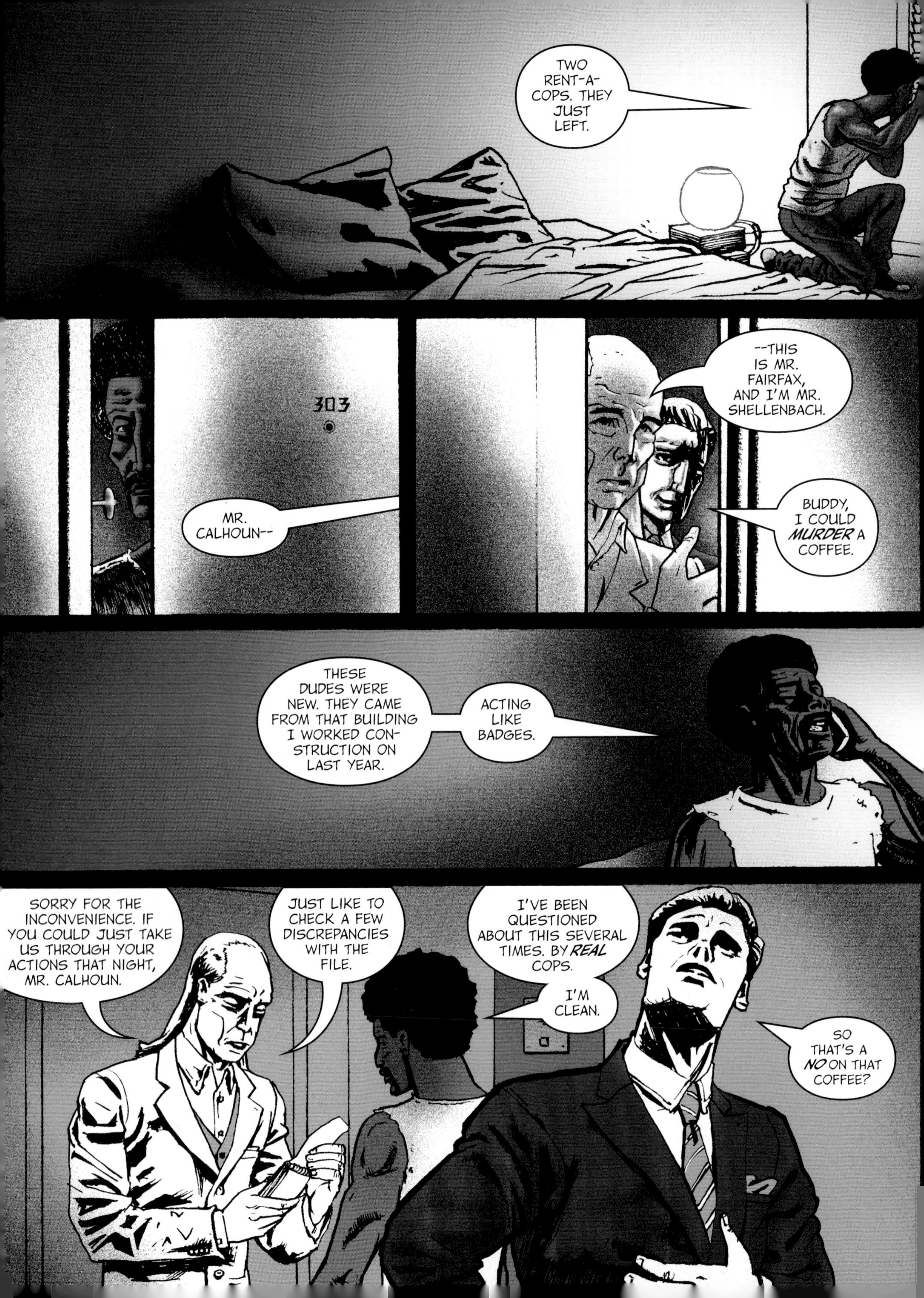
TWO RENT-A-COPS. THEY JUST LEFT.
MR. CALHOUN--
--THIS IS MR. FAIRFAX, AND I'M MR. SHELLENBACH.
BUDDY, I COULD *MURDER* A COFFEE.
THESE DUDES WERE NEW. THEY CAME FROM THAT BUILDING I WORKED CON-STRUCTION ON LAST YEAR.
ACTING LIKE BADGES.
SORRY FOR THE INCONVENIENCE. IF YOU COULD JUST TAKE US THROUGH YOUR ACTIONS THAT NIGHT, MR. CALHOUN.
JUST LIKE TO CHECK A FEW DISCREPANCIES WITH THE FILE.
I'VE BEEN QUESTIONED ABOUT THIS SEVERAL TIMES. BY *REAL* COPS.
I'M CLEAN.
SO THAT'S A *NO* ON THAT COFFEE?
303

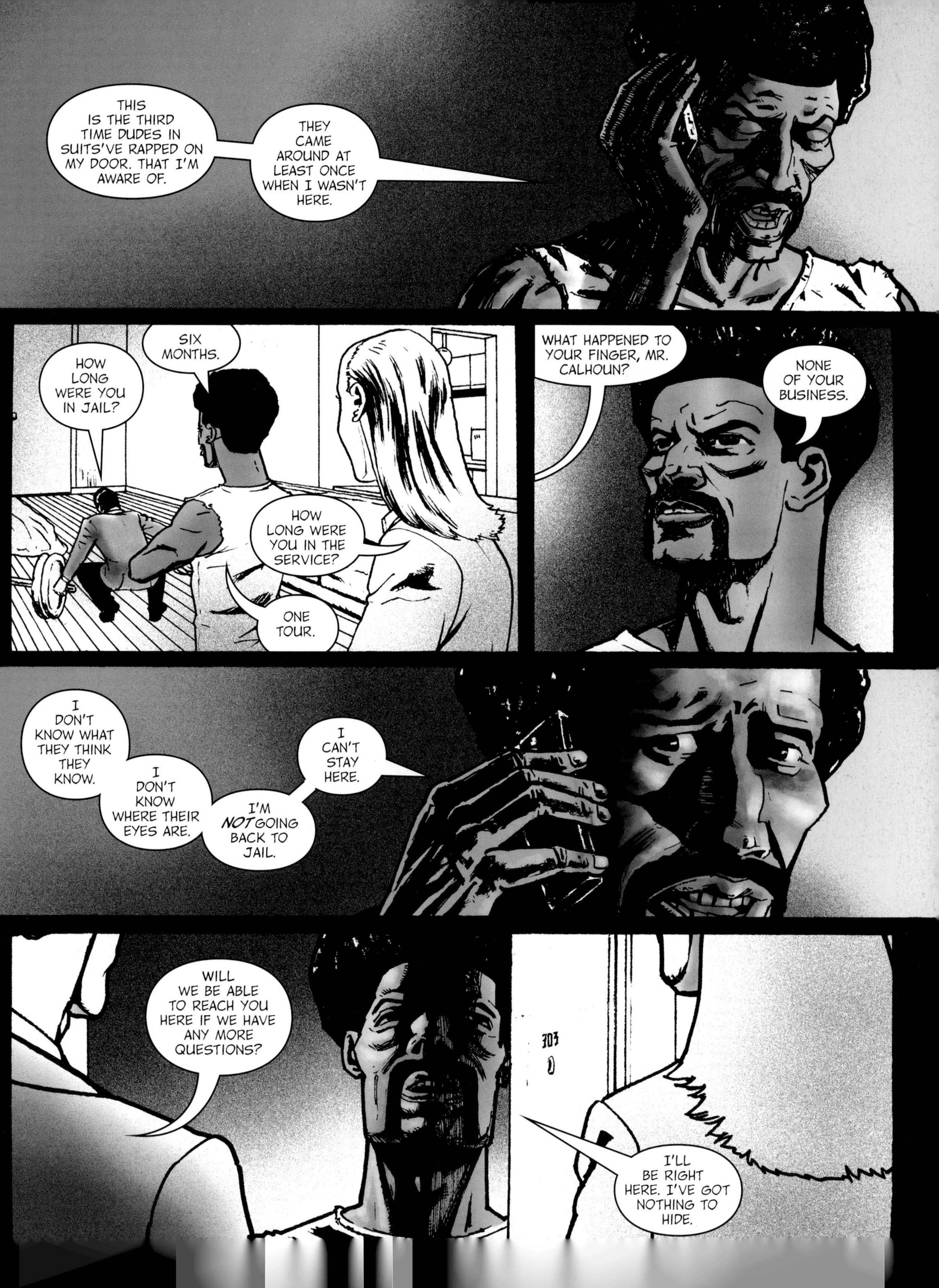
THIS IS THE THIRD TIME DUDES IN SUITS'VE RAPPED ON MY DOOR. THAT I'M AWARE OF.
THEY CAME AROUND AT LEAST ONCE WHEN I WASN'T HERE.
HOW LONG WERE YOU IN JAIL?
SIX MONTHS.
HOW LONG WERE YOU IN THE SERVICE?
ONE TOUR.
WHAT HAPPENED TO YOUR FINGER, MR. CALHOUN?
NONE OF YOUR BUSINESS.
I DON'T KNOW WHAT THEY THINK THEY KNOW.
I DON'T KNOW WHERE THEIR EYES ARE.
I'M *NOT* GOING BACK TO JAIL.
I CAN'T STAY HERE.
WILL WE BE ABLE TO REACH YOU HERE IF WE HAVE ANY MORE QUESTIONS?
303
I'LL BE RIGHT HERE. I'VE GOT NOTHING TO HIDE.

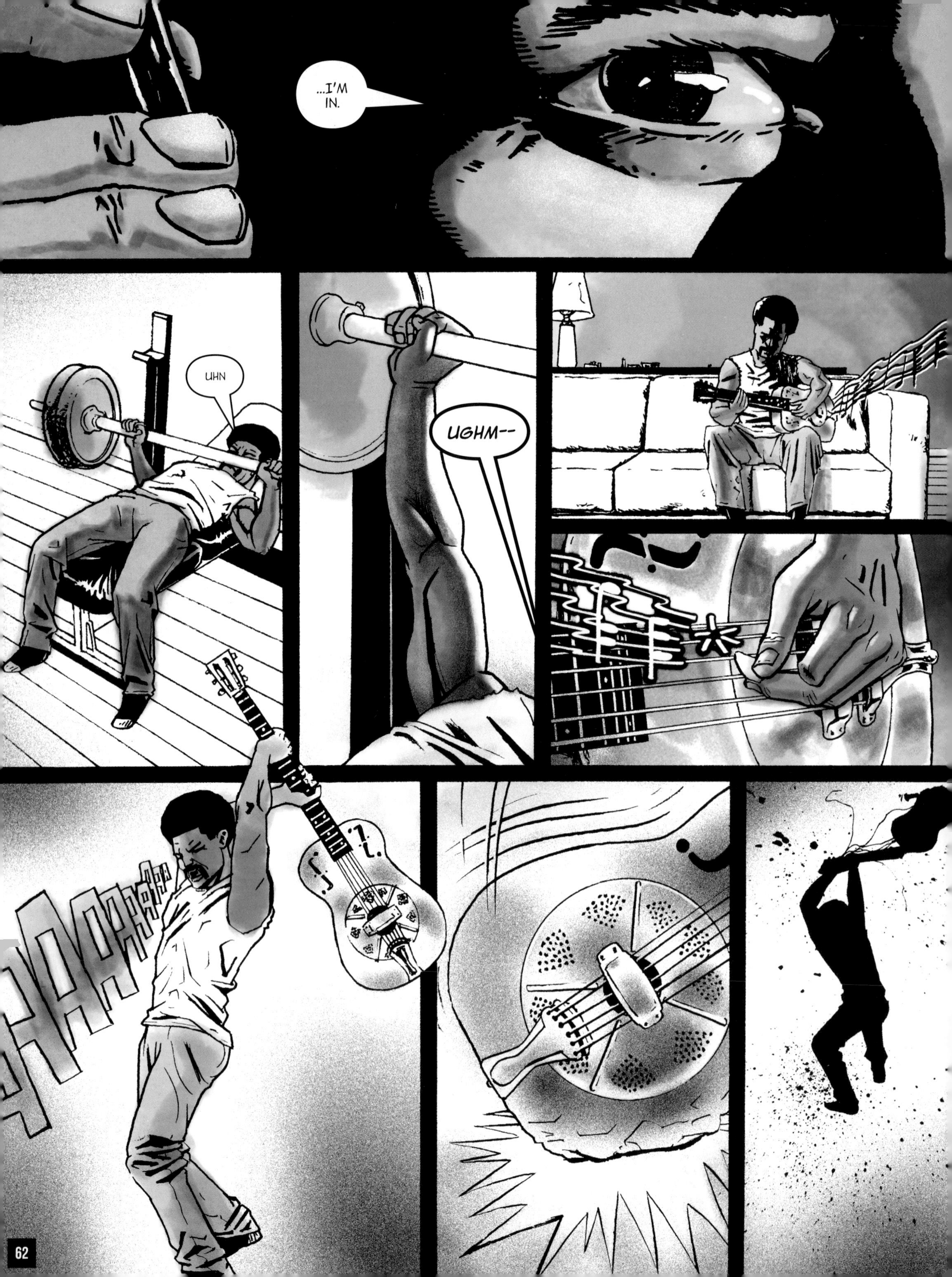
...I'M IN.
UHN
UGHM--

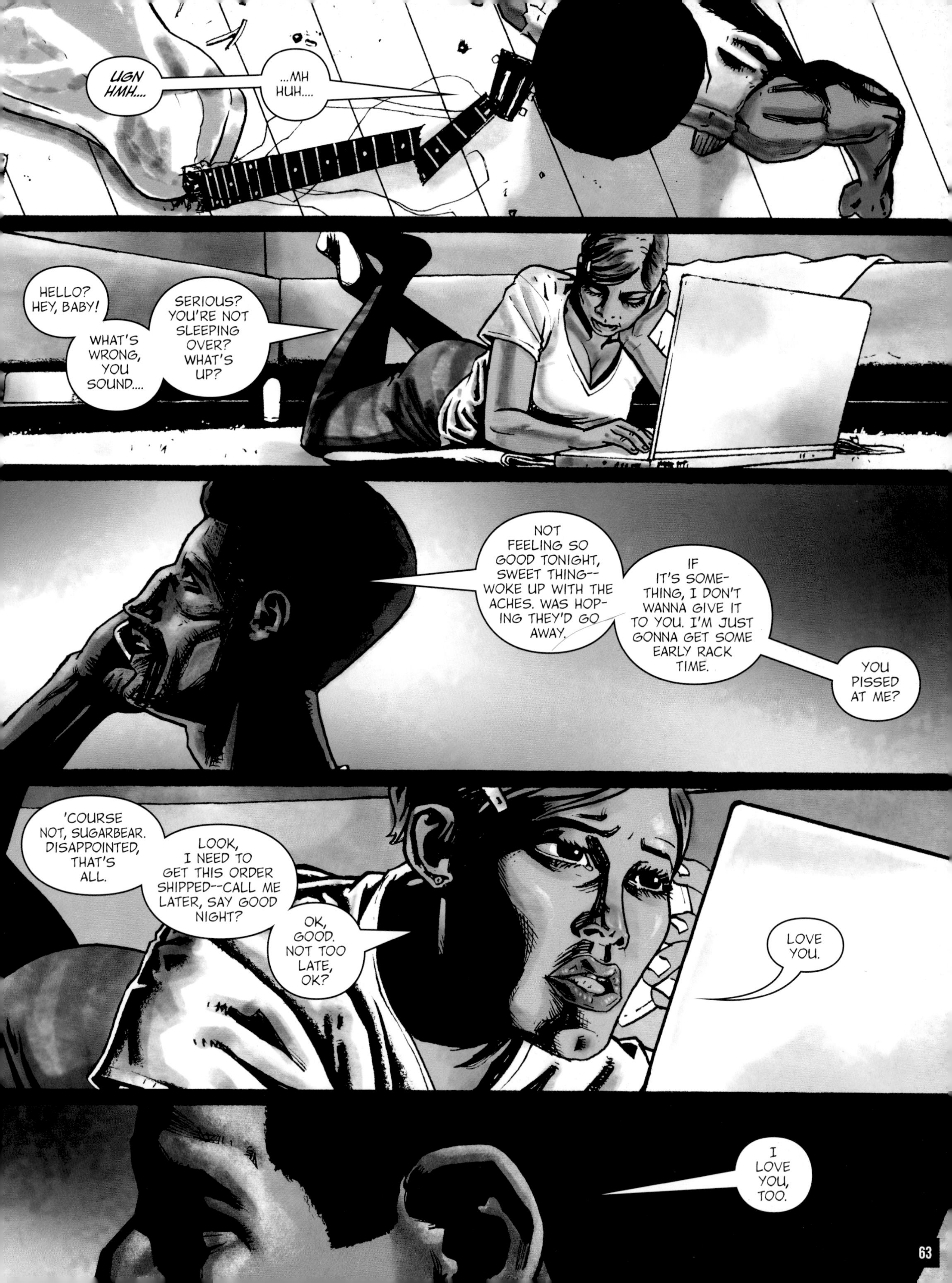

UGN HMH....
...MH HUH....
HELLO? HEY, BABY!
WHAT'S WRONG, YOU SOUND....
SERIOUS? YOU'RE NOT SLEEPING OVER? WHAT'S UP?
NOT FEELING SO GOOD TONIGHT, SWEET THING--WOKE UP WITH THE ACHES. WAS HOPING THEY'D GO AWAY.
IF IT'S SOMETHING, I DON'T WANNA GIVE IT TO YOU. I'M JUST GONNA GET SOME EARLY RACK TIME.
YOU PISSED AT ME?
'COURSE NOT, SUGARBEAR. DISAPPOINTED, THAT'S ALL.
LOOK, I NEED TO GET THIS ORDER SHIPPED--CALL ME LATER, SAY GOOD NIGHT?
OK, GOOD. NOT TOO LATE, OK?
LOVE YOU.
I LOVE YOU, TOO.

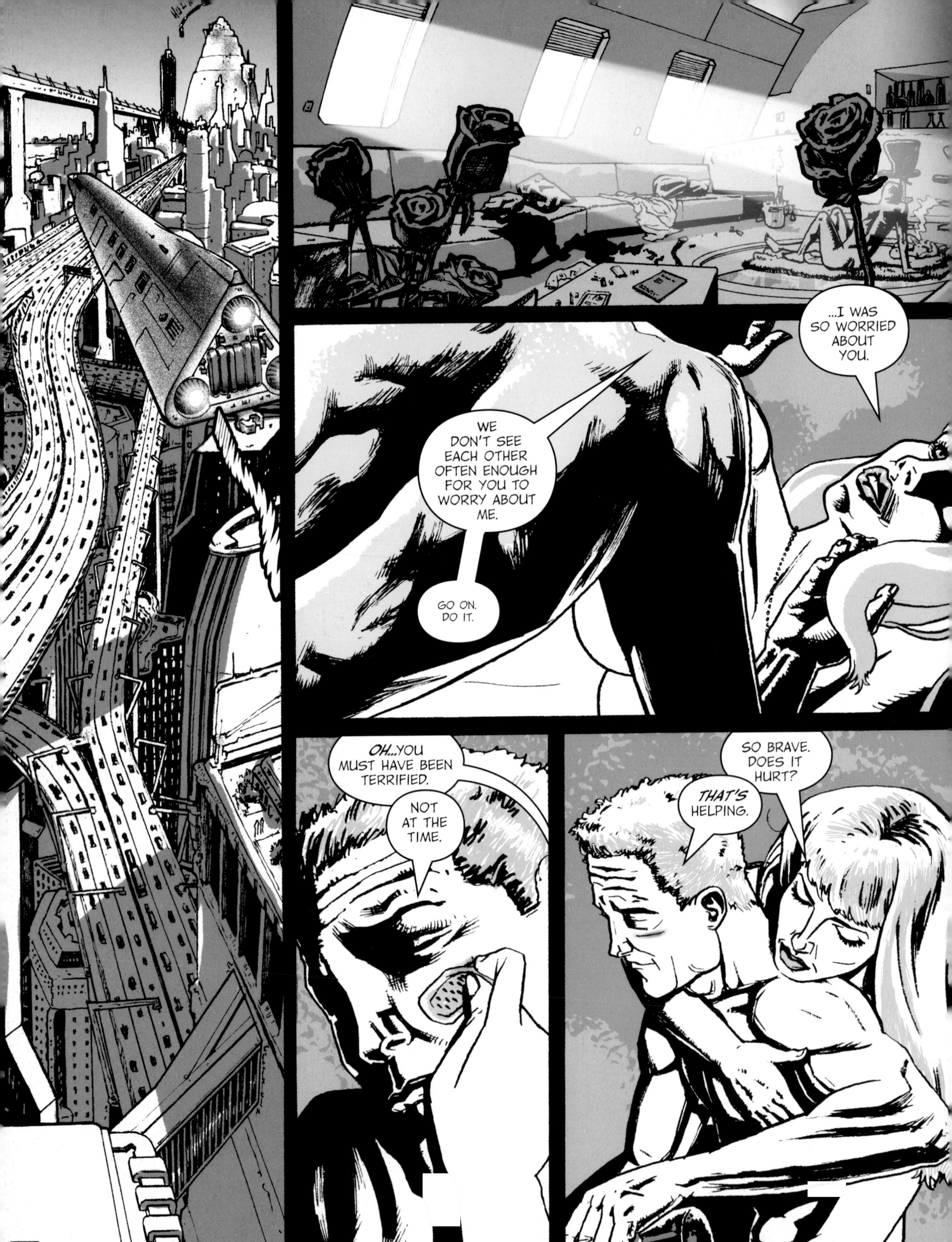

...I WAS SO WORRIED ABOUT YOU.
WE DON'T SEE EACH OTHER OFTEN ENOUGH FOR YOU TO WORRY ABOUT ME.
GO ON. DO IT.
OH...YOU MUST HAVE BEEN TERRIFIED.
NOT AT THE TIME.
SO BRAVE. DOES IT HURT?
THAT'S HELPING.

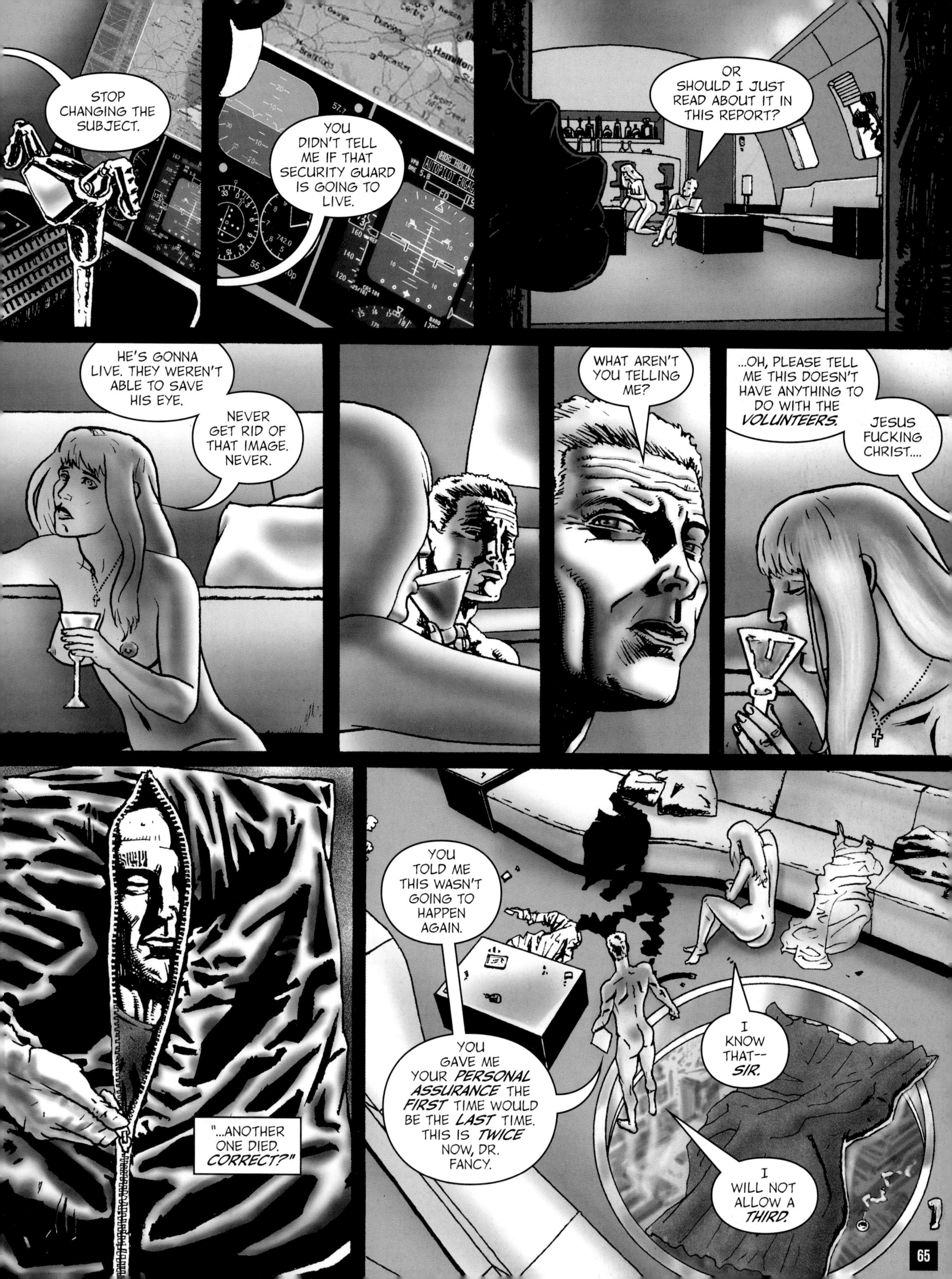
STOP CHANGING THE SUBJECT.
YOU DIDN'T TELL ME IF THAT SECURITY GUARD IS GOING TO LIVE.
OR SHOULD I JUST READ ABOUT IT IN THIS REPORT?
HE'S GONNA LIVE. THEY WEREN'T ABLE TO SAVE HIS EYE.
NEVER GET RID OF THAT IMAGE. NEVER.
WHAT AREN'T YOU TELLING ME?
...OH, PLEASE TELL ME THIS DOESN'T HAVE ANYTHING TO DO WITH THE *VOLUNTEERS.*
JESUS FUCKING CHRIST....
"...ANOTHER ONE DIED. *CORRECT?*"
YOU TOLD ME THIS WASN'T GOING TO HAPPEN AGAIN.
YOU GAVE ME YOUR *PERSONAL ASSURANCE* THE *FIRST* TIME WOULD BE THE *LAST* TIME. THIS IS *TWICE* NOW, DR. FANCY.
I KNOW THAT-- *SIR.*
I WILL NOT ALLOW A *THIRD.*

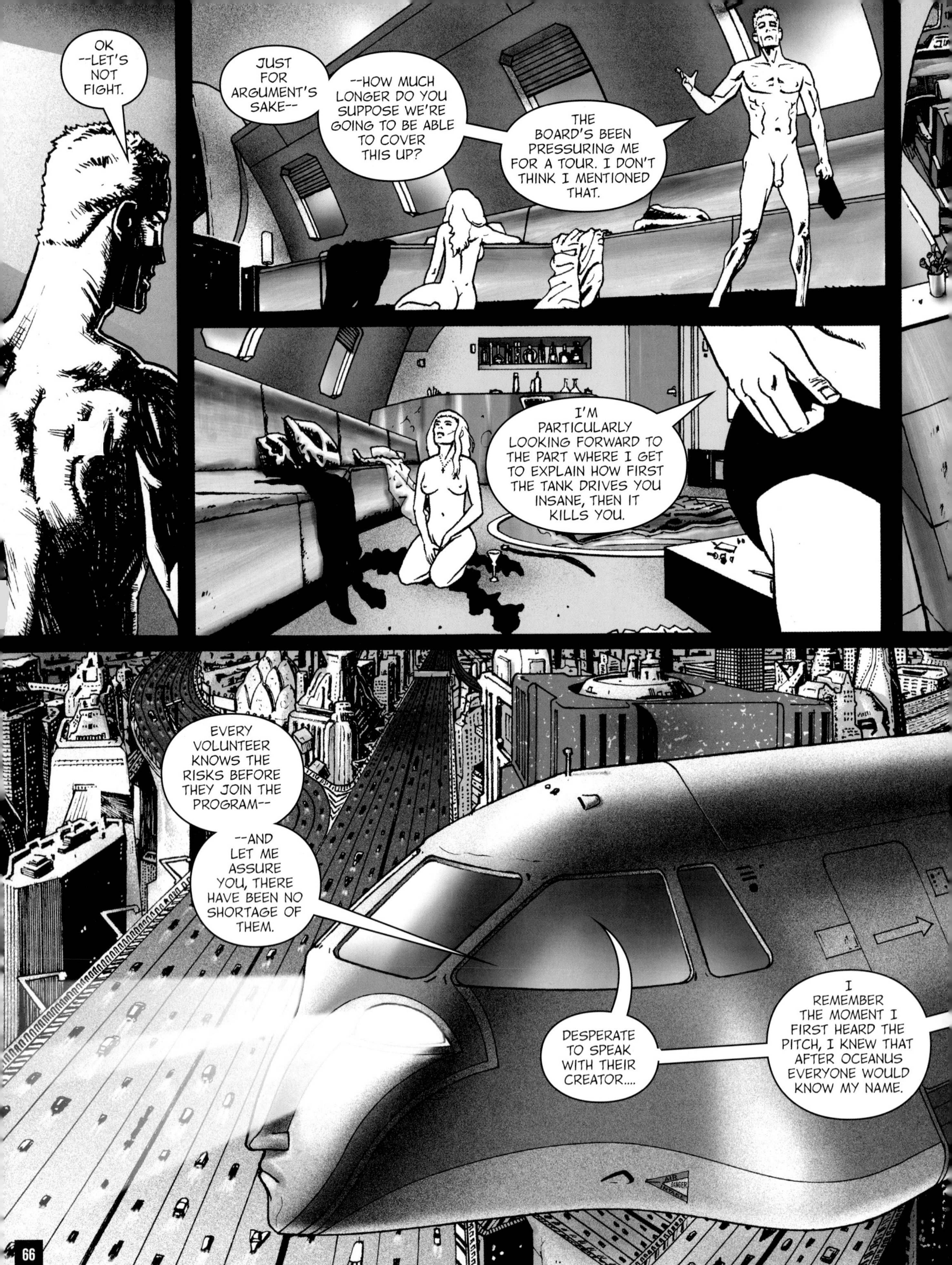

OK --LET'S NOT FIGHT.
JUST FOR ARGUMENT'S SAKE--
--HOW MUCH LONGER DO YOU SUPPOSE WE'RE GOING TO BE ABLE TO COVER THIS UP?
THE BOARD'S BEEN PRESSURING ME FOR A TOUR. I DON'T THINK I MENTIONED THAT.
I'M PARTICULARLY LOOKING FORWARD TO THE PART WHERE I GET TO EXPLAIN HOW FIRST THE TANK DRIVES YOU INSANE, THEN IT KILLS YOU.
EVERY VOLUNTEER KNOWS THE RISKS BEFORE THEY JOIN THE PROGRAM--
--AND LET ME ASSURE YOU, THERE HAVE BEEN NO SHORTAGE OF THEM.
DESPERATE TO SPEAK WITH THEIR CREATOR....
I REMEMBER THE MOMENT I FIRST HEARD THE PITCH, I KNEW THAT AFTER OCEANUS EVERYONE WOULD KNOW MY NAME.

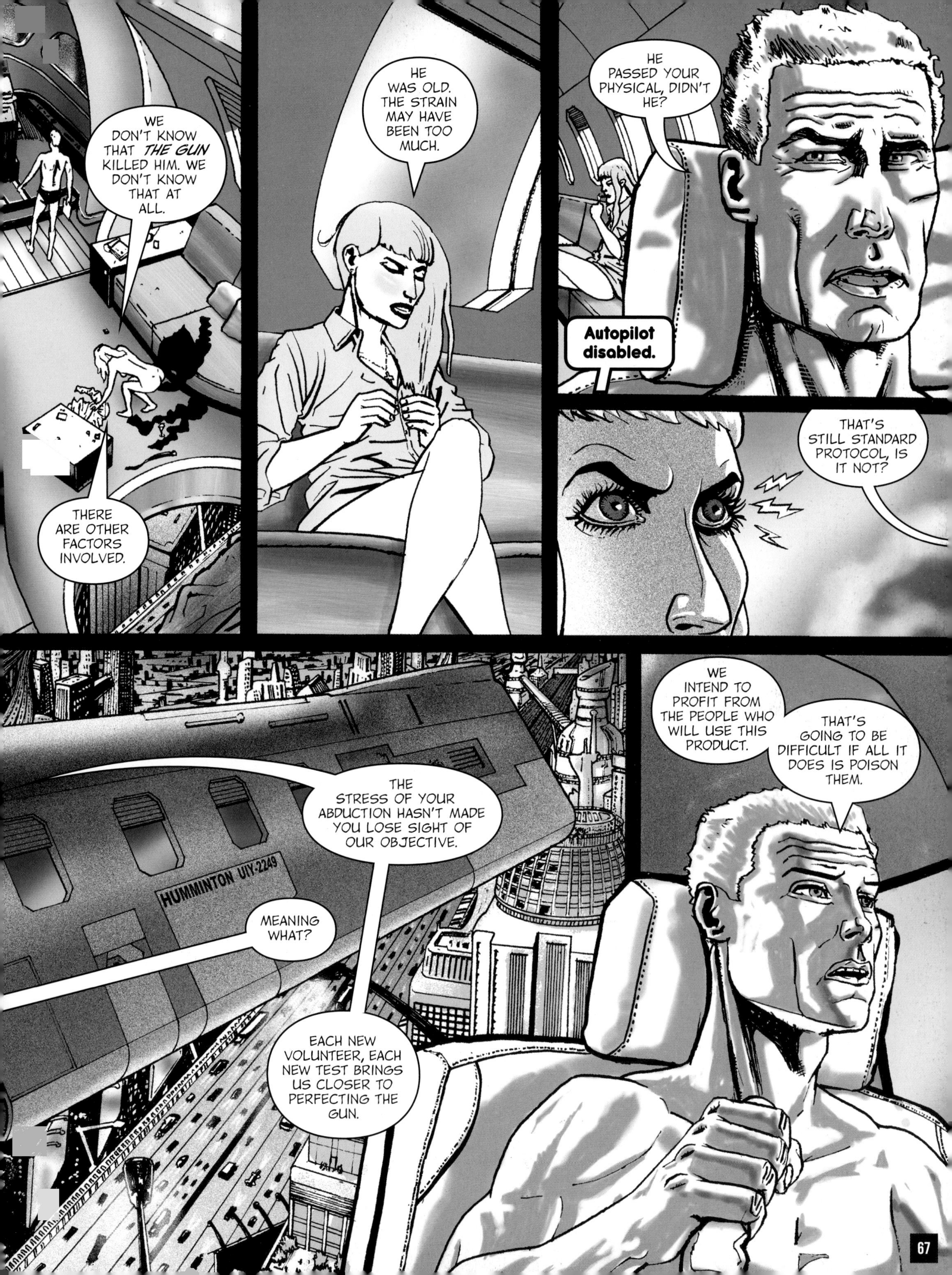
WE DON'T KNOW THAT *THE GUN* KILLED HIM. WE DON'T KNOW THAT AT ALL.
THERE ARE OTHER FACTORS INVOLVED.
HE WAS OLD. THE STRAIN MAY HAVE BEEN TOO MUCH.
HE PASSED YOUR PHYSICAL, DIDN'T HE?
Autopilot disabled.
THAT'S STILL STANDARD PROTOCOL, IS IT NOT?
THE STRESS OF YOUR ABDUCTION HASN'T MADE YOU LOSE SIGHT OF OUR OBJECTIVE.
MEANING WHAT?
EACH NEW VOLUNTEER, EACH NEW TEST BRINGS US CLOSER TO PERFECTING THE GUN.
HUMMINTON UIY-2249
WE INTEND TO PROFIT FROM THE PEOPLE WHO WILL USE THIS PRODUCT.
THAT'S GOING TO BE DIFFICULT IF ALL IT DOES IS POISON THEM.

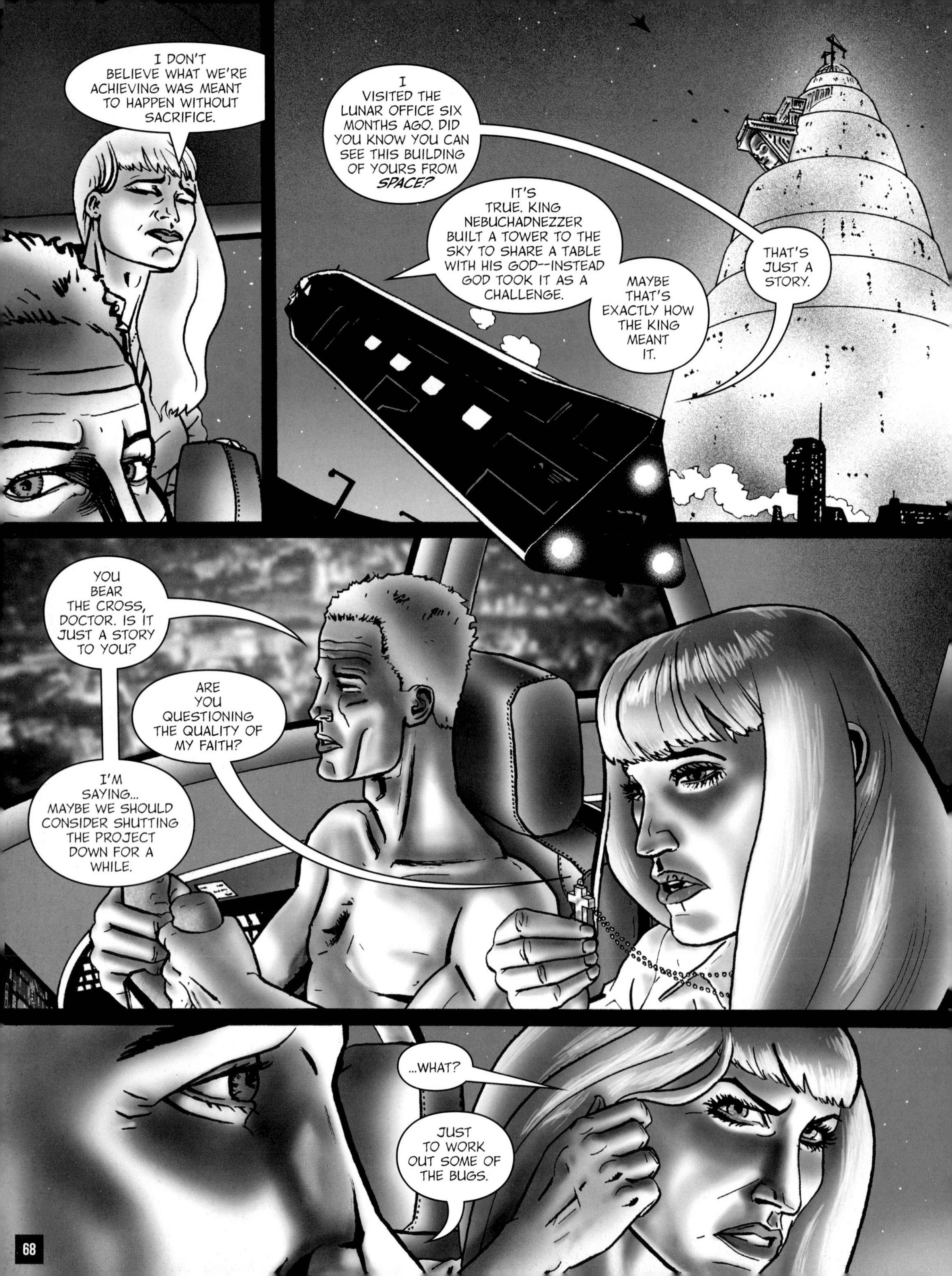
I DON'T BELIEVE WHAT WE'RE ACHIEVING WAS MEANT TO HAPPEN WITHOUT SACRIFICE.
I VISITED THE LUNAR OFFICE SIX MONTHS AGO. DID YOU KNOW YOU CAN SEE THIS BUILDING OF YOURS FROM *SPACE?*
THAT'S JUST A STORY.
IT'S TRUE. KING NEBUCHADNEZZER BUILT A TOWER TO THE SKY TO SHARE A TABLE WITH HIS GOD--INSTEAD GOD TOOK IT AS A CHALLENGE.
MAYBE THAT'S EXACTLY HOW THE KING MEANT IT.
YOU BEAR THE CROSS, DOCTOR. IS IT JUST A STORY TO YOU?
ARE YOU QUESTIONING THE QUALITY OF MY FAITH?
I'M SAYING... MAYBE WE SHOULD CONSIDER SHUTTING THE PROJECT DOWN FOR A WHILE.
...WHAT?
JUST TO WORK OUT SOME OF THE BUGS.

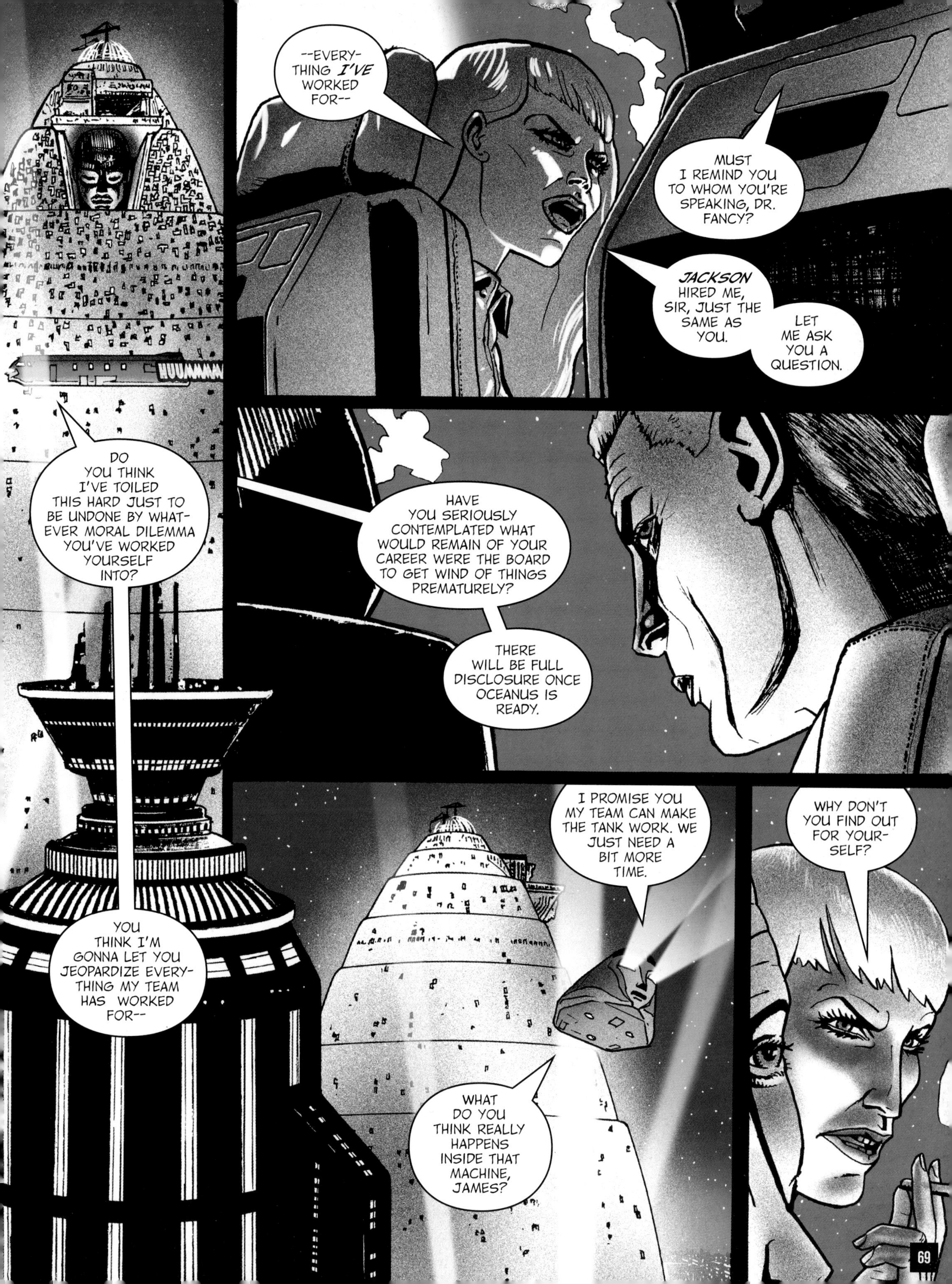

--EVERY-THING *I'VE* WORKED FOR--
MUST I REMIND YOU TO WHOM YOU'RE SPEAKING, DR. FANCY?
JACKSON HIRED ME, SIR, JUST THE SAME AS YOU.
LET ME ASK YOU A QUESTION.
HUUMMMM
DO YOU THINK I'VE TOILED THIS HARD JUST TO BE UNDONE BY WHAT-EVER MORAL DILEMMA YOU'VE WORKED YOURSELF INTO?
YOU THINK I'M GONNA LET YOU JEOPARDIZE EVERY-THING MY TEAM HAS WORKED FOR--
HAVE YOU SERIOUSLY CONTEMPLATED WHAT WOULD REMAIN OF YOUR CAREER WERE THE BOARD TO GET WIND OF THINGS PREMATURELY?
THERE WILL BE FULL DISCLOSURE ONCE OCEANUS IS READY.
I PROMISE YOU MY TEAM CAN MAKE THE TANK WORK. WE JUST NEED A BIT MORE TIME.
WHAT DO YOU THINK REALLY HAPPENS INSIDE THAT MACHINE, JAMES?
WHY DON'T YOU FIND OUT FOR YOUR-SELF?

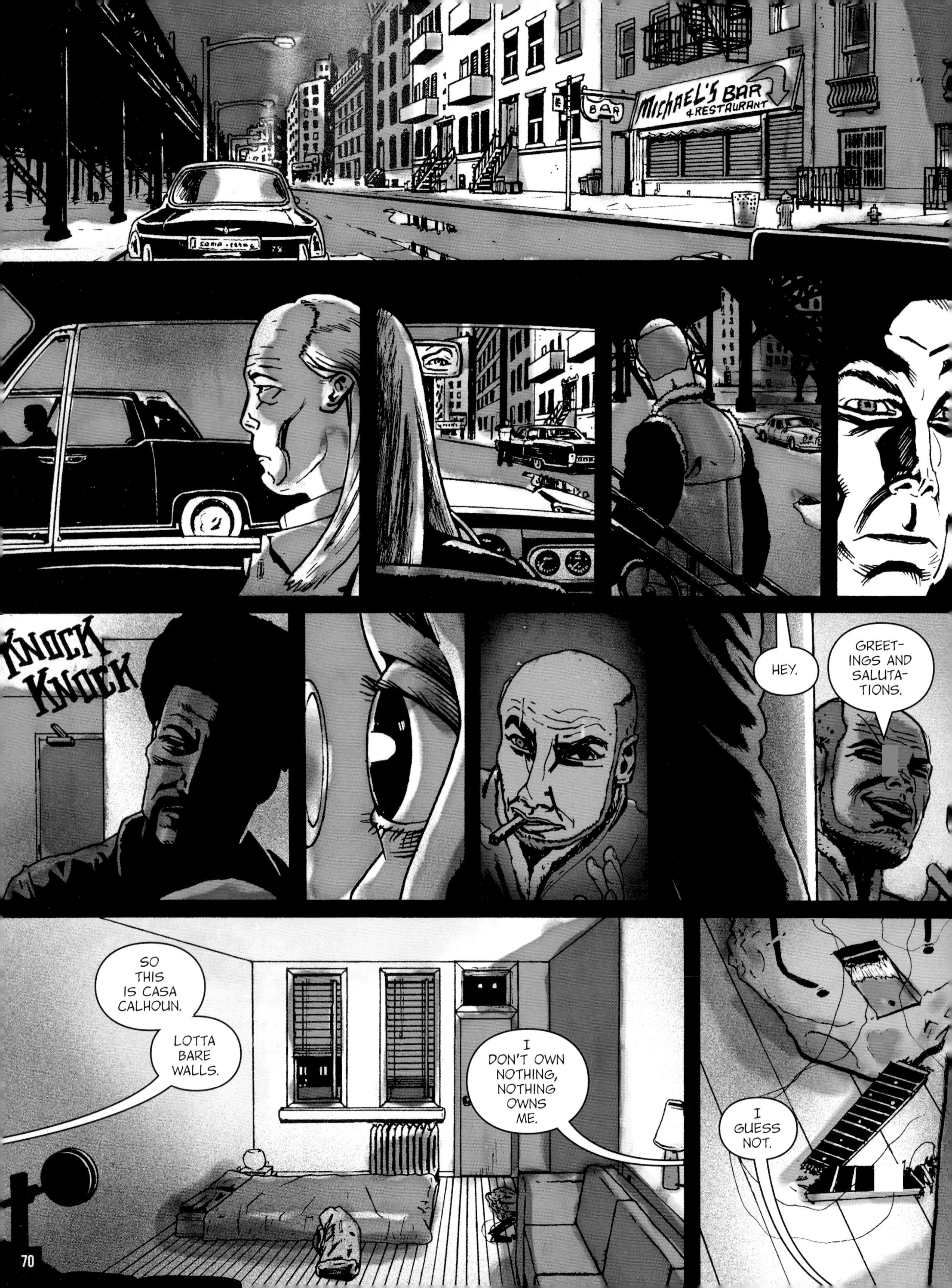
MICHAEL'S BAR
& RESTAURANT
BAR
KNOCK KNOCK
HEY.
GREETINGS AND SALUTATIONS.
SO THIS IS CASA CALHOUN.
LOTTA BARE WALLS.
I DON'T OWN NOTHING, NOTHING OWNS ME.
I GUESS NOT.

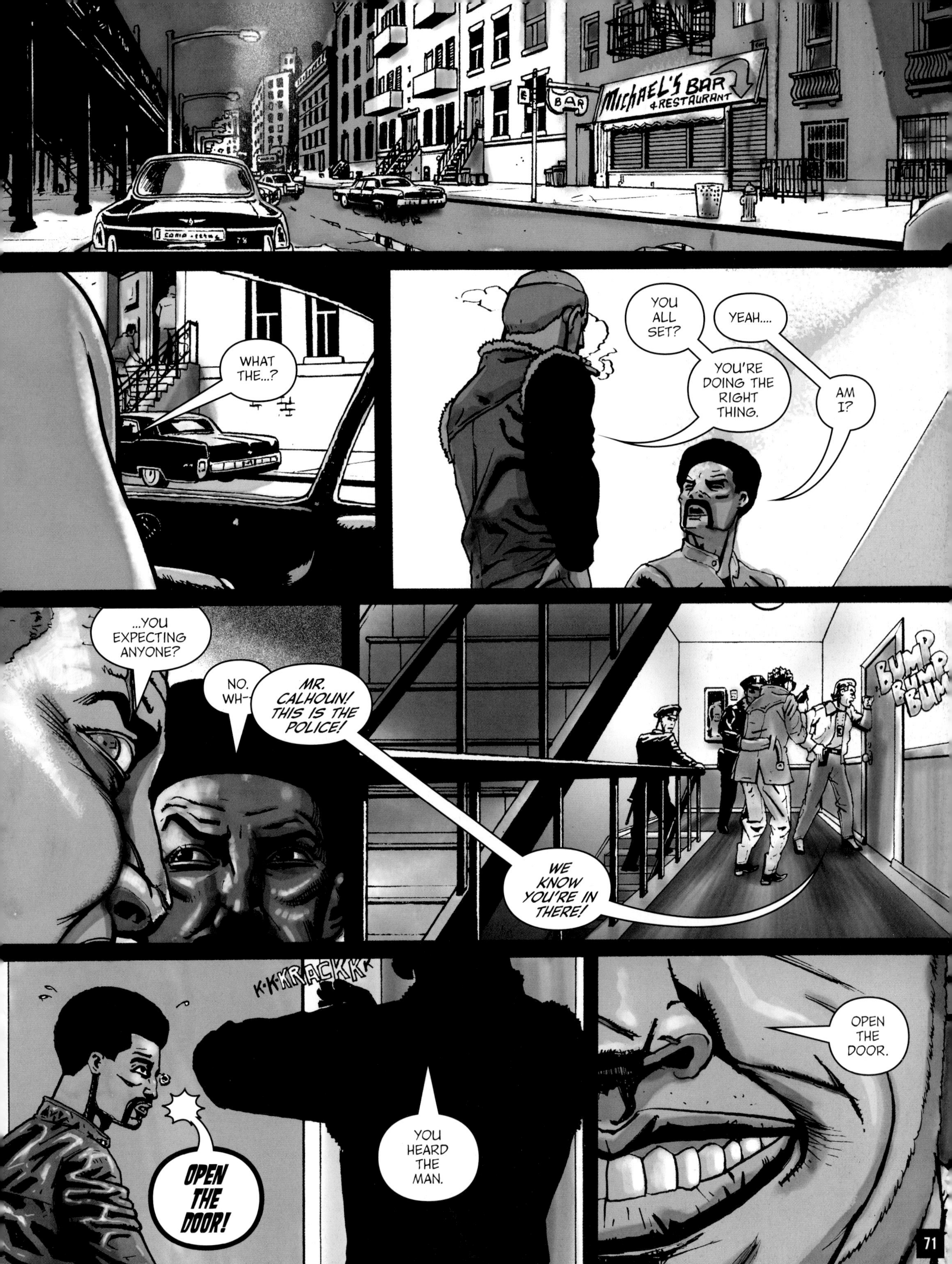
MICHAEL'S BAR
& RESTAURANT
BAR
WHAT THE...?
YOU ALL SET?
YOU'RE DOING THE RIGHT THING.
YEAH....
AM I?
...YOU EXPECTING ANYONE?
NO. WH-
MR. CALHOUN! THIS IS THE POLICE!
WE KNOW YOU'RE IN THERE!
BUMP BUMP BUM
K-K-KRACKK
OPEN THE DOOR!
YOU HEARD THE MAN.
OPEN THE DOOR.

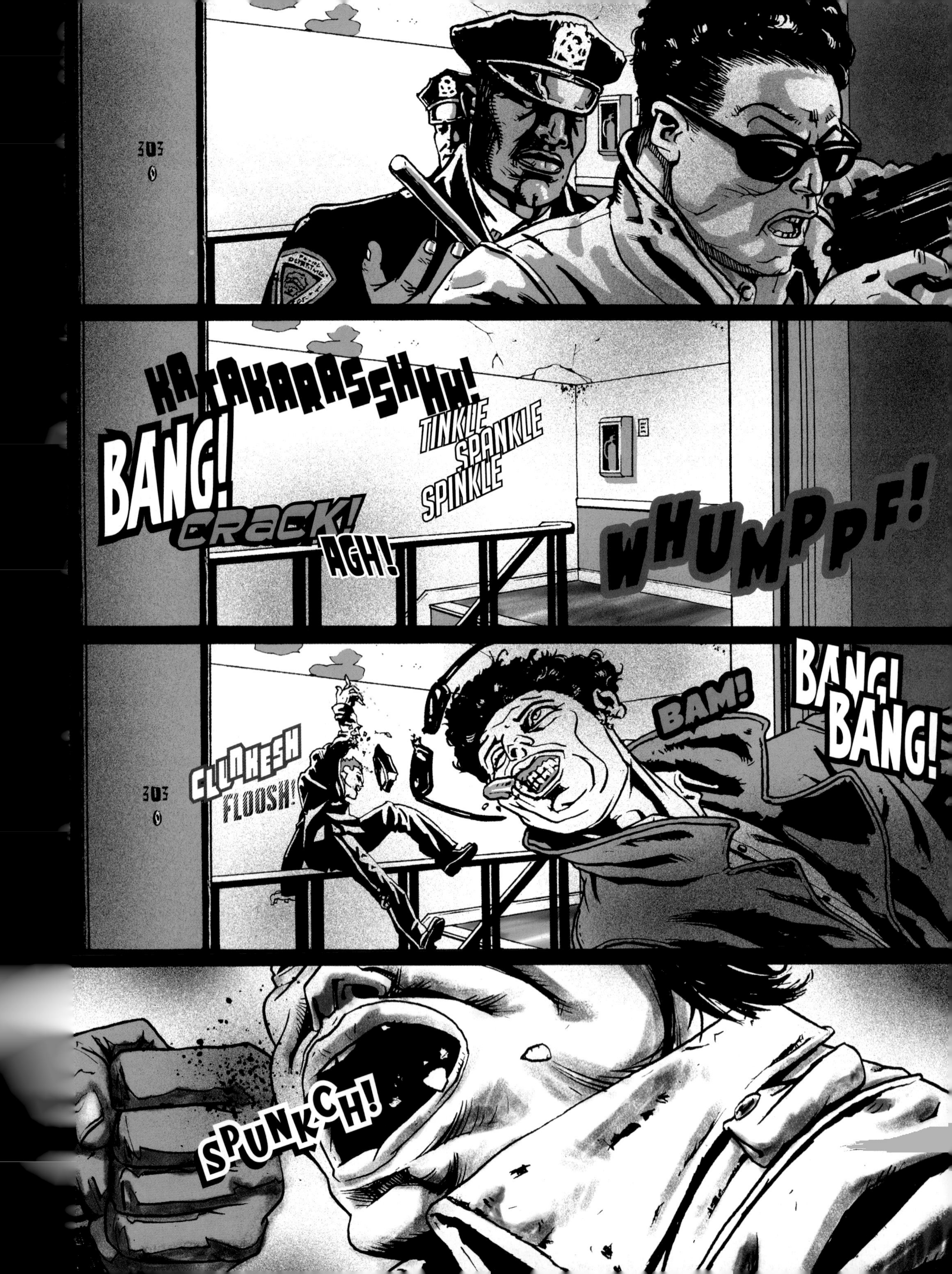

303
KAKAKAKARASSHHH!
BANG!
CRACK!
AGH!
TINKLE
SPANKLE
SPINKLE
WHUMPPF!
303
CLUNKESH
FLOOSH!
BAM!
BANG!
BANG!
SPUNKCH!

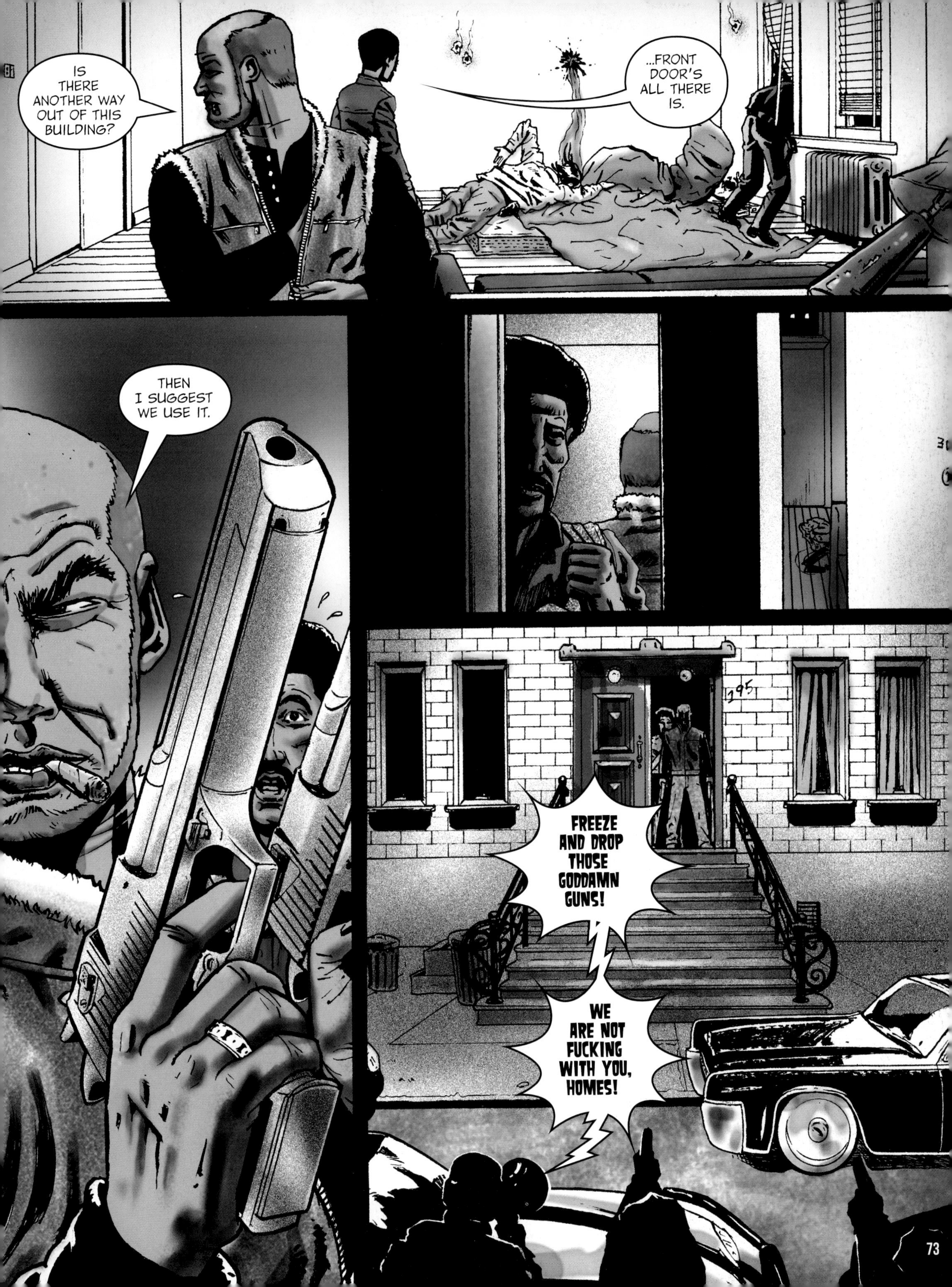
IS THERE ANOTHER WAY OUT OF THIS BUILDING?
...FRONT DOOR'S ALL THERE IS.
THEN I SUGGEST WE USE IT.
FREEZE AND DROP THOSE GODDAMN GUNS!
WE ARE NOT FUCKING WITH YOU, HOMES!

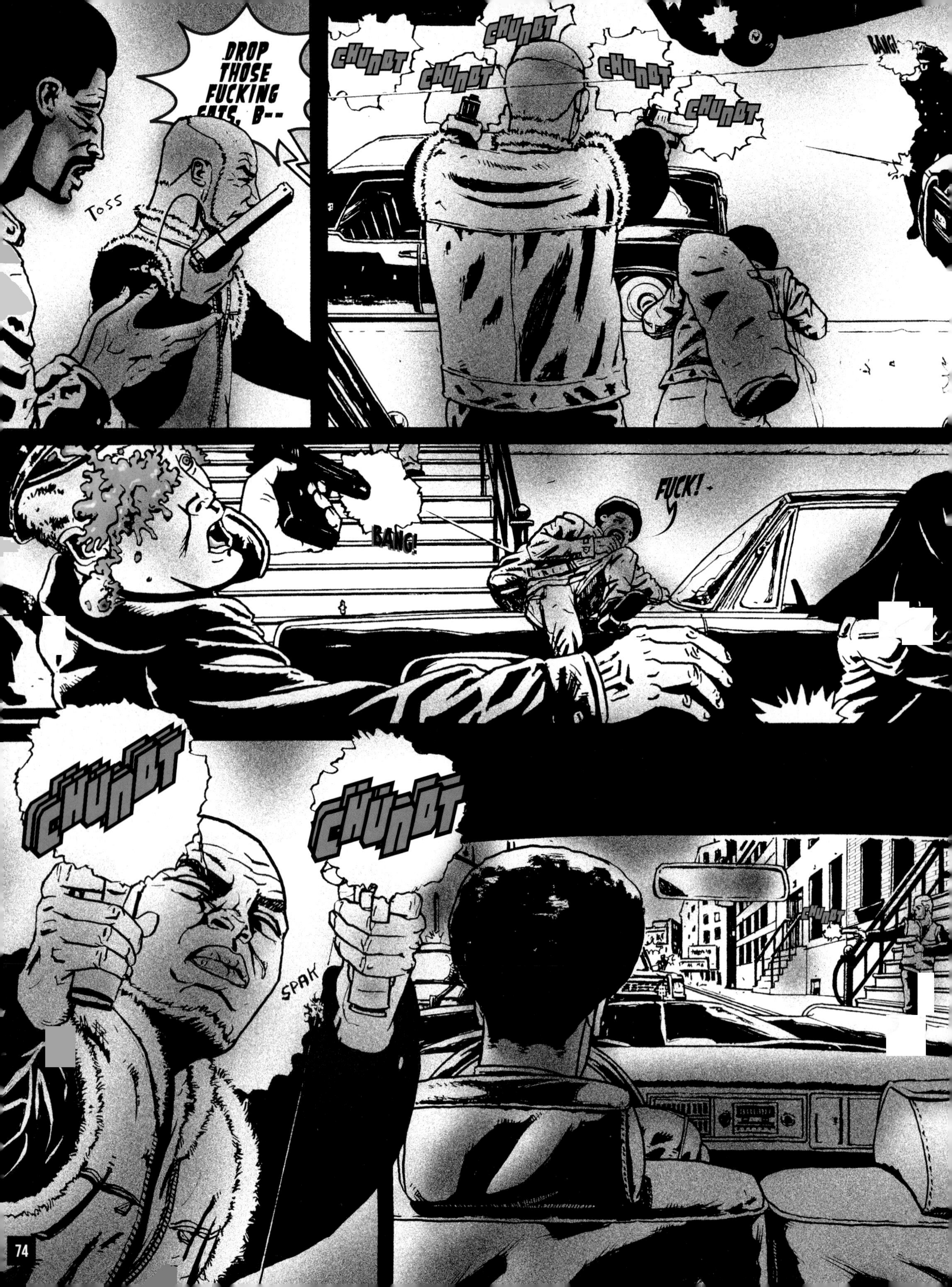

DROP THOSE FUCKING GATS, B--
TOSS
CHUNDT
CHUNDT
CHUNDT
CHUNDT
CHUNDT
BANG!
BANG!
FUCK!
CHUNDT
CHUNDT
SPAK
CHUNDT

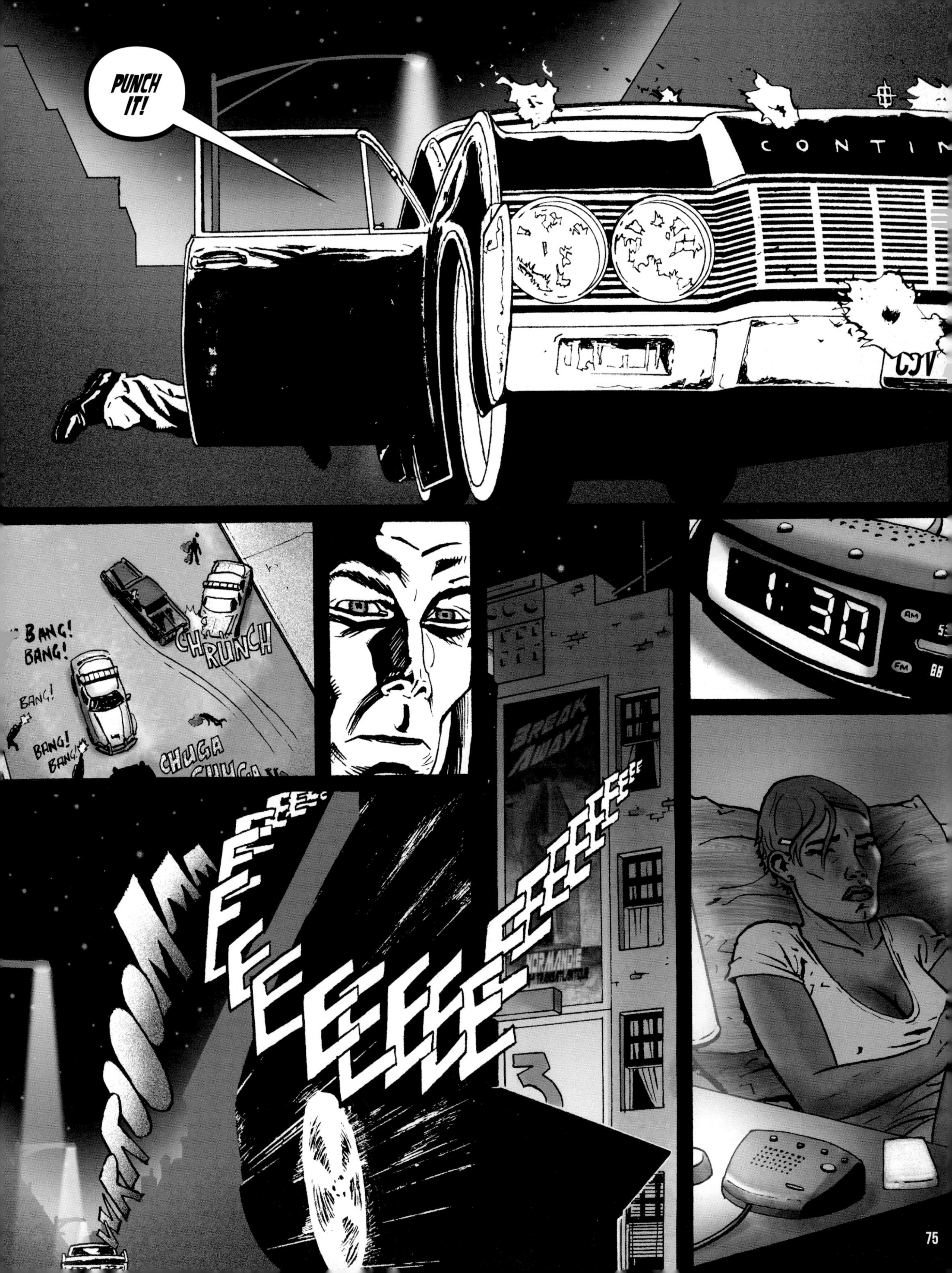
PUNCH IT!
CONTIN
CJV
BANG! BANG!
BANG!
BANG! BANG!
CHRUNCH
CHUGA
1:30
AM
FM
BREAK AWAY!
NORMANDIE

"As men migrated from the east, they said to one another, 'Come, let us build ourselves a city, and a tower with its top in the heavens, and let us make a name for ourselves, lest we be scattered abroad upon the face of the whole earth.'"

— GENESIS 11:19

NEXT:
CITY AND SAND

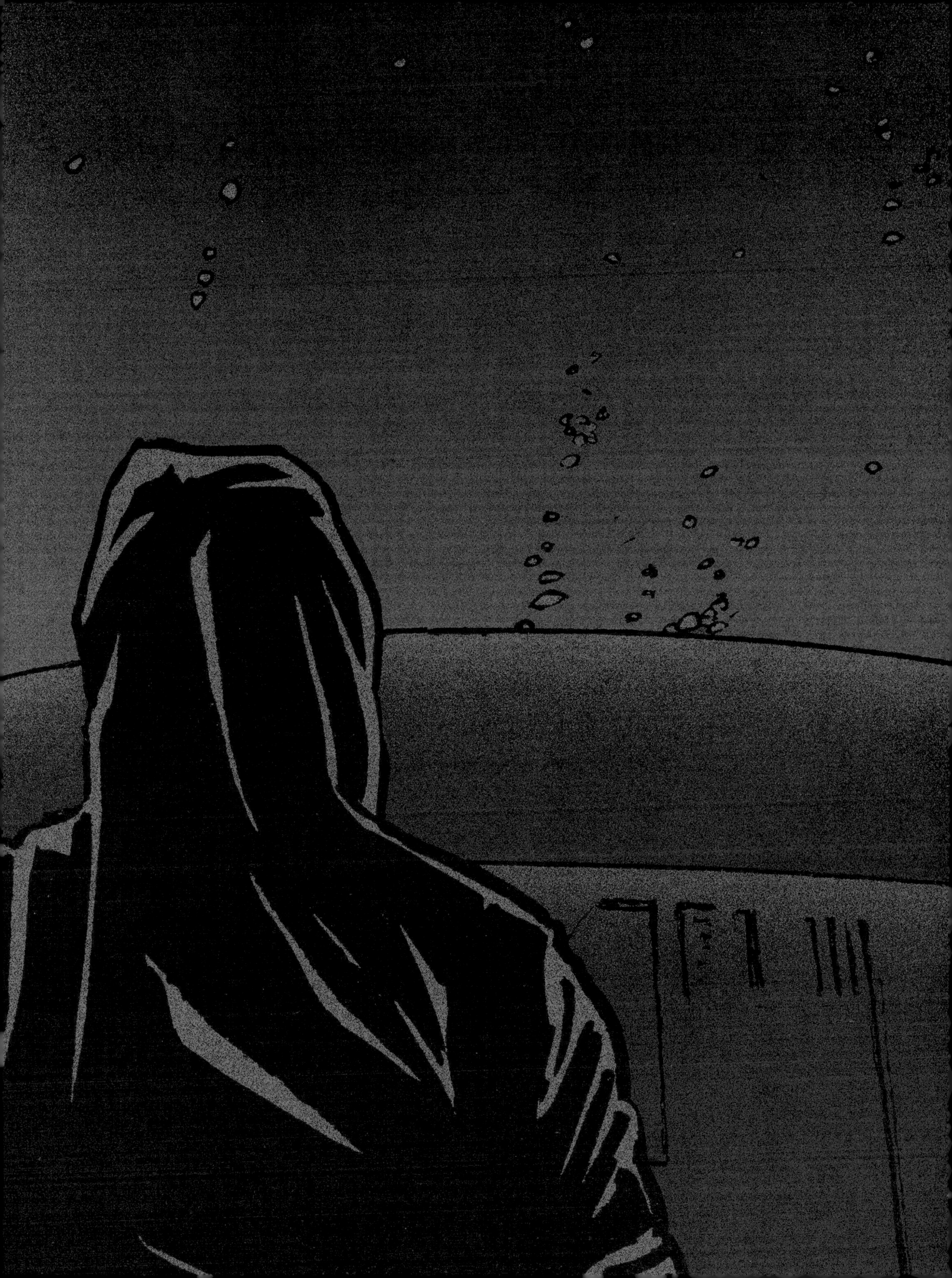

CHAPTER 2 CITY AND SAND

HO CHE ANDERSON
WRITER/ARTIST

GARY GROTH
EDITOR

PRESTON WHITE
PRODUCTION

JACQ COHEN
PROMOTIONS

GARY GROTH
ERIC REYNOLDS
PUBLISHERS

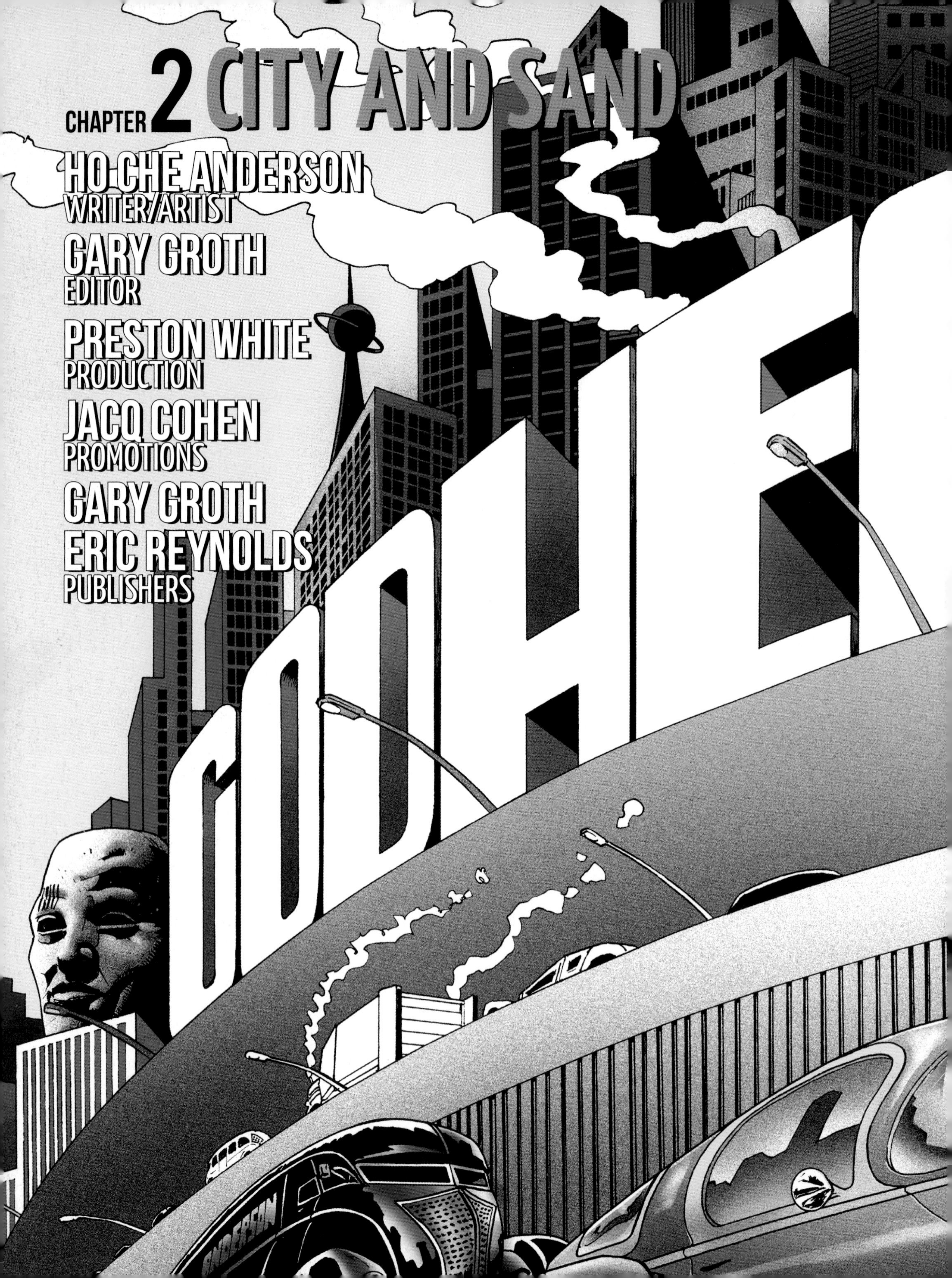

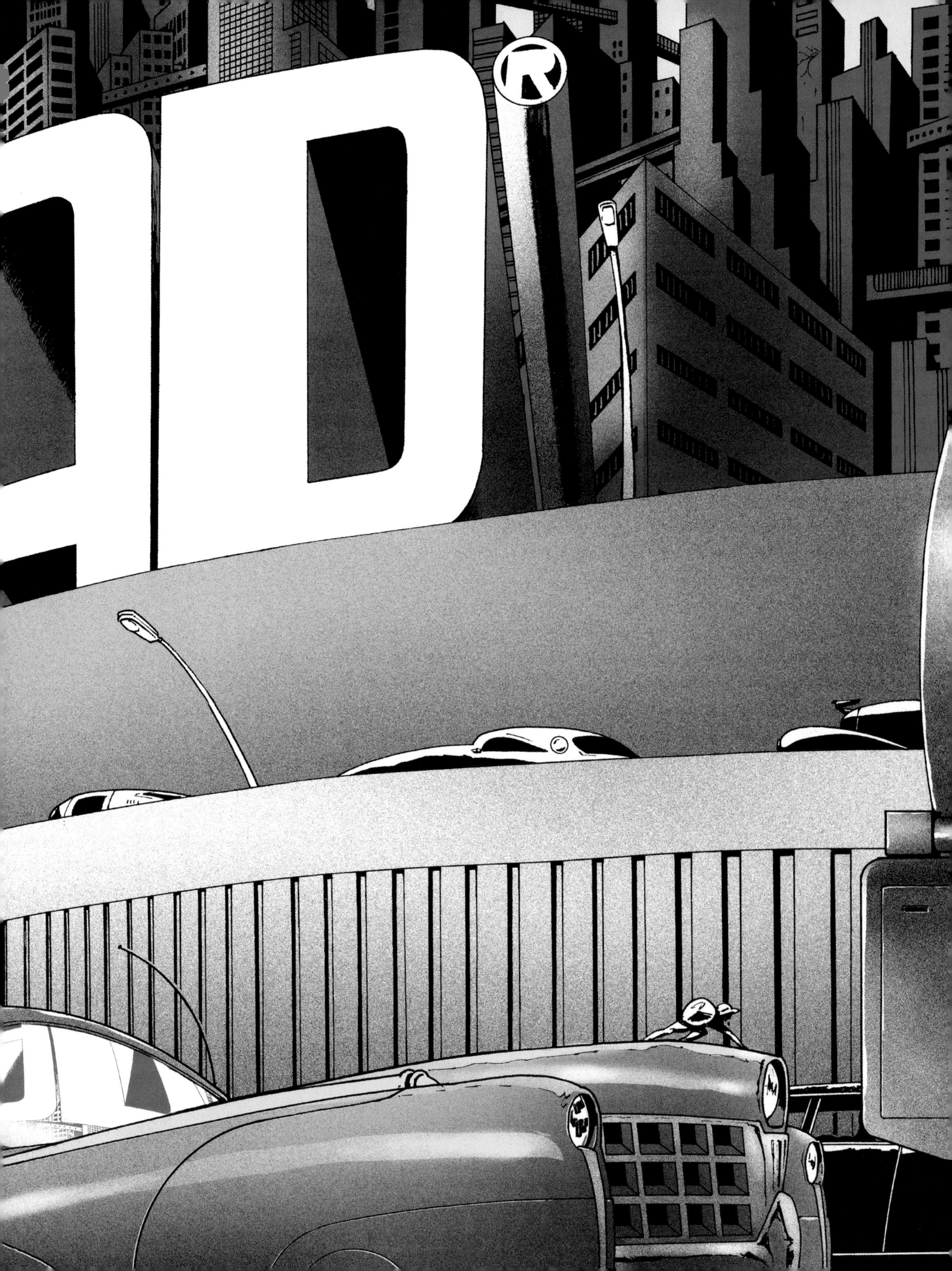

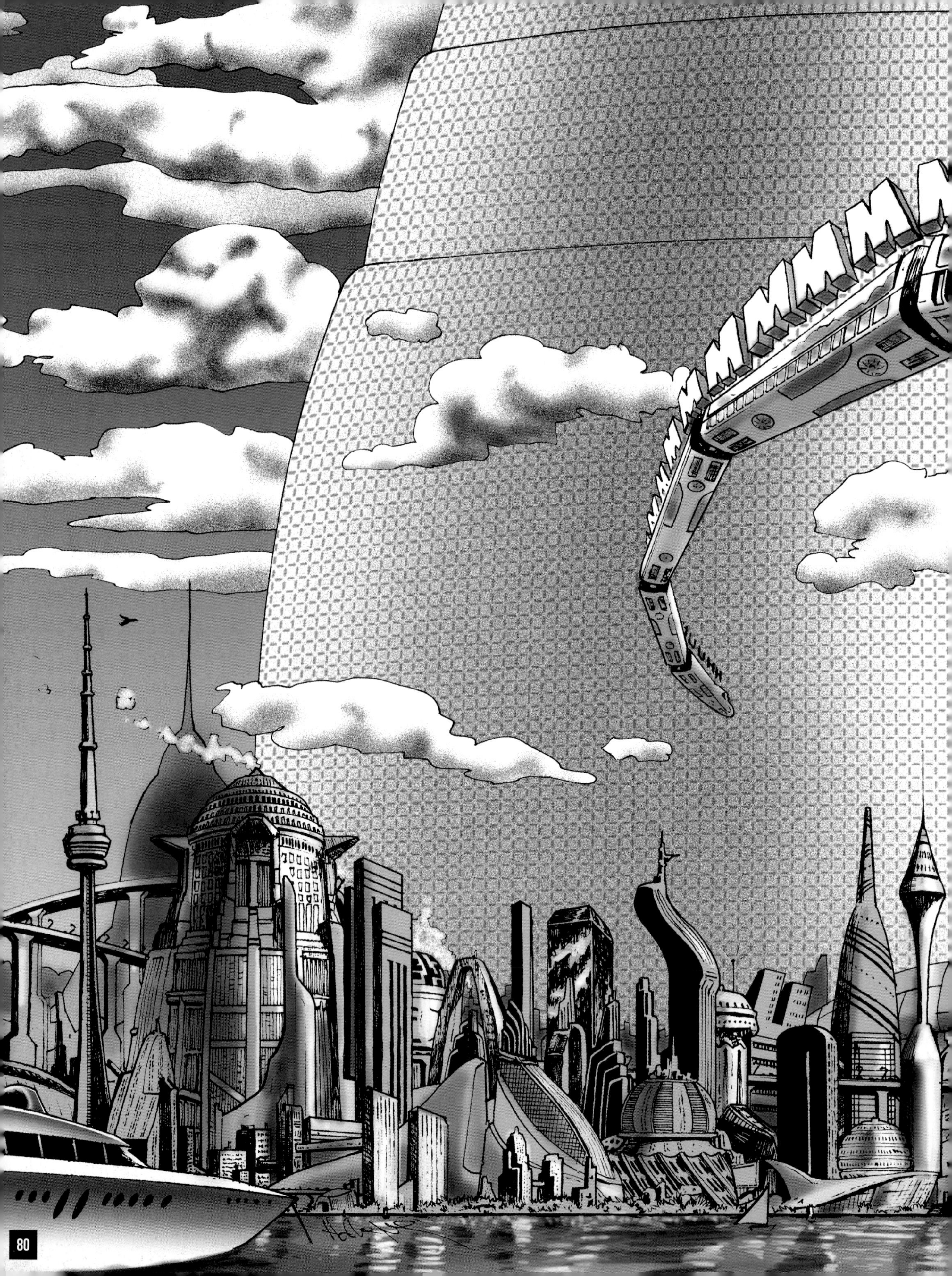

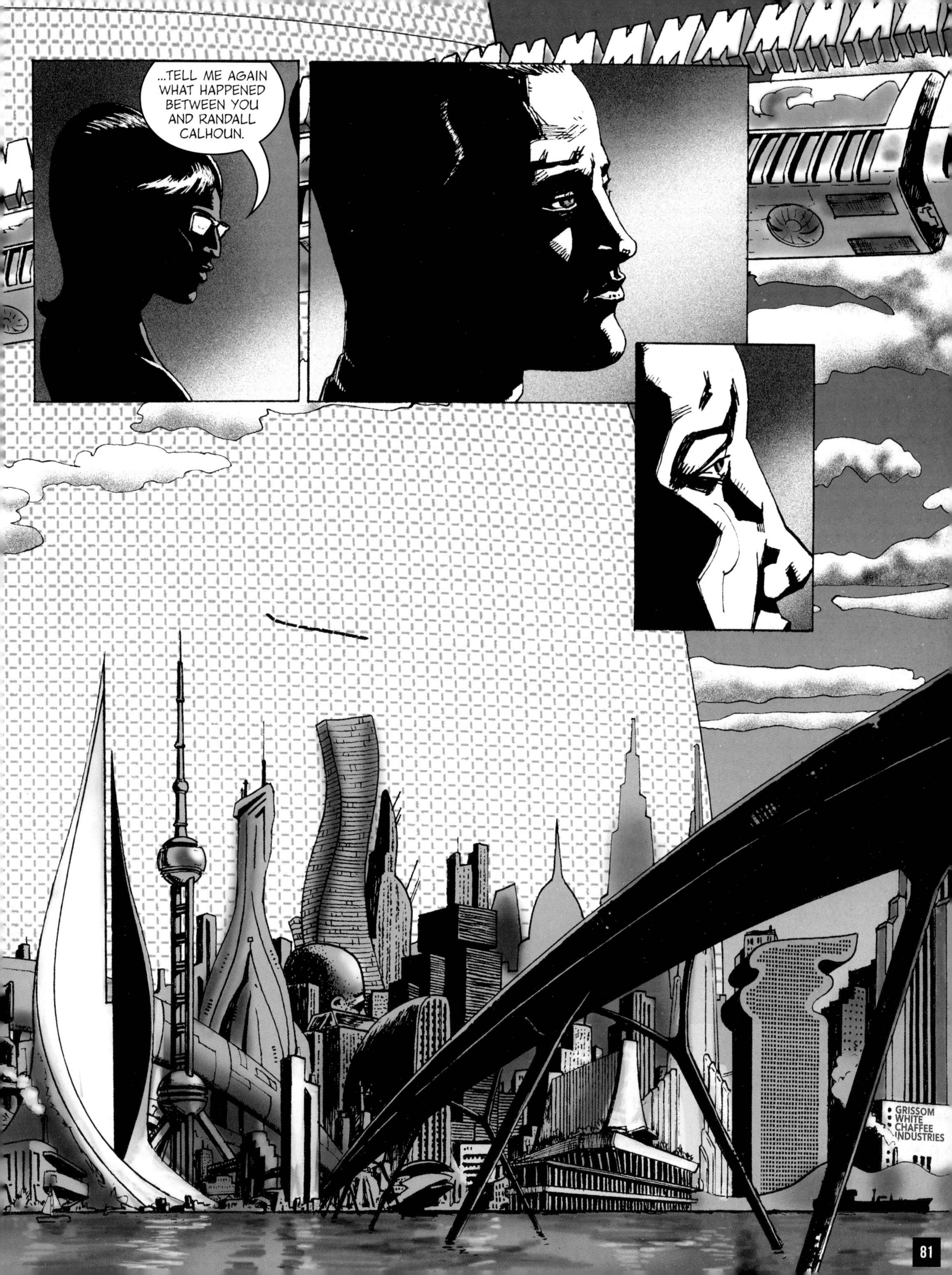
...TELL ME AGAIN WHAT HAPPENED BETWEEN YOU AND RANDALL CALHOUN.
GRISSOM WHITE CHAFFEE INDUSTRIES

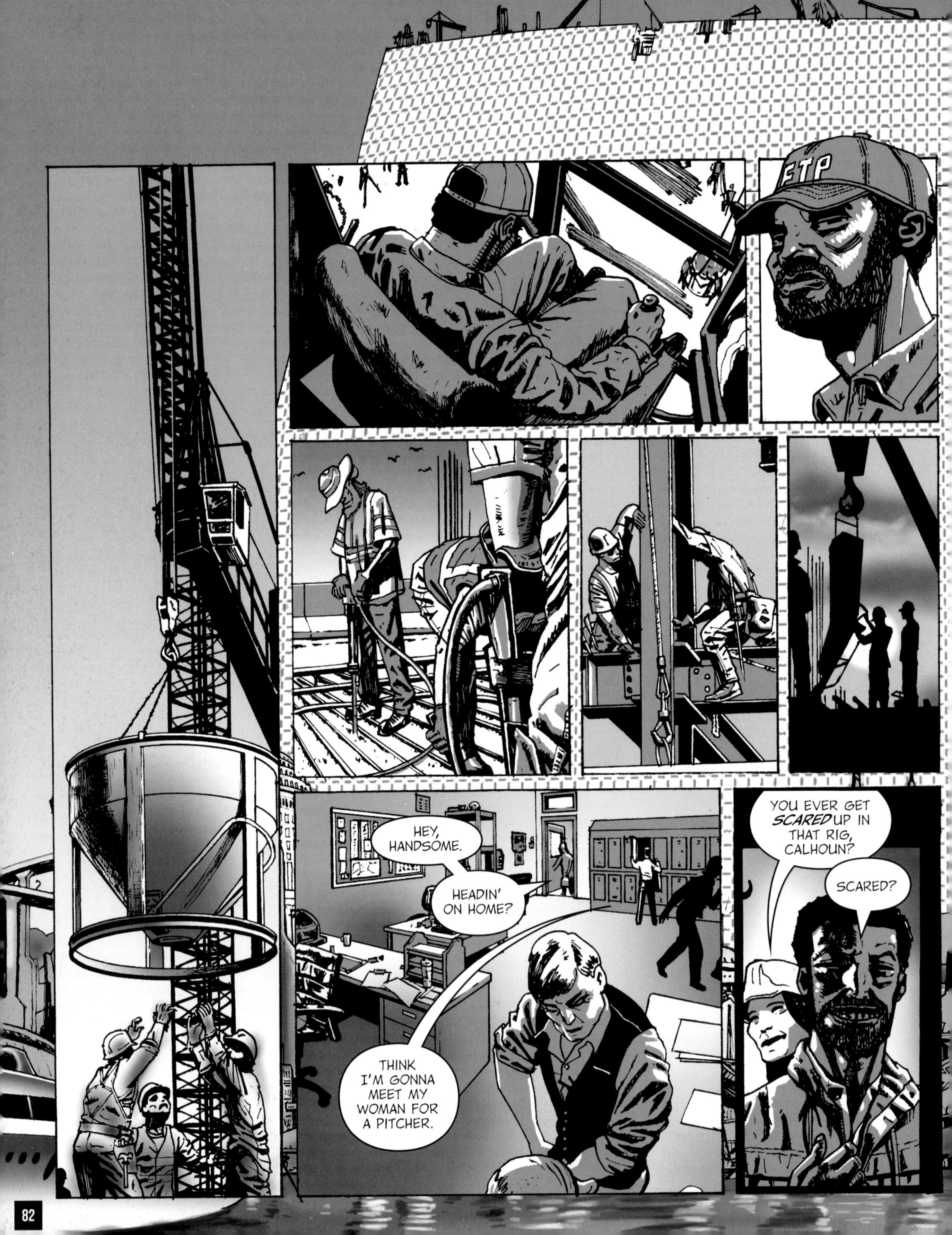
HEY, HANDSOME.
HEADIN' ON HOME?
THINK I'M GONNA MEET MY WOMAN FOR A PITCHER.
YOU EVER GET SCARED UP IN THAT RIG, CALHOUN?
SCARED?

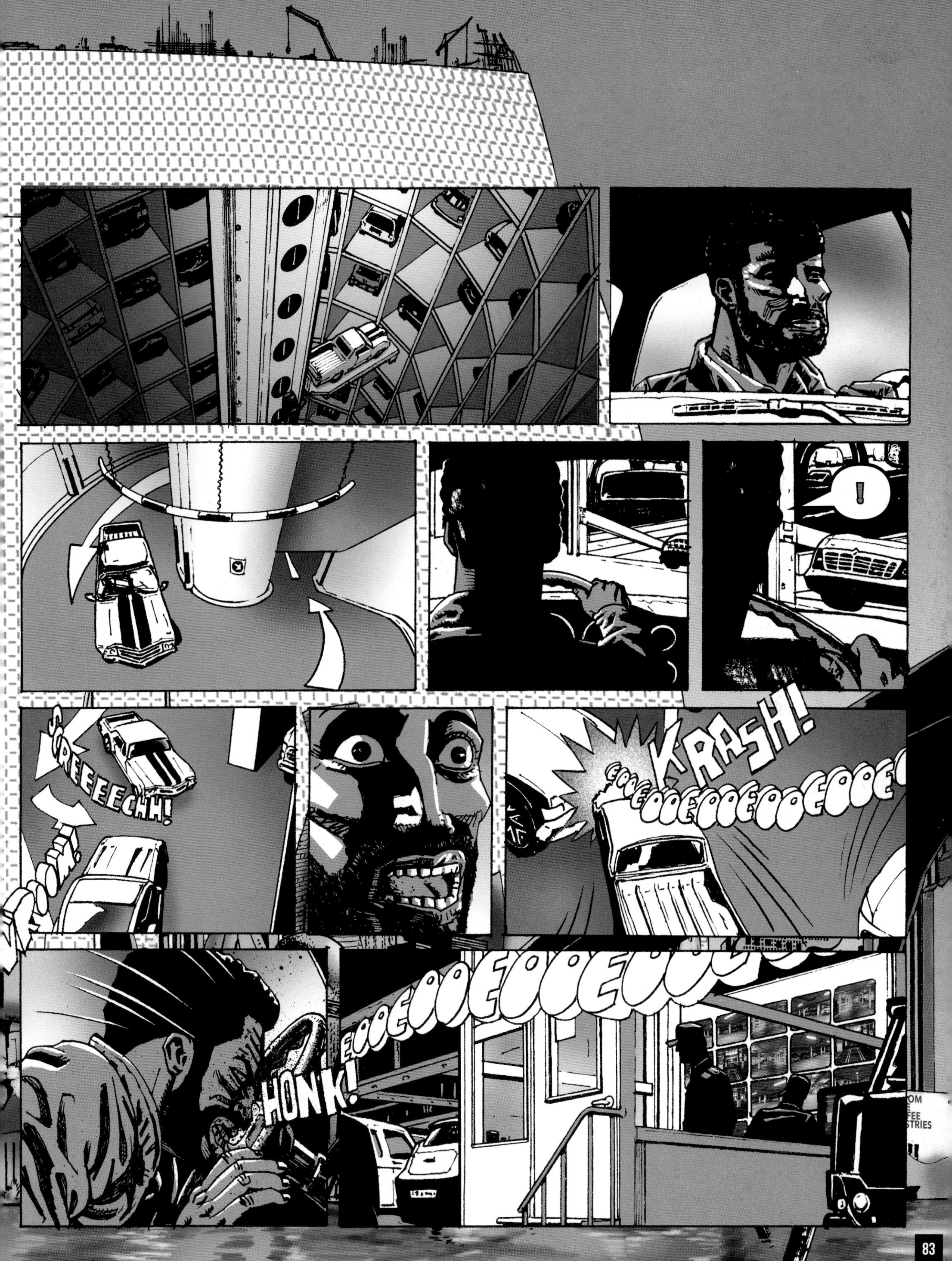
!
SCREEEEECHH!
KRASH!
HONK!

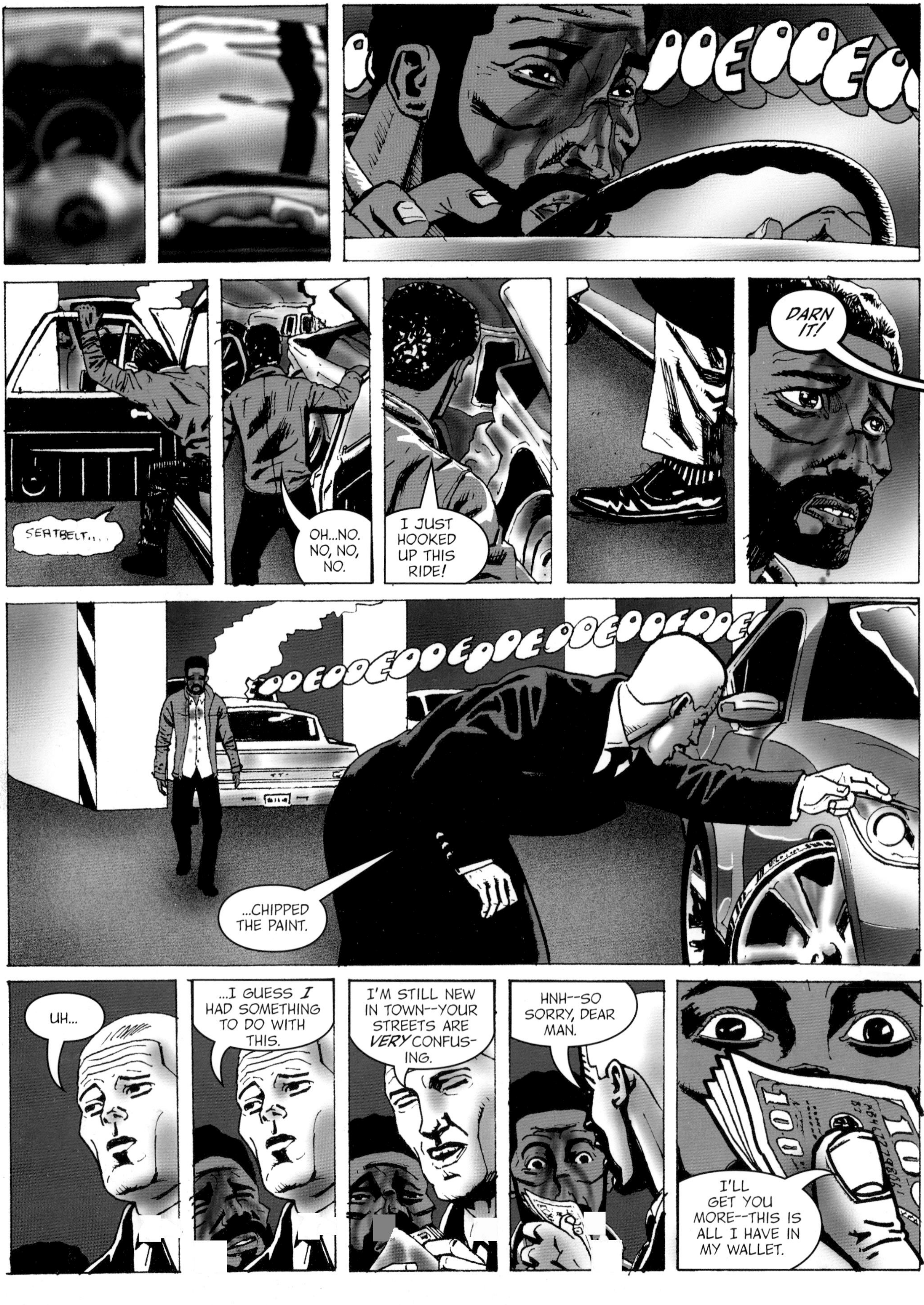
SEATBELT....
OH...NO. NO, NO, NO.
I JUST HOOKED UP THIS RIDE!
DARN IT!
...CHIPPED THE PAINT.
UH...
...I GUESS I HAD SOMETHING TO DO WITH THIS.
I'M STILL NEW IN TOWN--YOUR STREETS ARE VERY CONFUS-ING.
HNH--SO SORRY, DEAR MAN.
I'LL GET YOU MORE--THIS IS ALL I HAVE IN MY WALLET.

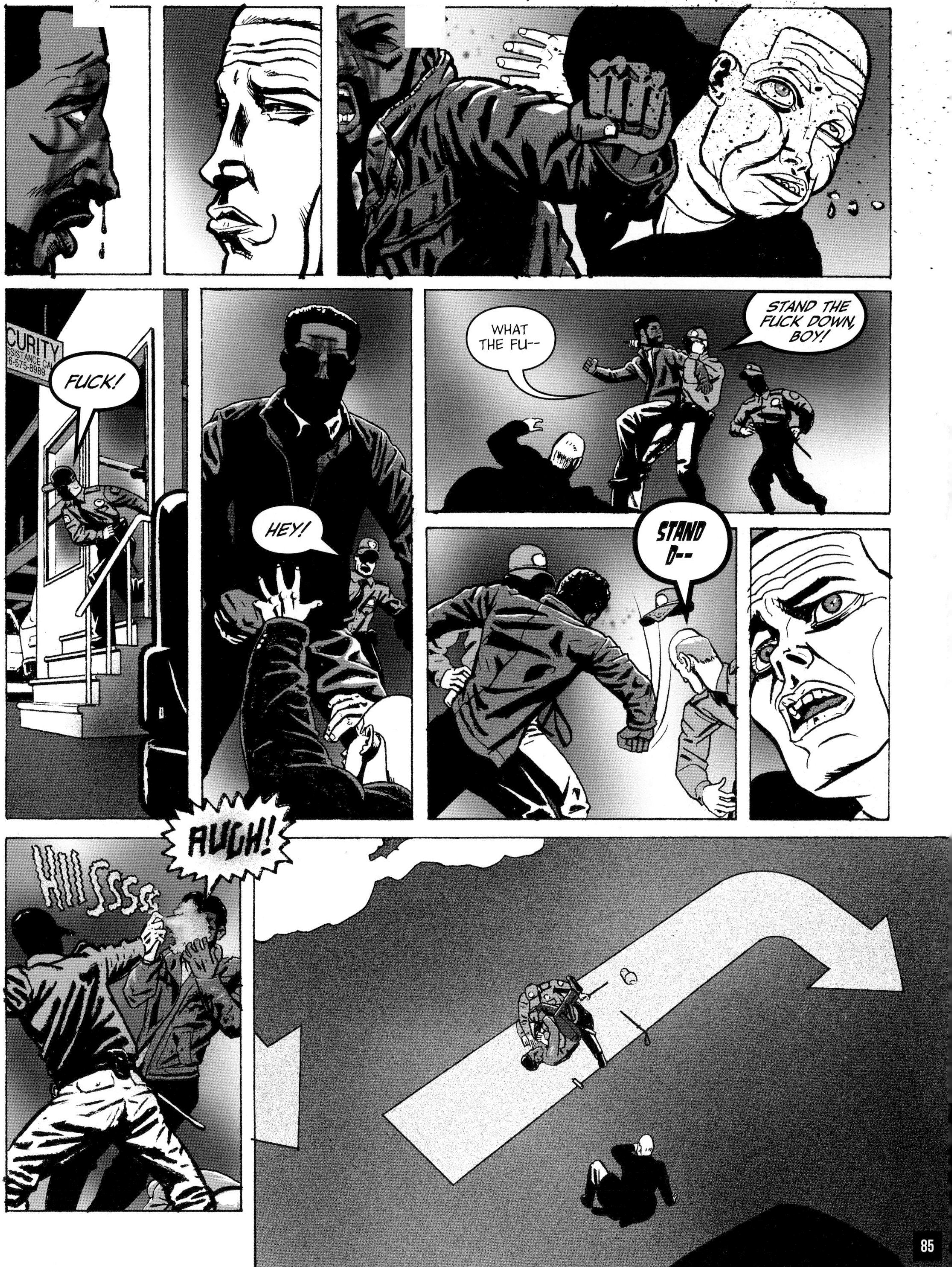
CURITY
SSISTANCE CA
6-575-8989
FUCK!
HEY!
WHAT THE FU--
STAND THE FUCK DOWN, BOY!
STAND D--
AUGH!

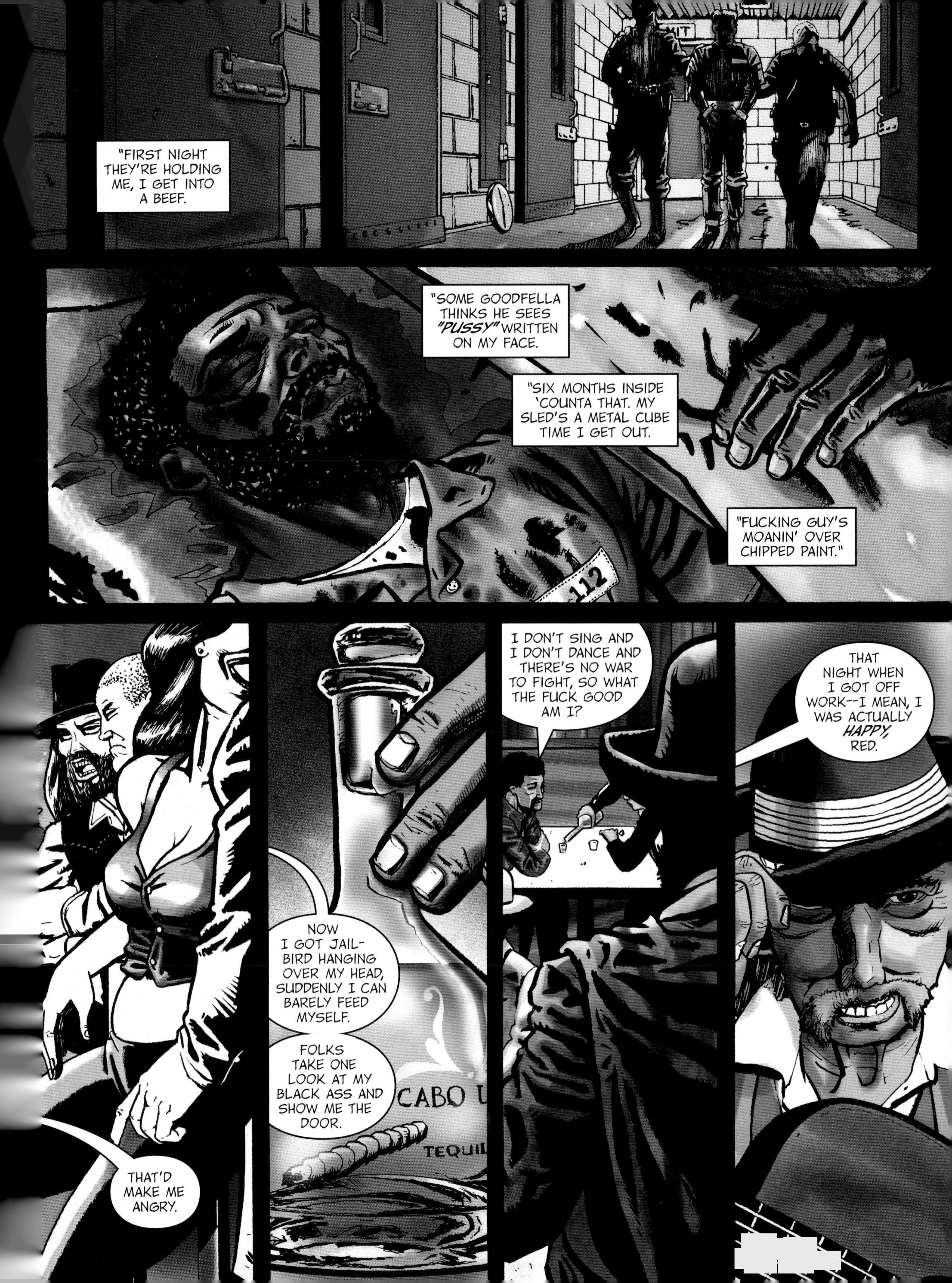
"FIRST NIGHT THEY'RE HOLDING ME, I GET INTO A BEEF.
"SOME GOODFELLA THINKS HE SEES "PUSSY" WRITTEN ON MY FACE.
"SIX MONTHS INSIDE 'COUNTA THAT. MY SLED'S A METAL CUBE TIME I GET OUT.
"FUCKING GUY'S MOANIN' OVER CHIPPED PAINT."
112
THAT'D MAKE ME ANGRY.
NOW I GOT JAIL-BIRD HANGING OVER MY HEAD, SUDDENLY I CAN BARELY FEED MYSELF.
FOLKS TAKE ONE LOOK AT MY BLACK ASS AND SHOW ME THE DOOR.
CABO
I DON'T SING AND I DON'T DANCE AND THERE'S NO WAR TO FIGHT, SO WHAT THE FUCK GOOD AM I?
THAT NIGHT WHEN I GOT OFF WORK--I MEAN, I WAS ACTUALLY HAPPY, RED.

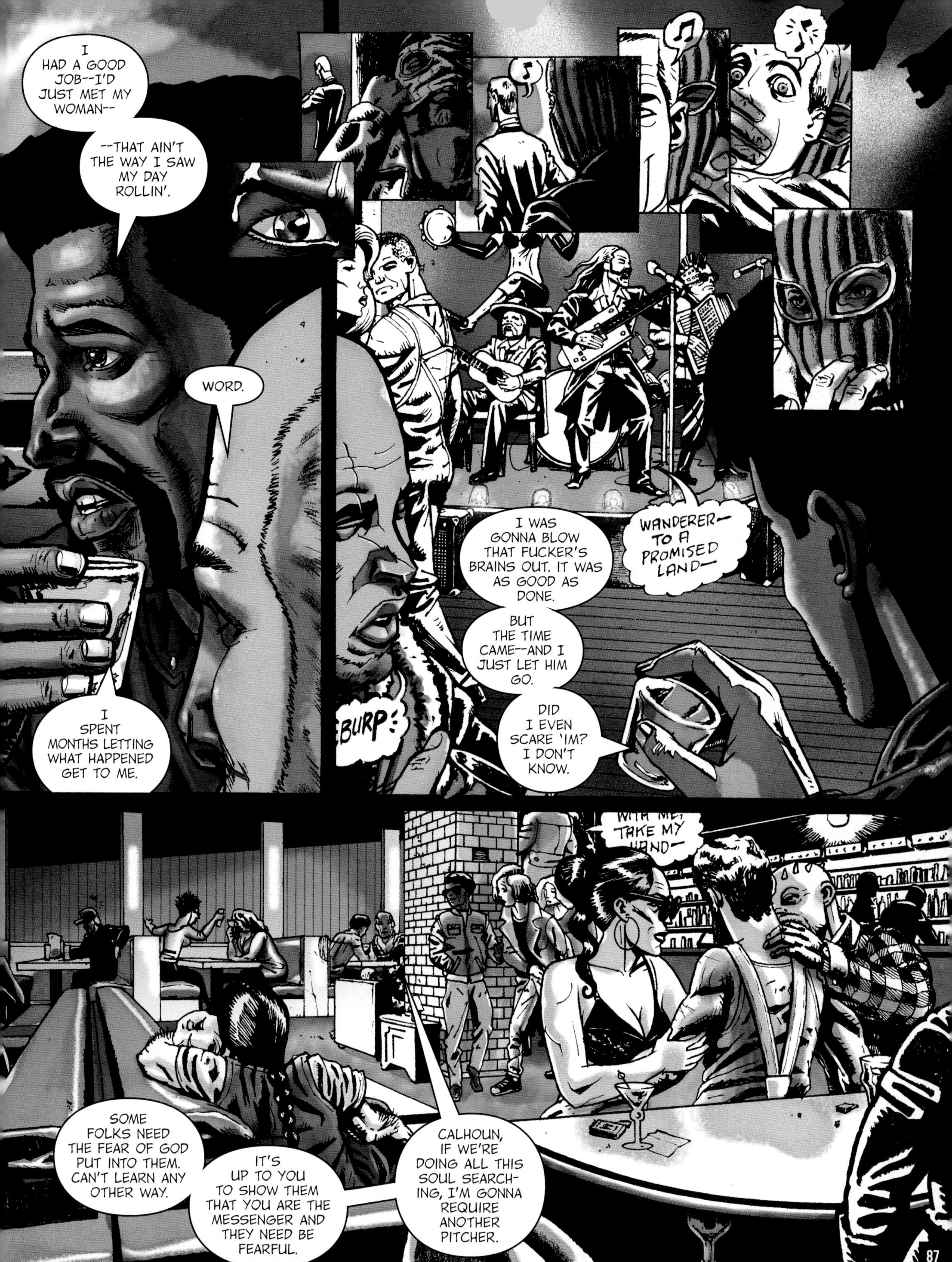
I HAD A GOOD JOB--I'D JUST MET MY WOMAN--
--THAT AIN'T THE WAY I SAW MY DAY ROLLIN'.
WORD.
I SPENT MONTHS LETTING WHAT HAPPENED GET TO ME.
I WAS GONNA BLOW THAT FUCKER'S BRAINS OUT. IT WAS AS GOOD AS DONE.
WANDERER— TO A PROMISED LAND—
BUT THE TIME CAME--AND I JUST LET HIM GO.
BURP
DID I EVEN SCARE 'IM? I DON'T KNOW.
TAKE MY
SOME FOLKS NEED THE FEAR OF GOD PUT INTO THEM. CAN'T LEARN ANY OTHER WAY.
IT'S UP TO YOU TO SHOW THEM THAT YOU ARE THE MESSENGER AND THEY NEED BE FEARFUL.
CALHOUN, IF WE'RE DOING ALL THIS SOUL SEARCH-ING, I'M GONNA REQUIRE ANOTHER PITCHER.

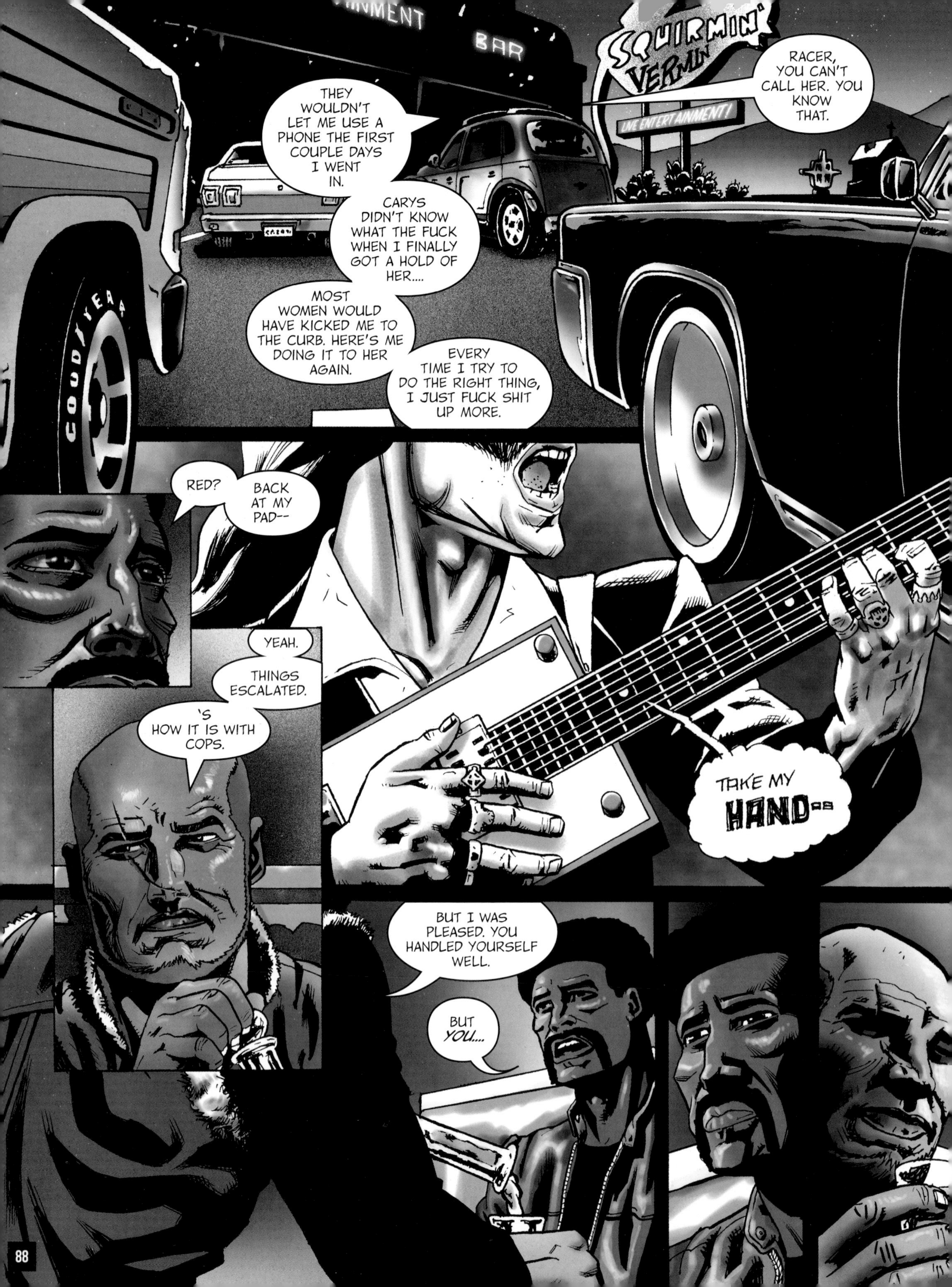

...AINMENT
BAR
SQUIRMIN' VERMIN
LIVE ENTERTAINMENT!
THEY WOULDN'T LET ME USE A PHONE THE FIRST COUPLE DAYS I WENT IN.
RACER, YOU CAN'T CALL HER. YOU KNOW THAT.
CARYS DIDN'T KNOW WHAT THE FUCK WHEN I FINALLY GOT A HOLD OF HER....
MOST WOMEN WOULD HAVE KICKED ME TO THE CURB. HERE'S ME DOING IT TO HER AGAIN.
EVERY TIME I TRY TO DO THE RIGHT THING, I JUST FUCK SHIT UP MORE.
GOODYEAR
RED?
BACK AT MY PAD--
YEAH.
THINGS ESCALATED.
'S HOW IT IS WITH COPS.
TAKE MY HAND--
BUT I WAS PLEASED. YOU HANDLED YOURSELF WELL.
BUT *YOU*....

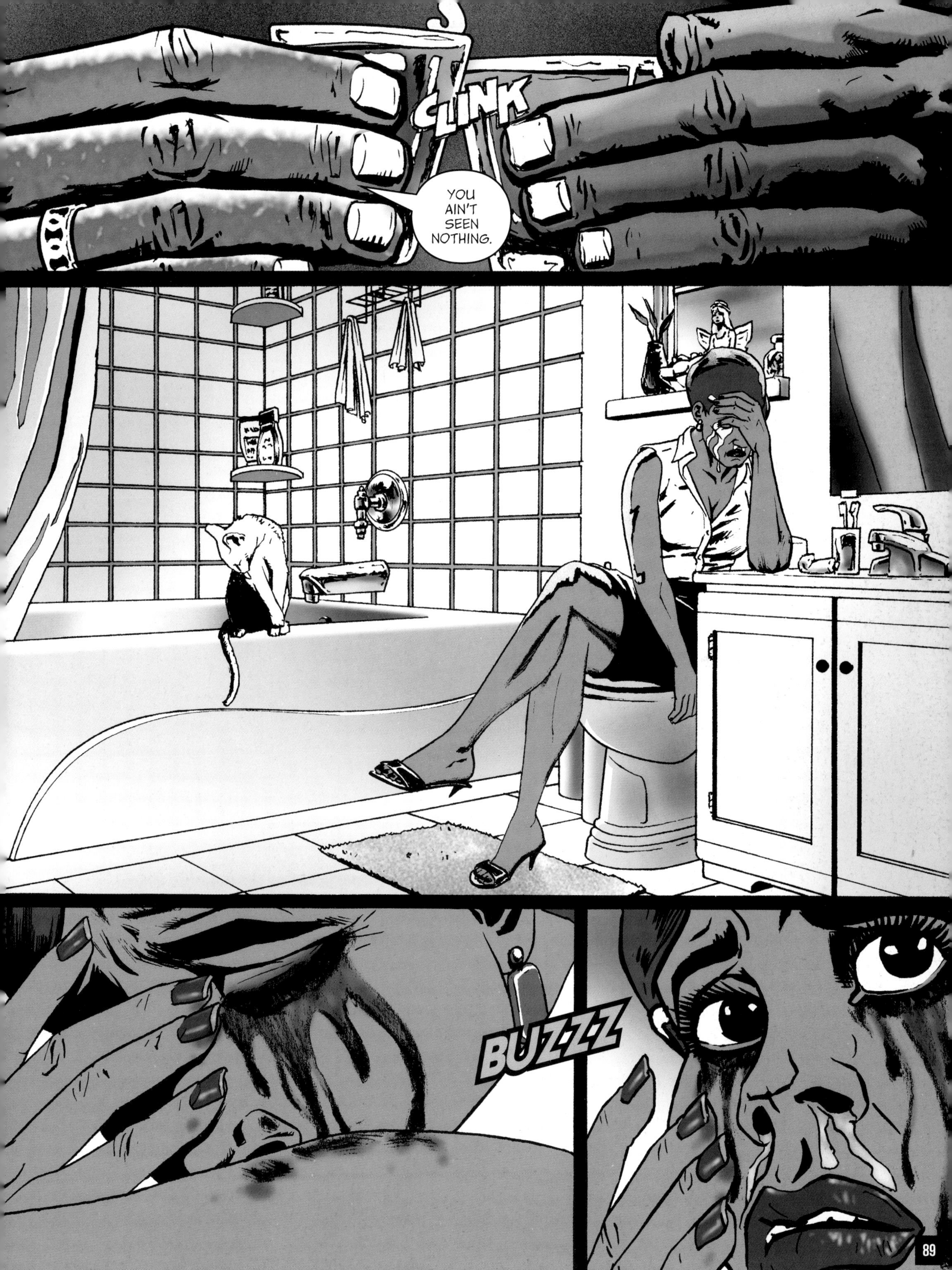
CLINK
YOU AIN'T SEEN NOTHING.
BUZZZ

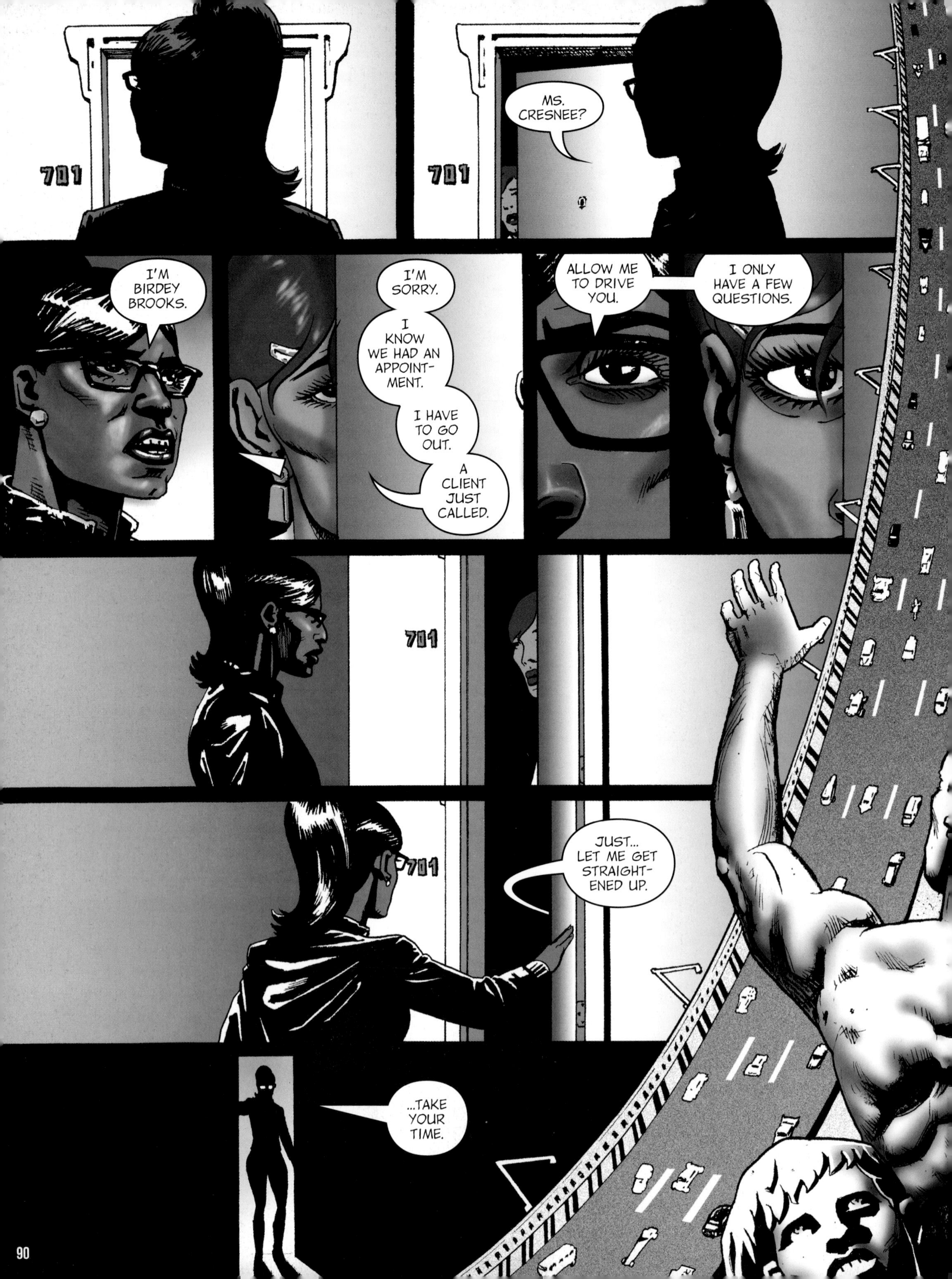
701
701
MS. CRESNEE?
I'M BIRDEY BROOKS.
I'M SORRY.
I KNOW WE HAD AN APPOINT-MENT.
I HAVE TO GO OUT.
A CLIENT JUST CALLED.
ALLOW ME TO DRIVE YOU.
I ONLY HAVE A FEW QUESTIONS.
701
701
JUST... LET ME GET STRAIGHT-ENED UP.
...TAKE YOUR TIME.

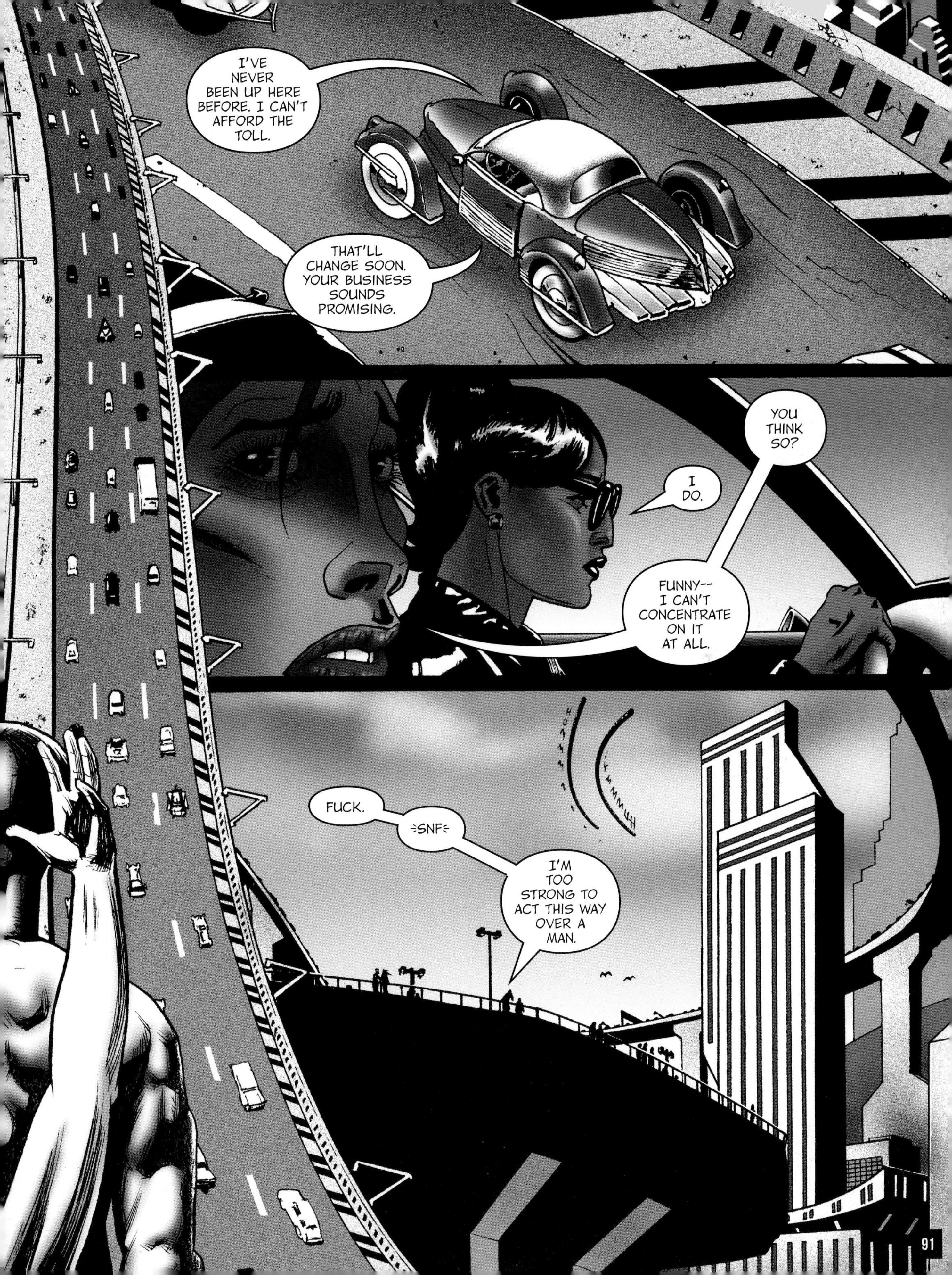
I'VE NEVER BEEN UP HERE BEFORE. I CAN'T AFFORD THE TOLL.
THAT'LL CHANGE SOON. YOUR BUSINESS SOUNDS PROMISING.
YOU THINK SO?
I DO.
FUNNY-- I CAN'T CONCENTRATE ON IT AT ALL.
FUCK.
SNF
I'M TOO STRONG TO ACT THIS WAY OVER A MAN.

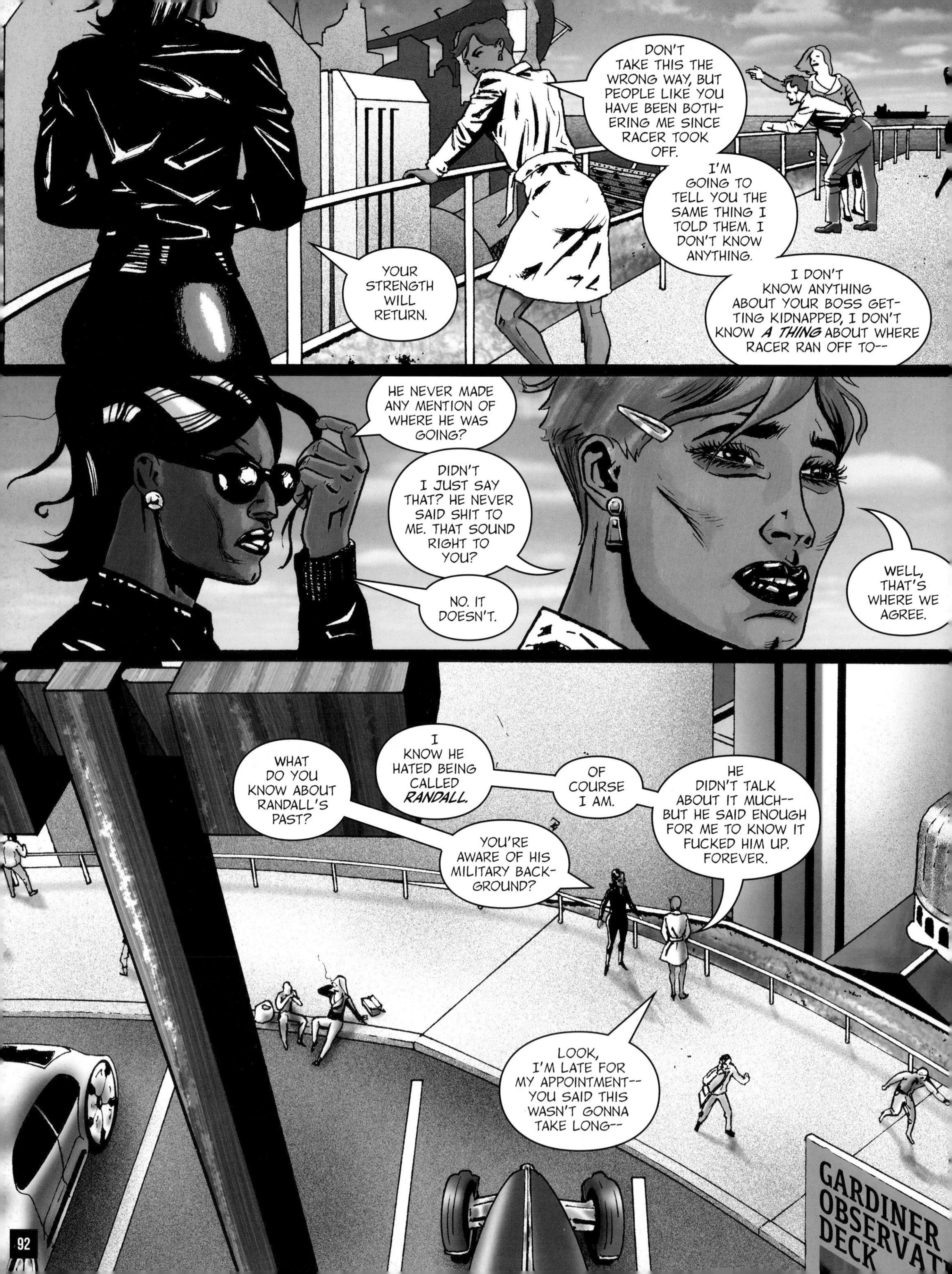

DON'T TAKE THIS THE WRONG WAY, BUT PEOPLE LIKE YOU HAVE BEEN BOTHERING ME SINCE RACER TOOK OFF.
I'M GOING TO TELL YOU THE SAME THING I TOLD THEM. I DON'T KNOW ANYTHING.
YOUR STRENGTH WILL RETURN.
I DON'T KNOW ANYTHING ABOUT YOUR BOSS GETTING KIDNAPPED, I DON'T KNOW *A THING* ABOUT WHERE RACER RAN OFF TO--
HE NEVER MADE ANY MENTION OF WHERE HE WAS GOING?
DIDN'T I JUST SAY THAT? HE NEVER SAID SHIT TO ME. THAT SOUND RIGHT TO YOU?
NO. IT DOESN'T.
WELL, THAT'S WHERE WE AGREE.
WHAT DO YOU KNOW ABOUT RANDALL'S PAST?
I KNOW HE HATED BEING CALLED *RANDALL.*
YOU'RE AWARE OF HIS MILITARY BACKGROUND?
OF COURSE I AM.
HE DIDN'T TALK ABOUT IT MUCH-- BUT HE SAID ENOUGH FOR ME TO KNOW IT FUCKED HIM UP. FOREVER.
LOOK, I'M LATE FOR MY APPOINTMENT-- YOU SAID THIS WASN'T GONNA TAKE LONG--
GARDINER OBSERVAT DECK

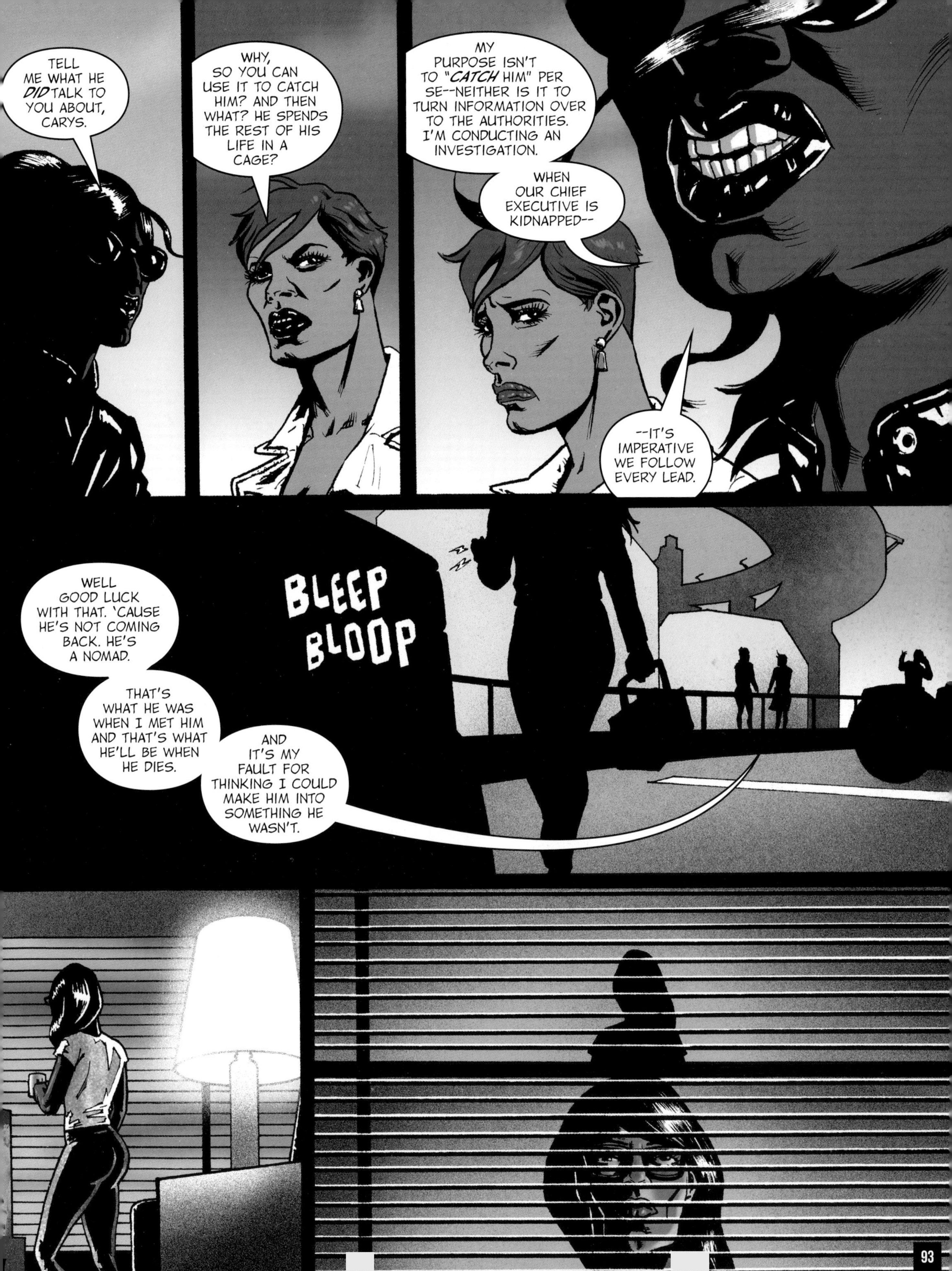

TELL ME WHAT HE *DID* TALK TO YOU ABOUT, CARYS.
WHY, SO YOU CAN USE IT TO CATCH HIM? AND THEN WHAT? HE SPENDS THE REST OF HIS LIFE IN A CAGE?
MY PURPOSE ISN'T TO "*CATCH* HIM" PER SE--NEITHER IS IT TO TURN INFORMATION OVER TO THE AUTHORITIES. I'M CONDUCTING AN INVESTIGATION.
WHEN OUR CHIEF EXECUTIVE IS KIDNAPPED--
--IT'S IMPERATIVE WE FOLLOW EVERY LEAD.
BLEEP BLOOP
WELL GOOD LUCK WITH THAT. 'CAUSE HE'S NOT COMING BACK. HE'S A NOMAD.
THAT'S WHAT HE WAS WHEN I MET HIM AND THAT'S WHAT HE'LL BE WHEN HE DIES.
AND IT'S MY FAULT FOR THINKING I COULD MAKE HIM INTO SOMETHING HE WASN'T.

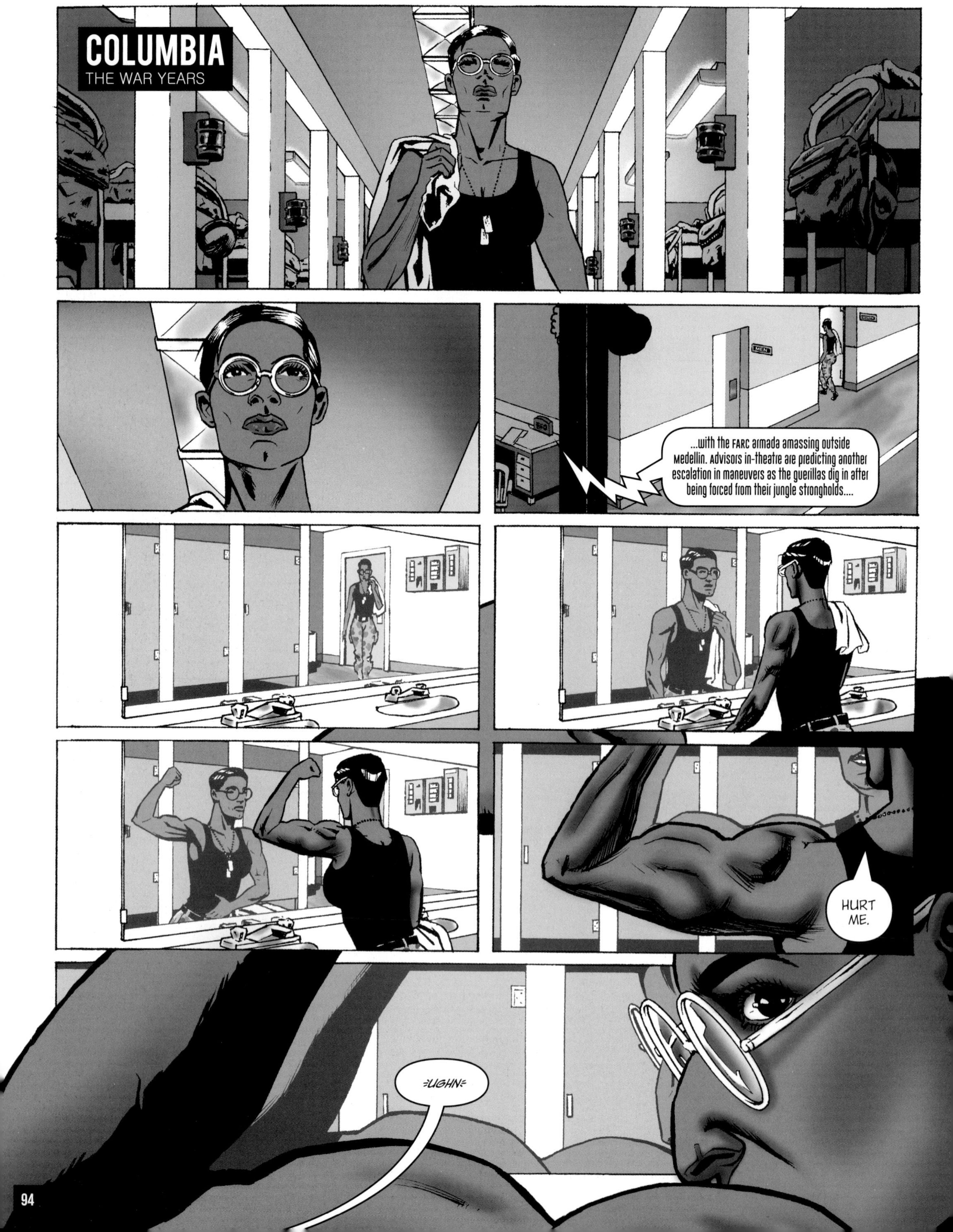
COLUMBIA
THE WAR YEARS
...with the FARC armada amassing outside Medellin. Advisors in-theatre are predicting another escalation in maneuvers as the guerillas dig in after being forced from their jungle strongholds....
HURT ME.
UGHN

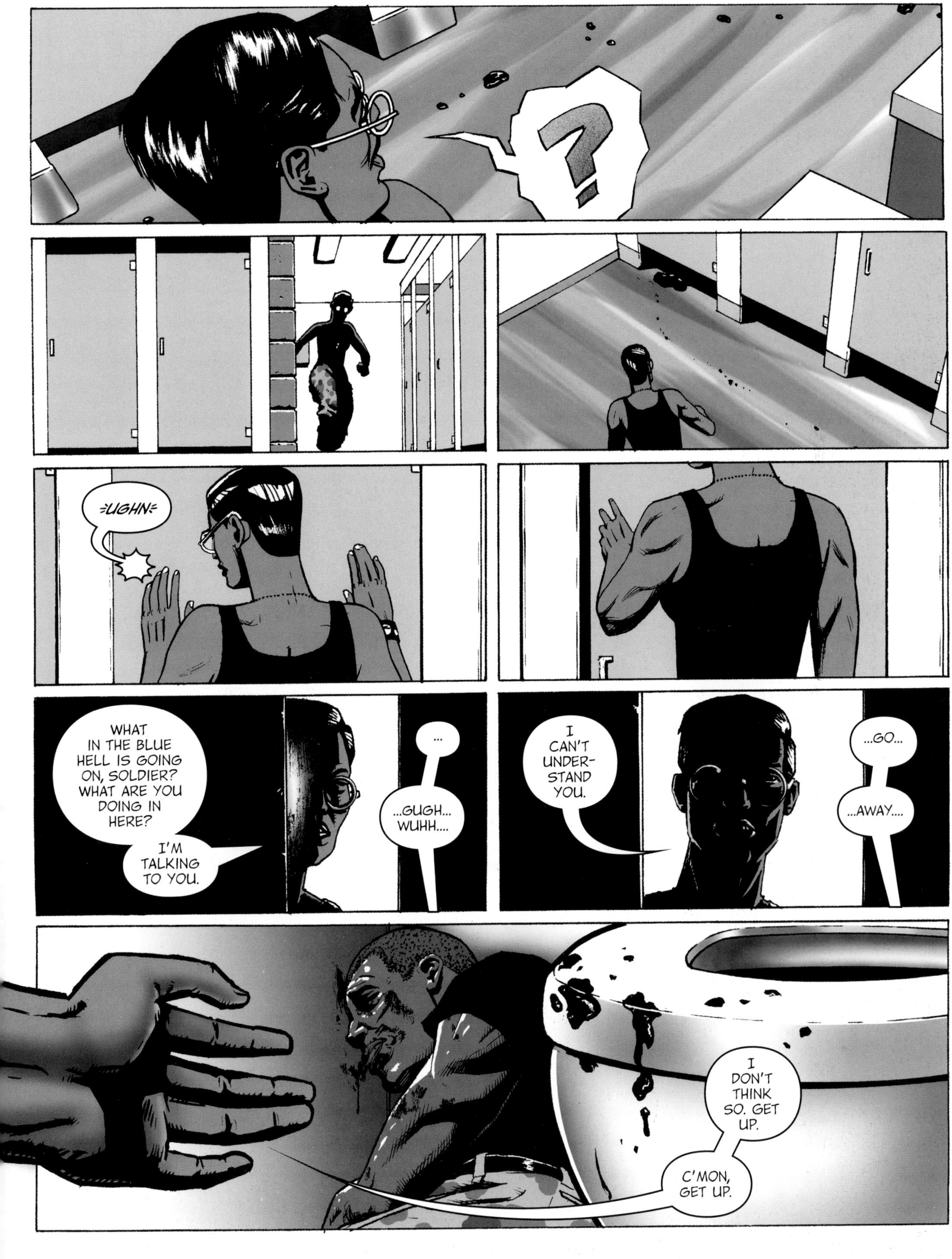
?
UGHN
WHAT IN THE BLUE HELL IS GOING ON, SOLDIER? WHAT ARE YOU DOING IN HERE?
I'M TALKING TO YOU.
...
...GUGH... WUHH....
I CAN'T UNDER-STAND YOU.
...GO...
...AWAY....
I DON'T THINK SO. GET UP.
C'MON, GET UP.

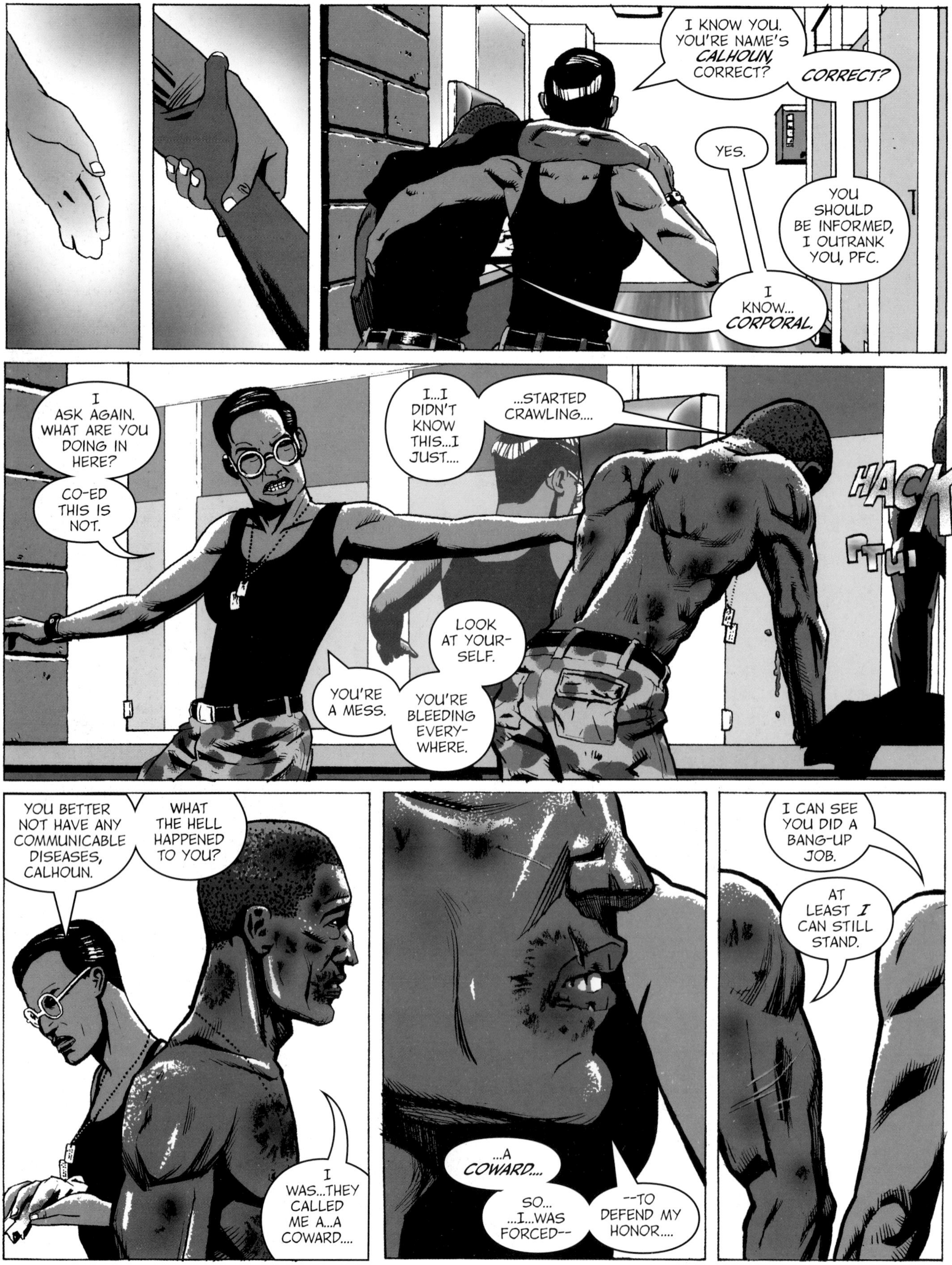
I KNOW YOU. YOU'RE NAME'S *CALHOUN,* CORRECT?
CORRECT?
YES.
YOU SHOULD BE INFORMED, I OUTRANK YOU, PFC.
I KNOW... *CORPORAL.*
I ASK AGAIN. WHAT ARE YOU DOING IN HERE?
CO-ED THIS IS NOT.
I...I DIDN'T KNOW THIS...I JUST....
...STARTED CRAWLING....
HACK!
PTUI
LOOK AT YOURSELF.
YOU'RE A MESS.
YOU'RE BLEEDING EVERYWHERE.
YOU BETTER NOT HAVE ANY COMMUNICABLE DISEASES, CALHOUN.
WHAT THE HELL HAPPENED TO YOU?
I WAS...THEY CALLED ME A...A COWARD....
...A *COWARD....*
SO... ...I...WAS FORCED--
--TO DEFEND MY HONOR....
I CAN SEE YOU DID A BANG-UP JOB.
AT LEAST *I* CAN STILL STAND.

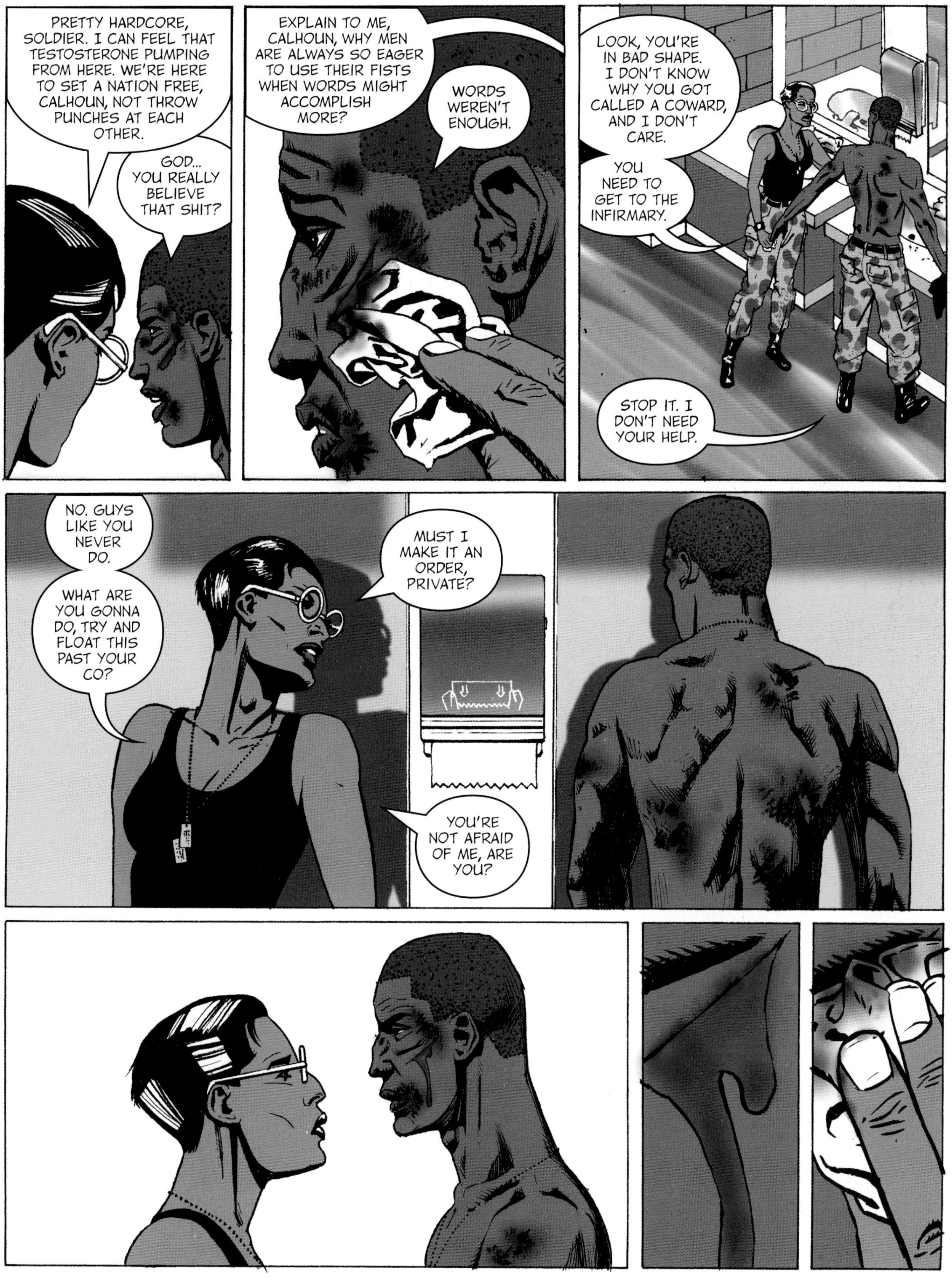
PRETTY HARDCORE, SOLDIER. I CAN FEEL THAT TESTOSTERONE PUMPING FROM HERE. WE'RE HERE TO SET A NATION FREE, CALHOUN, NOT THROW PUNCHES AT EACH OTHER.
GOD... YOU REALLY BELIEVE THAT SHIT?
EXPLAIN TO ME, CALHOUN, WHY MEN ARE ALWAYS SO EAGER TO USE THEIR FISTS WHEN WORDS MIGHT ACCOMPLISH MORE?
WORDS WEREN'T ENOUGH.
LOOK, YOU'RE IN BAD SHAPE. I DON'T KNOW WHY YOU GOT CALLED A COWARD, AND I DON'T CARE.
YOU NEED TO GET TO THE INFIRMARY.
STOP IT. I DON'T NEED YOUR HELP.
NO. GUYS LIKE YOU NEVER DO.
WHAT ARE YOU GONNA DO, TRY AND FLOAT THIS PAST YOUR CO?
MUST I MAKE IT AN ORDER, PRIVATE?
YOU'RE NOT AFRAID OF ME, ARE YOU?

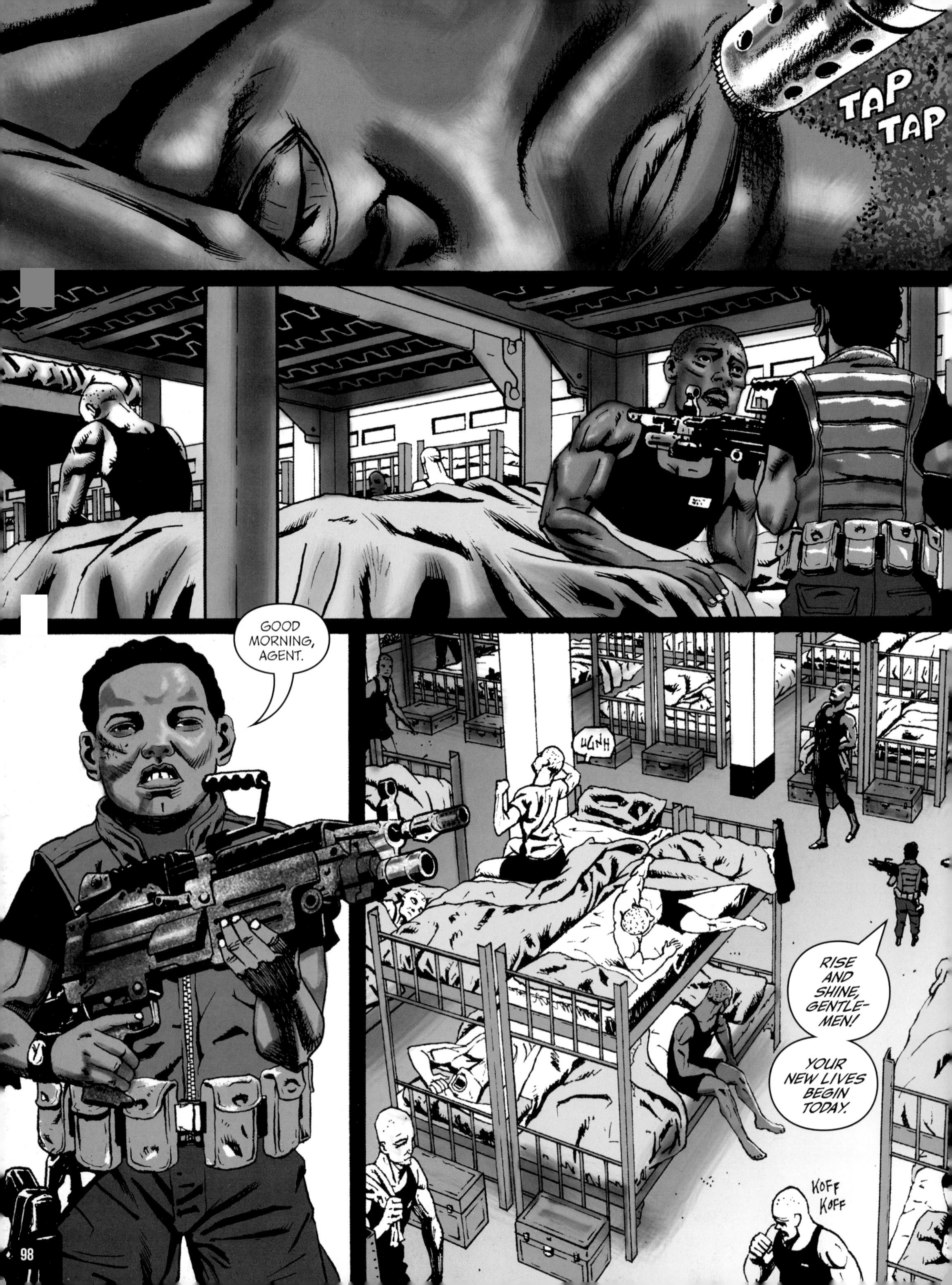
TAP TAP
GOOD MORNING, AGENT.
UGNH
RISE AND SHINE, GENTLEMEN!
YOUR NEW LIVES BEGIN TODAY.
KOFF KOFF

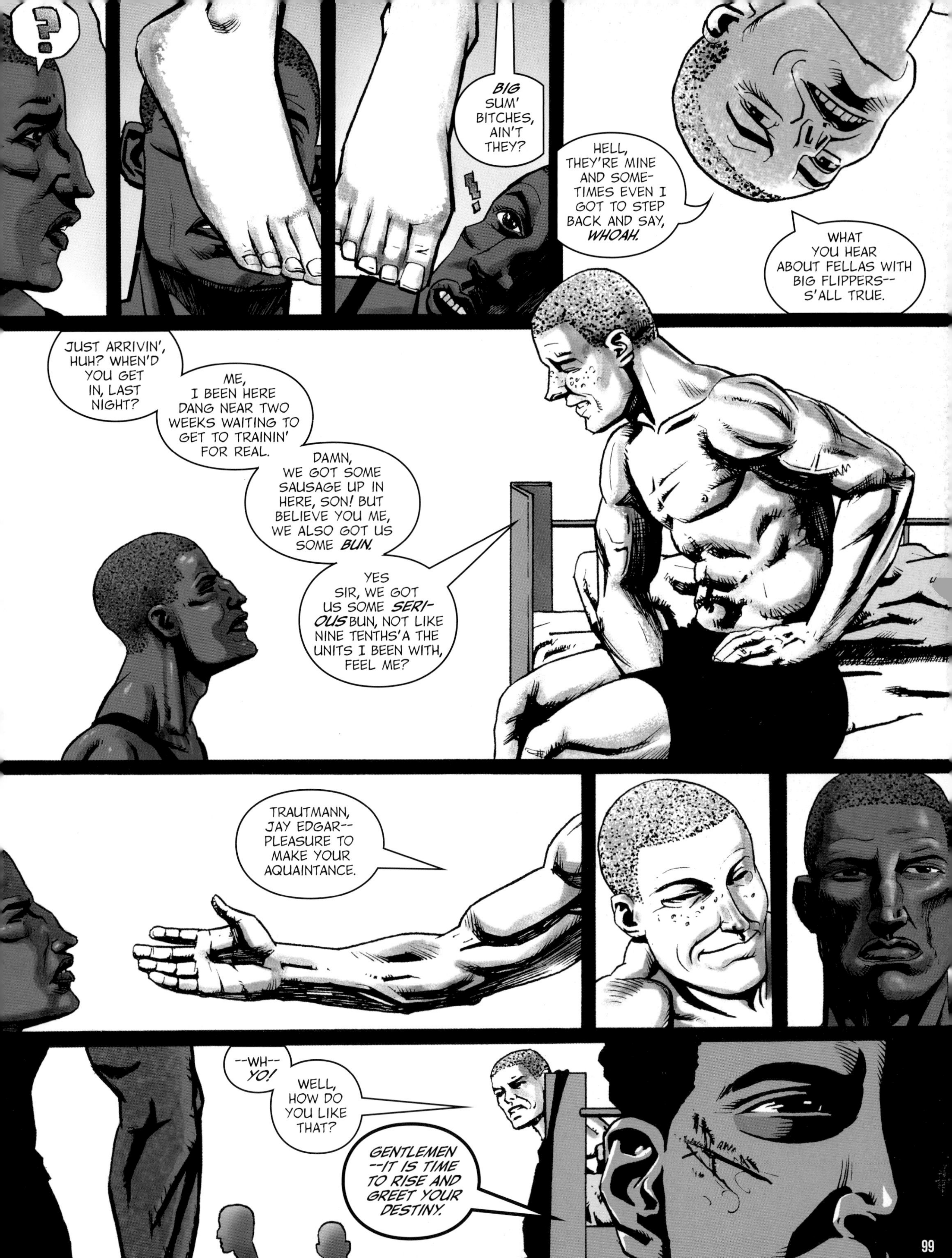

?
BIG SUM' BITCHES, AIN'T THEY?
HELL, THEY'RE MINE AND SOME-TIMES EVEN I GOT TO STEP BACK AND SAY, WHOAH.
WHAT YOU HEAR ABOUT FELLAS WITH BIG FLIPPERS-- S'ALL TRUE.
JUST ARRIVIN', HUH? WHEN'D YOU GET IN, LAST NIGHT?
ME, I BEEN HERE DANG NEAR TWO WEEKS WAITING TO GET TO TRAININ' FOR REAL.
DAMN, WE GOT SOME SAUSAGE UP IN HERE, SON! BUT BELIEVE YOU ME, WE ALSO GOT US SOME BUN.
YES SIR, WE GOT US SOME SERI-OUS BUN, NOT LIKE NINE TENTHS'A THE UNITS I BEEN WITH, FEEL ME?
TRAUTMANN, JAY EDGAR-- PLEASURE TO MAKE YOUR AQUAINTANCE.
--WH-- YO!
WELL, HOW DO YOU LIKE THAT?
GENTLEMEN --IT IS TIME TO RISE AND GREET YOUR DESTINY.

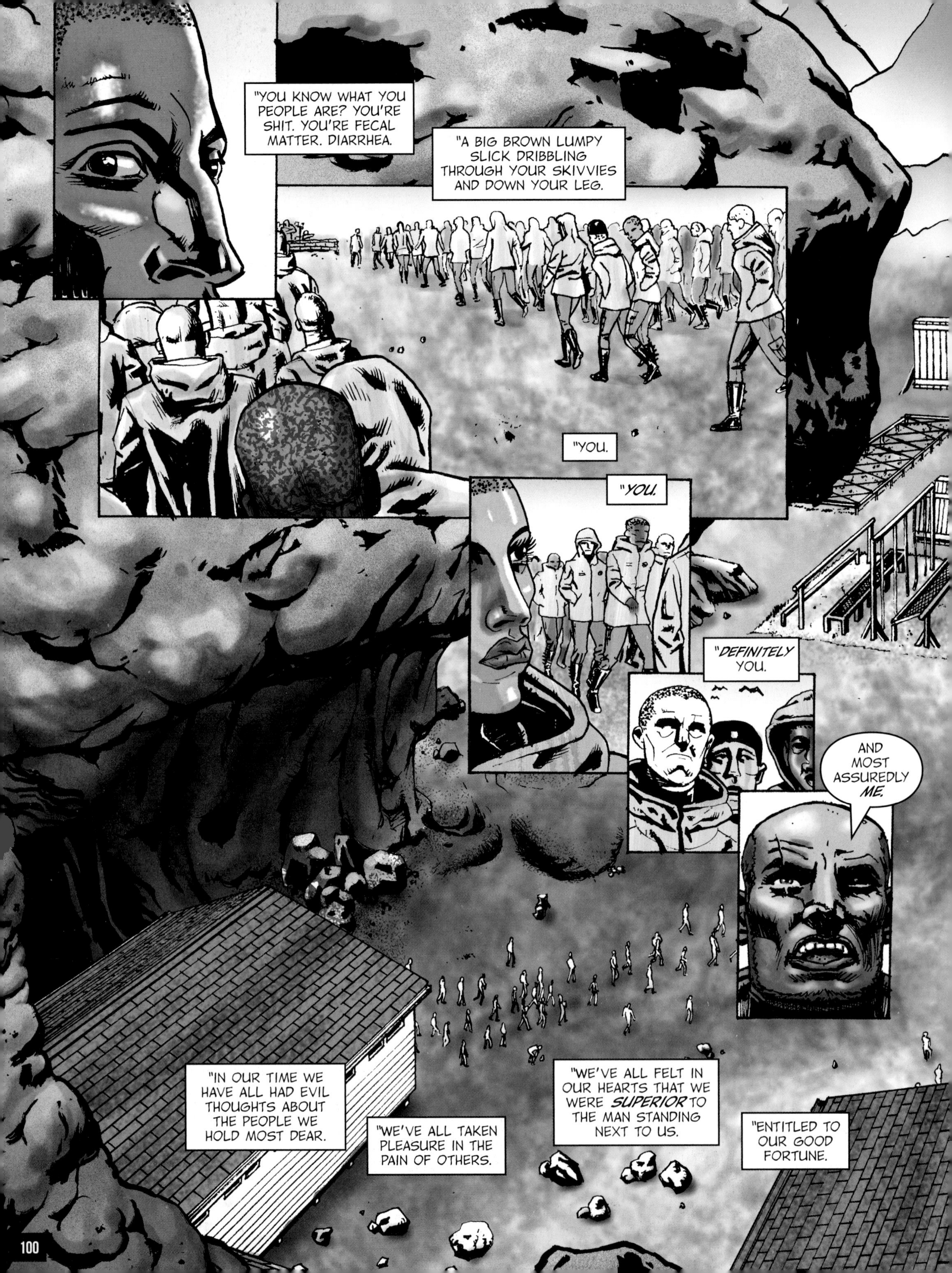

"YOU KNOW WHAT YOU PEOPLE ARE? YOU'RE SHIT. YOU'RE FECAL MATTER. DIARRHEA.
"A BIG BROWN LUMPY SLICK DRIBBLING THROUGH YOUR SKIVVIES AND DOWN YOUR LEG.
"YOU.
"YOU.
"DEFINITELY YOU.
AND MOST ASSUREDLY ME.
"IN OUR TIME WE HAVE ALL HAD EVIL THOUGHTS ABOUT THE PEOPLE WE HOLD MOST DEAR.
"WE'VE ALL TAKEN PLEASURE IN THE PAIN OF OTHERS.
"WE'VE ALL FELT IN OUR HEARTS THAT WE WERE SUPERIOR TO THE MAN STANDING NEXT TO US.
"ENTITLED TO OUR GOOD FORTUNE.

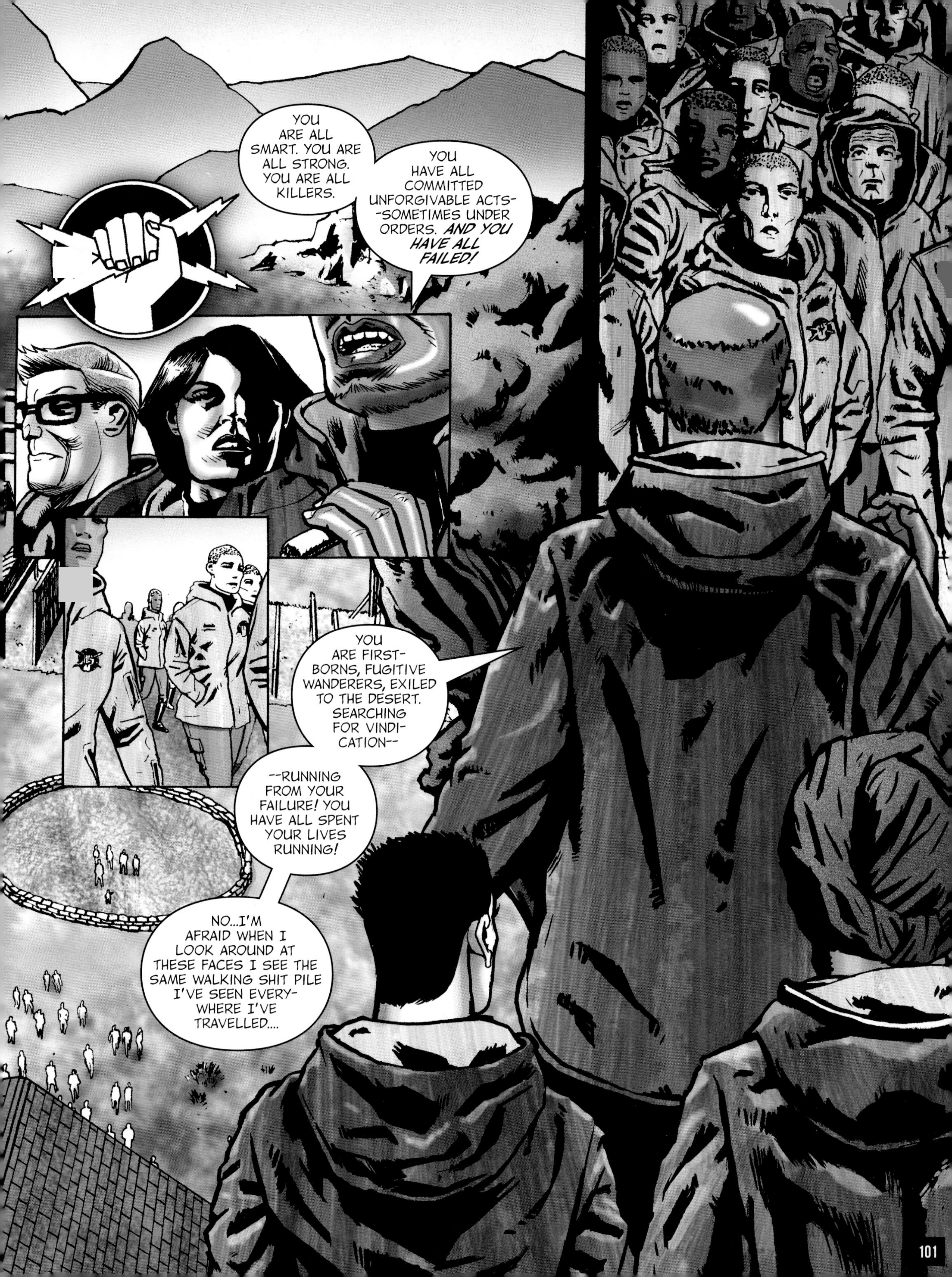

YOU ARE ALL SMART. YOU ARE ALL STRONG. YOU ARE ALL KILLERS.
YOU HAVE ALL COMMITTED UNFORGIVABLE ACTS--SOMETIMES UNDER ORDERS. AND YOU HAVE ALL FAILED!
YOU ARE FIRST-BORNS, FUGITIVE WANDERERS, EXILED TO THE DESERT. SEARCHING FOR VINDI-CATION--
--RUNNING FROM YOUR FAILURE! YOU HAVE ALL SPENT YOUR LIVES RUNNING!
NO...I'M AFRAID WHEN I LOOK AROUND AT THESE FACES I SEE THE SAME WALKING SHIT PILE I'VE SEEN EVERY-WHERE I'VE TRAVELLED....

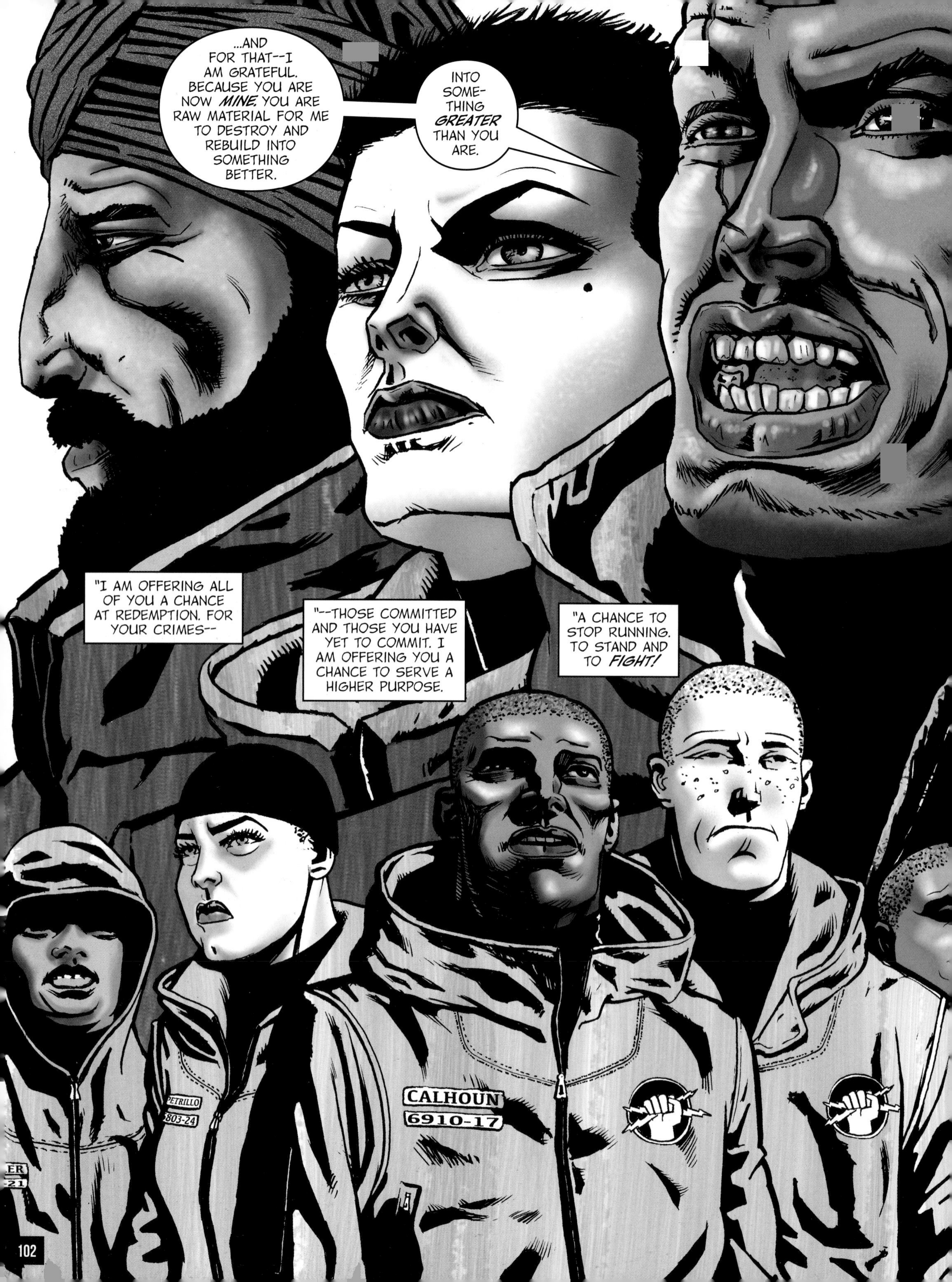
...AND FOR THAT--I AM GRATEFUL. BECAUSE YOU ARE NOW *MINE.* YOU ARE RAW MATERIAL FOR ME TO DESTROY AND REBUILD INTO SOMETHING BETTER.
INTO SOME-THING *GREATER* THAN YOU ARE.
"I AM OFFERING ALL OF YOU A CHANCE AT REDEMPTION. FOR YOUR CRIMES--
"--THOSE COMMITTED AND THOSE YOU HAVE YET TO COMMIT. I AM OFFERING YOU A CHANCE TO SERVE A HIGHER PURPOSE.
"A CHANCE TO STOP RUNNING. TO STAND AND TO *FIGHT!*
PETRILLO
803-24
CALHOUN
6910-17

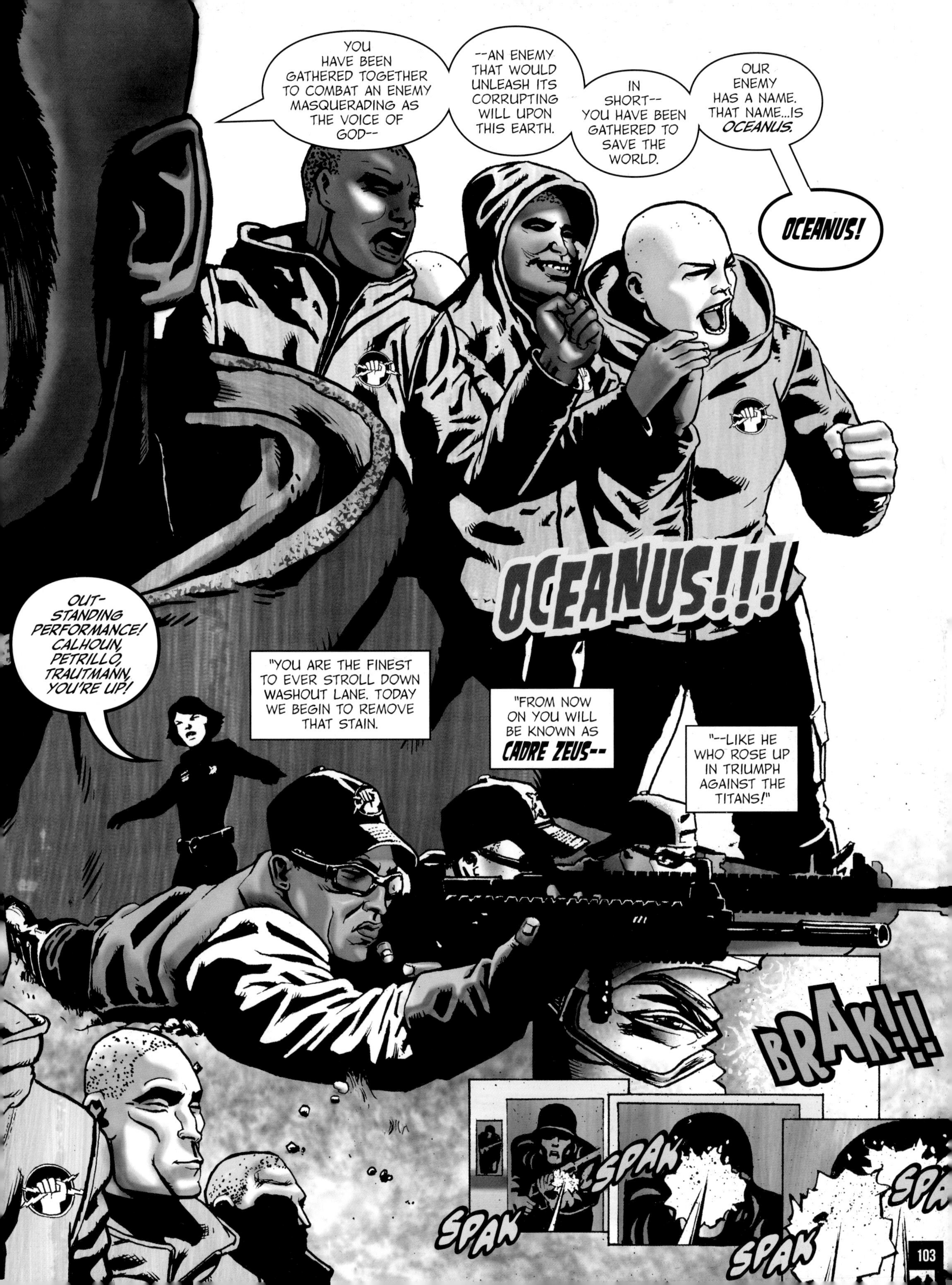

YOU HAVE BEEN GATHERED TOGETHER TO COMBAT AN ENEMY MASQUERADING AS THE VOICE OF GOD--
--AN ENEMY THAT WOULD UNLEASH ITS CORRUPTING WILL UPON THIS EARTH.
IN SHORT-- YOU HAVE BEEN GATHERED TO SAVE THE WORLD.
OUR ENEMY HAS A NAME. THAT NAME...IS *OCEANUS.*
OCEANUS!
OCEANUS!!!
OUT-STANDING PERFORMANCE! CALHOUN, PETRILLO, TRAUTMANN, YOU'RE UP!
"YOU ARE THE FINEST TO EVER STROLL DOWN WASHOUT LANE. TODAY WE BEGIN TO REMOVE THAT STAIN.
"FROM NOW ON YOU WILL BE KNOWN AS CADRE ZEUS--
"--LIKE HE WHO ROSE UP IN TRIUMPH AGAINST THE TITANS!"
BRAK!!!
SPAK
SPAK
SPAK
SPAK

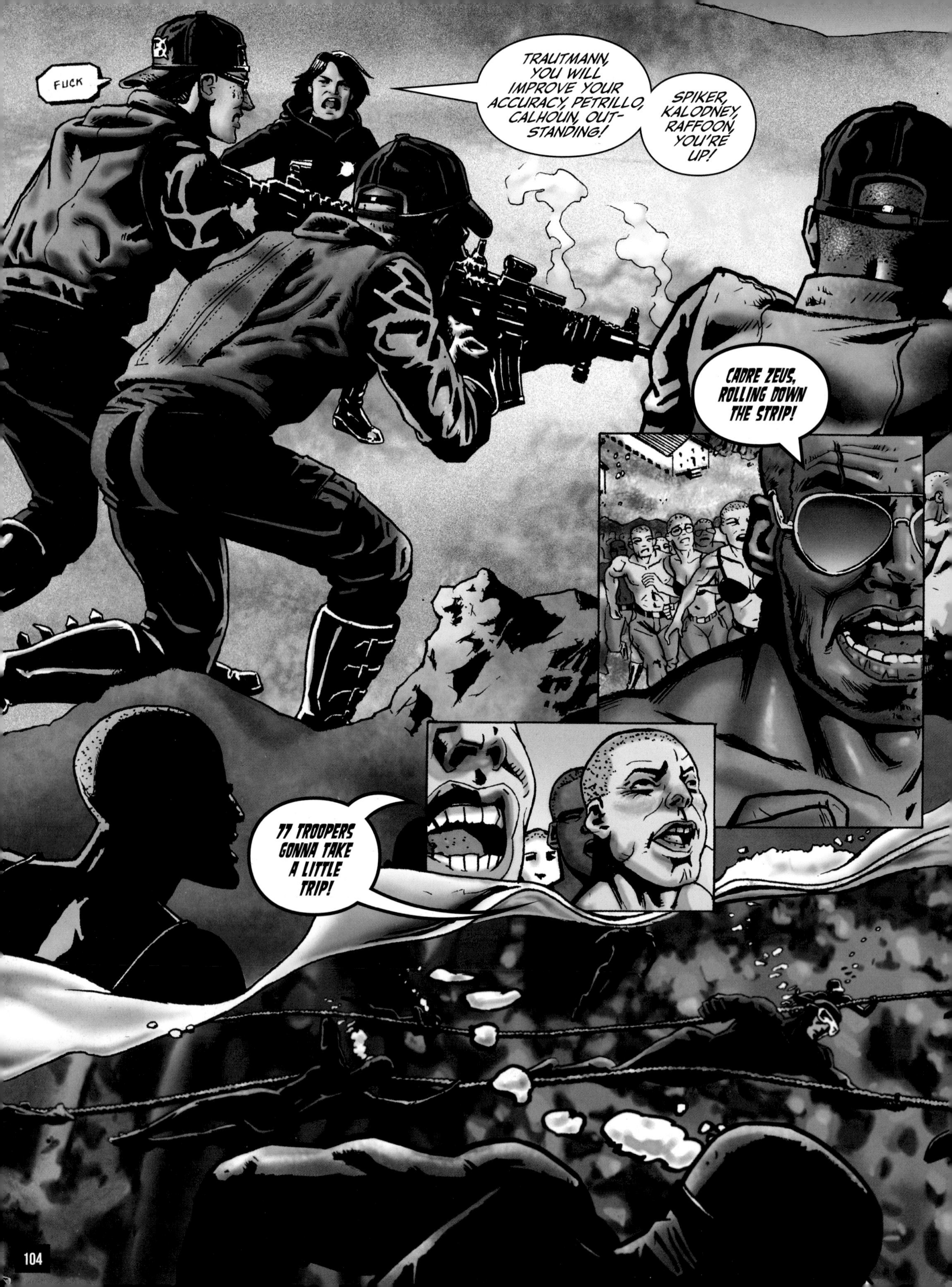
FUCK
TRAUTMANN, YOU WILL IMPROVE YOUR ACCURACY, PETRILLO, CALHOUN, OUT-STANDING!
SPIKER, KALODNEY, RAFFOON, YOU'RE UP!
CADRE ZEUS, ROLLING DOWN THE STRIP!
77 TROOPERS GONNA TAKE A LITTLE TRIP!

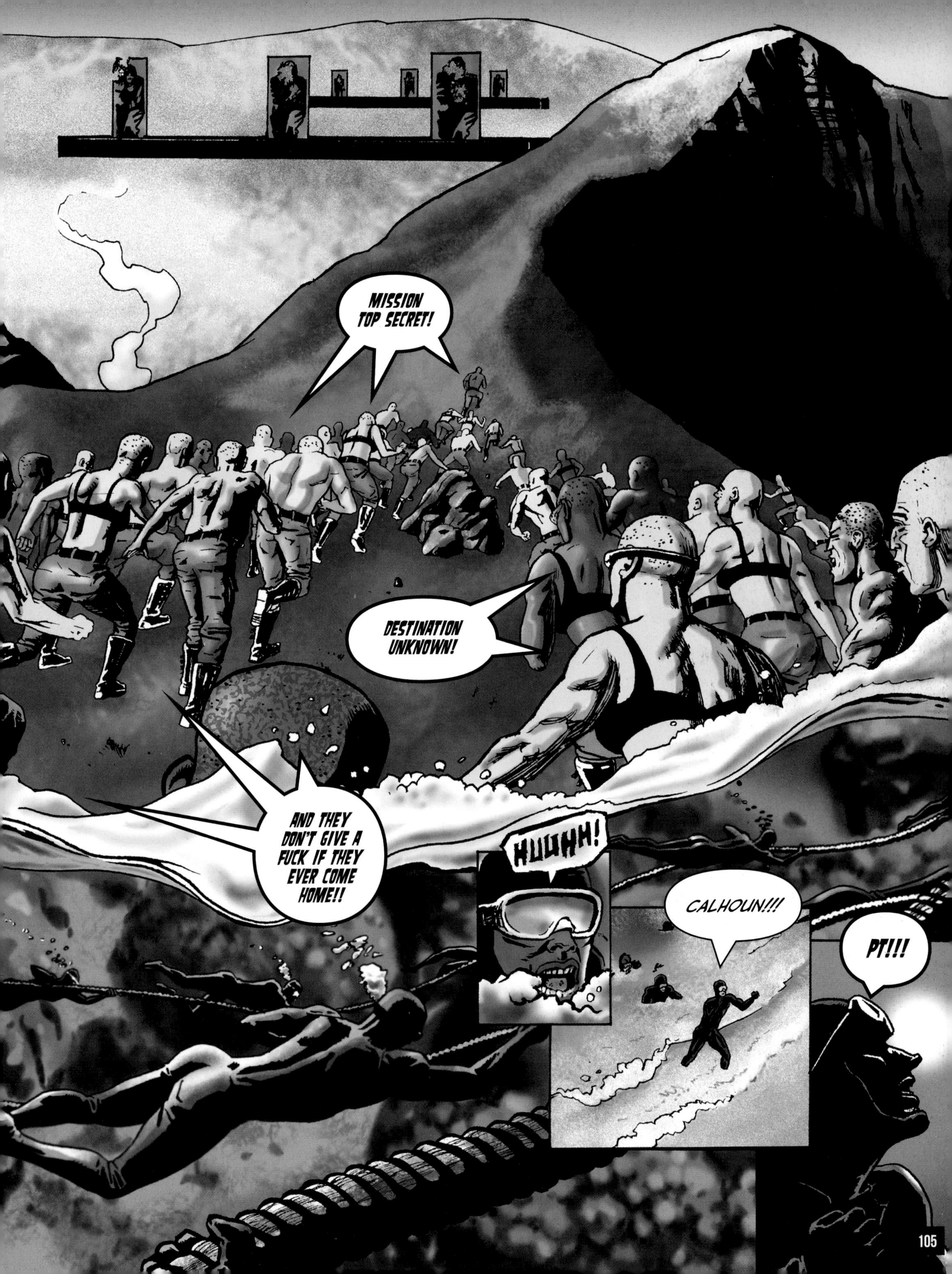
MISSION TOP SECRET!
DESTINATION UNKNOWN!
AND THEY DON'T GIVE A FUCK IF THEY EVER COME HOME!!
HUUHH!
CALHOUN!!!
PT!!!

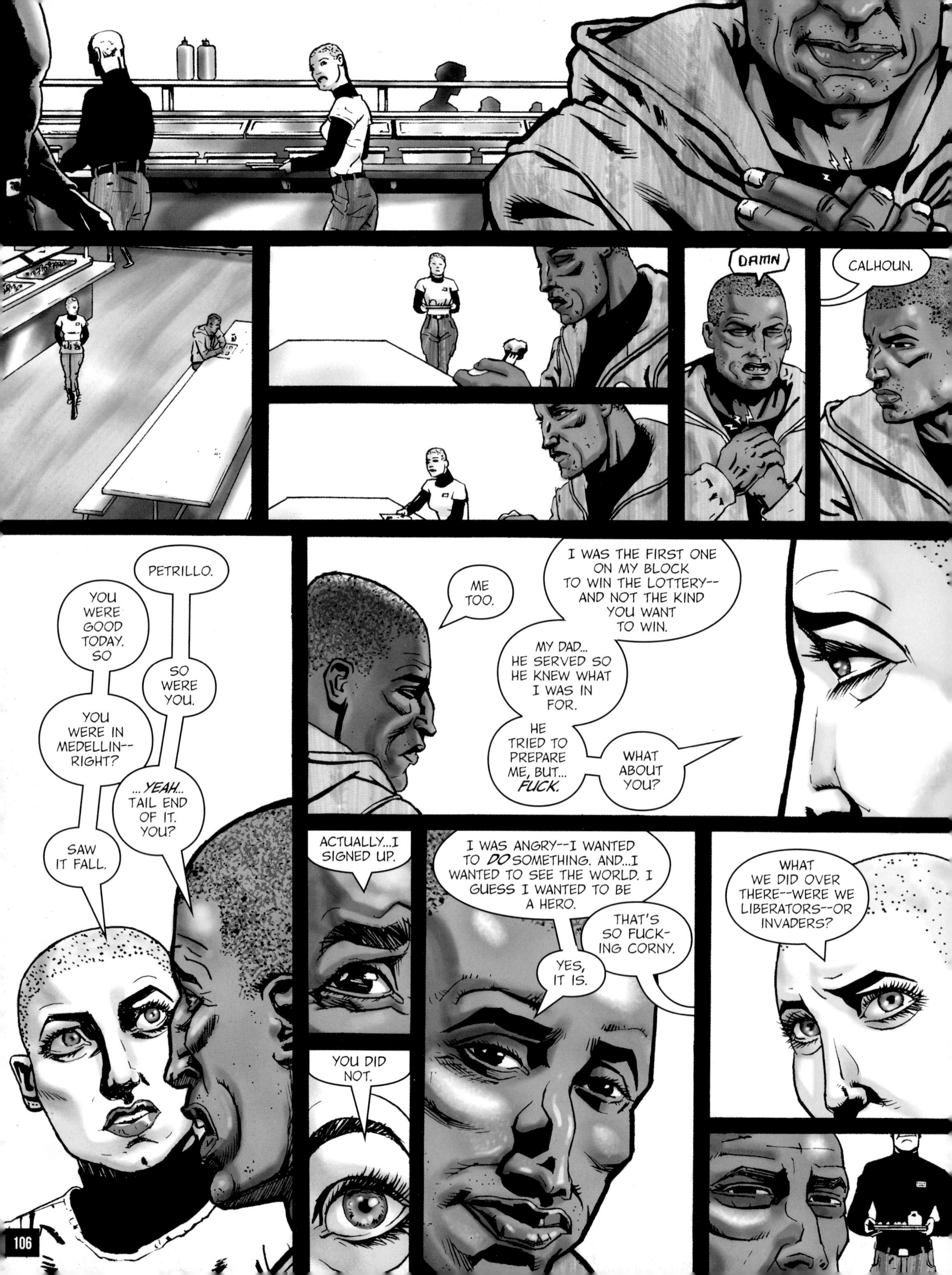
DAMN
CALHOUN.
PETRILLO.
YOU WERE GOOD TODAY. SO
SO WERE YOU.
YOU WERE IN MEDELLIN-- RIGHT?
...YEAH... TAIL END OF IT. YOU?
SAW IT FALL.
ME TOO.
I WAS THE FIRST ONE ON MY BLOCK TO WIN THE LOTTERY-- AND NOT THE KIND YOU WANT TO WIN.
MY DAD... HE SERVED SO HE KNEW WHAT I WAS IN FOR.
HE TRIED TO PREPARE ME, BUT... FUCK.
WHAT ABOUT YOU?
ACTUALLY...I SIGNED UP.
YOU DID NOT.
I WAS ANGRY--I WANTED TO DO SOMETHING. AND...I WANTED TO SEE THE WORLD. I GUESS I WANTED TO BE A HERO.
THAT'S SO FUCK-ING CORNY.
YES, IT IS.
WHAT WE DID OVER THERE--WERE WE LIBERATORS--OR INVADERS?

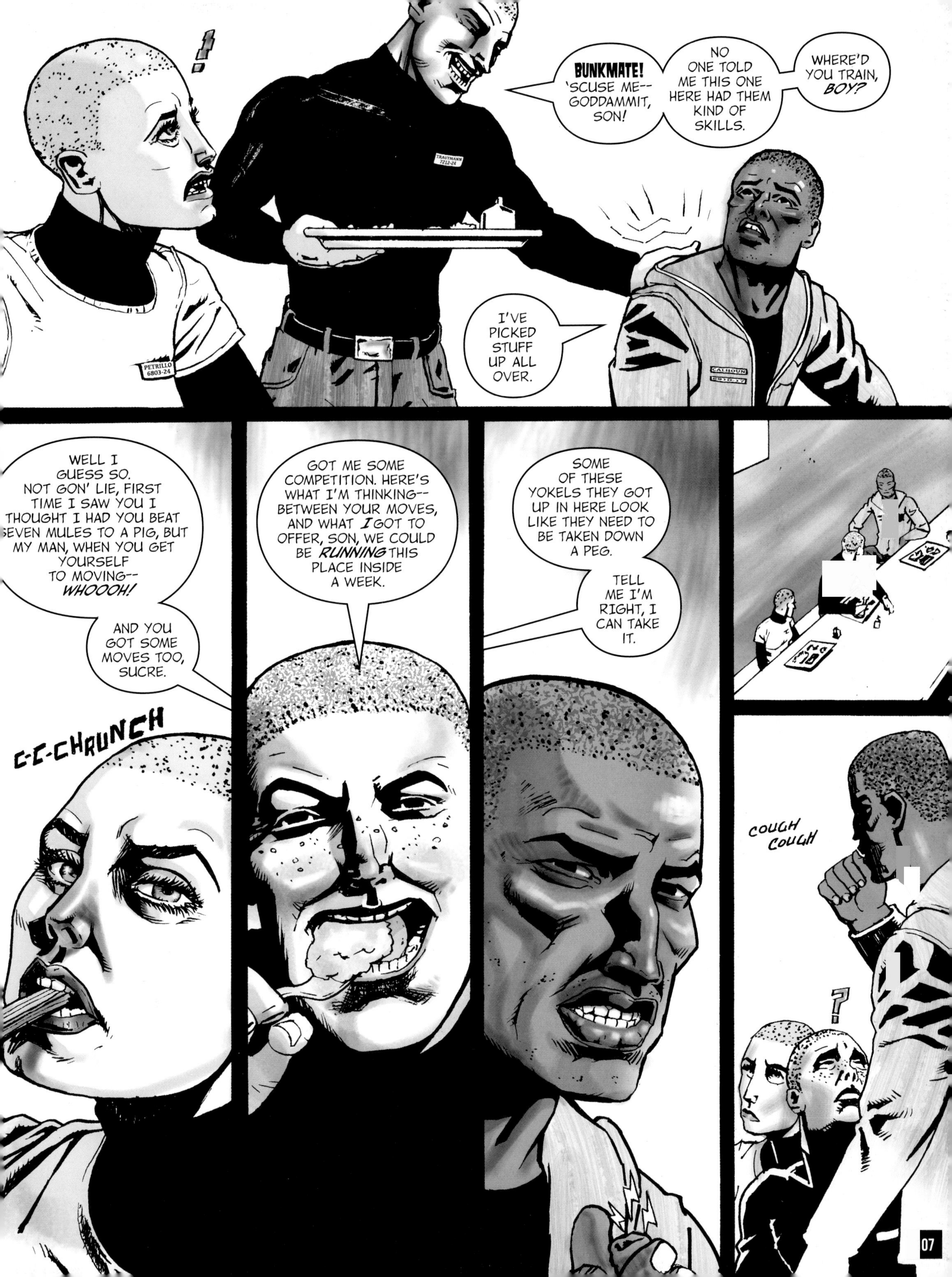
!
BUNKMATE! 'SCUSE ME-- GODDAMMIT, SON!
NO ONE TOLD ME THIS ONE HERE HAD THEM KIND OF SKILLS.
WHERE'D YOU TRAIN, *BOY?*
TRAUTMANN 7212-24
PETRILLO 6803-24
CALHOUN
I'VE PICKED STUFF UP ALL OVER.
WELL I GUESS SO. NOT GON' LIE, FIRST TIME I SAW YOU I THOUGHT I HAD YOU BEAT SEVEN MULES TO A PIG, BUT MY MAN, WHEN YOU GET YOURSELF TO MOVING-- *WHOOOH!*
AND YOU GOT SOME MOVES TOO, SUCRE.
C-C-CHRUNCH
GOT ME SOME COMPETITION. HERE'S WHAT I'M THINKING-- BETWEEN YOUR MOVES, AND WHAT *I* GOT TO OFFER, SON, WE COULD BE *RUNNING* THIS PLACE INSIDE A WEEK.
SOME OF THESE YOKELS THEY GOT UP IN HERE LOOK LIKE THEY NEED TO BE TAKEN DOWN A PEG.
TELL ME I'M RIGHT, I CAN TAKE IT.
COUGH COUGH
?

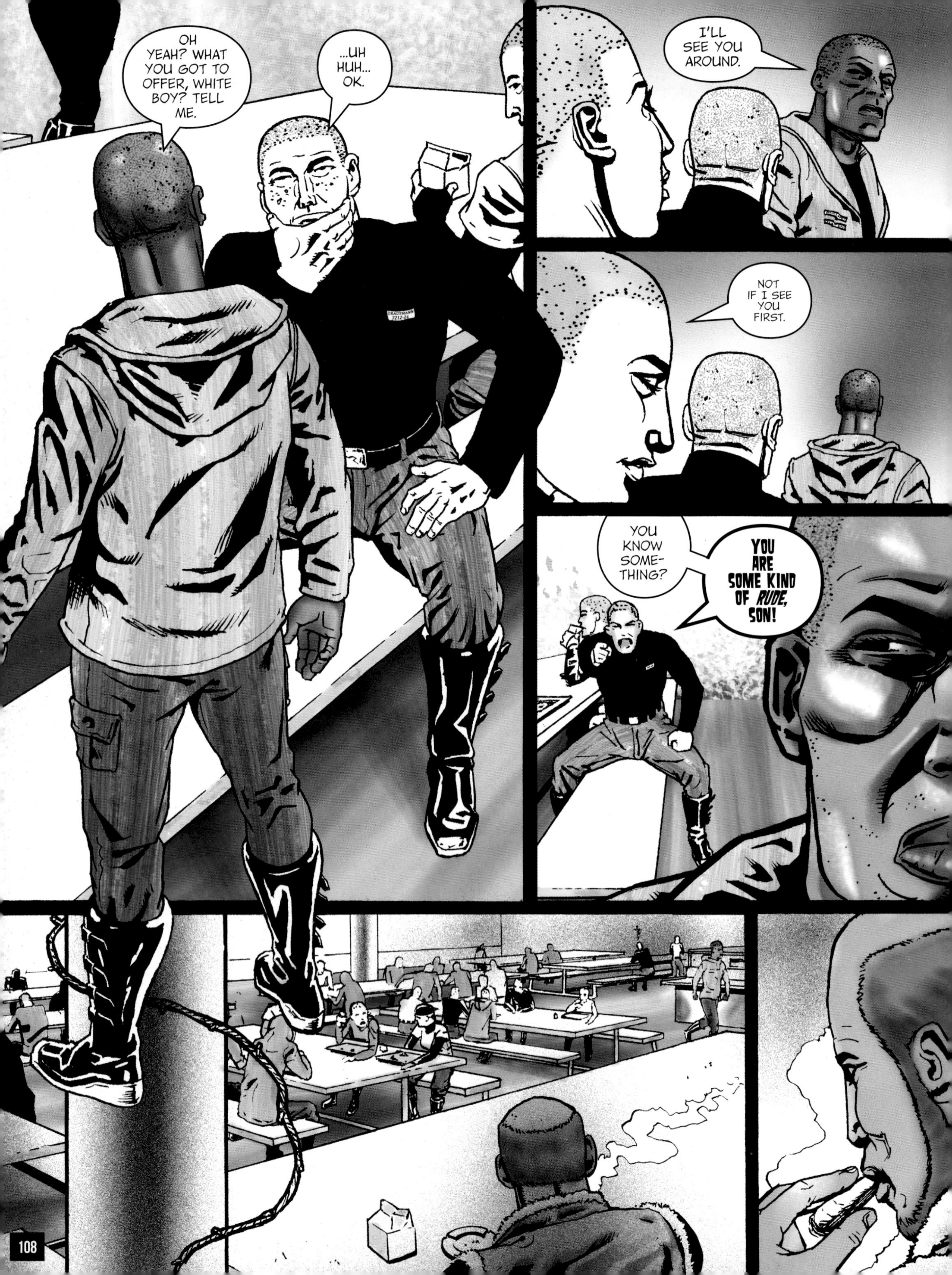
OH YEAH? WHAT YOU GOT TO OFFER, WHITE BOY? TELL ME.
...UH HUH... OK.
TRAUTMANN 7212-24
I'LL SEE YOU AROUND.
NOT IF I SEE YOU FIRST.
YOU KNOW SOME-THING?
YOU ARE SOME KIND OF *RUDE*, SON!

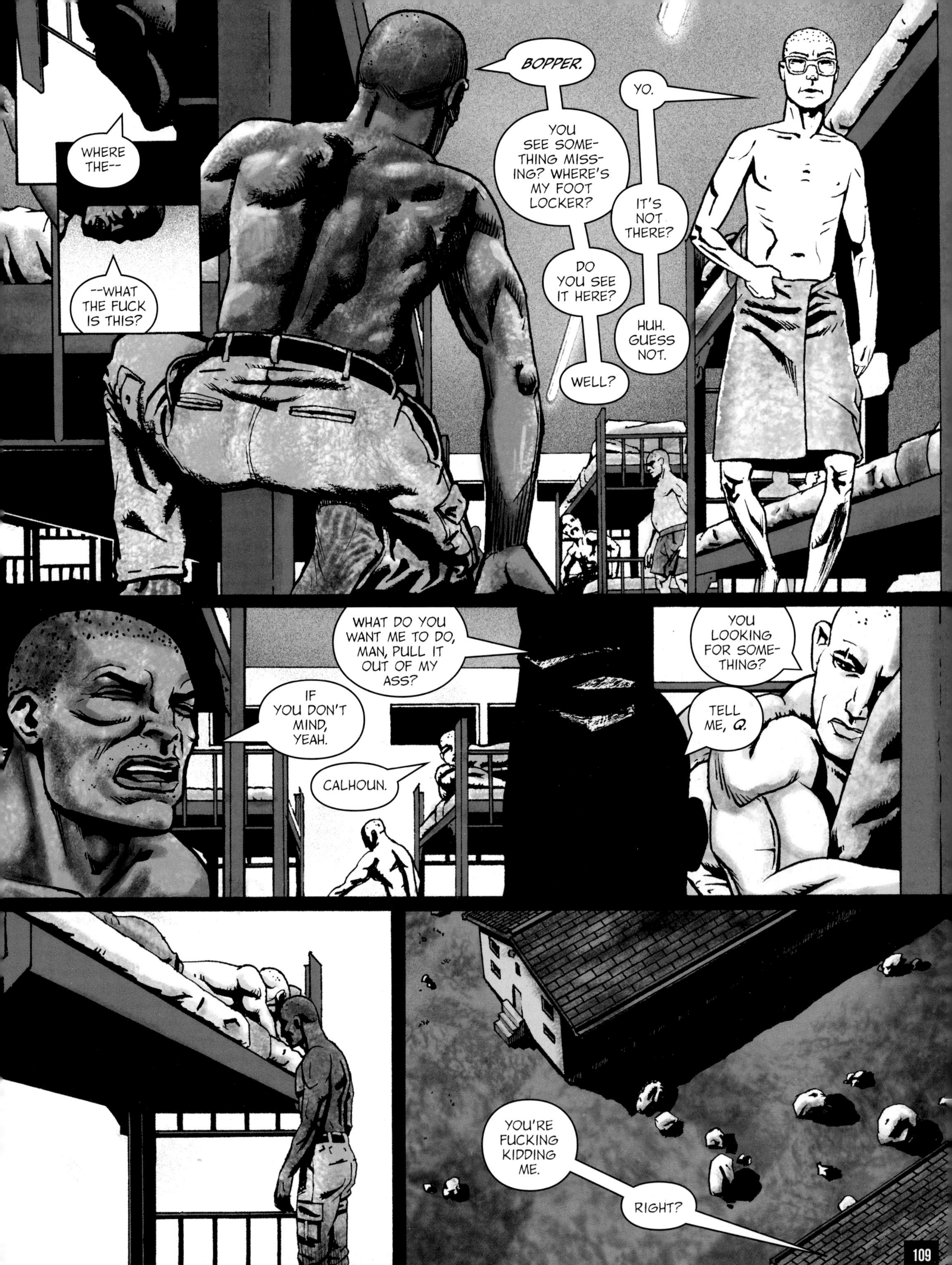
WHERE THE--
--WHAT THE FUCK IS THIS?
BOPPER.
YOU SEE SOME-THING MISS-ING? WHERE'S MY FOOT LOCKER?
YO.
IT'S NOT THERE?
DO YOU SEE IT HERE?
HUH. GUESS NOT.
WELL?
WHAT DO YOU WANT ME TO DO, MAN, PULL IT OUT OF MY ASS?
IF YOU DON'T MIND, YEAH.
CALHOUN.
YOU LOOKING FOR SOME-THING?
TELL ME, Q.
YOU'RE FUCKING KIDDING ME.
RIGHT?

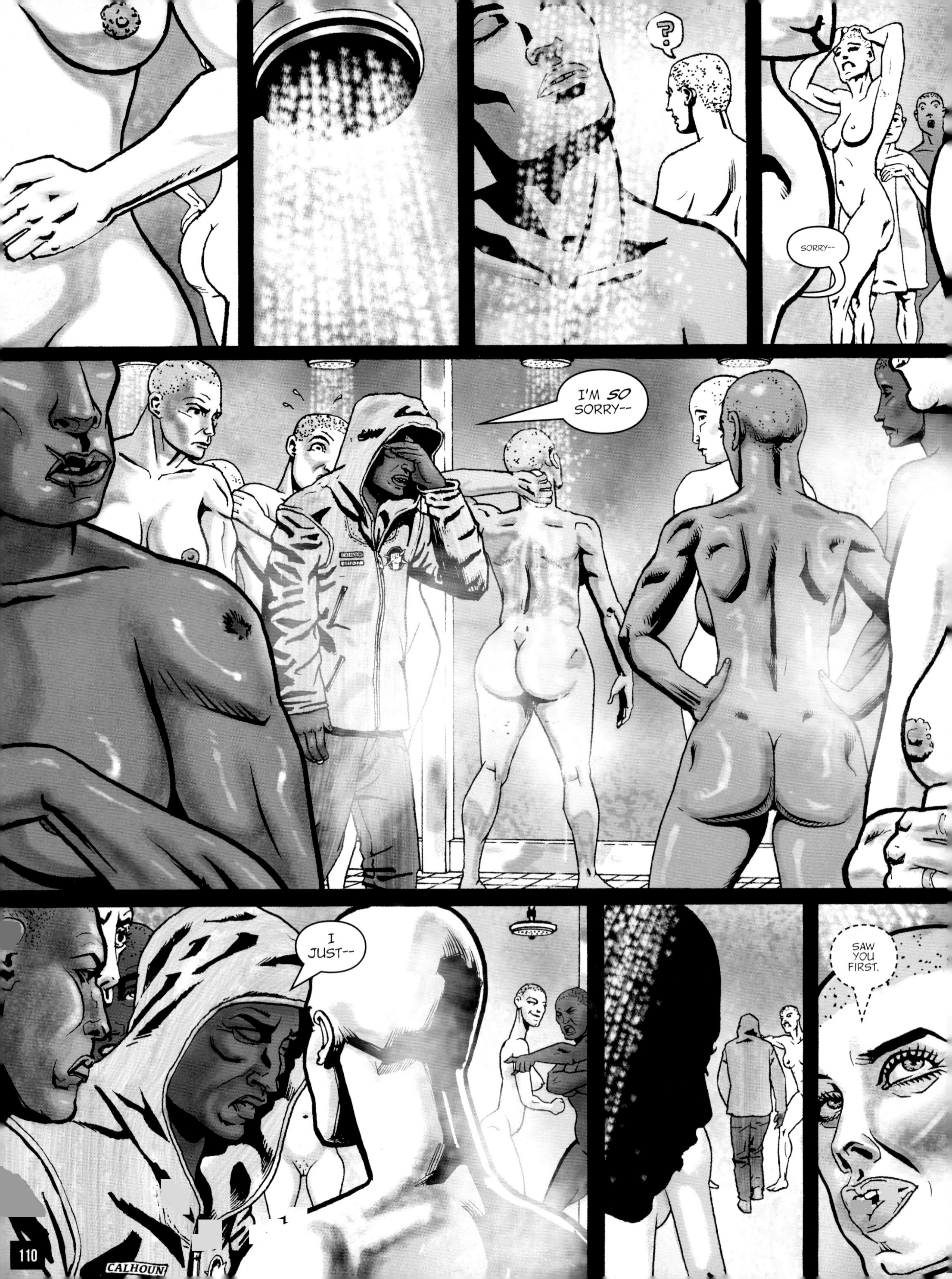
?
SORRY--
I'M *SO* SORRY--
I JUST--
SAW YOU FIRST.
CALHOUN

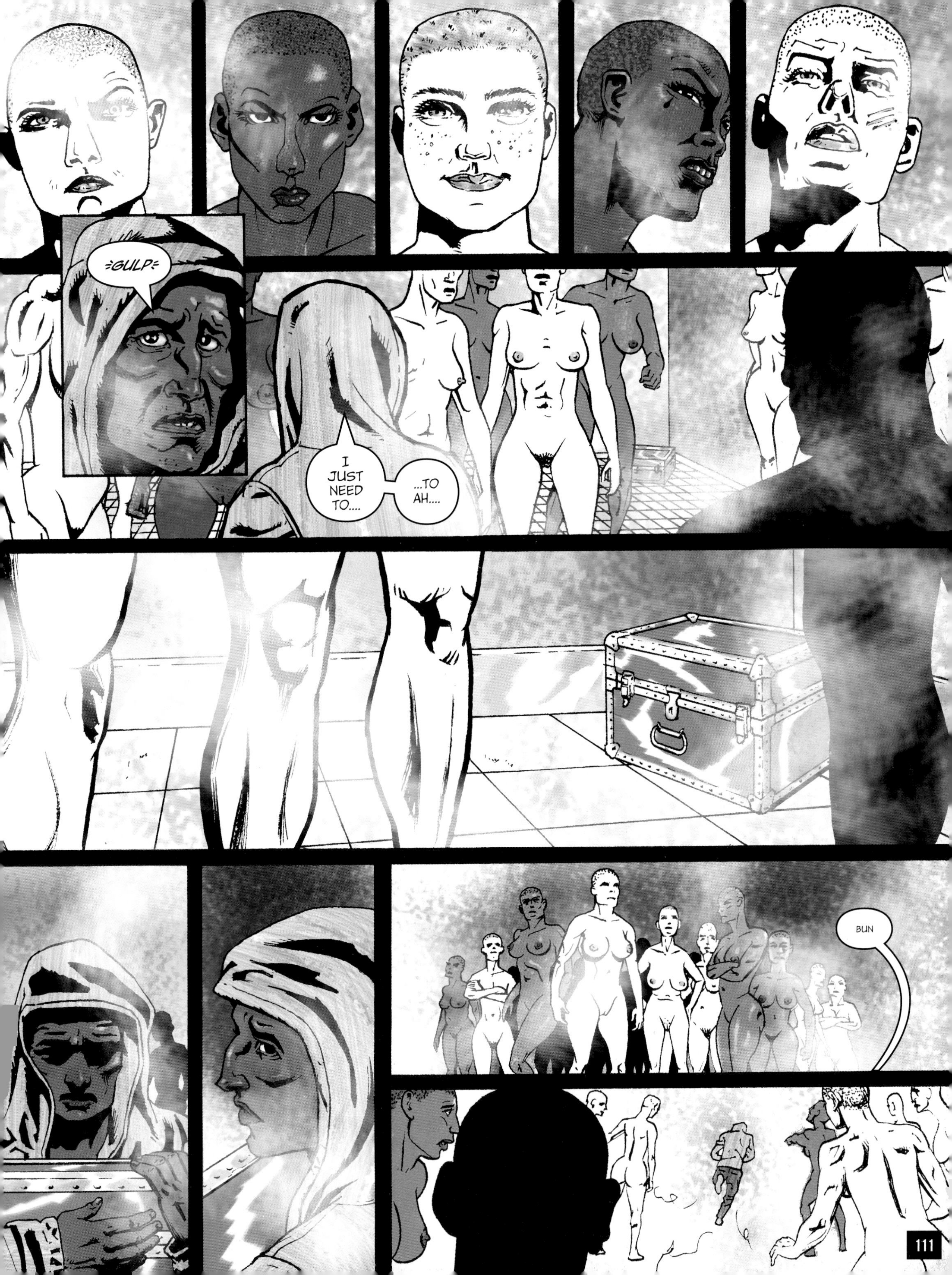
GULP
I JUST NEED TO....
...TO AH....
BUN

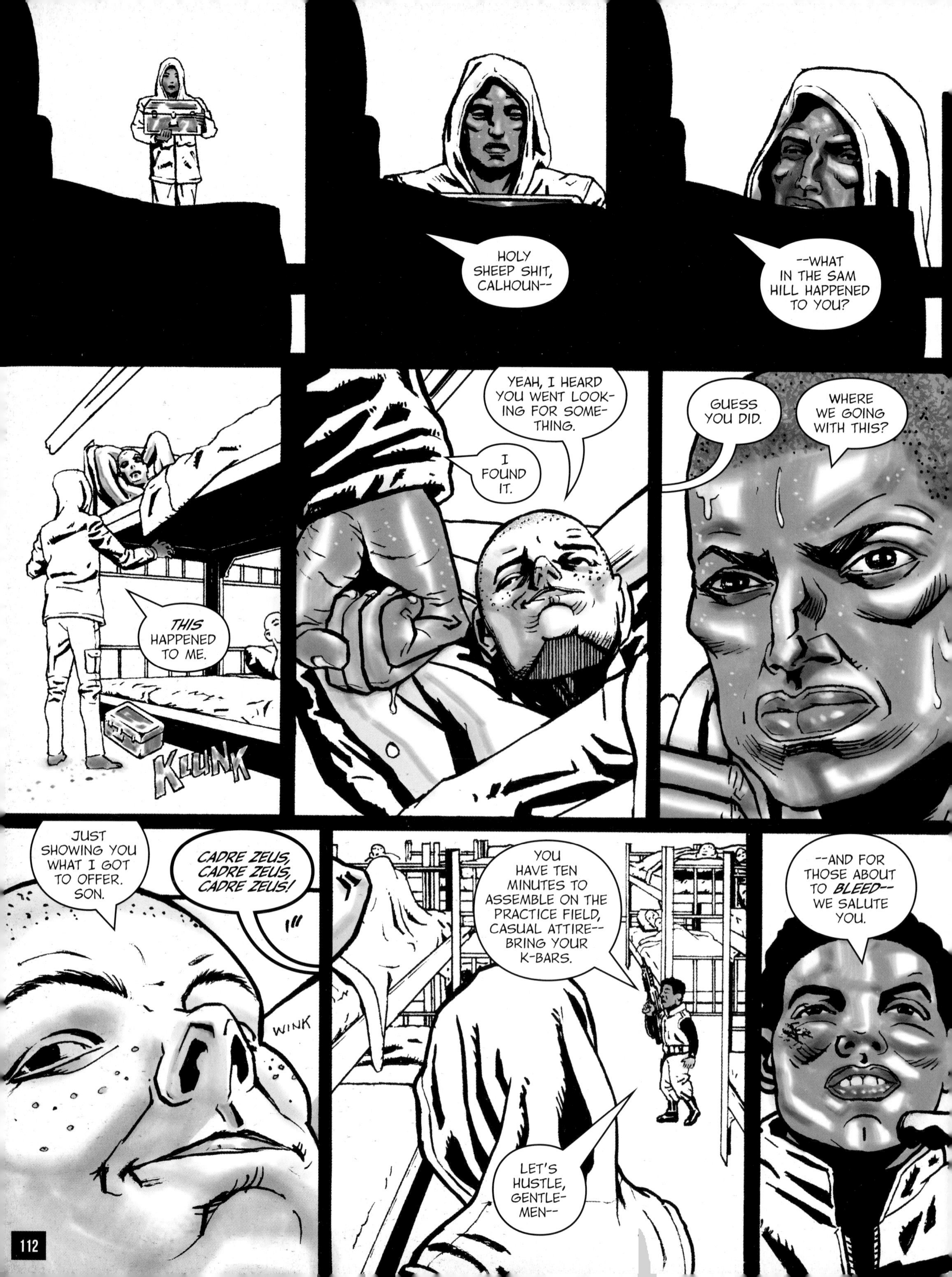

HOLY SHEEP SHIT, CALHOUN--
--WHAT IN THE SAM HILL HAPPENED TO YOU?
THIS HAPPENED TO ME.
KLUNK
YEAH, I HEARD YOU WENT LOOKING FOR SOMETHING.
I FOUND IT.
GUESS YOU DID.
WHERE WE GOING WITH THIS?
JUST SHOWING YOU WHAT I GOT TO OFFER. SON.
CADRE ZEUS, CADRE ZEUS, CADRE ZEUS!
WINK
YOU HAVE TEN MINUTES TO ASSEMBLE ON THE PRACTICE FIELD, CASUAL ATTIRE-- BRING YOUR K-BARS.
LET'S HUSTLE, GENTLEMEN--
--AND FOR THOSE ABOUT TO BLEED-- WE SALUTE YOU.

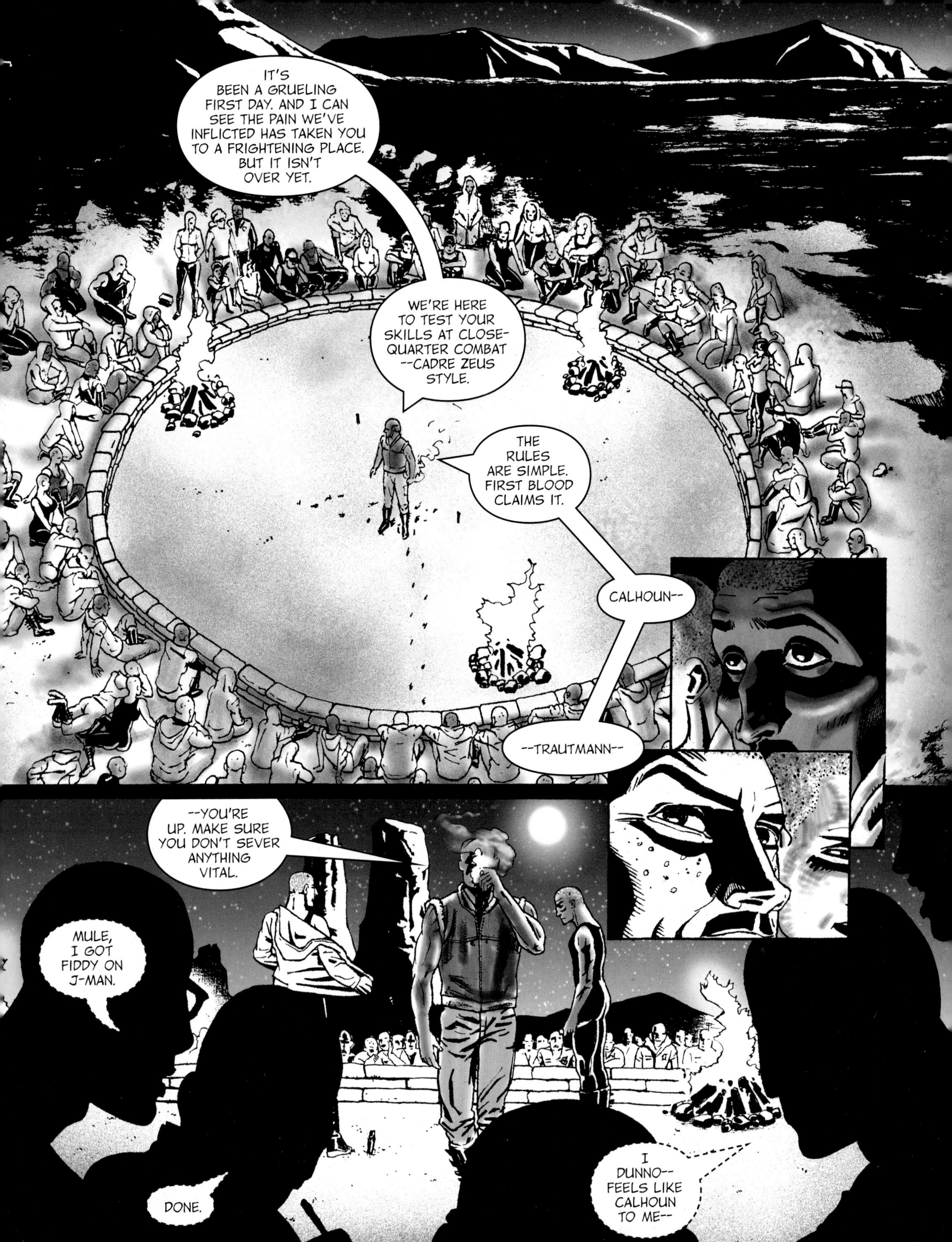
IT'S BEEN A GRUELING FIRST DAY. AND I CAN SEE THE PAIN WE'VE INFLICTED HAS TAKEN YOU TO A FRIGHTENING PLACE. BUT IT ISN'T OVER YET.
WE'RE HERE TO TEST YOUR SKILLS AT CLOSE-QUARTER COMBAT --CADRE ZEUS STYLE.
THE RULES ARE SIMPLE. FIRST BLOOD CLAIMS IT.
CALHOUN--
--TRAUTMANN--
--YOU'RE UP. MAKE SURE YOU DON'T SEVER ANYTHING VITAL.
MULE, I GOT FIDDY ON J-MAN.
DONE.
I DUNNO-- FEELS LIKE CALHOUN TO ME--

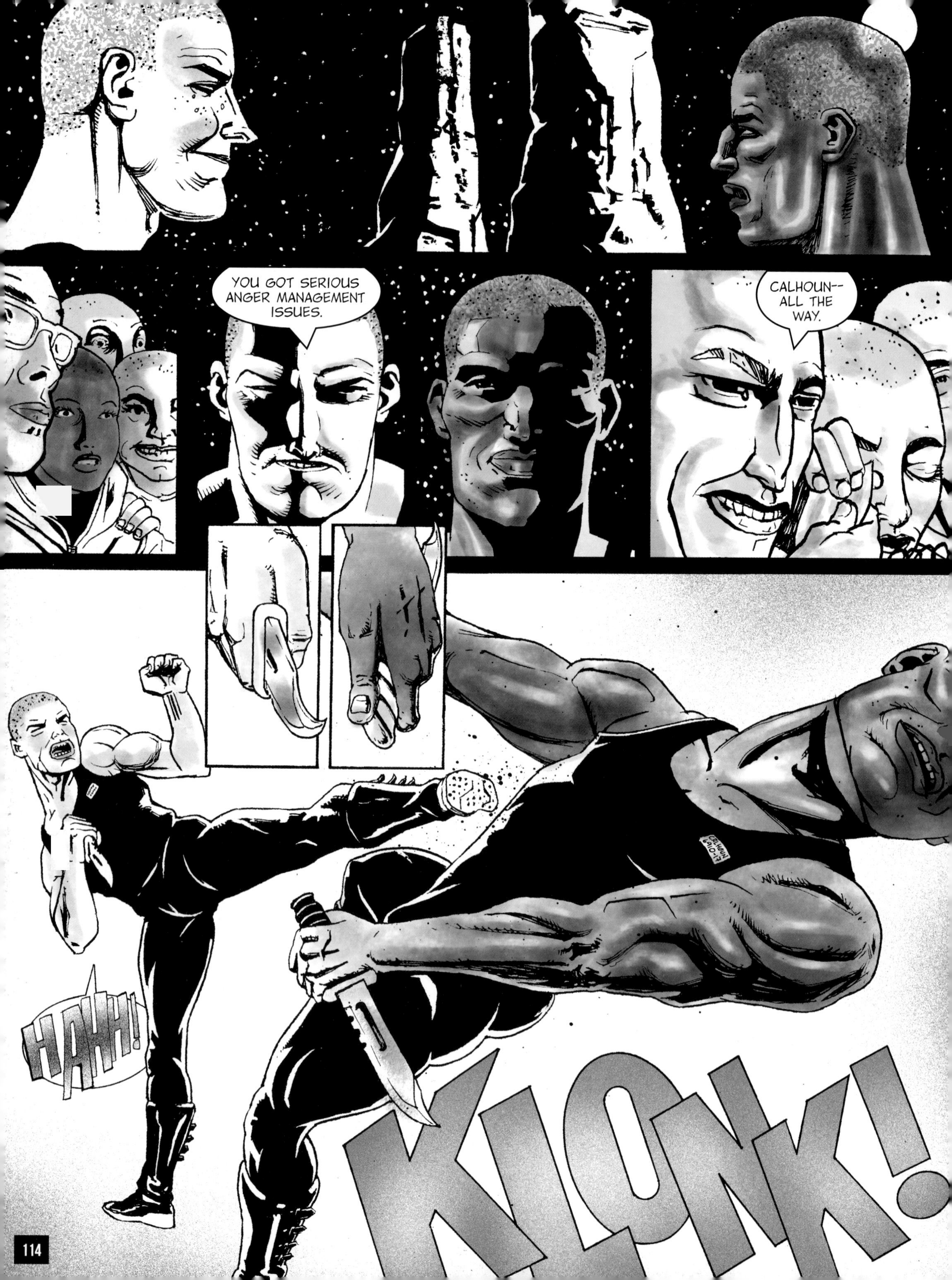
YOU GOT SERIOUS ANGER MANAGEMENT ISSUES.
CALHOUN-- ALL THE WAY.
HAHH!
KLONK!

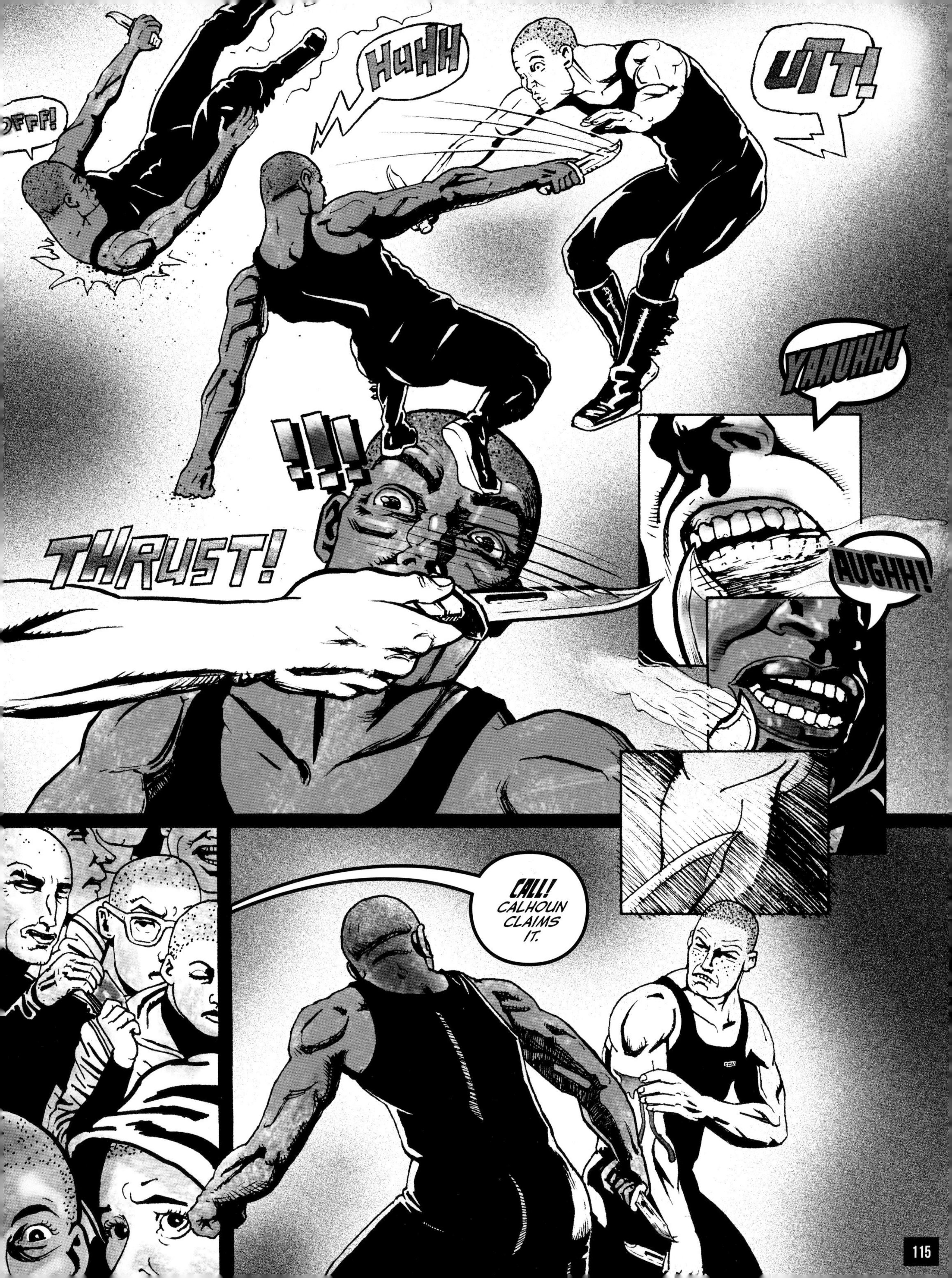
OFFF!
HuHH
UTT!
YAAUHH!
THRUST!
AUGHH!
CALL! CALHOUN CLAIMS IT.

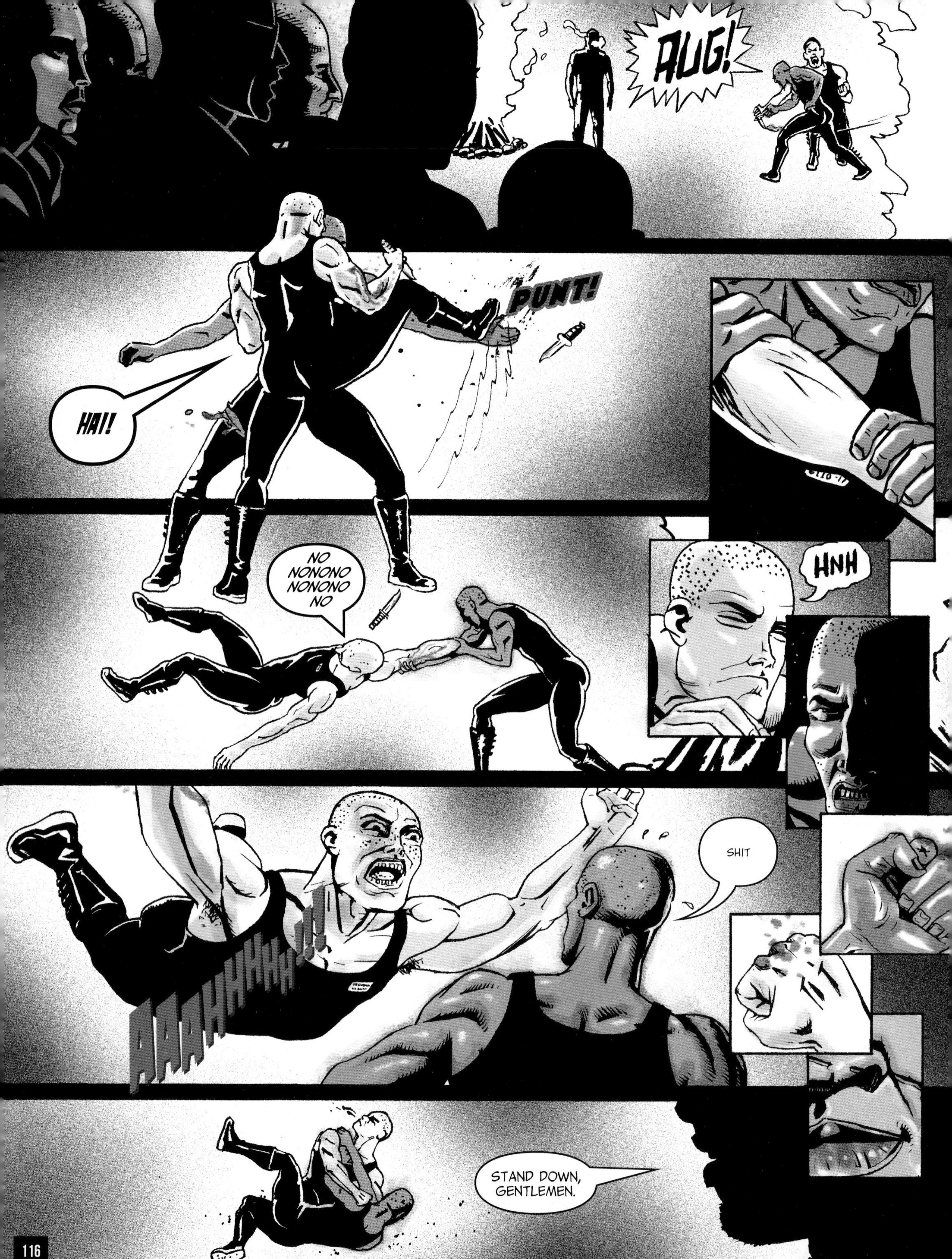
AUG!
PUNT!
HAI!
NO NONONO NONONO NO
HNH
SHIT
AAAHHHHH!!!
STAND DOWN, GENTLEMEN.

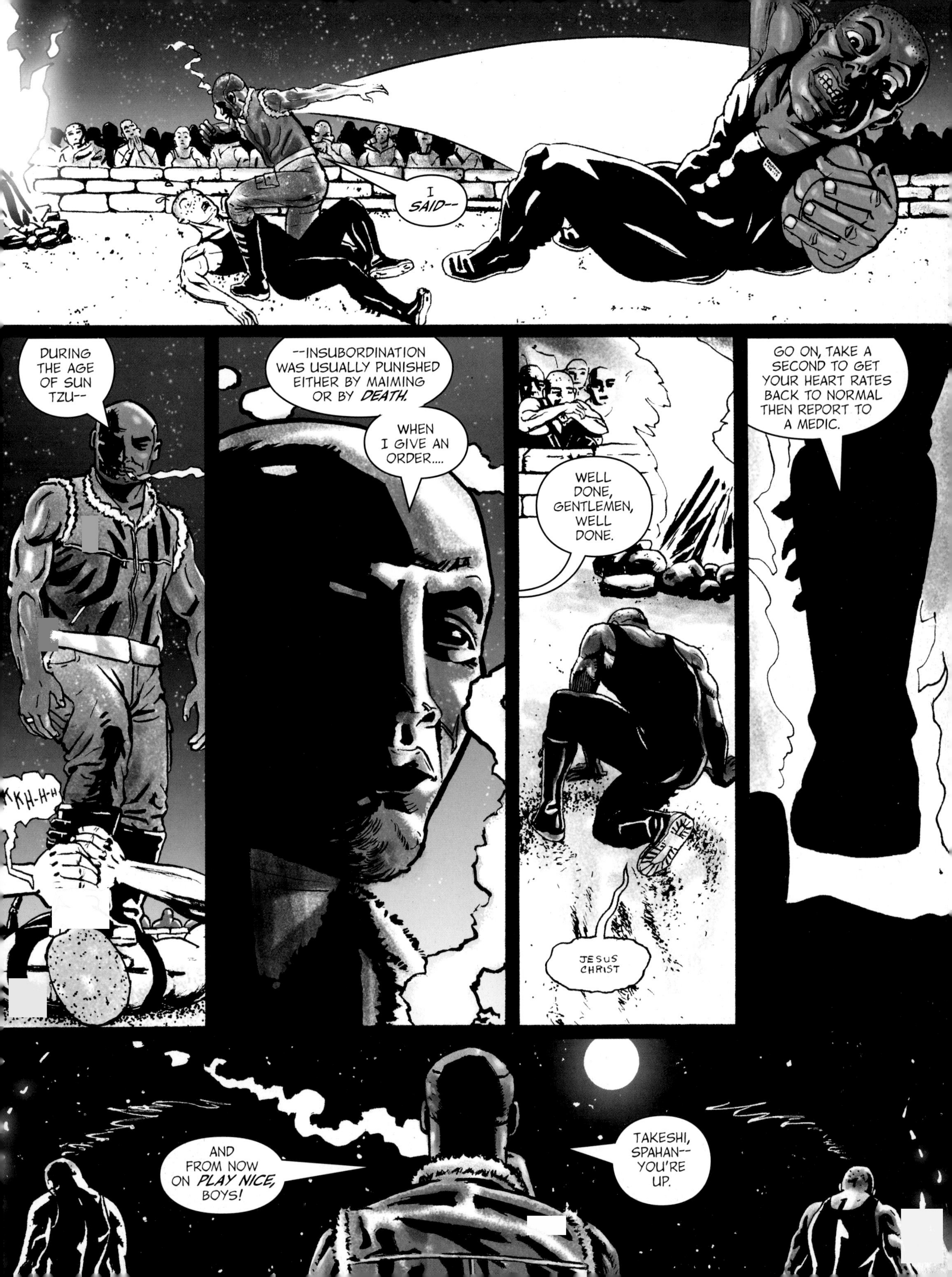
I SAID--
DURING THE AGE OF SUN TZU--
--INSUBORDINATION WAS USUALLY PUNISHED EITHER BY MAIMING OR BY DEATH.
WHEN I GIVE AN ORDER....
KKH-H-H
WELL DONE, GENTLEMEN, WELL DONE.
JESUS CHRIST
GO ON, TAKE A SECOND TO GET YOUR HEART RATES BACK TO NORMAL THEN REPORT TO A MEDIC.
TAKESHI, SPAHAN-- YOU'RE UP.
AND FROM NOW ON PLAY NICE, BOYS!

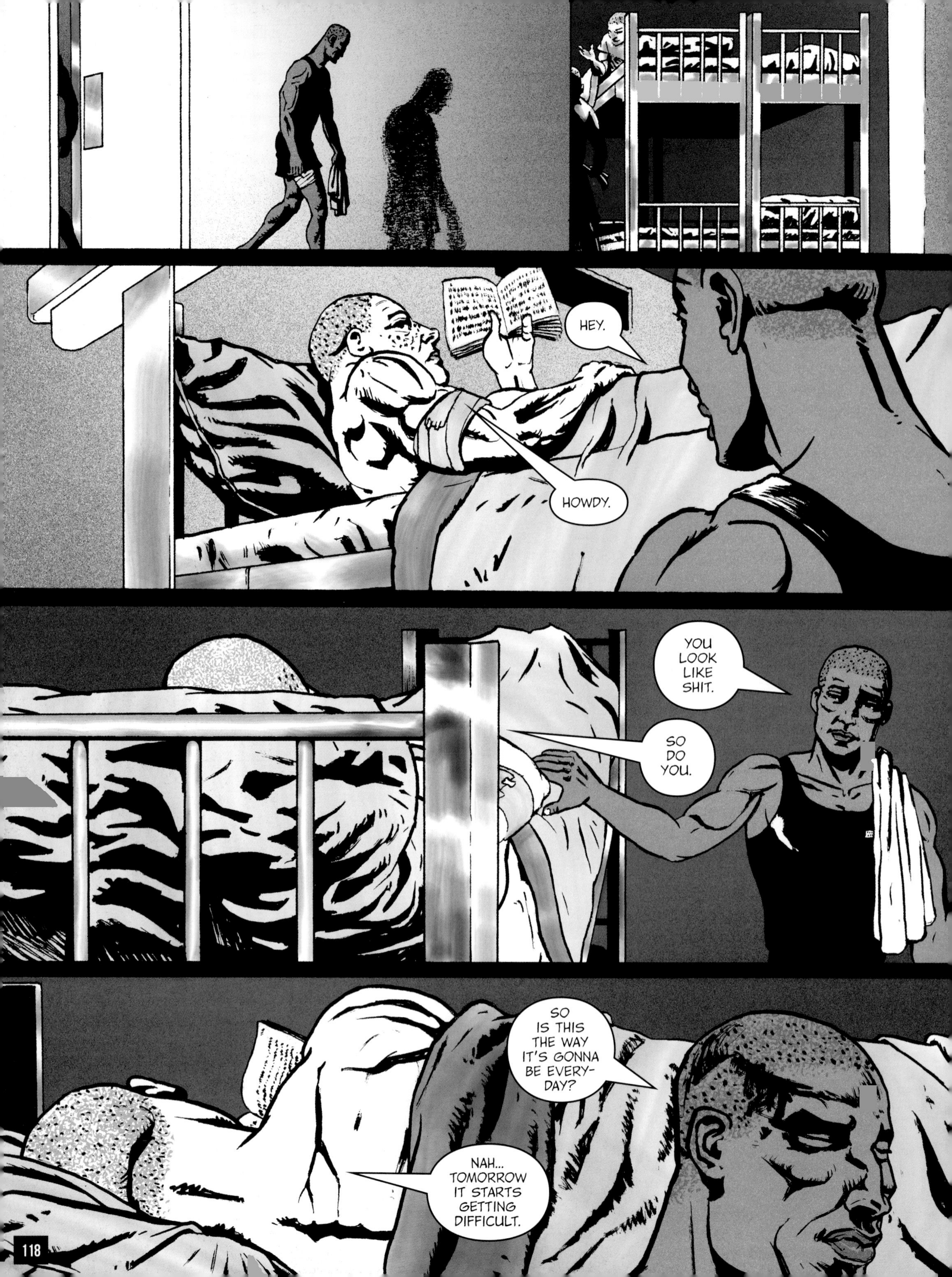
HEY.
HOWDY.
YOU LOOK LIKE SHIT.
SO DO YOU.
SO IS THIS THE WAY IT'S GONNA BE EVERY-DAY?
NAH... TOMORROW IT STARTS GETTING DIFFICULT.

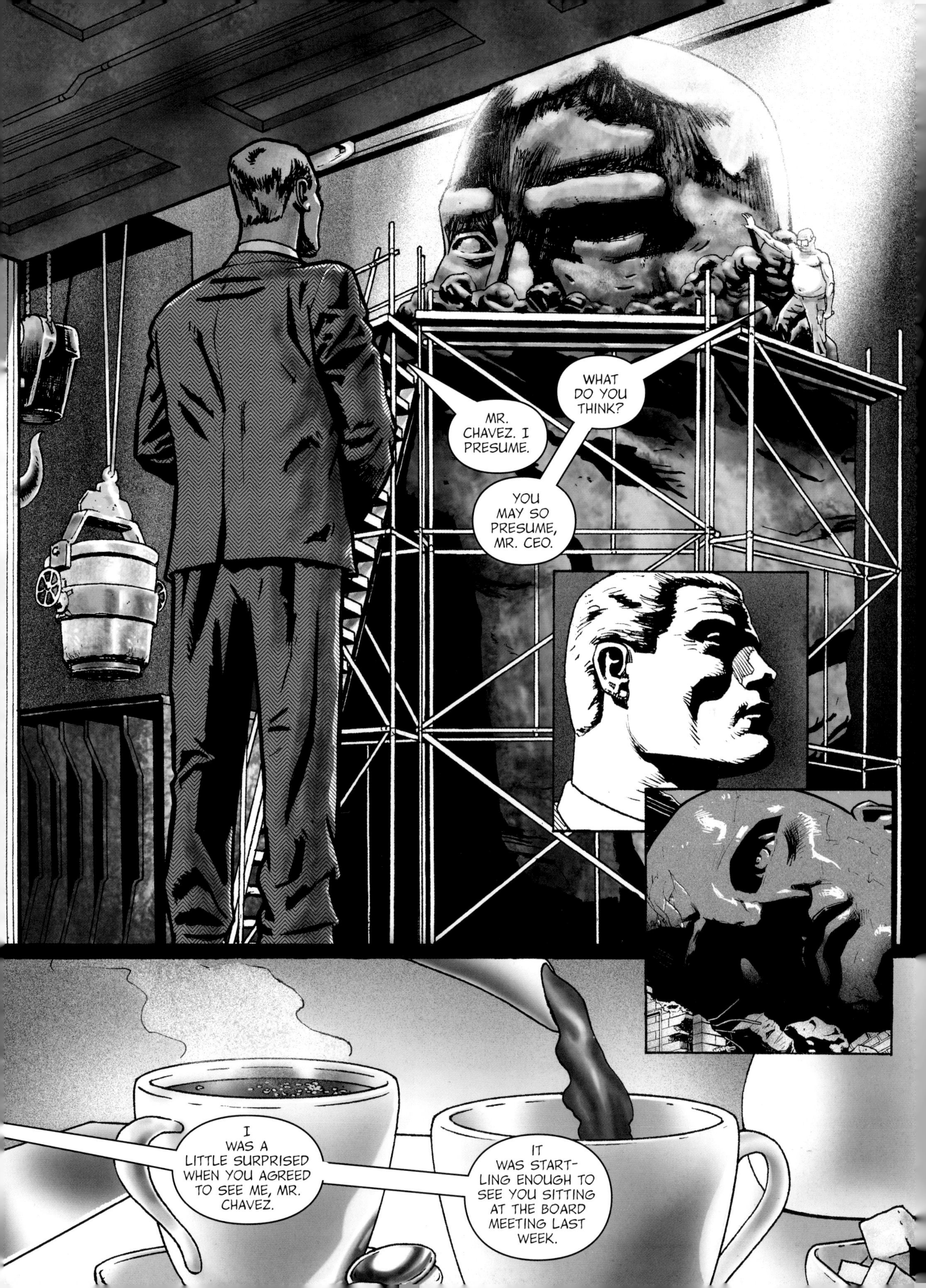

MR. CHAVEZ. I PRESUME.
WHAT DO YOU THINK?
YOU MAY SO PRESUME, MR. CEO.
I WAS A LITTLE SURPRISED WHEN YOU AGREED TO SEE ME, MR. CHAVEZ.
IT WAS START-LING ENOUGH TO SEE YOU SITTING AT THE BOARD MEETING LAST WEEK.

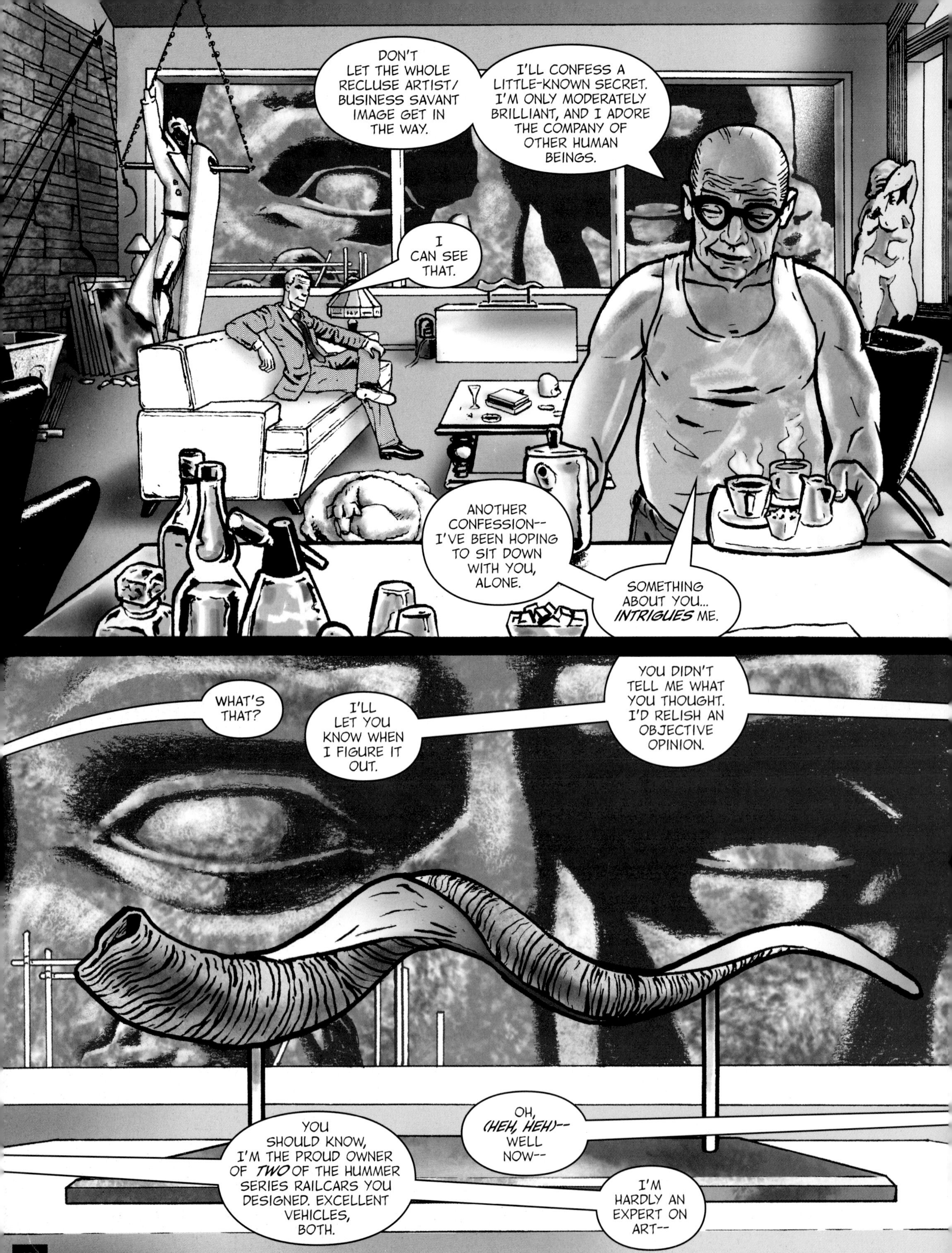
DON'T LET THE WHOLE RECLUSE ARTIST/ BUSINESS SAVANT IMAGE GET IN THE WAY.
I'LL CONFESS A LITTLE-KNOWN SECRET. I'M ONLY MODERATELY BRILLIANT, AND I ADORE THE COMPANY OF OTHER HUMAN BEINGS.
I CAN SEE THAT.
ANOTHER CONFESSION-- I'VE BEEN HOPING TO SIT DOWN WITH YOU, ALONE.
SOMETHING ABOUT YOU... *INTRIGUES* ME.
WHAT'S THAT?
YOU DIDN'T TELL ME WHAT YOU THOUGHT. I'D RELISH AN OBJECTIVE OPINION.
I'LL LET YOU KNOW WHEN I FIGURE IT OUT.
OH, *(HEH, HEH)*-- WELL NOW--
I'M HARDLY AN EXPERT ON ART--
YOU SHOULD KNOW, I'M THE PROUD OWNER OF *TWO* OF THE HUMMER SERIES RAILCARS YOU DESIGNED. EXCELLENT VEHICLES, BOTH.

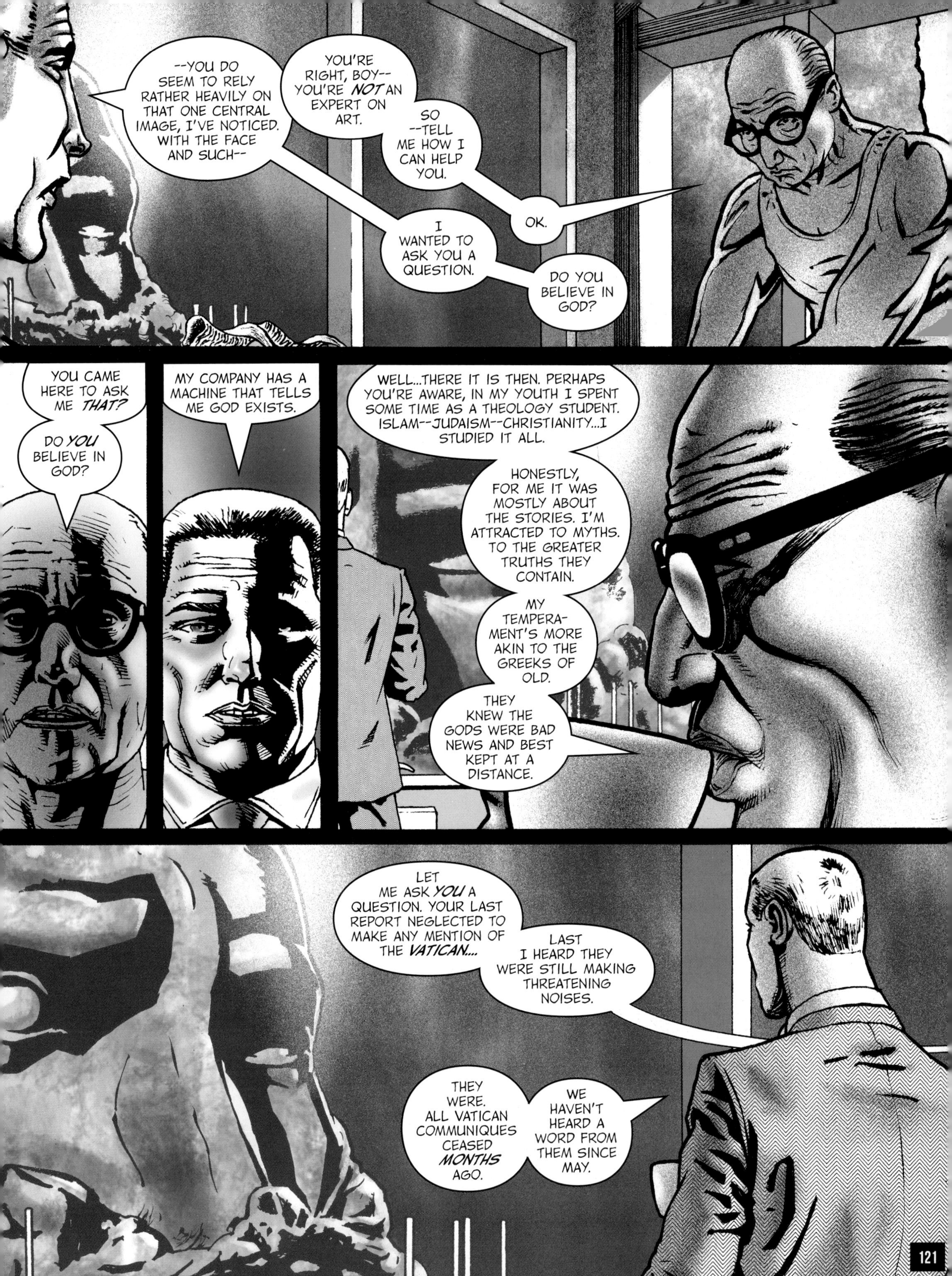
--YOU DO SEEM TO RELY RATHER HEAVILY ON THAT ONE CENTRAL IMAGE, I'VE NOTICED. WITH THE FACE AND SUCH--
YOU'RE RIGHT, BOY-- YOU'RE *NOT* AN EXPERT ON ART.
SO --TELL ME HOW I CAN HELP YOU.
OK.
I WANTED TO ASK YOU A QUESTION.
DO YOU BELIEVE IN GOD?
YOU CAME HERE TO ASK ME *THAT?*
DO *YOU* BELIEVE IN GOD?
MY COMPANY HAS A MACHINE THAT TELLS ME GOD EXISTS.
WELL...THERE IT IS THEN. PERHAPS YOU'RE AWARE, IN MY YOUTH I SPENT SOME TIME AS A THEOLOGY STUDENT. ISLAM--JUDAISM--CHRISTIANITY...I STUDIED IT ALL.
HONESTLY, FOR ME IT WAS MOSTLY ABOUT THE STORIES. I'M ATTRACTED TO MYTHS. TO THE GREATER TRUTHS THEY CONTAIN.
MY TEMPERA-MENT'S MORE AKIN TO THE GREEKS OF OLD.
THEY KNEW THE GODS WERE BAD NEWS AND BEST KEPT AT A DISTANCE.
LET ME ASK *YOU* A QUESTION. YOUR LAST REPORT NEGLECTED TO MAKE ANY MENTION OF THE *VATICAN....*
LAST I HEARD THEY WERE STILL MAKING THREATENING NOISES.
THEY WERE. ALL VATICAN COMMUNIQUES CEASED *MONTHS* AGO.
WE HAVEN'T HEARD A WORD FROM THEM SINCE MAY.

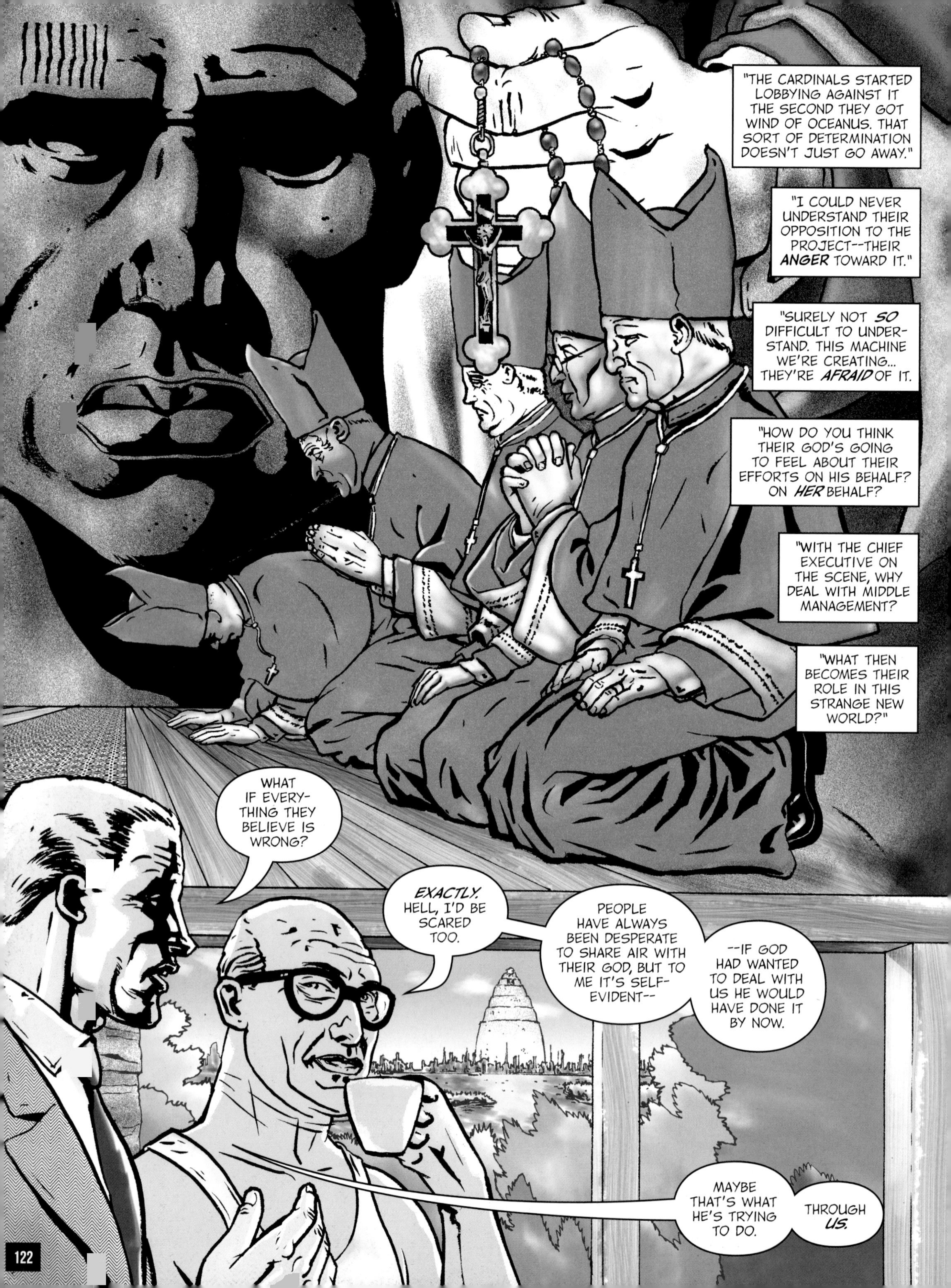
"THE CARDINALS STARTED LOBBYING AGAINST IT THE SECOND THEY GOT WIND OF OCEANUS. THAT SORT OF DETERMINATION DOESN'T JUST GO AWAY."
"I COULD NEVER UNDERSTAND THEIR OPPOSITION TO THE PROJECT--THEIR ANGER TOWARD IT."
"SURELY NOT SO DIFFICULT TO UNDER-STAND. THIS MACHINE WE'RE CREATING... THEY'RE AFRAID OF IT.
"HOW DO YOU THINK THEIR GOD'S GOING TO FEEL ABOUT THEIR EFFORTS ON HIS BEHALF? ON HER BEHALF?
"WITH THE CHIEF EXECUTIVE ON THE SCENE, WHY DEAL WITH MIDDLE MANAGEMENT?
"WHAT THEN BECOMES THEIR ROLE IN THIS STRANGE NEW WORLD?"
WHAT IF EVERY-THING THEY BELIEVE IS WRONG?
EXACTLY. HELL, I'D BE SCARED TOO.
PEOPLE HAVE ALWAYS BEEN DESPERATE TO SHARE AIR WITH THEIR GOD, BUT TO ME IT'S SELF-EVIDENT--
--IF GOD HAD WANTED TO DEAL WITH US HE WOULD HAVE DONE IT BY NOW.
MAYBE THAT'S WHAT HE'S TRYING TO DO.
THROUGH US.

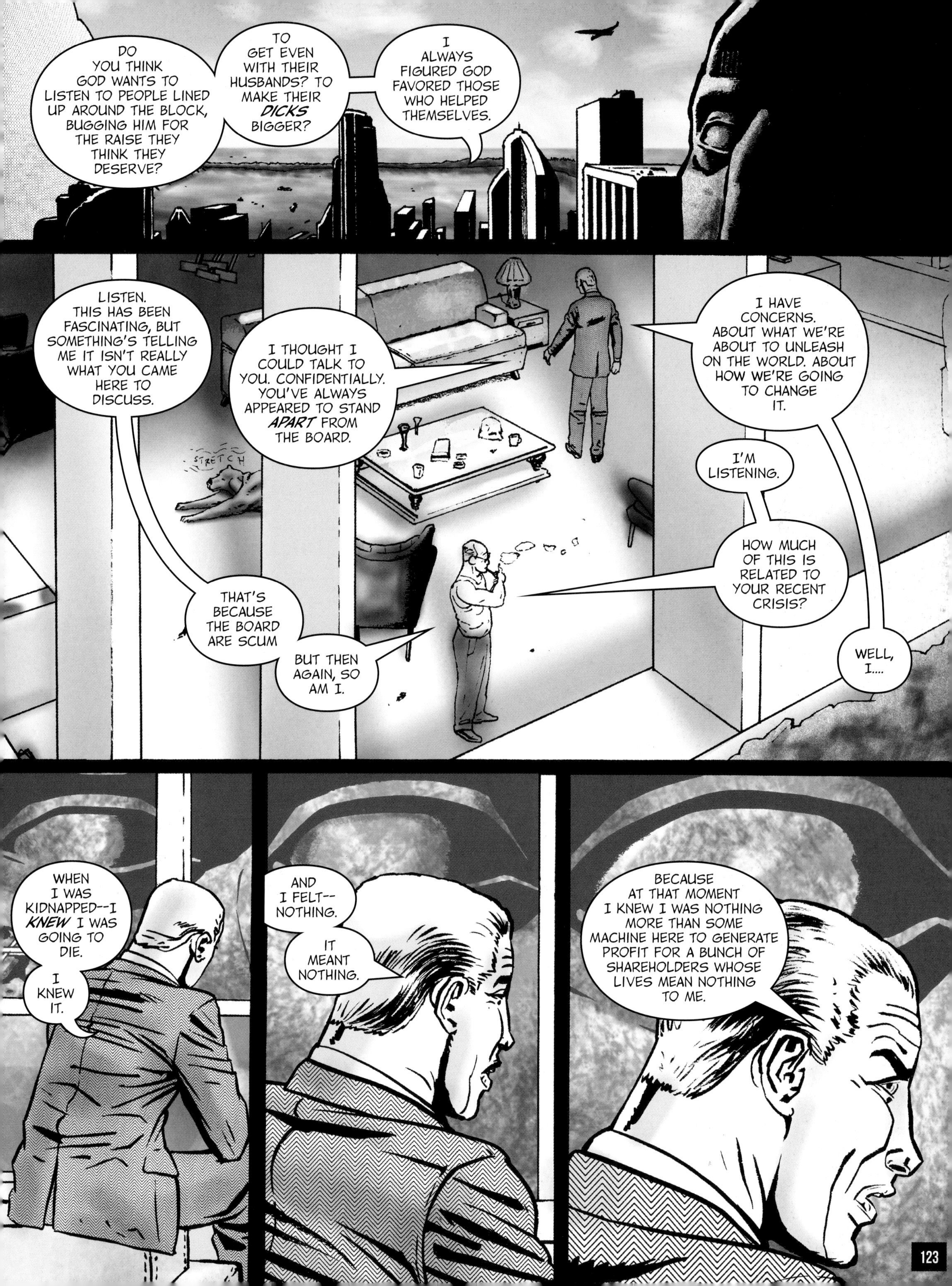
DO YOU THINK GOD WANTS TO LISTEN TO PEOPLE LINED UP AROUND THE BLOCK, BUGGING HIM FOR THE RAISE THEY THINK THEY DESERVE?
TO GET EVEN WITH THEIR HUSBANDS? TO MAKE THEIR *DICKS* BIGGER?
I ALWAYS FIGURED GOD FAVORED THOSE WHO HELPED THEMSELVES.
LISTEN. THIS HAS BEEN FASCINATING, BUT SOMETHING'S TELLING ME IT ISN'T REALLY WHAT YOU CAME HERE TO DISCUSS.
I THOUGHT I COULD TALK TO YOU. CONFIDENTIALLY. YOU'VE ALWAYS APPEARED TO STAND *APART* FROM THE BOARD.
THAT'S BECAUSE THE BOARD ARE SCUM
BUT THEN AGAIN, SO AM I.
STRETCH
I HAVE CONCERNS. ABOUT WHAT WE'RE ABOUT TO UNLEASH ON THE WORLD. ABOUT HOW WE'RE GOING TO CHANGE IT.
I'M LISTENING.
HOW MUCH OF THIS IS RELATED TO YOUR RECENT CRISIS?
WELL, I....
WHEN I WAS KIDNAPPED--I *KNEW* I WAS GOING TO DIE.
I KNEW IT.
AND I FELT--NOTHING.
IT MEANT NOTHING.
BECAUSE AT THAT MOMENT I KNEW I WAS NOTHING MORE THAN SOME MACHINE HERE TO GENERATE PROFIT FOR A BUNCH OF SHAREHOLDERS WHOSE LIVES MEAN NOTHING TO ME.

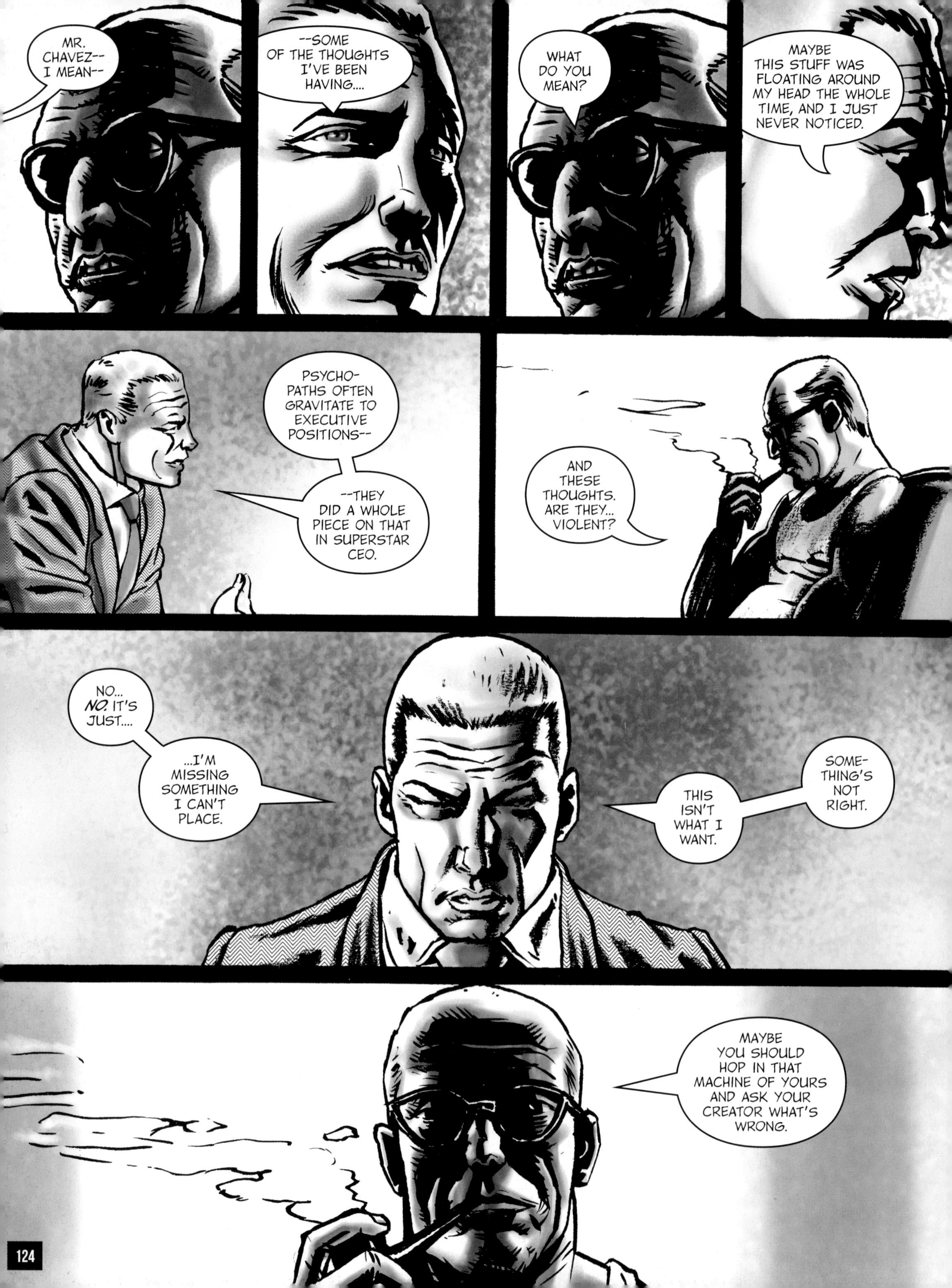
MR. CHAVEZ-- I MEAN--
--SOME OF THE THOUGHTS I'VE BEEN HAVING....
WHAT DO YOU MEAN?
MAYBE THIS STUFF WAS FLOATING AROUND MY HEAD THE WHOLE TIME, AND I JUST NEVER NOTICED.
PSYCHO-PATHS OFTEN GRAVITATE TO EXECUTIVE POSITIONS--
--THEY DID A WHOLE PIECE ON THAT IN SUPERSTAR CEO.
AND THESE THOUGHTS. ARE THEY... VIOLENT?
NO... *NO.* IT'S JUST....
...I'M MISSING SOMETHING I CAN'T PLACE.
THIS ISN'T WHAT I WANT.
SOME-THING'S NOT RIGHT.
MAYBE YOU SHOULD HOP IN THAT MACHINE OF YOURS AND ASK YOUR CREATOR WHAT'S WRONG.

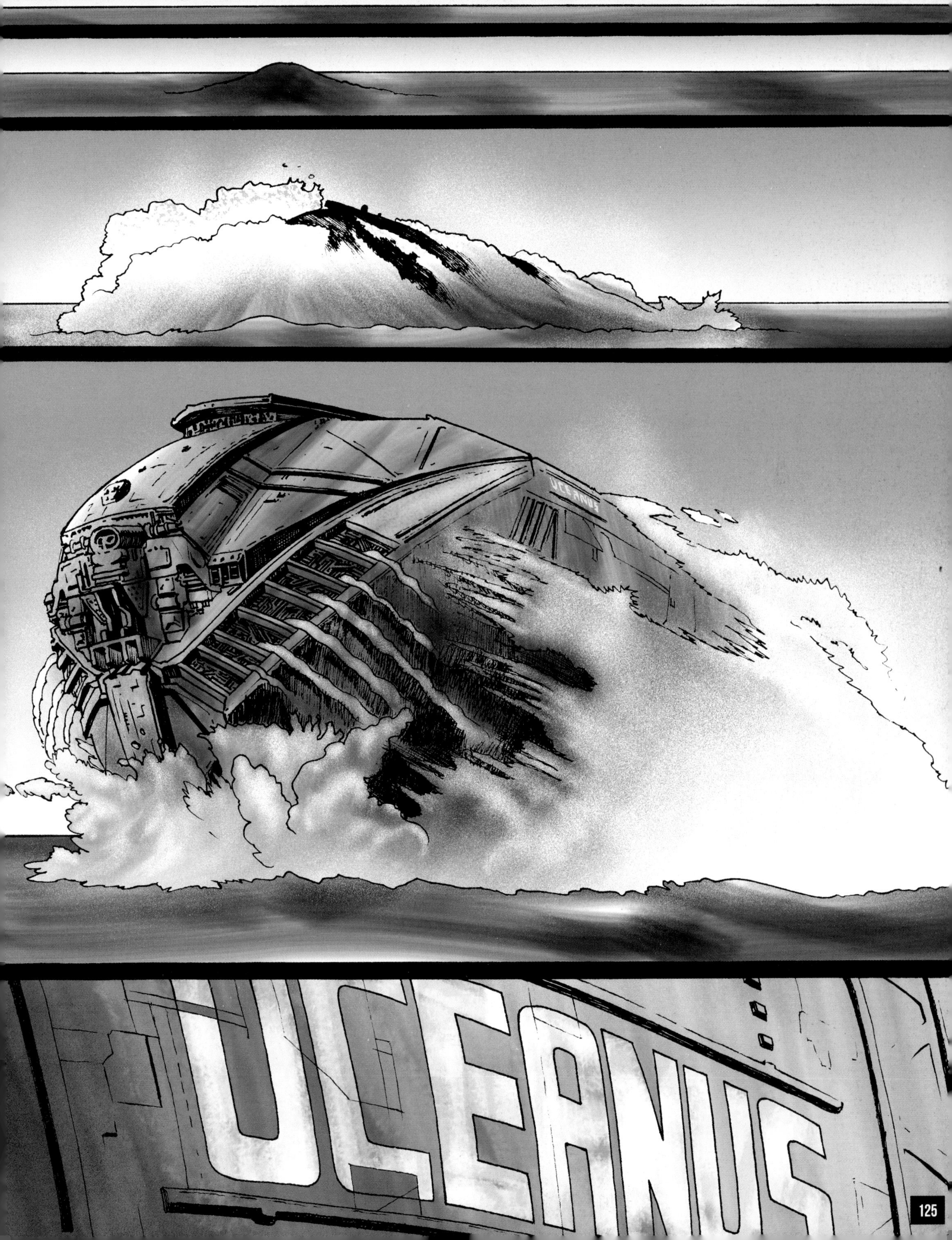
OCEANUS

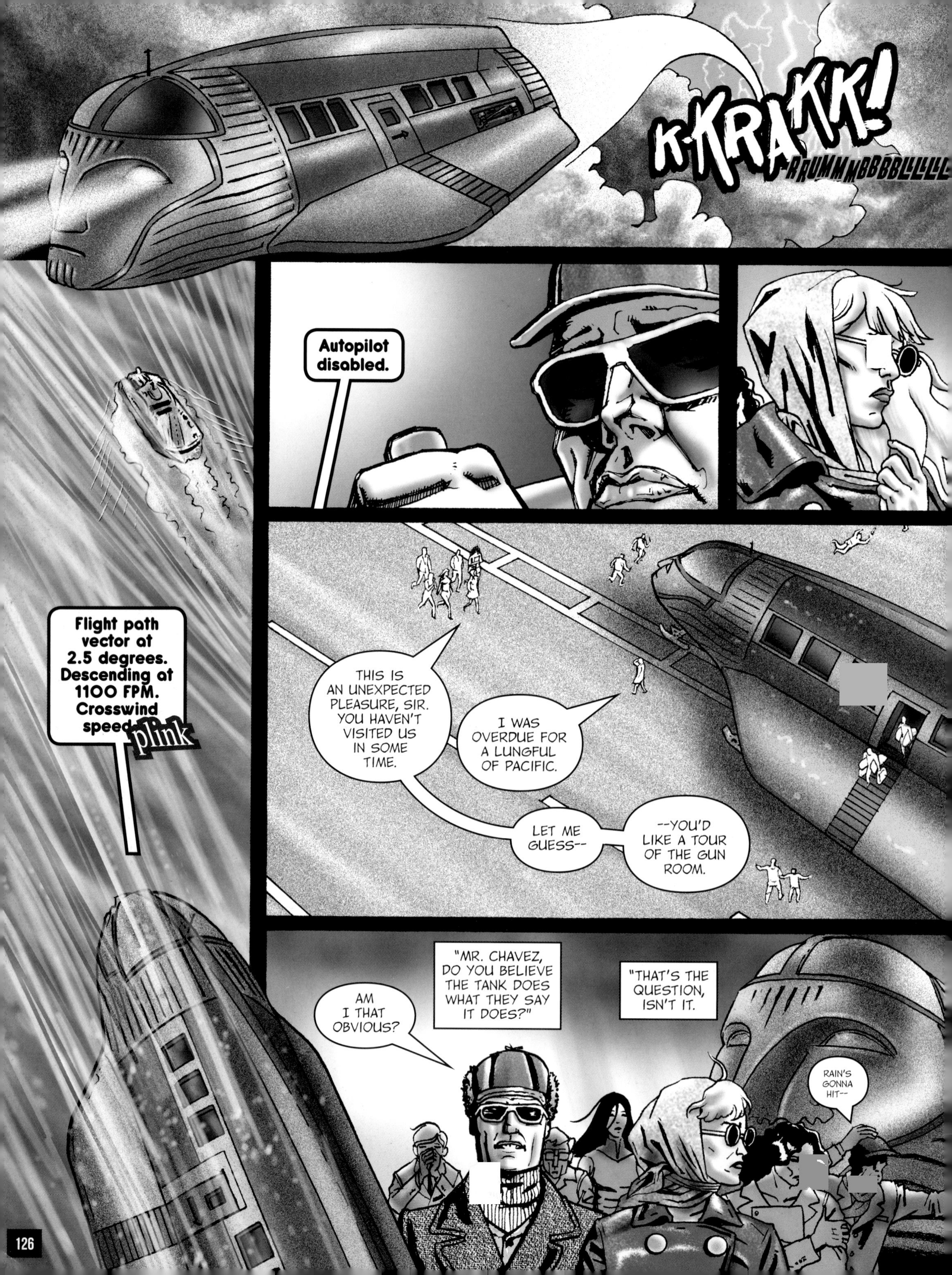
K-KRAKK!
RRUMMMBBBBLLLLLL
Autopilot disabled.
Flight path vector at 2.5 degrees. Descending at 1100 FPM. Crosswind speed
plink
THIS IS AN UNEXPECTED PLEASURE, SIR. YOU HAVEN'T VISITED US IN SOME TIME.
I WAS OVERDUE FOR A LUNGFUL OF PACIFIC.
LET ME GUESS--
--YOU'D LIKE A TOUR OF THE GUN ROOM.
AM I THAT OBVIOUS?
"MR. CHAVEZ, DO YOU BELIEVE THE TANK DOES WHAT THEY SAY IT DOES?"
"THAT'S THE QUESTION, ISN'T IT.
RAIN'S GONNA HIT--

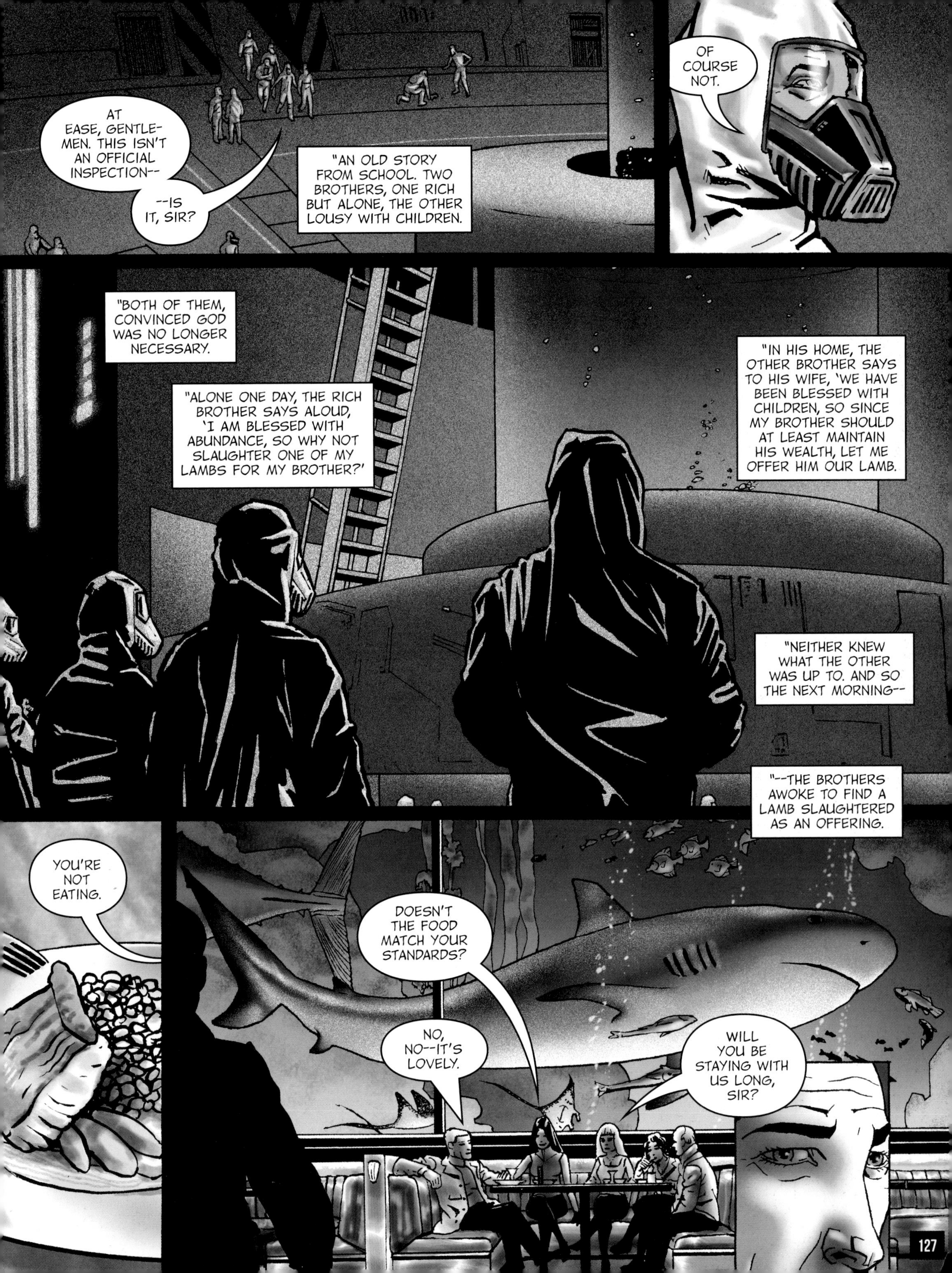
AT EASE, GENTLEMEN. THIS ISN'T AN OFFICIAL INSPECTION--
--IS IT, SIR?
"AN OLD STORY FROM SCHOOL. TWO BROTHERS, ONE RICH BUT ALONE, THE OTHER LOUSY WITH CHILDREN.
OF COURSE NOT.
"BOTH OF THEM, CONVINCED GOD WAS NO LONGER NECESSARY.
"ALONE ONE DAY, THE RICH BROTHER SAYS ALOUD, 'I AM BLESSED WITH ABUNDANCE, SO WHY NOT SLAUGHTER ONE OF MY LAMBS FOR MY BROTHER?'
"IN HIS HOME, THE OTHER BROTHER SAYS TO HIS WIFE, 'WE HAVE BEEN BLESSED WITH CHILDREN, SO SINCE MY BROTHER SHOULD AT LEAST MAINTAIN HIS WEALTH, LET ME OFFER HIM OUR LAMB.
"NEITHER KNEW WHAT THE OTHER WAS UP TO. AND SO THE NEXT MORNING--
"--THE BROTHERS AWOKE TO FIND A LAMB SLAUGHTERED AS AN OFFERING.
YOU'RE NOT EATING.
DOESN'T THE FOOD MATCH YOUR STANDARDS?
NO, NO--IT'S LOVELY.
WILL YOU BE STAYING WITH US LONG, SIR?

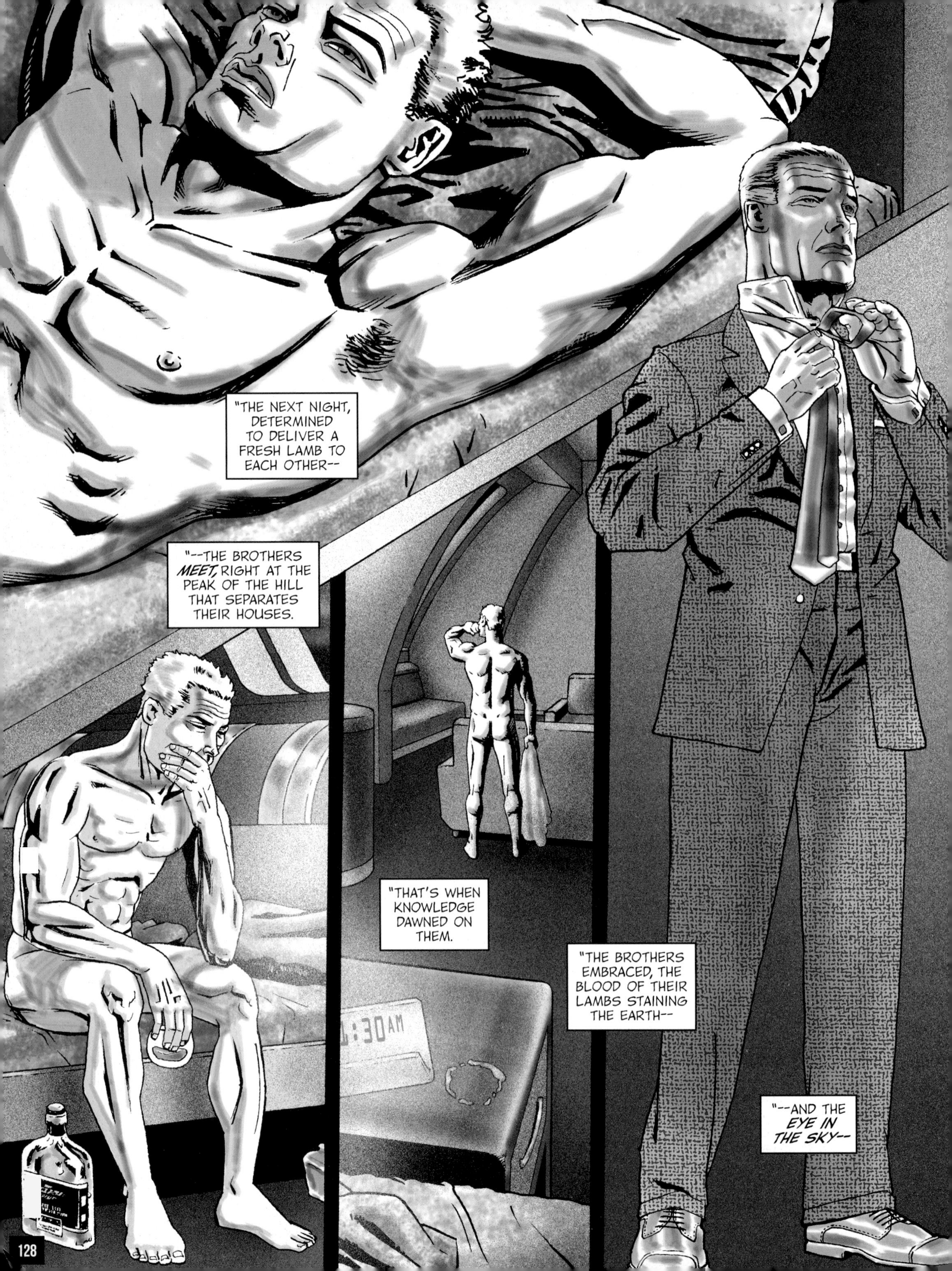
"THE NEXT NIGHT, DETERMINED TO DELIVER A FRESH LAMB TO EACH OTHER--
"--THE BROTHERS *MEET,* RIGHT AT THE PEAK OF THE HILL THAT SEPARATES THEIR HOUSES.
"THAT'S WHEN KNOWLEDGE DAWNED ON THEM.
"THE BROTHERS EMBRACED, THE BLOOD OF THEIR LAMBS STAINING THE EARTH--
"--AND THE *EYE IN THE SKY--*

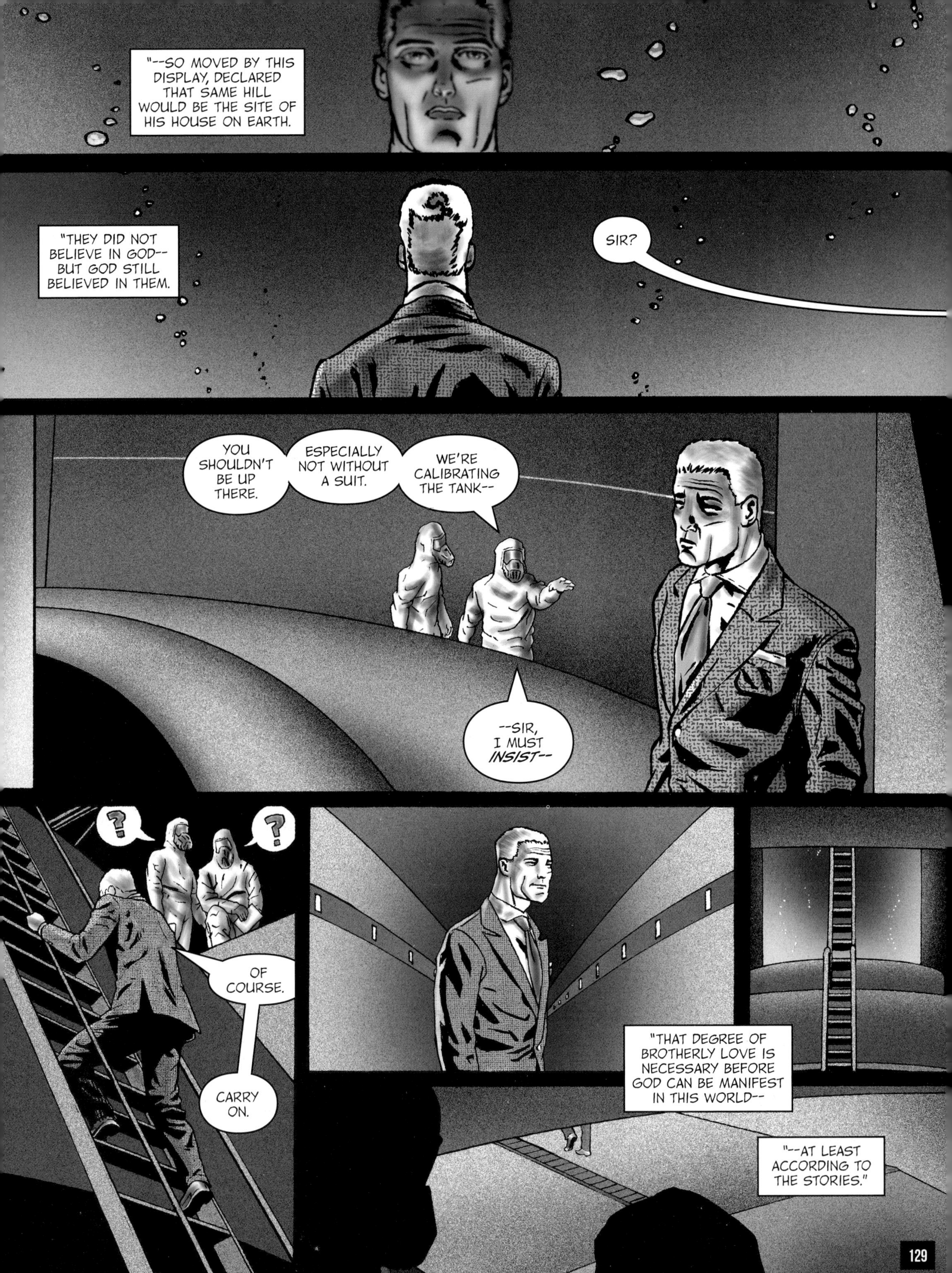
"--SO MOVED BY THIS DISPLAY, DECLARED THAT SAME HILL WOULD BE THE SITE OF HIS HOUSE ON EARTH.
"THEY DID NOT BELIEVE IN GOD-- BUT GOD STILL BELIEVED IN THEM.
SIR?
YOU SHOULDN'T BE UP THERE.
ESPECIALLY NOT WITHOUT A SUIT.
WE'RE CALIBRATING THE TANK--
--SIR, I MUST *INSIST*--
?
?
OF COURSE.
CARRY ON.
"THAT DEGREE OF BROTHERLY LOVE IS NECESSARY BEFORE GOD CAN BE MANIFEST IN THIS WORLD--
"--AT LEAST ACCORDING TO THE STORIES."

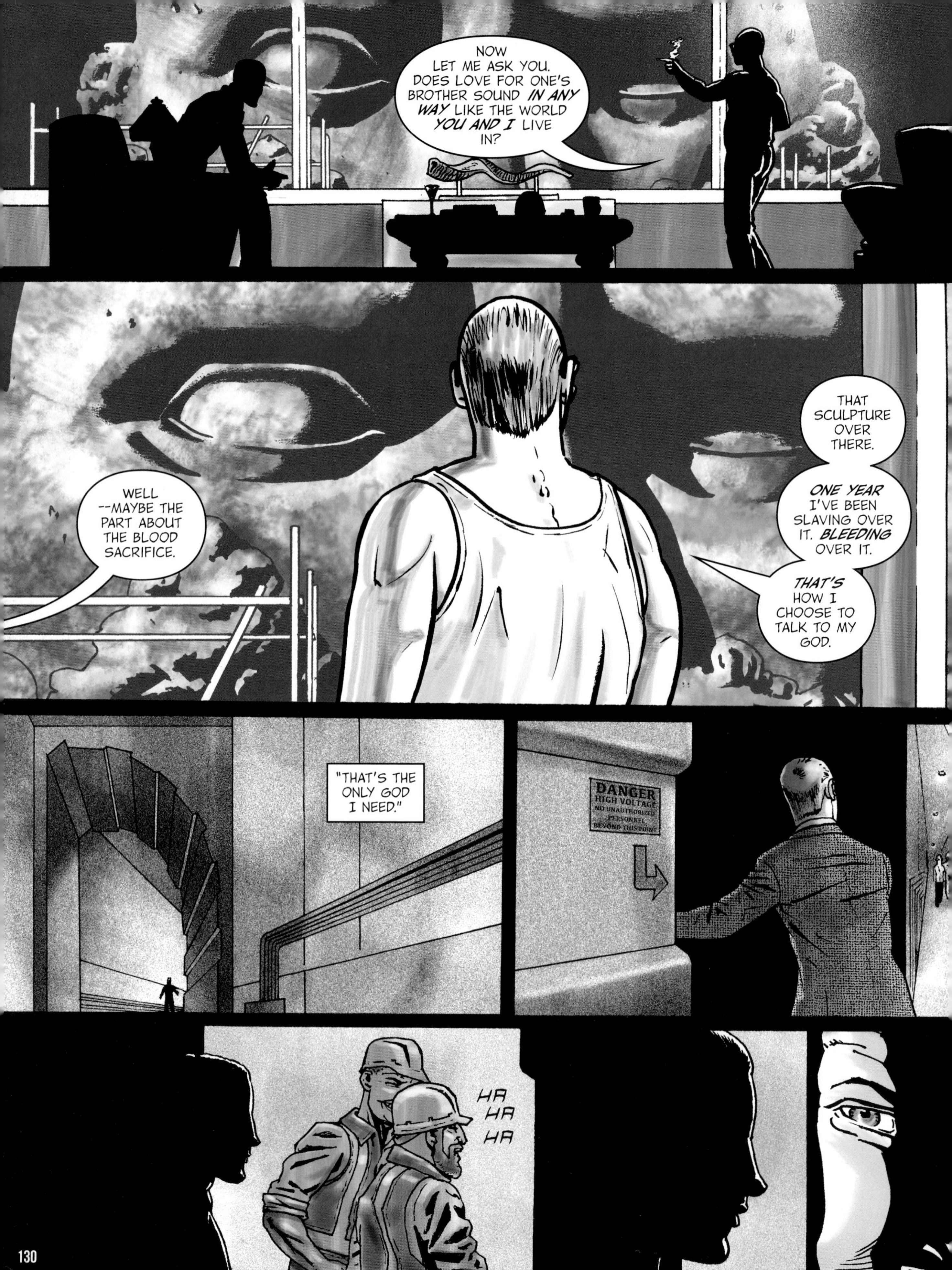
NOW LET ME ASK YOU. DOES LOVE FOR ONE'S BROTHER SOUND IN ANY WAY LIKE THE WORLD YOU AND I LIVE IN?
WELL --MAYBE THE PART ABOUT THE BLOOD SACRIFICE.
THAT SCULPTURE OVER THERE.
ONE YEAR I'VE BEEN SLAVING OVER IT. BLEEDING OVER IT.
THAT'S HOW I CHOOSE TO TALK TO MY GOD.
"THAT'S THE ONLY GOD I NEED."
DANGER HIGH VOLTAGE NO UNAUTHORIZED PERSONNEL BEYOND THIS POINT
HA HA HA

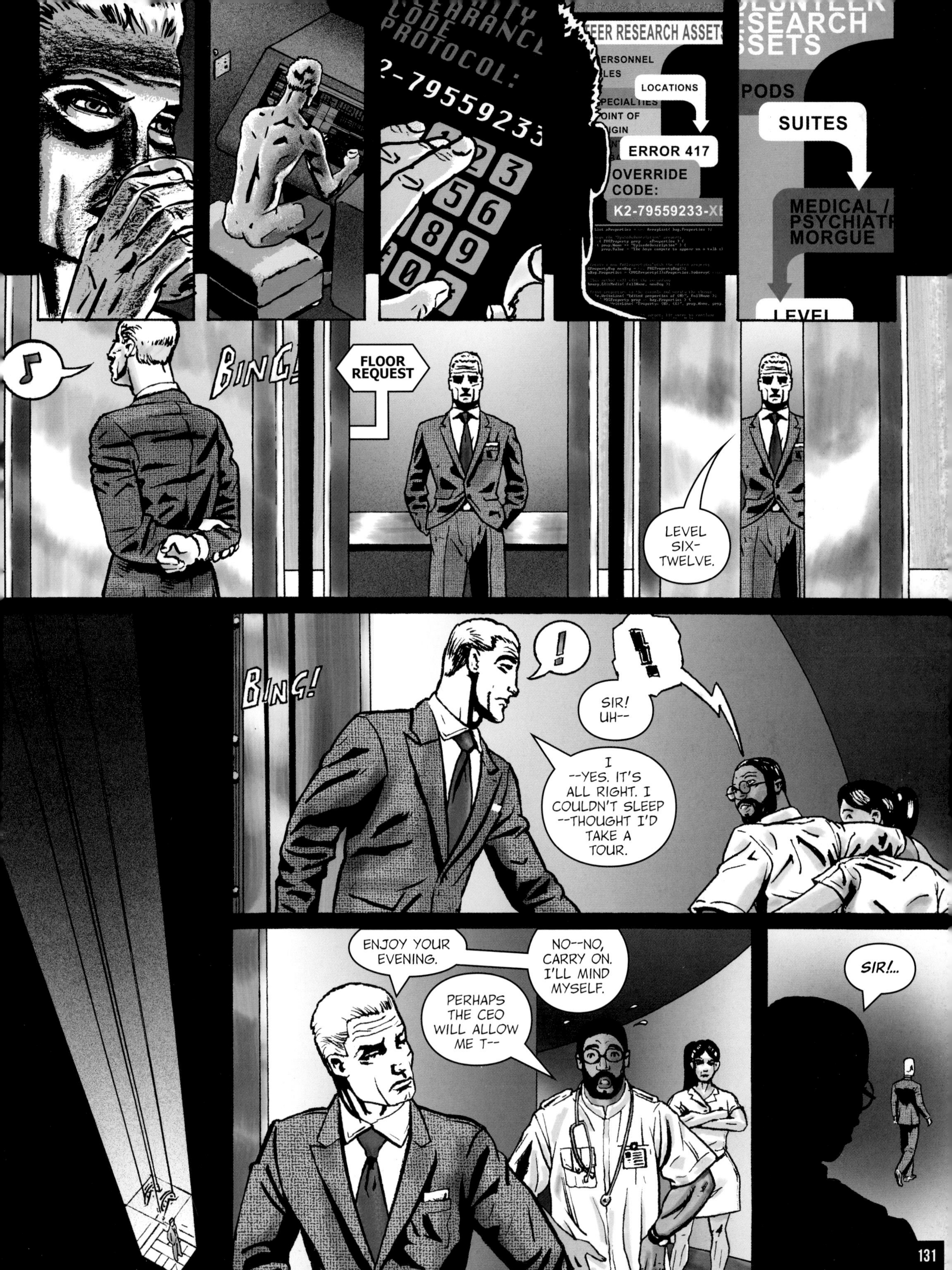

CODE
PROTOCOL:
ERSONNEL
LOCATIONS
ERROR 417
OVERRIDE CODE:
K2-79559233-X
PODS
SUITES
MEDICAL /
PSYCHIATR
MORGUE
LEVEL
♪
BING!
FLOOR REQUEST
LEVEL SIX-TWELVE.
BING!
!
!
SIR! UH--
I --YES. IT'S ALL RIGHT. I COULDN'T SLEEP --THOUGHT I'D TAKE A TOUR.
NO--NO, CARRY ON. I'LL MIND MYSELF.
PERHAPS THE CEO WILL ALLOW ME T--
ENJOY YOUR EVENING.
SIR!...

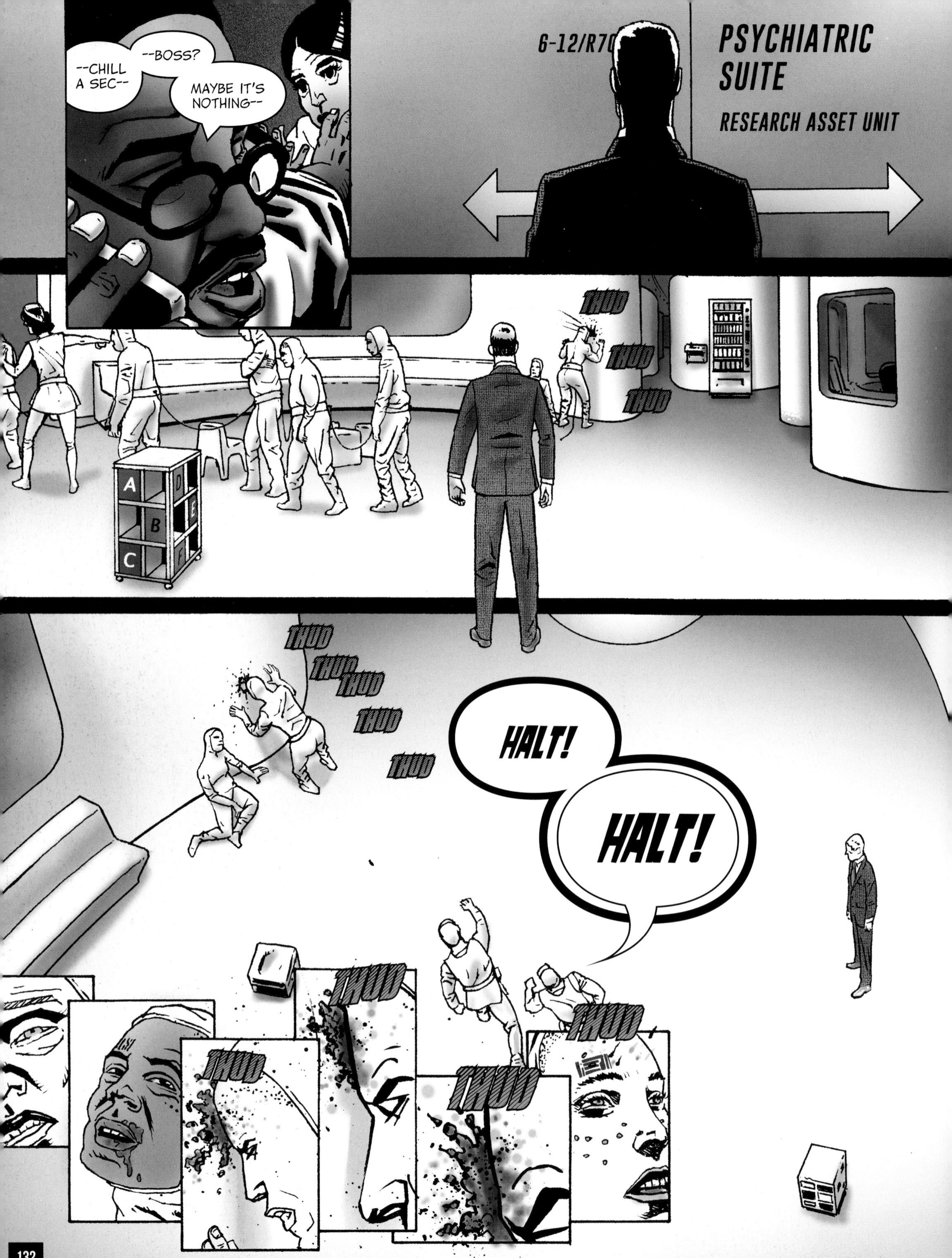
--CHILL A SEC--
--BOSS?
MAYBE IT'S NOTHING--
6-12/R70
PSYCHIATRIC SUITE
RESEARCH ASSET UNIT
THUD
THUD
THUD
A
B
C
THUD
THUD
THUD
THUD
THUD
HALT!
HALT!
THUD
THUD
THUD
THUD

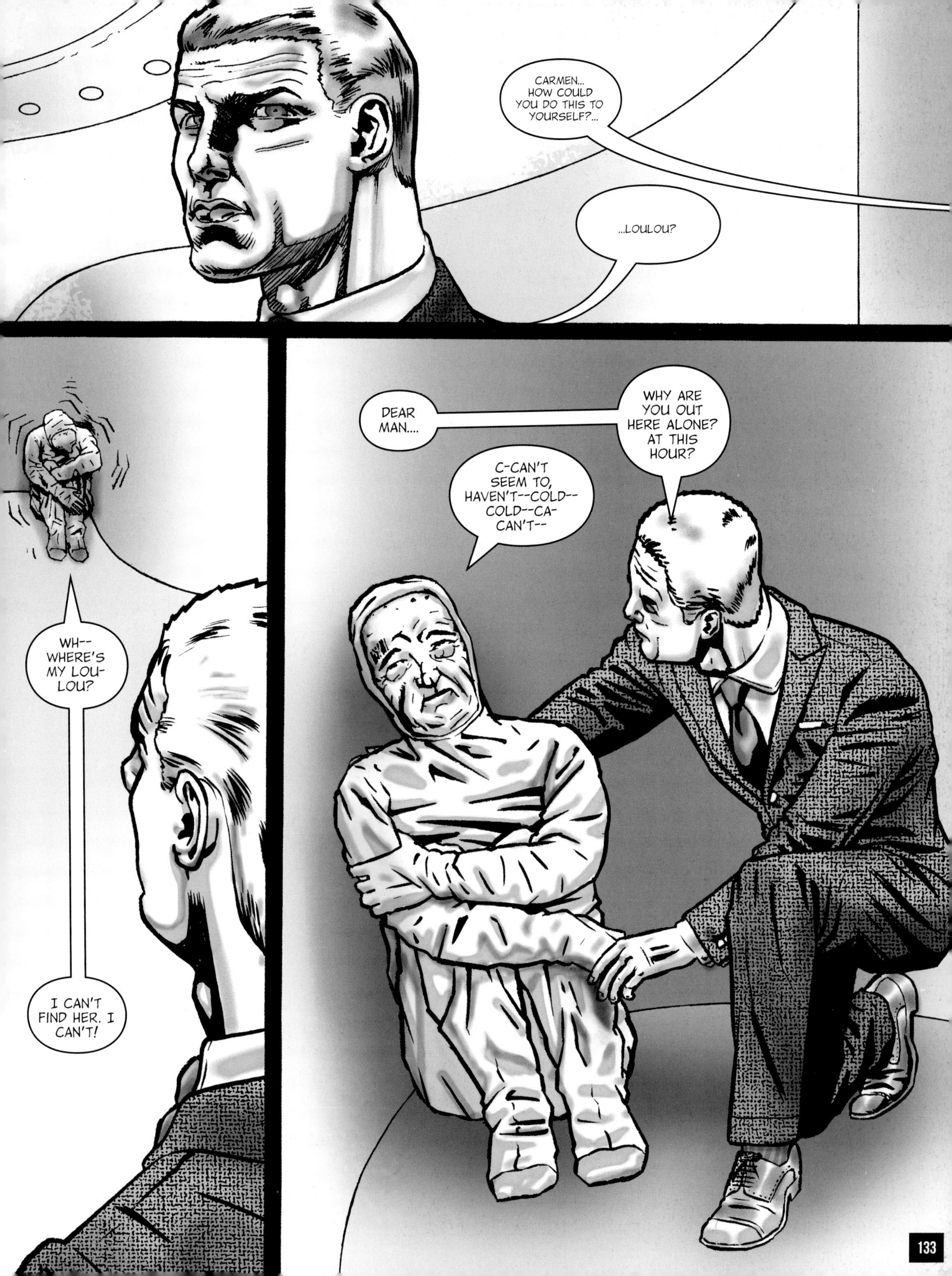

CARMEN... HOW COULD YOU DO THIS TO YOURSELF?...
...LOULOU?
WH-- WHERE'S MY LOU-LOU?
I CAN'T FIND HER. I CAN'T!
DEAR MAN....
WHY ARE YOU OUT HERE ALONE? AT THIS HOUR?
C-CAN'T SEEM TO, HAVEN'T--COLD--COLD--CA-CAN'T--

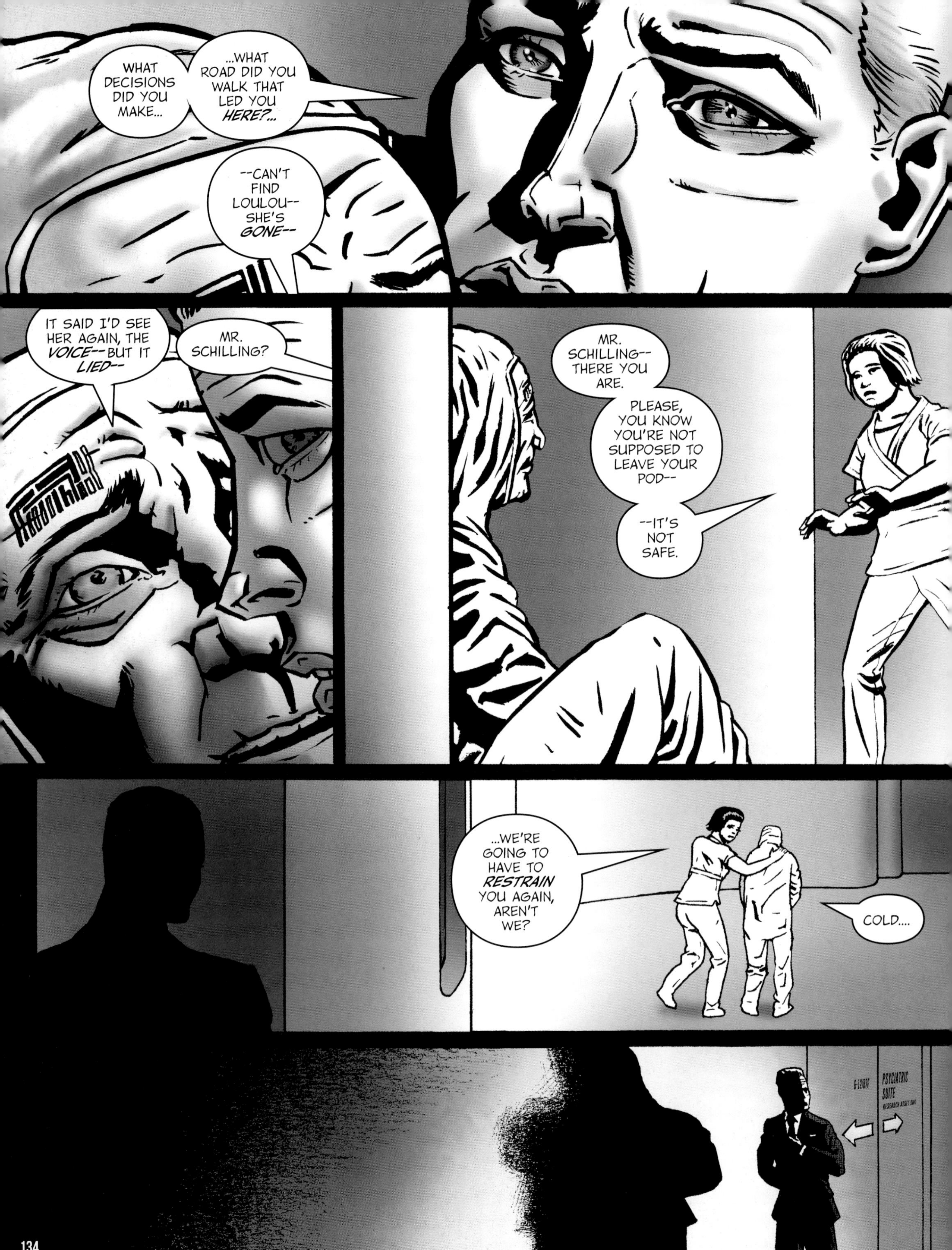
WHAT DECISIONS DID YOU MAKE...
...WHAT ROAD DID YOU WALK THAT LED YOU *HERE?...*
--CAN'T FIND LOULOU--SHE'S *GONE*--
IT SAID I'D SEE HER AGAIN, THE *VOICE*--BUT IT *LIED*--
MR. SCHILLING?
MR. SCHILLING--THERE YOU ARE.
PLEASE, YOU KNOW YOU'RE NOT SUPPOSED TO LEAVE YOUR POD--
--IT'S NOT SAFE.
...WE'RE GOING TO HAVE TO *RESTRAIN* YOU AGAIN, AREN'T WE?
COLD....
PSYCIATRIC SUITE

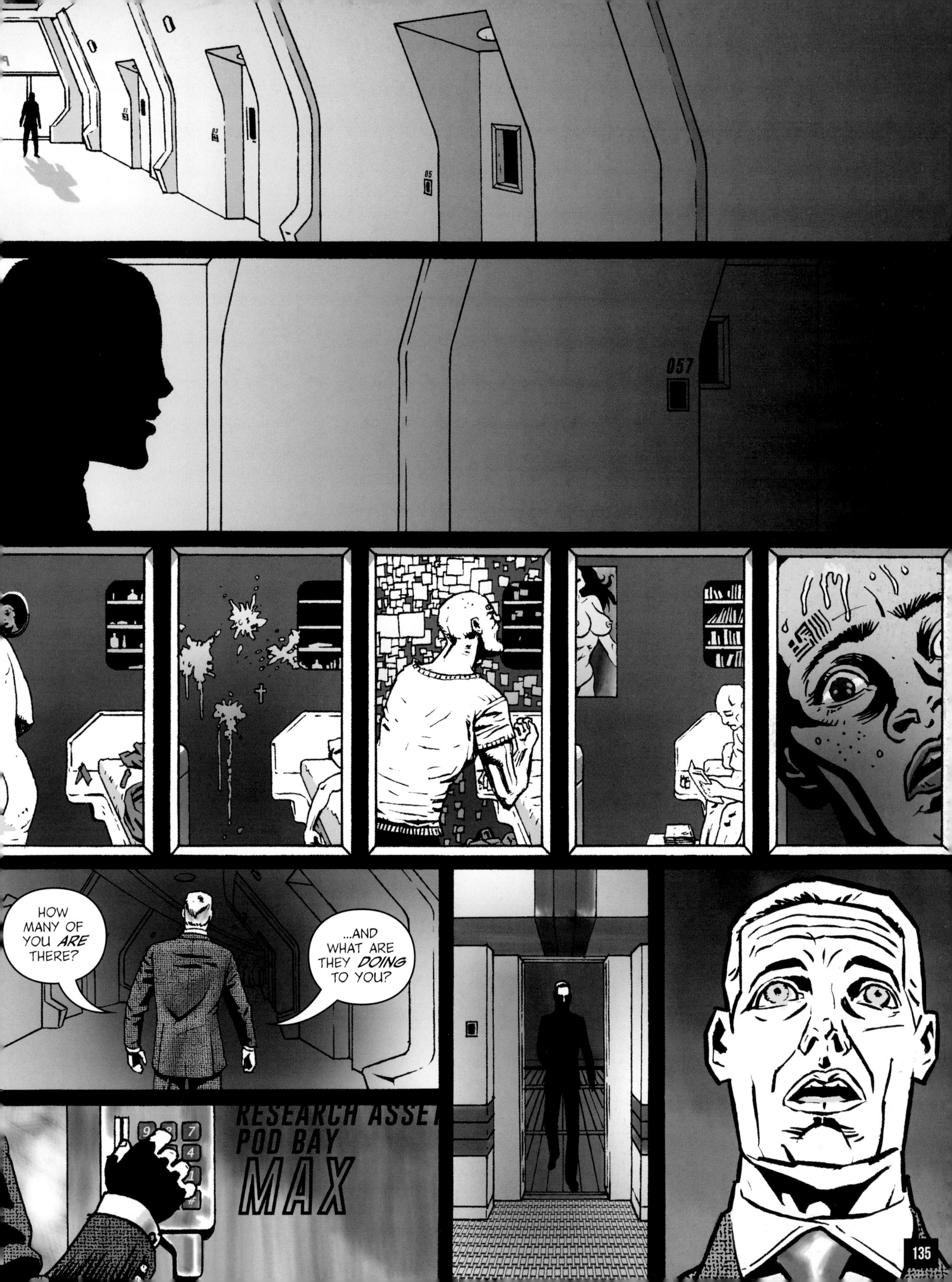
057
HOW MANY OF YOU *ARE* THERE?
...AND WHAT ARE THEY *DOING* TO YOU?
RESEARCH ASSET POD BAY
MAX

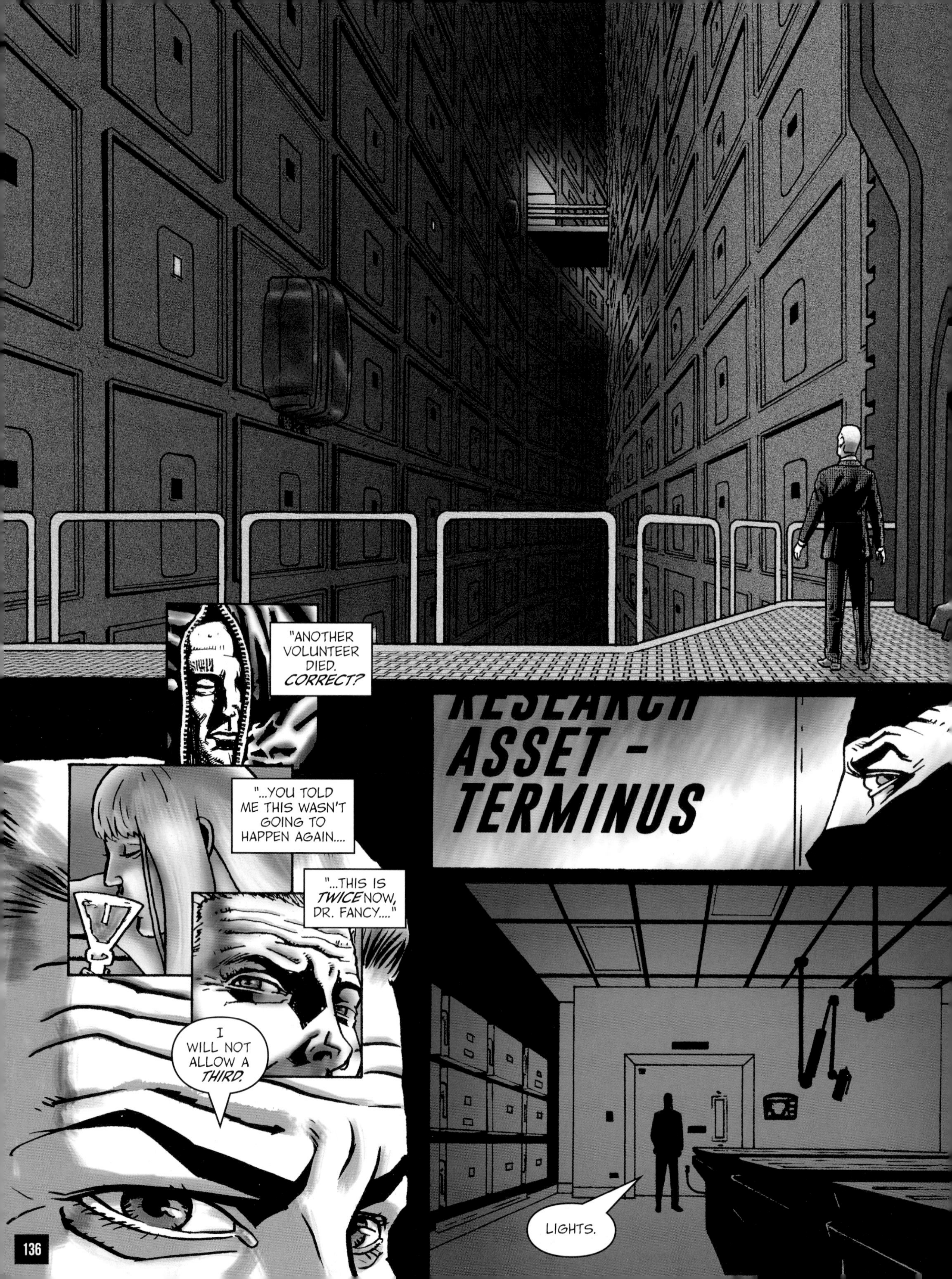
"ANOTHER VOLUNTEER DIED. CORRECT?
ASSET - TERMINUS
"...YOU TOLD ME THIS WASN'T GOING TO HAPPEN AGAIN....
"...THIS IS TWICE NOW, DR. FANCY...."
I WILL NOT ALLOW A THIRD.
LIGHTS.

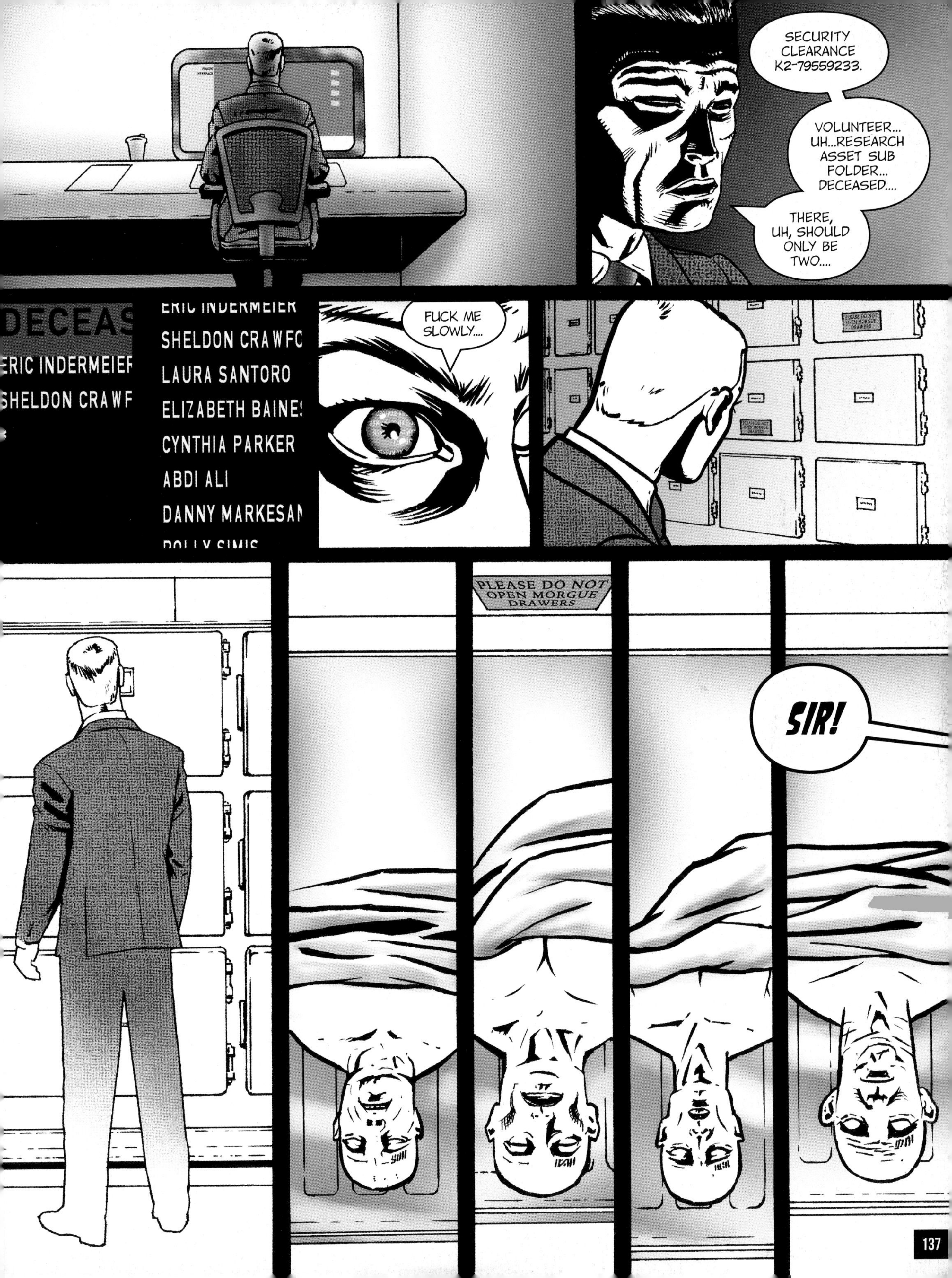
SECURITY CLEARANCE K2-79559233.
VOLUNTEER... UH...RESEARCH ASSET SUB FOLDER... DECEASED....
THERE, UH, SHOULD ONLY BE TWO....
DECEAS
ERIC INDERMEIER
SHELDON CRAWF
SHELDON CRAWFO
LAURA SANTORO
ELIZABETH BAINES
CYNTHIA PARKER
ABDI ALI
DANNY MARKESAN
FUCK ME SLOWLY....
PLEASE DO NOT OPEN MORGUE DRAWERS
PLEASE DO NOT OPEN MORGUE DRAWERS
SIR!

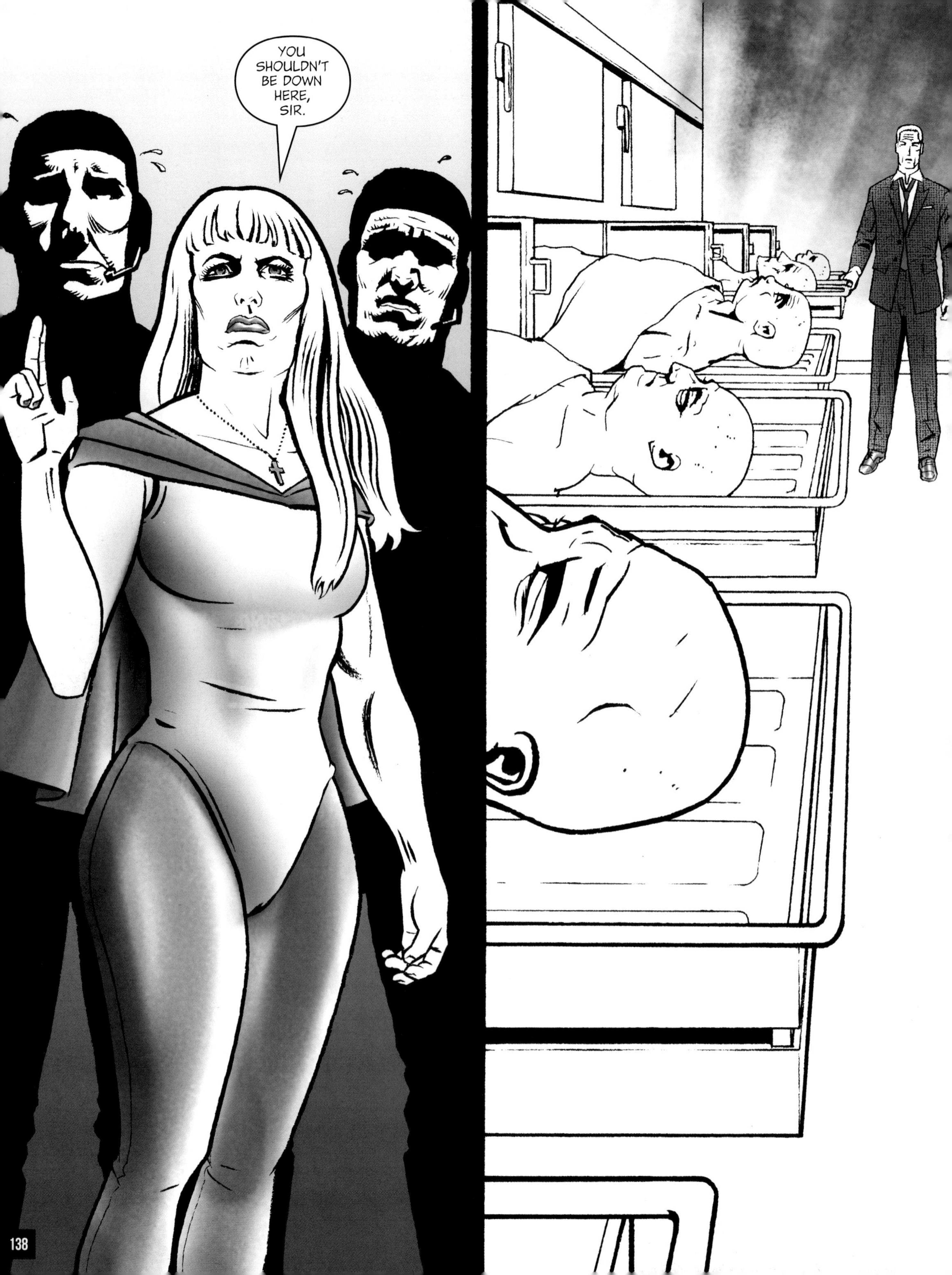
YOU SHOULDN'T BE DOWN HERE, SIR.

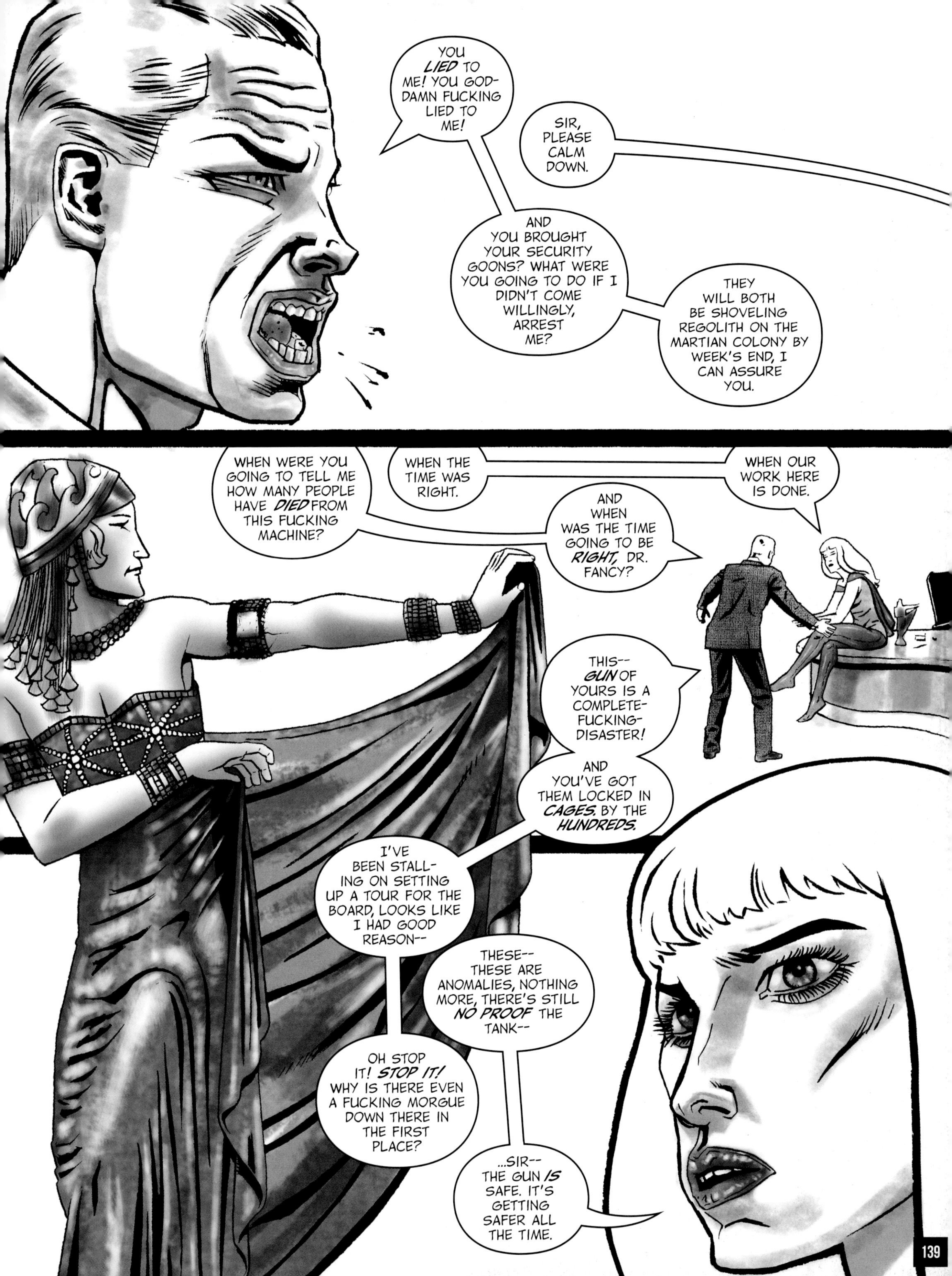
YOU *LIED* TO ME! YOU GOD-DAMN FUCKING LIED TO ME!
SIR, PLEASE CALM DOWN.
AND YOU BROUGHT YOUR SECURITY GOONS? WHAT WERE YOU GOING TO DO IF I DIDN'T COME WILLINGLY, ARREST ME?
THEY WILL BOTH BE SHOVELING REGOLITH ON THE MARTIAN COLONY BY WEEK'S END, I CAN ASSURE YOU.
WHEN WERE YOU GOING TO TELL ME HOW MANY PEOPLE HAVE *DIED* FROM THIS FUCKING MACHINE?
WHEN THE TIME WAS RIGHT.
WHEN OUR WORK HERE IS DONE.
AND WHEN WAS THE TIME GOING TO BE *RIGHT,* DR. FANCY?
THIS-- *GUN* OF YOURS IS A COMPLETE-FUCKING-DISASTER!
AND YOU'VE GOT THEM LOCKED IN *CAGES.* BY THE *HUNDREDS.*
I'VE BEEN STALLING ON SETTING UP A TOUR FOR THE BOARD, LOOKS LIKE I HAD GOOD REASON--
THESE-- THESE ARE ANOMALIES, NOTHING MORE, THERE'S STILL *NO PROOF* THE TANK--
OH STOP IT! *STOP IT!* WHY IS THERE EVEN A FUCKING MORGUE DOWN THERE IN THE FIRST PLACE?
...SIR-- THE GUN *IS* SAFE. IT'S GETTING SAFER ALL THE TIME.

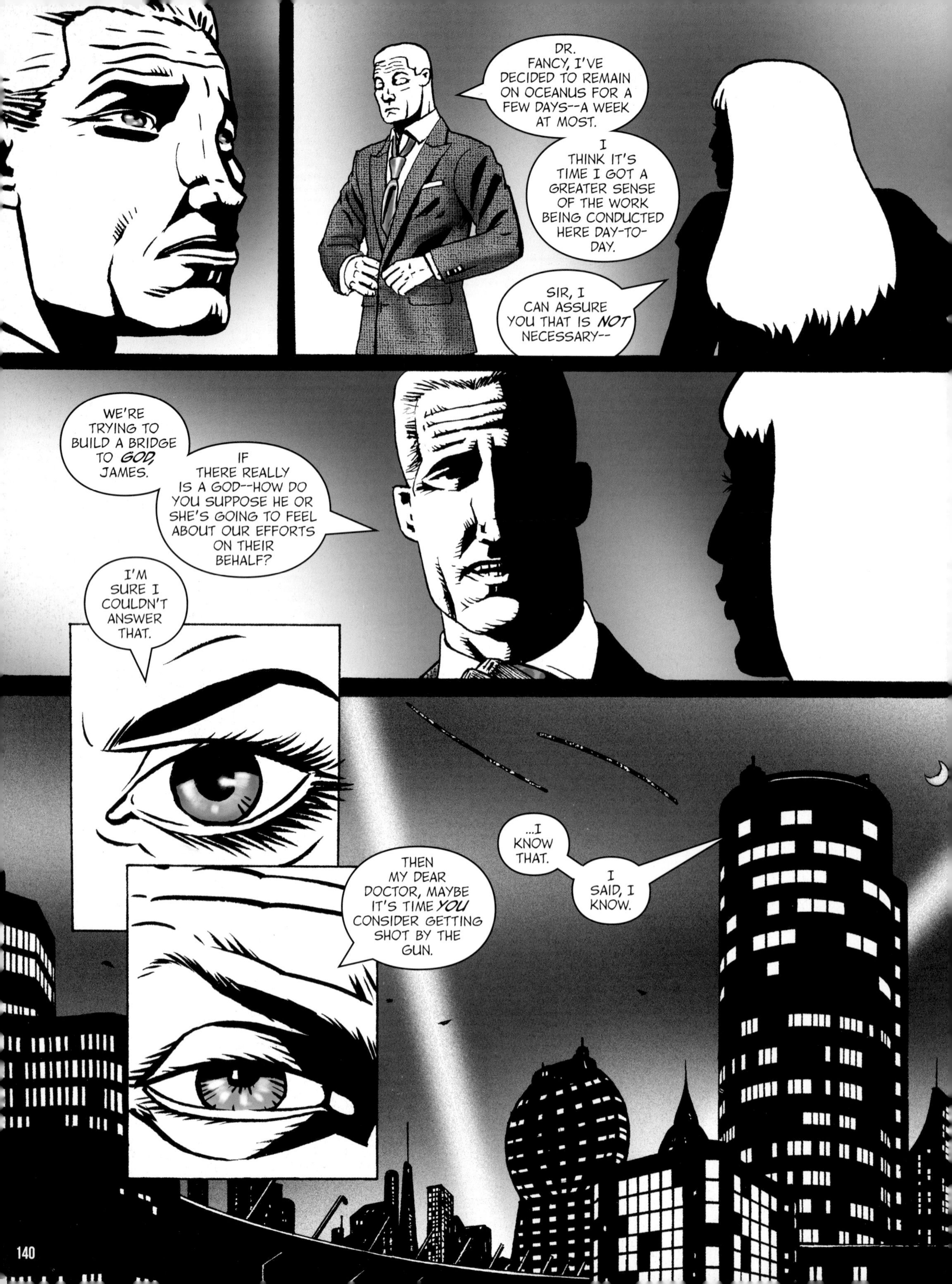
DR. FANCY, I'VE DECIDED TO REMAIN ON OCEANUS FOR A FEW DAYS--A WEEK AT MOST.
I THINK IT'S TIME I GOT A GREATER SENSE OF THE WORK BEING CONDUCTED HERE DAY-TO-DAY.
SIR, I CAN ASSURE YOU THAT IS *NOT* NECESSARY--
WE'RE TRYING TO BUILD A BRIDGE TO *GOD,* JAMES.
IF THERE REALLY IS A GOD--HOW DO YOU SUPPOSE HE OR SHE'S GOING TO FEEL ABOUT OUR EFFORTS ON THEIR BEHALF?
I'M SURE I COULDN'T ANSWER THAT.
THEN MY DEAR DOCTOR, MAYBE IT'S TIME *YOU* CONSIDER GETTING SHOT BY THE GUN.
...I KNOW THAT.
I SAID, I KNOW.

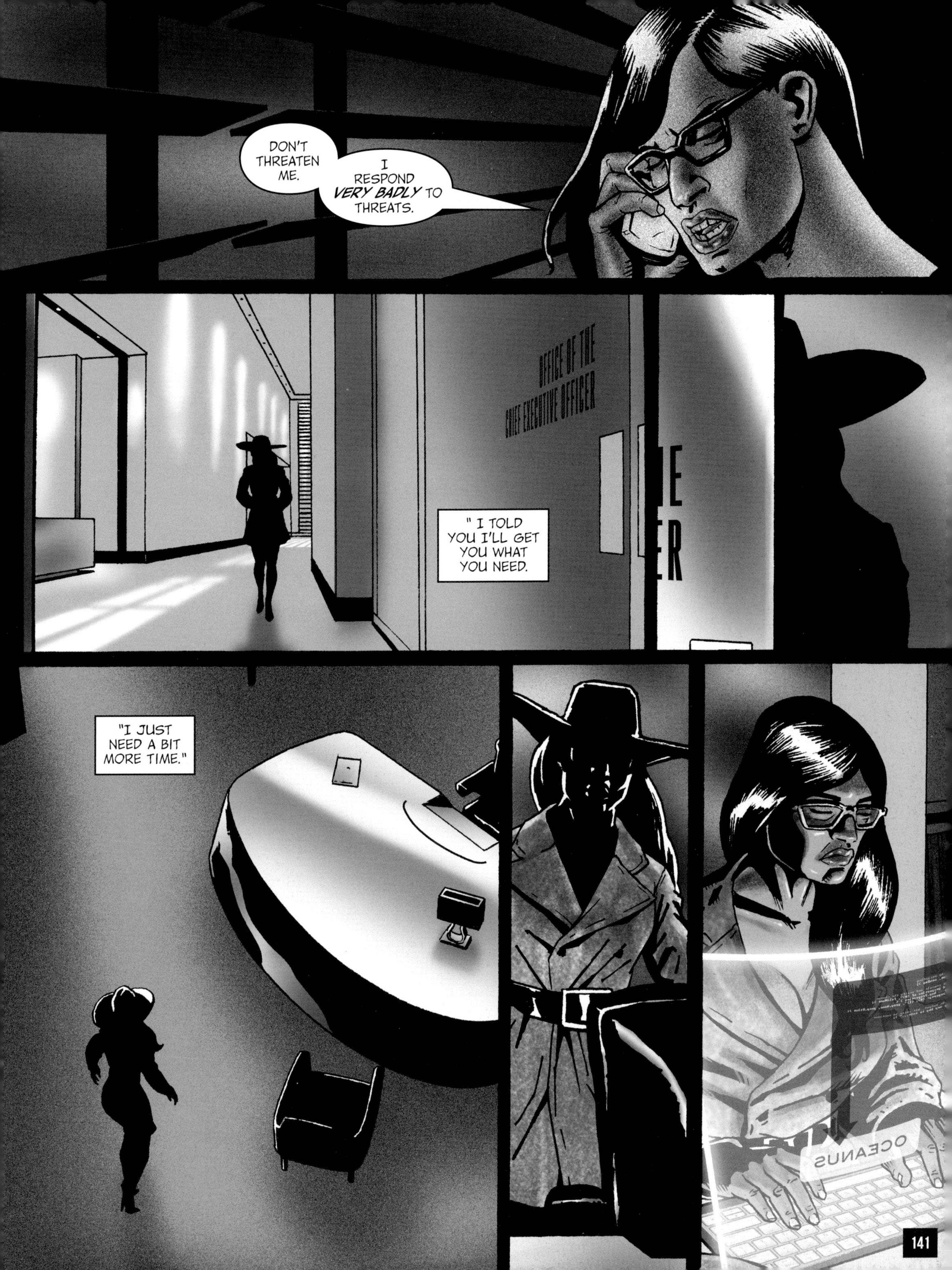
DON'T THREATEN ME.
I RESPOND VERY BADLY TO THREATS.
OFFICE OF THE CHIEF EXECUTIVE OFFICER
" I TOLD YOU I'LL GET YOU WHAT YOU NEED.
"I JUST NEED A BIT MORE TIME."
OCEANUS

"Wanderer through a promised land

Walk with me, take my hand

Lest thy blood stain the sand

We live or die by fate's command

O wanderer to a promised land"

— PROVERB, AUTHOR UNKNOWN

NEXT:
OUR BRAND IS MADNESS

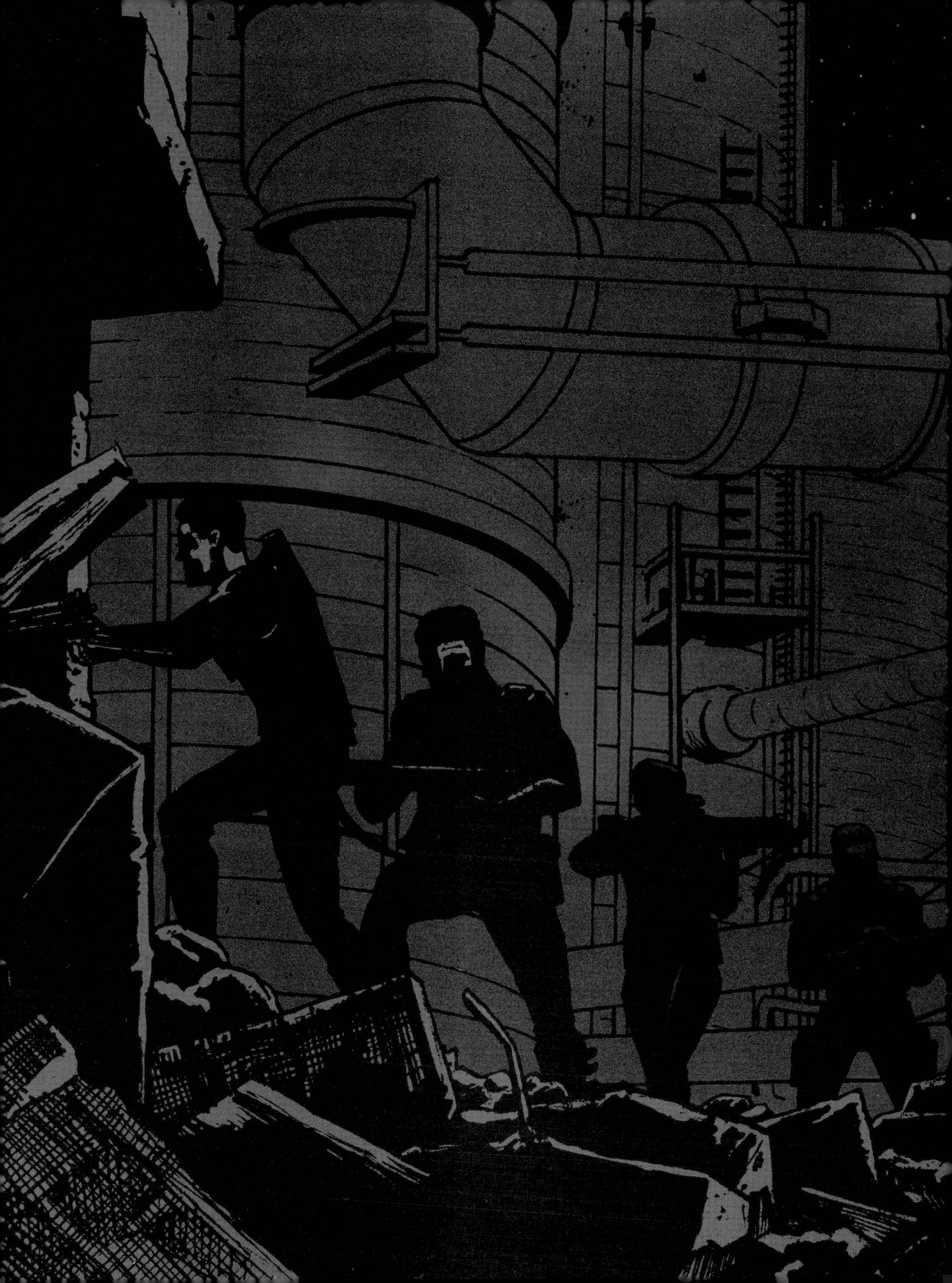

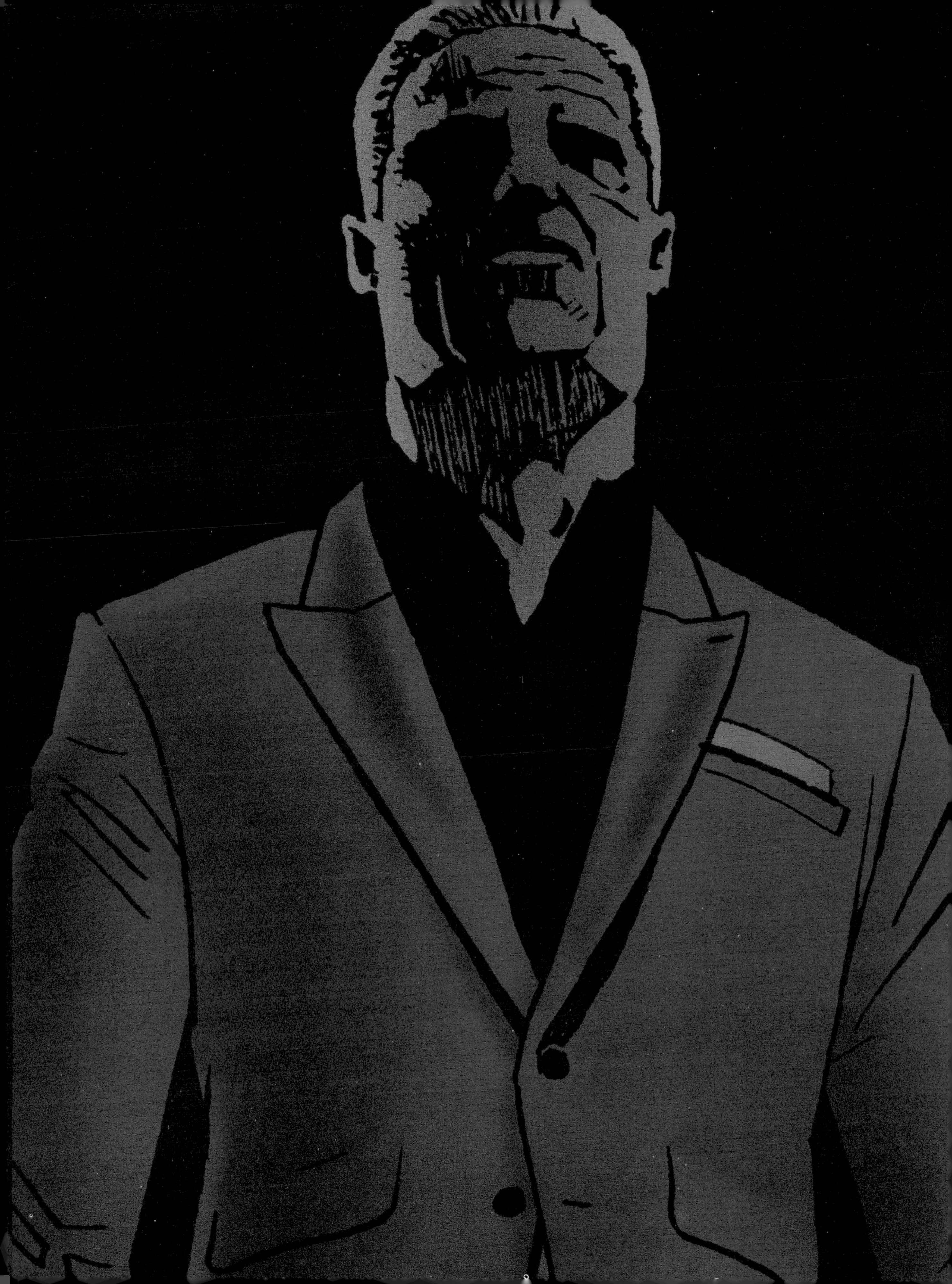

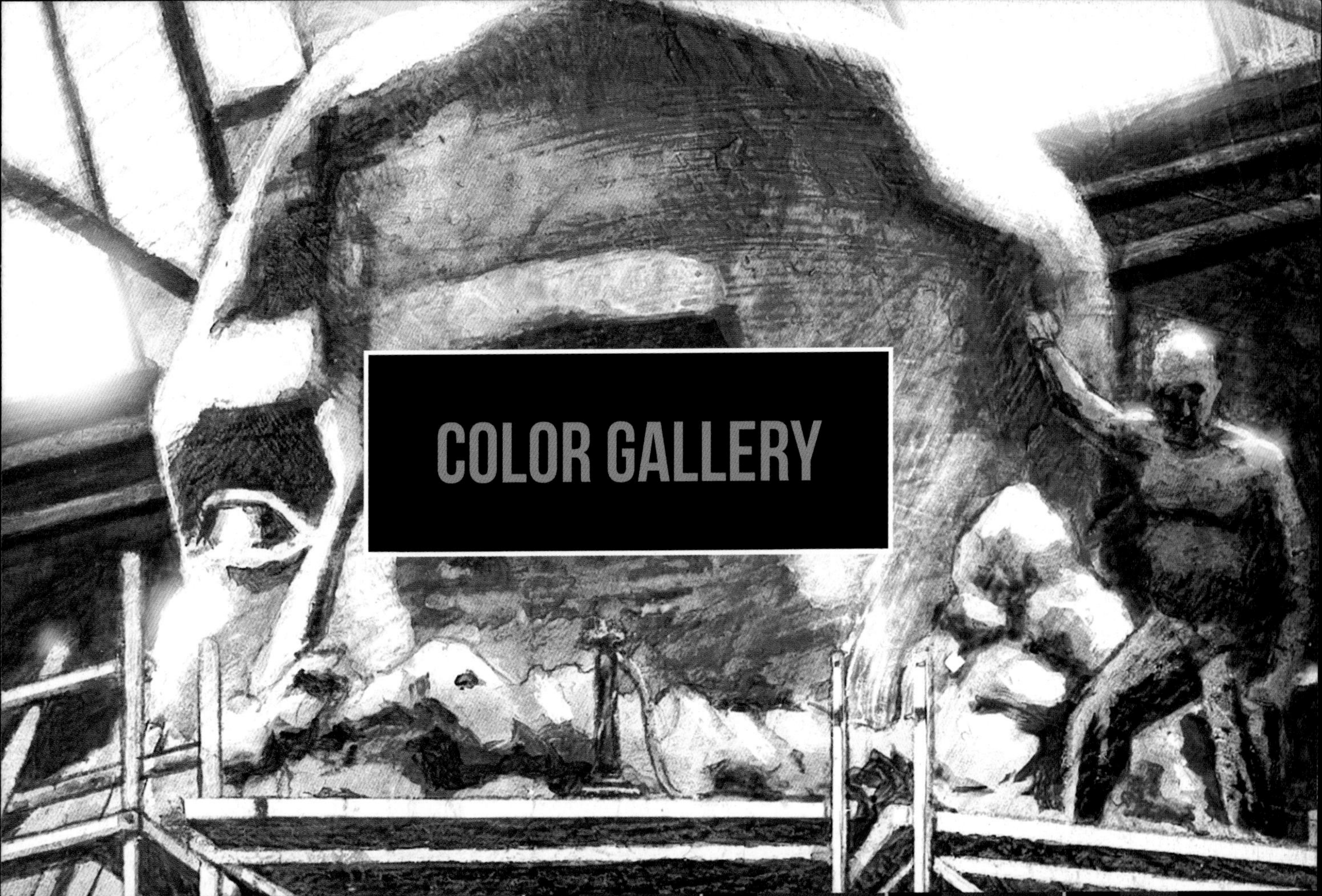

COLOR GALLERY

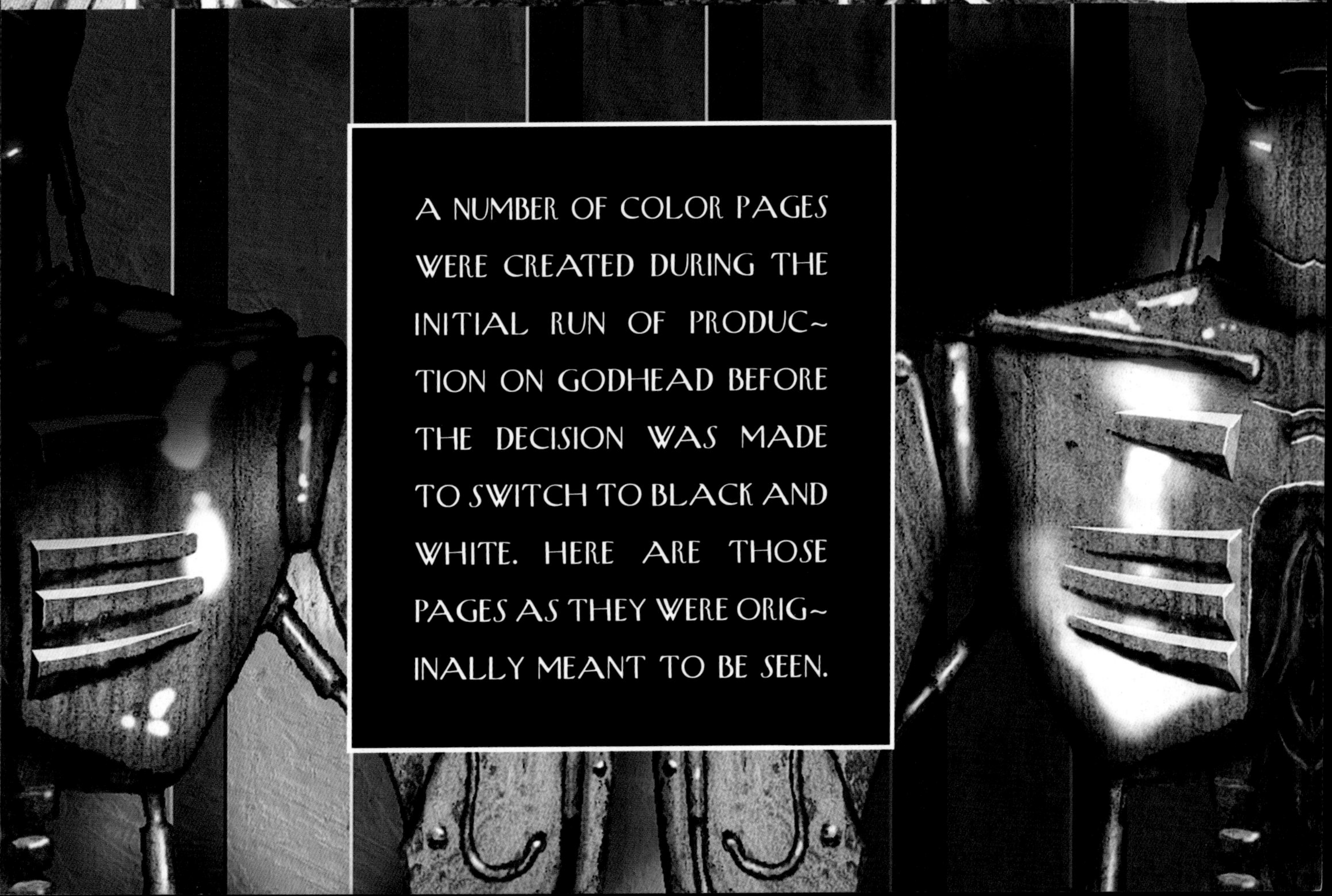

A NUMBER OF COLOR PAGES WERE CREATED DURING THE INITIAL RUN OF PRODUCTION ON GODHEAD BEFORE THE DECISION WAS MADE TO SWITCH TO BLACK AND WHITE. HERE ARE THOSE PAGES AS THEY WERE ORIGINALLY MEANT TO BE SEEN.

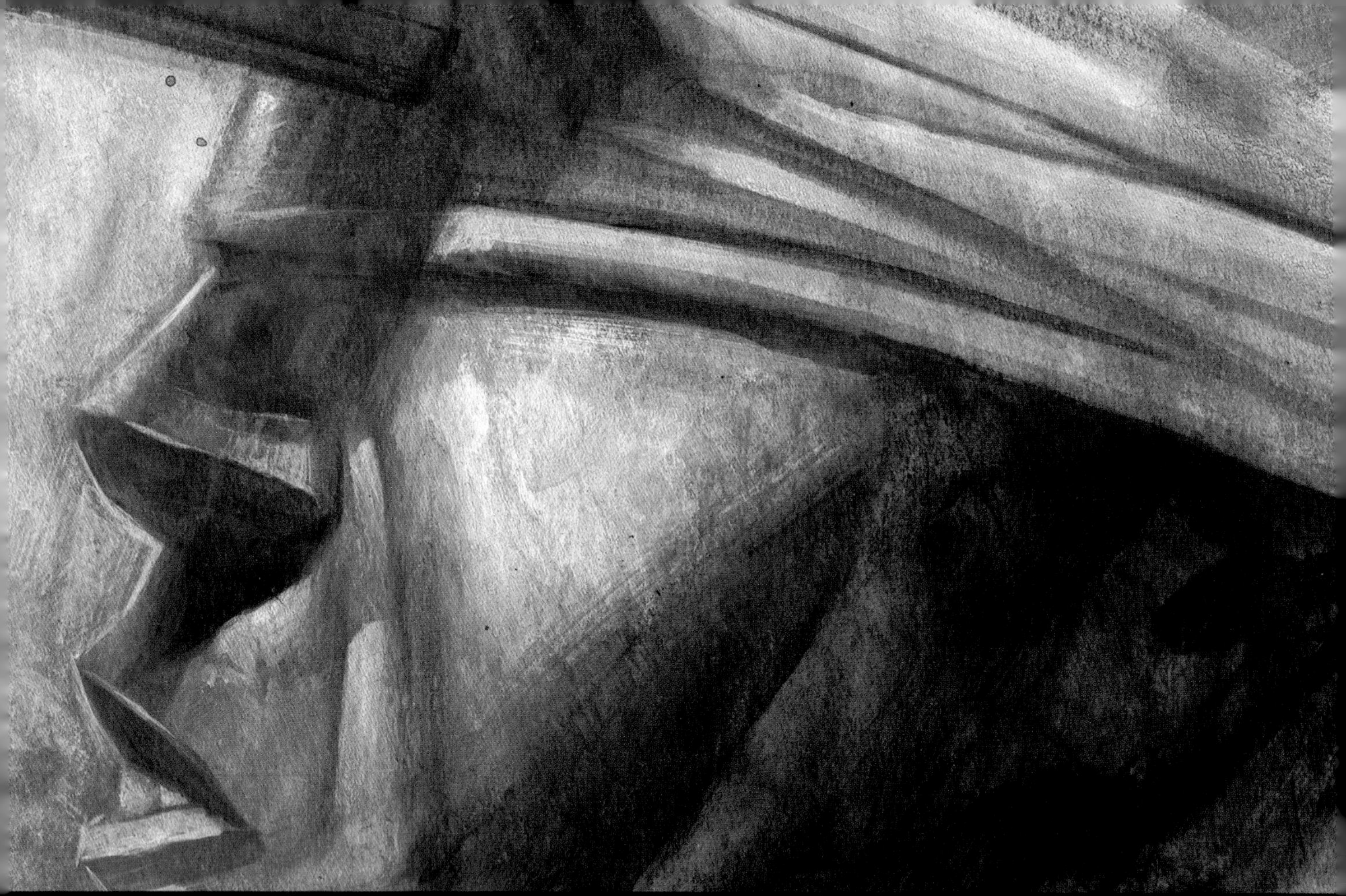

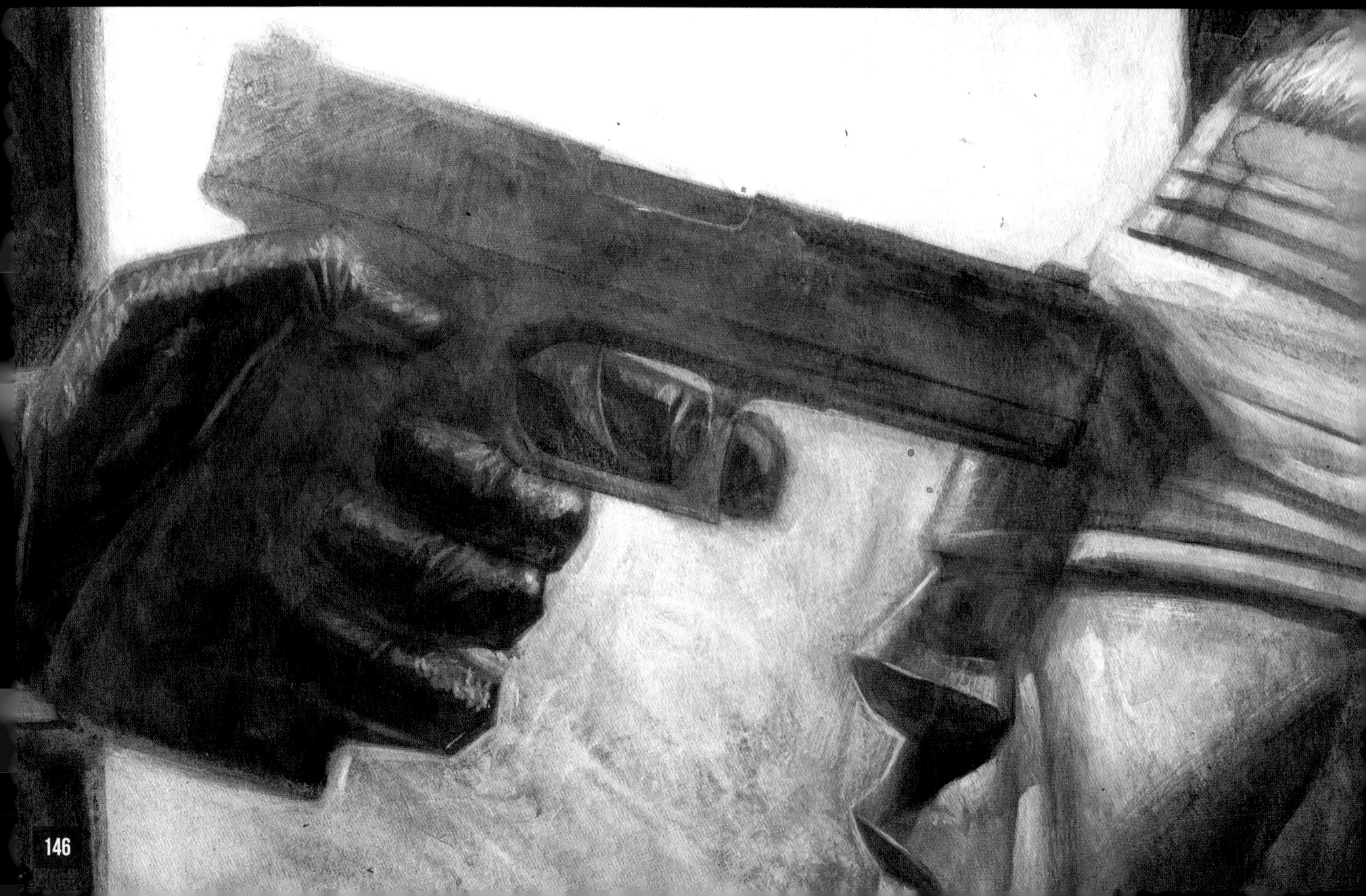

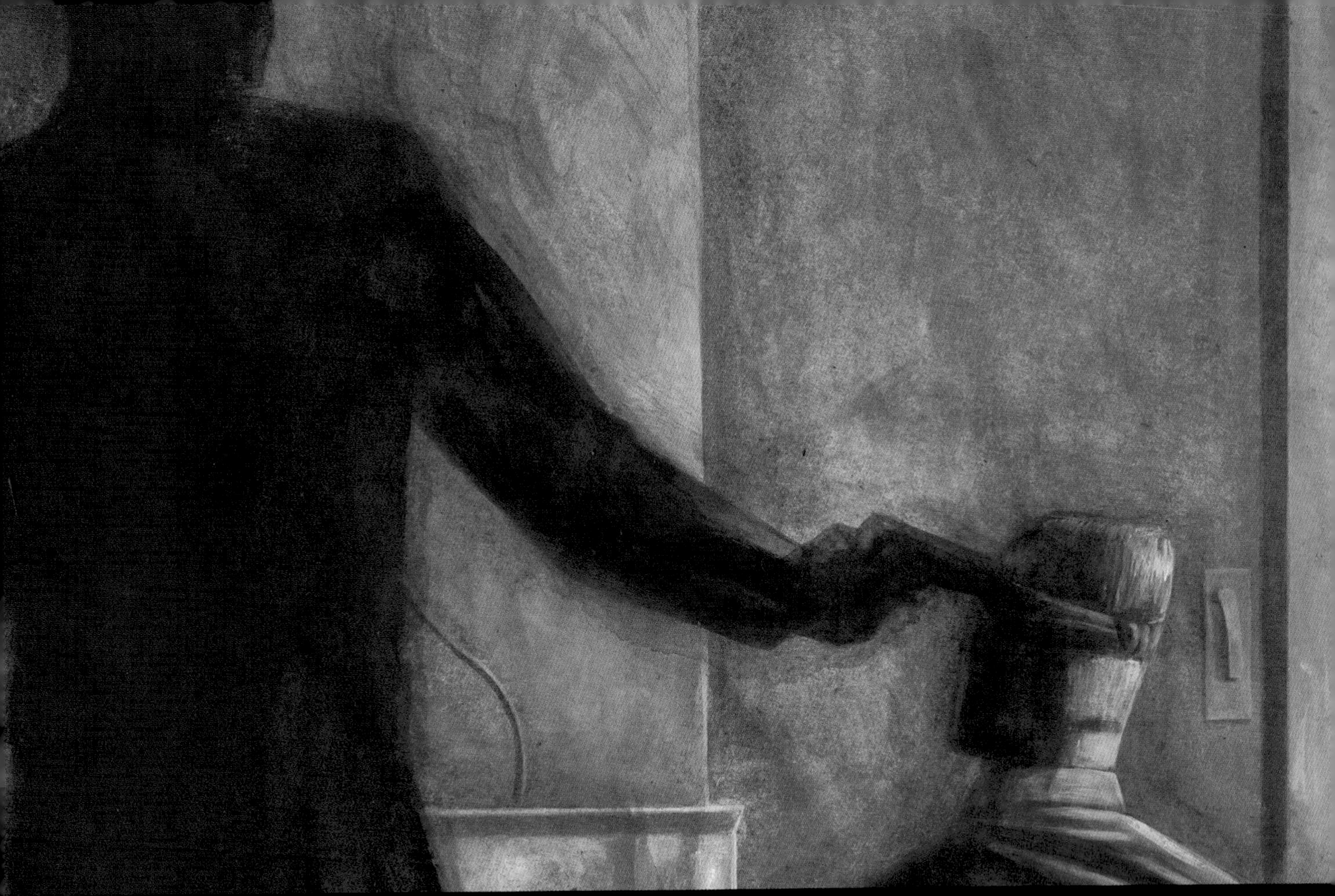

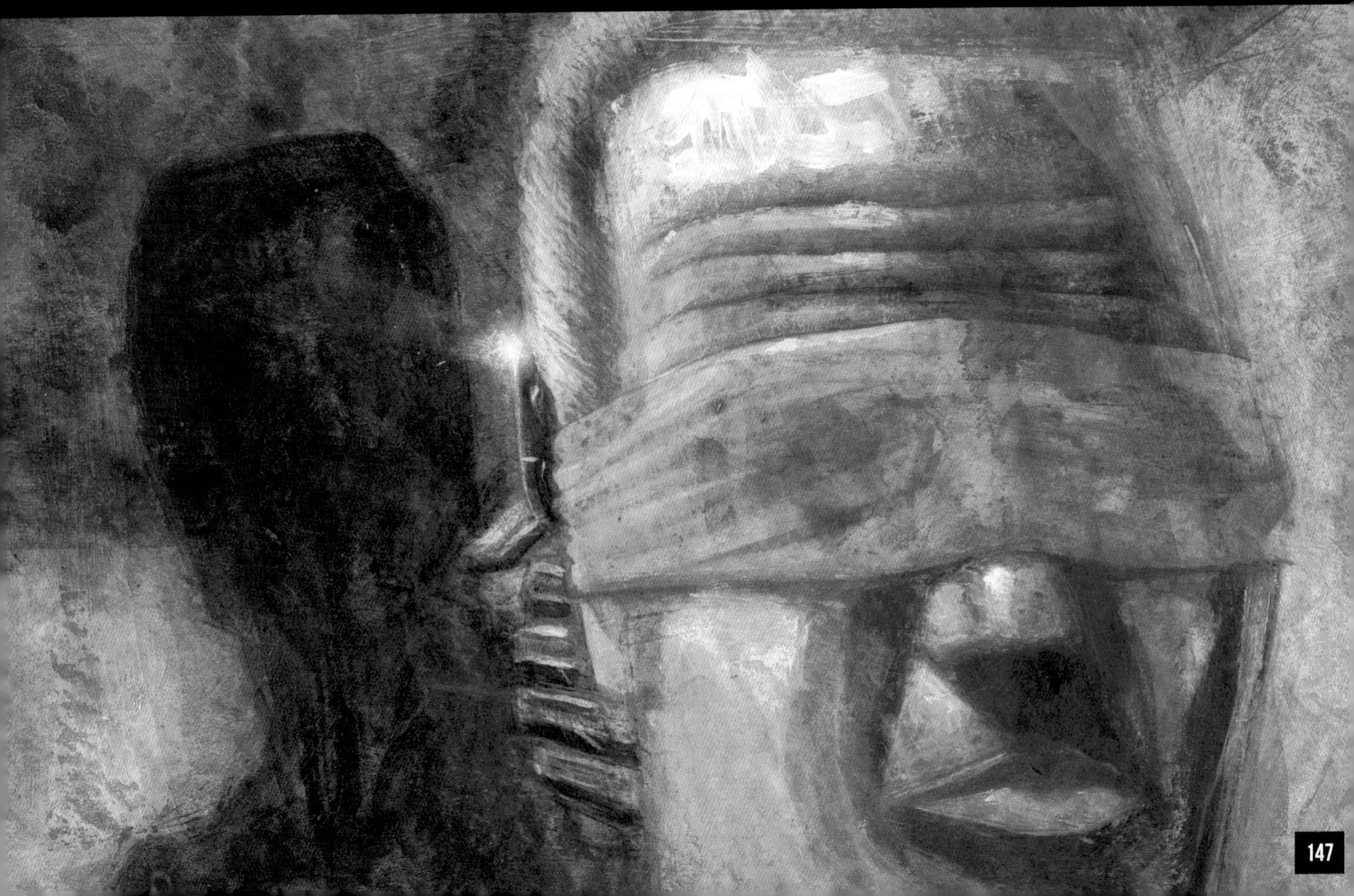

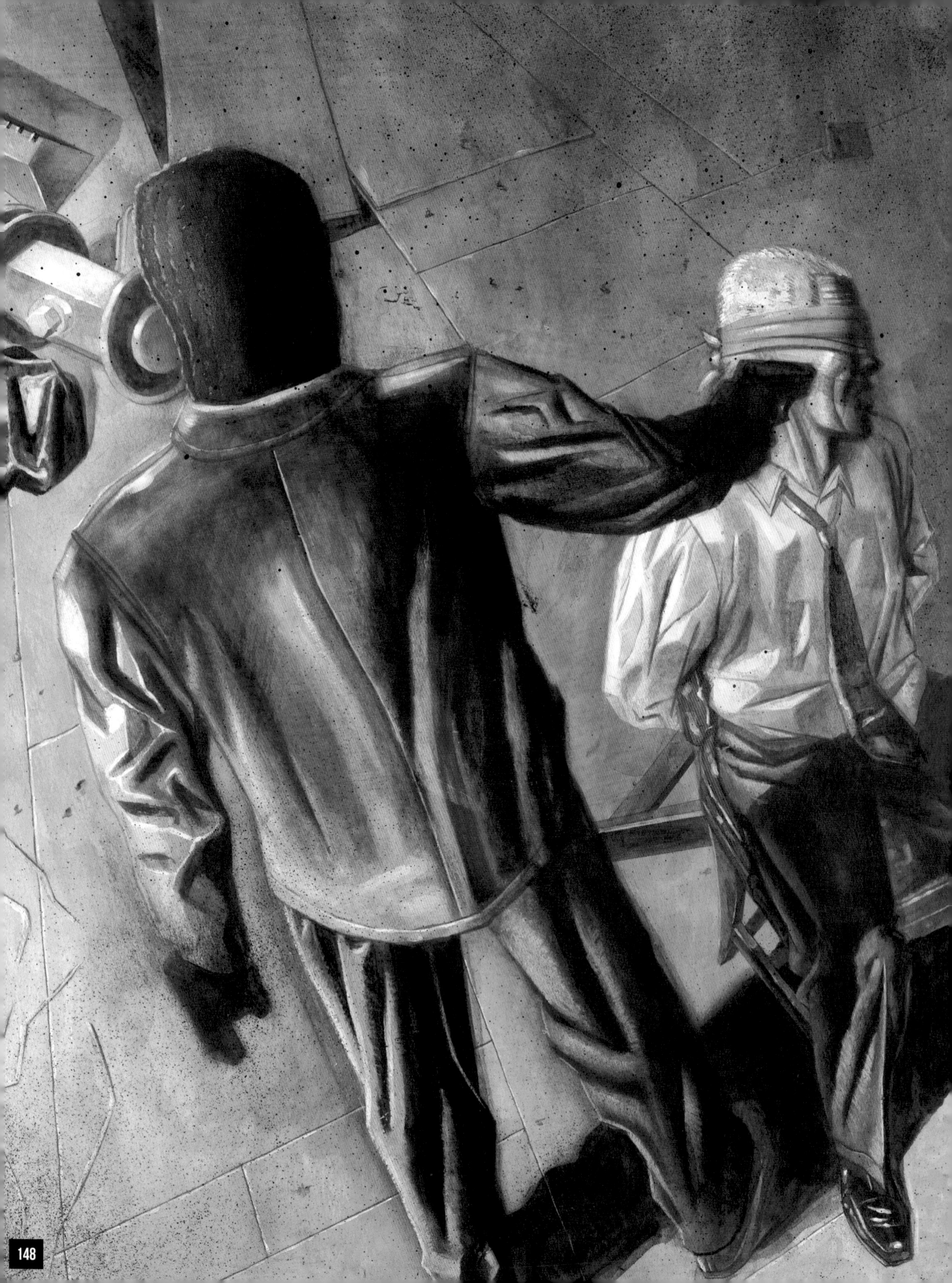

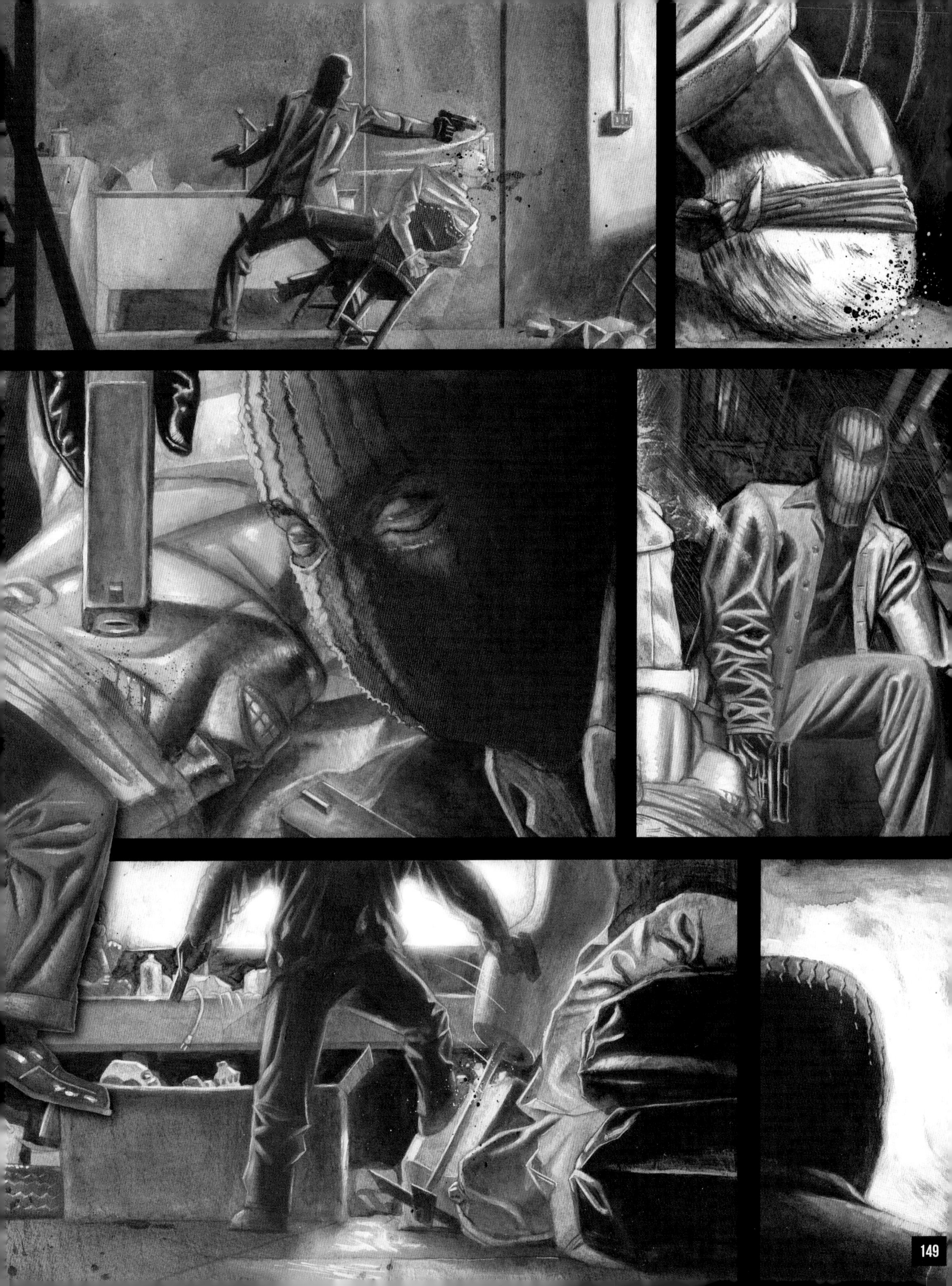

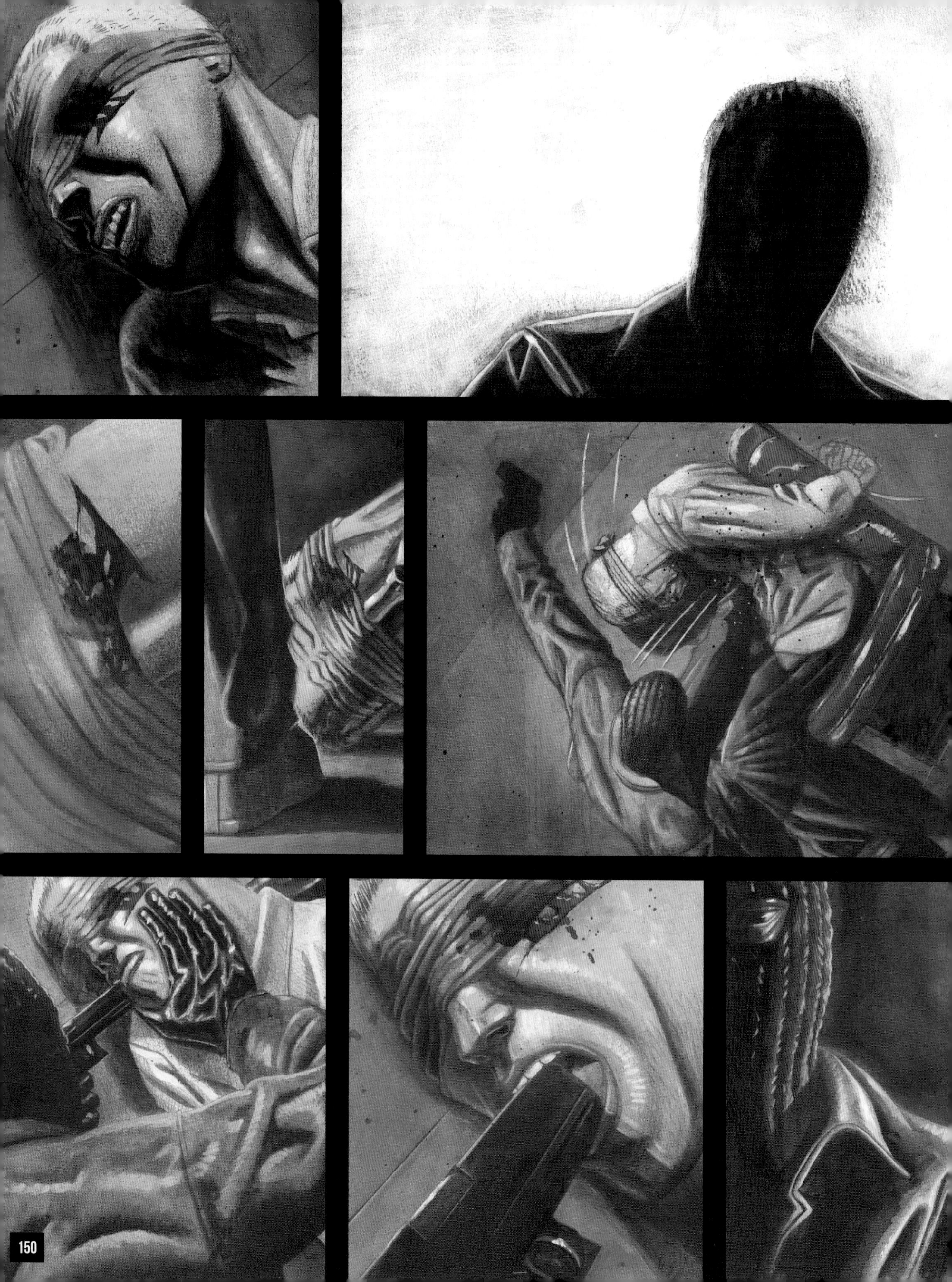

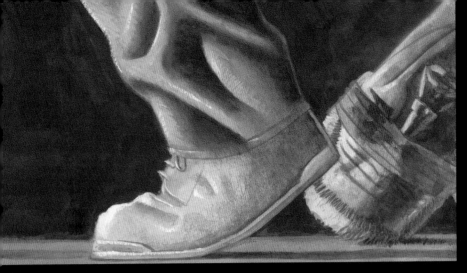

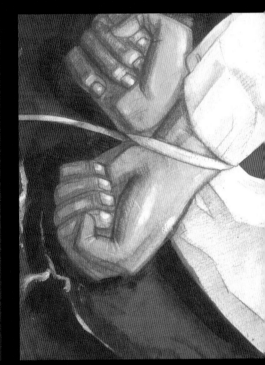
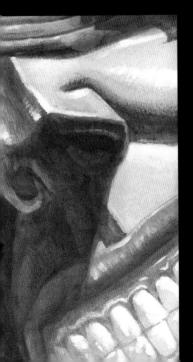
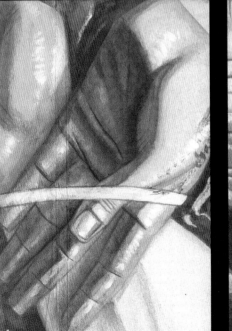
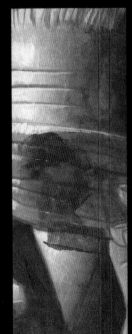

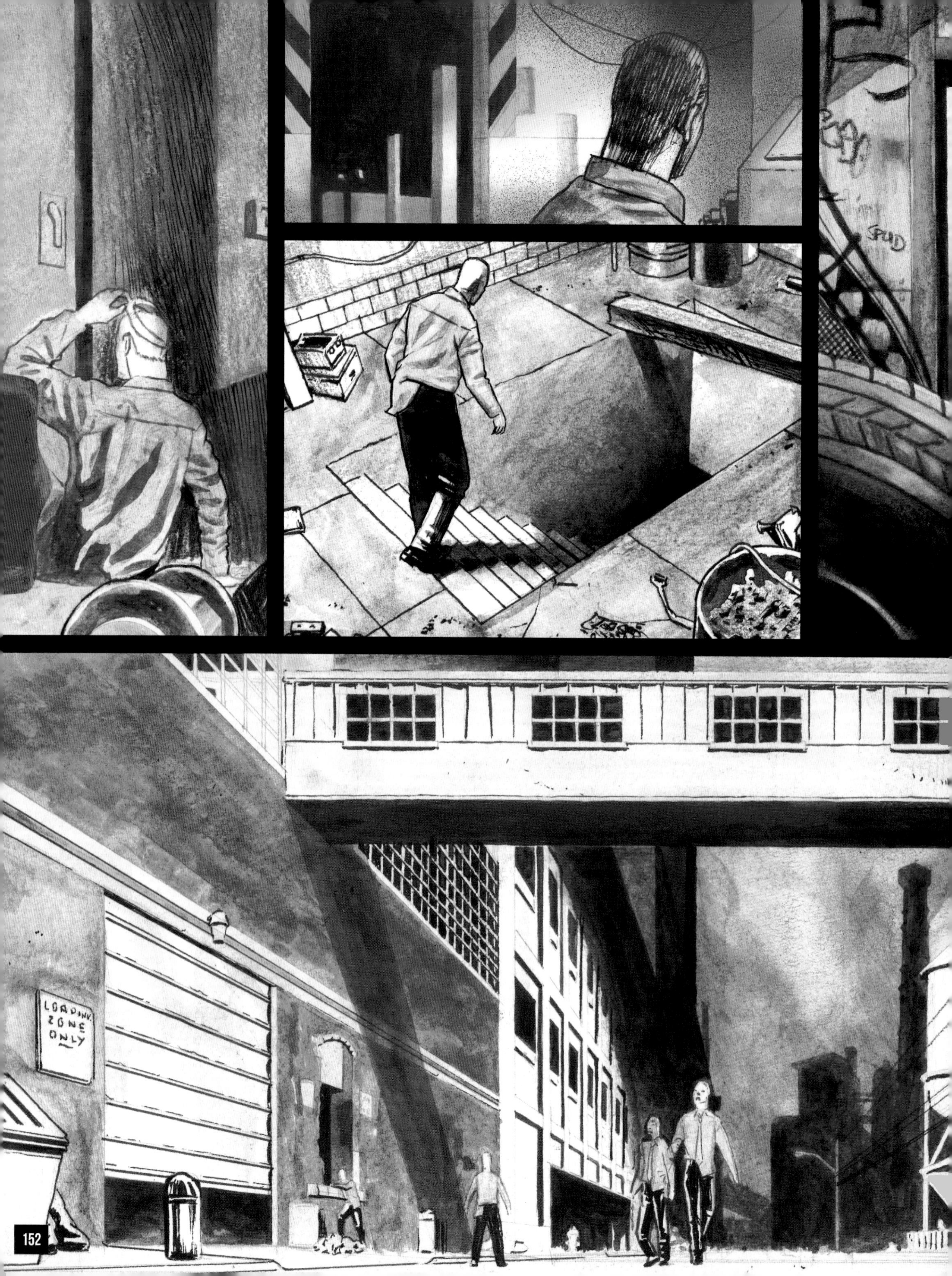
LOADING ZONE ONLY

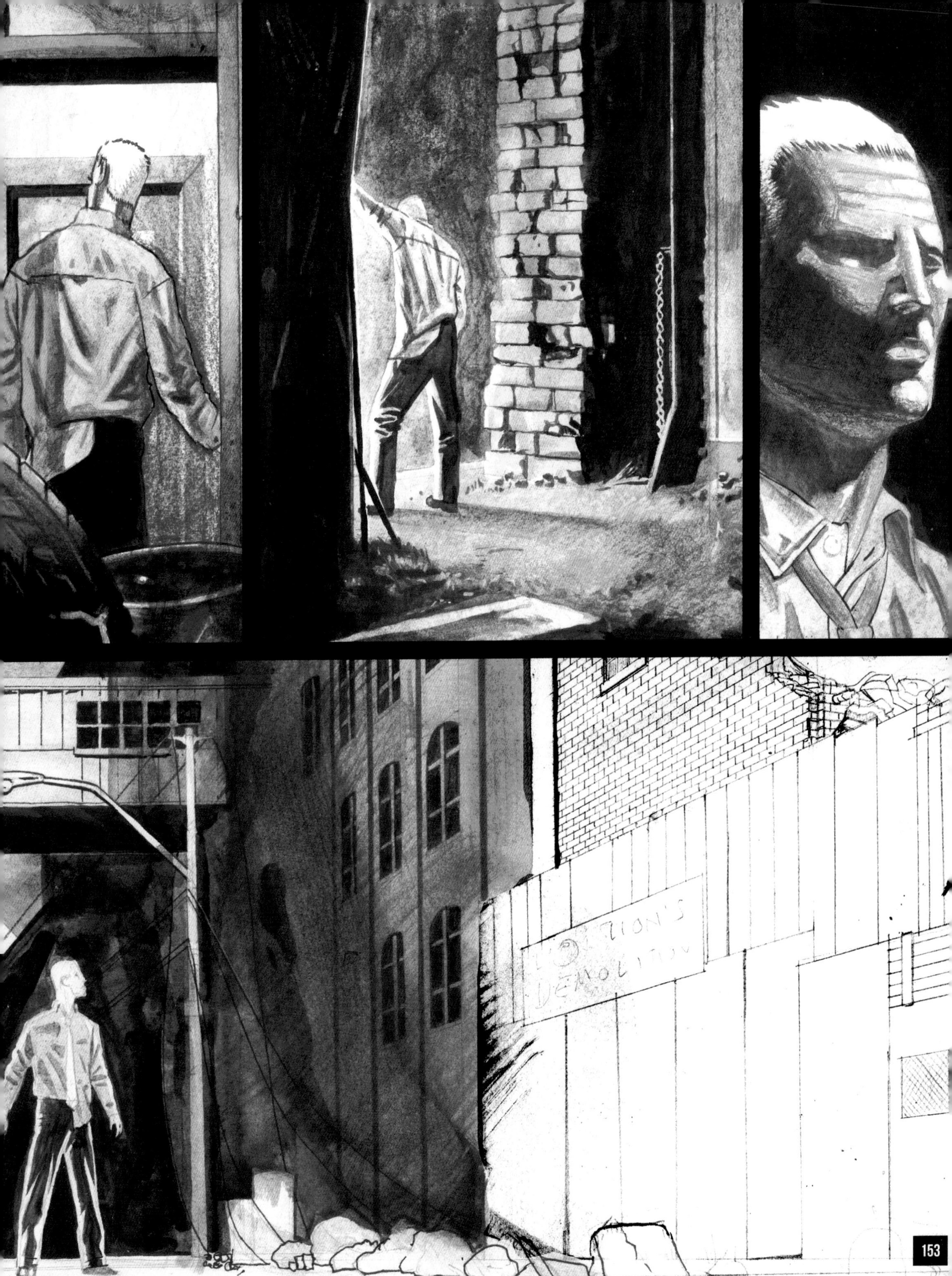
TION'S
DEMOLITION

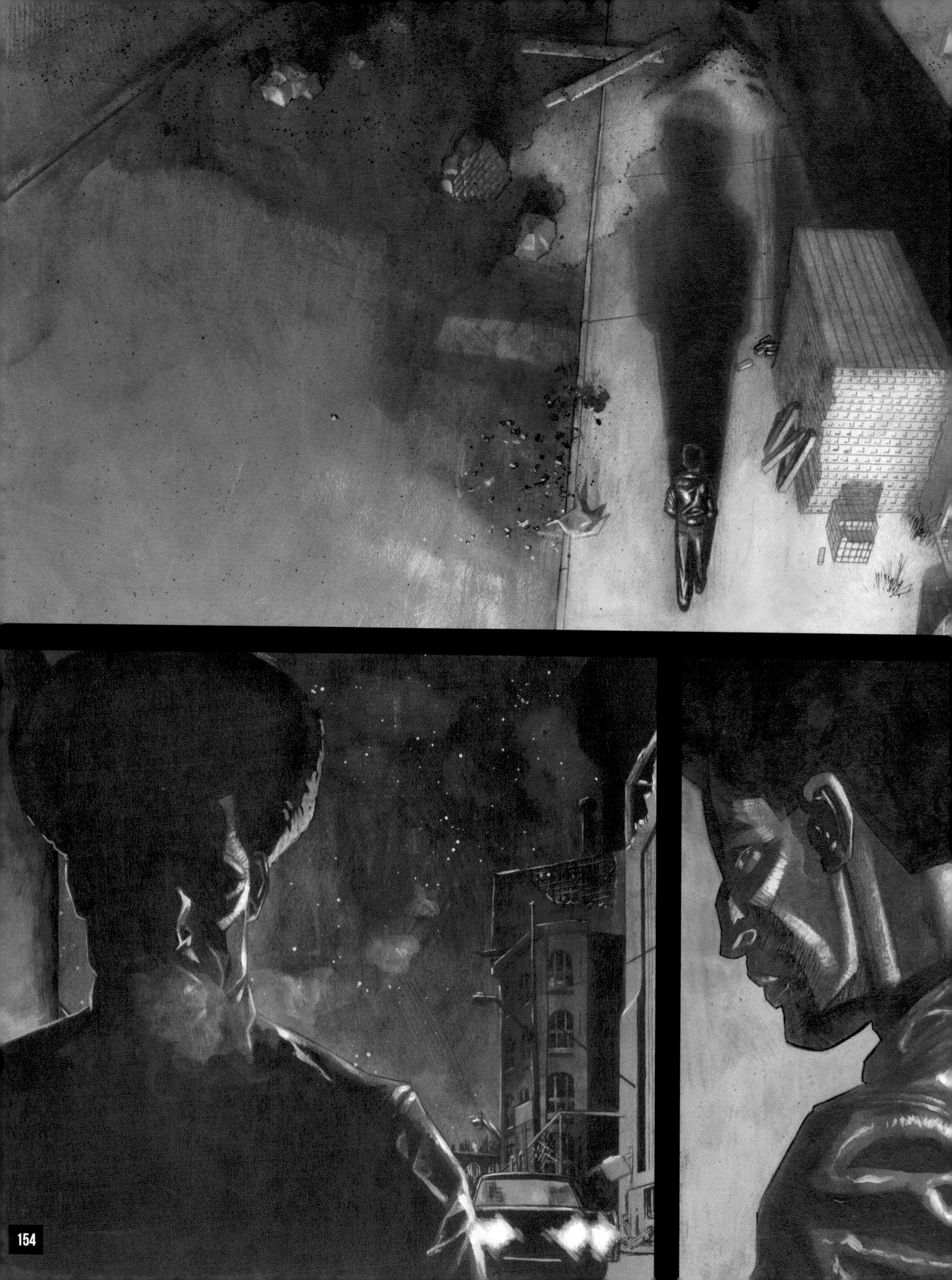

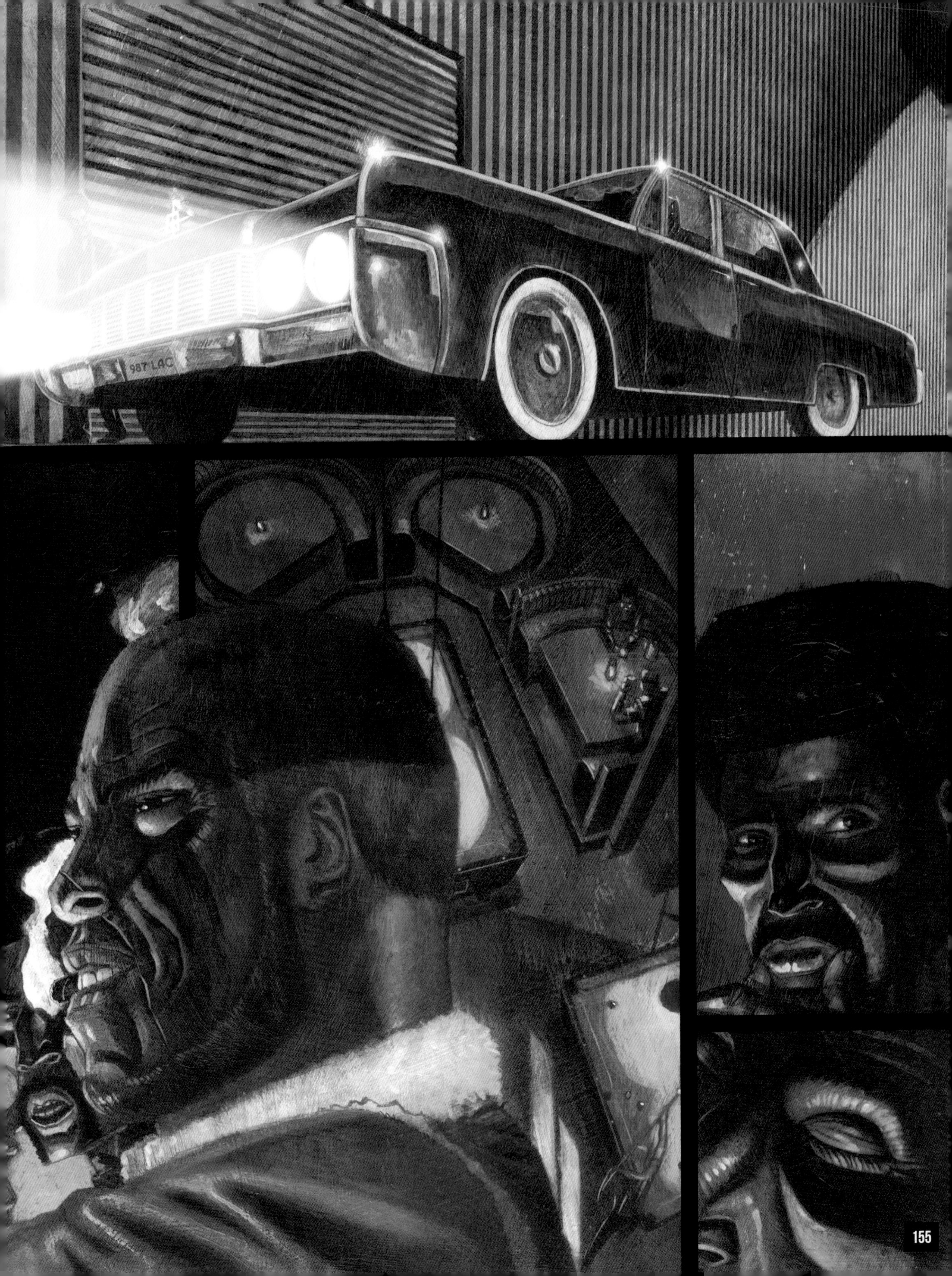
987 LAC

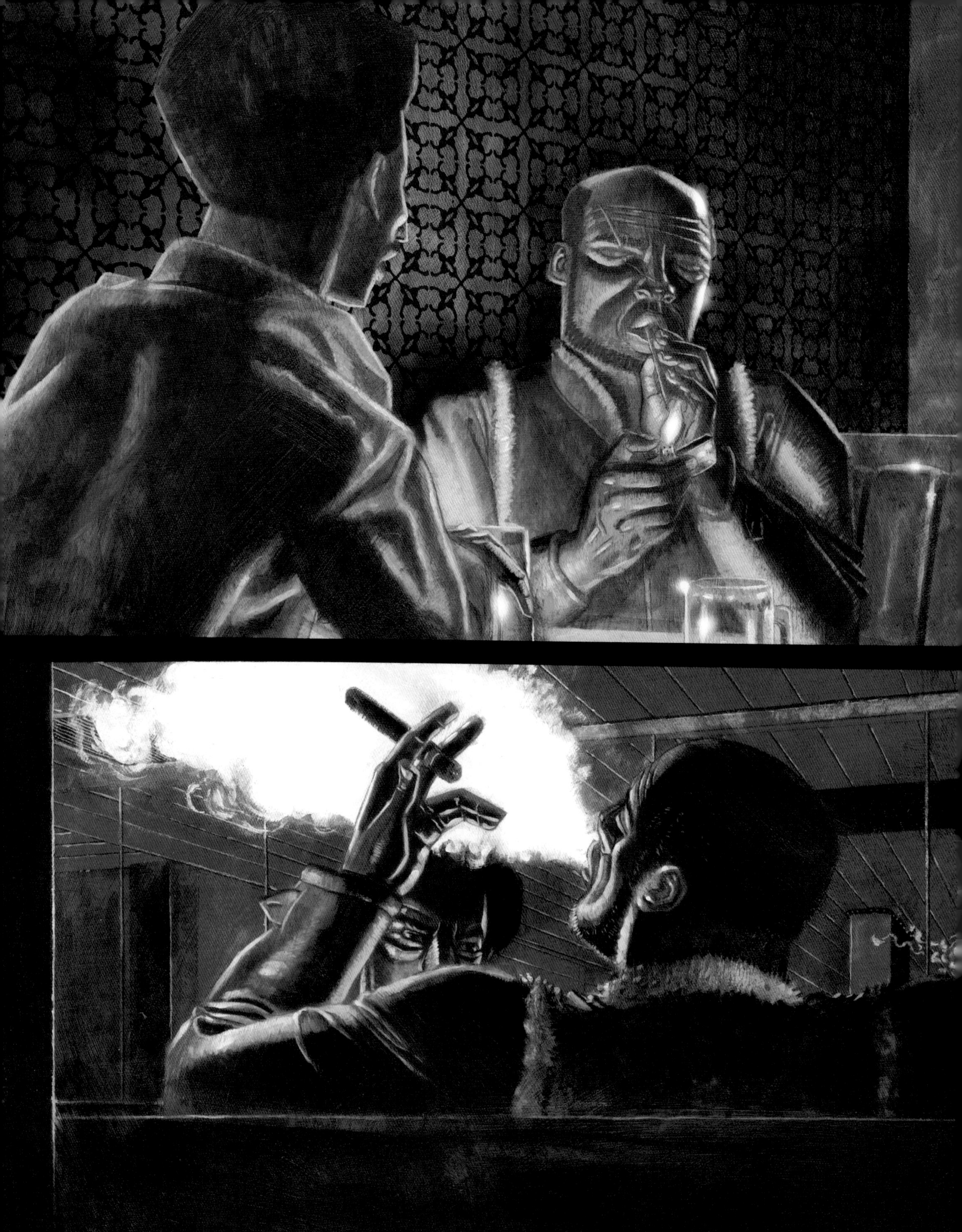

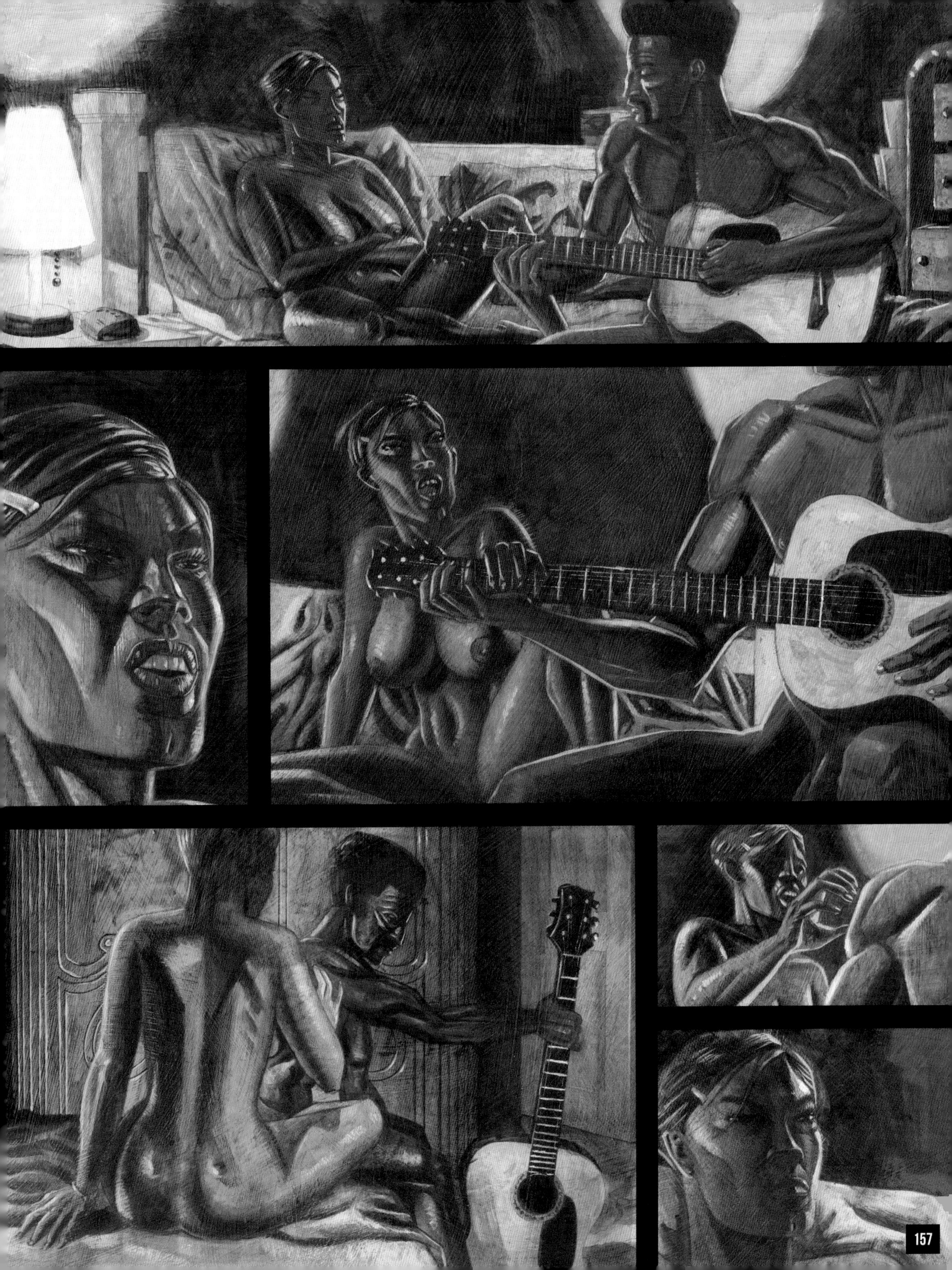

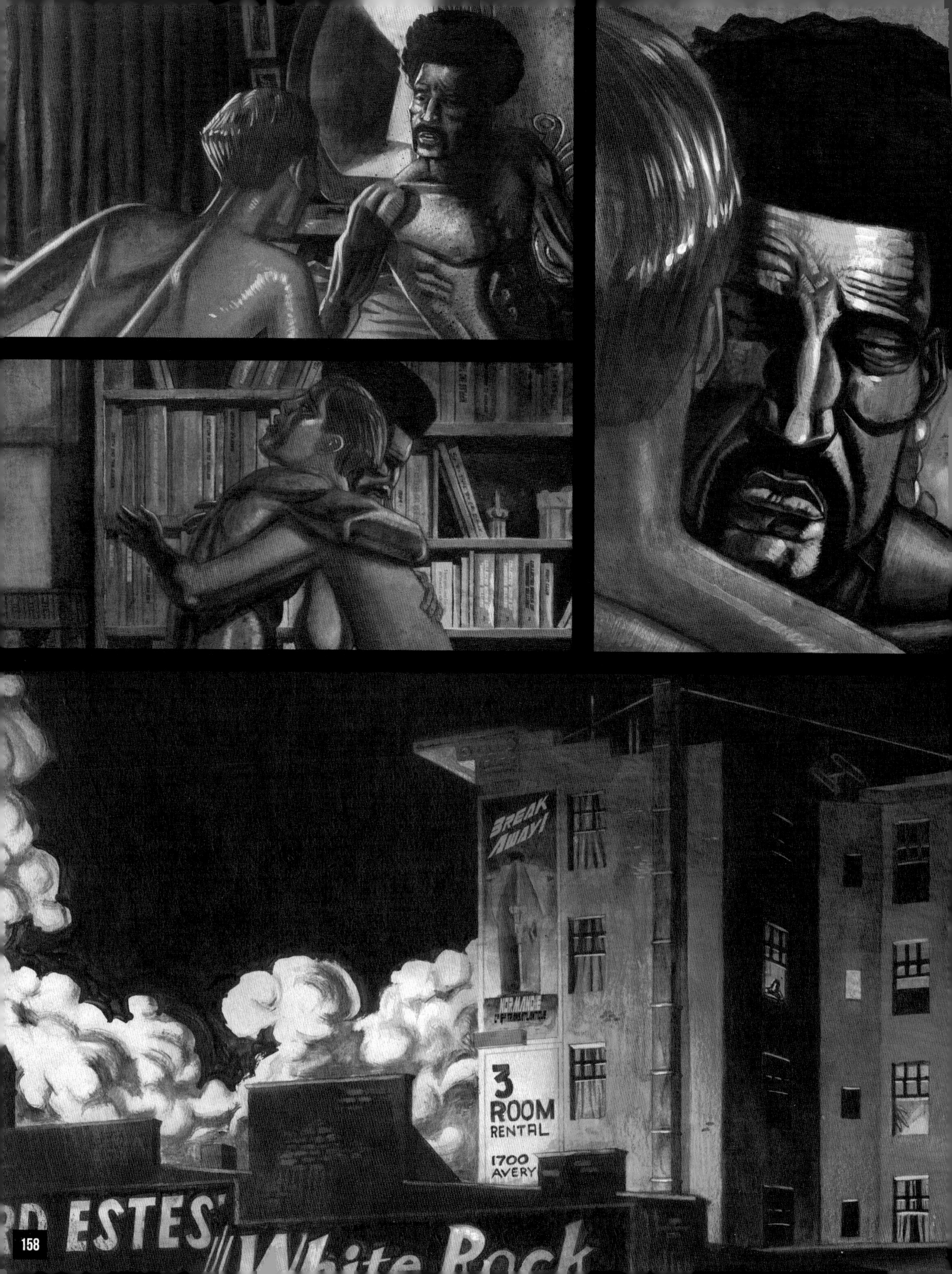
BREAK AWAY!
NORMANDIE
3 ROOM RENTAL
1700 AVERY
D ESTES
White Rock

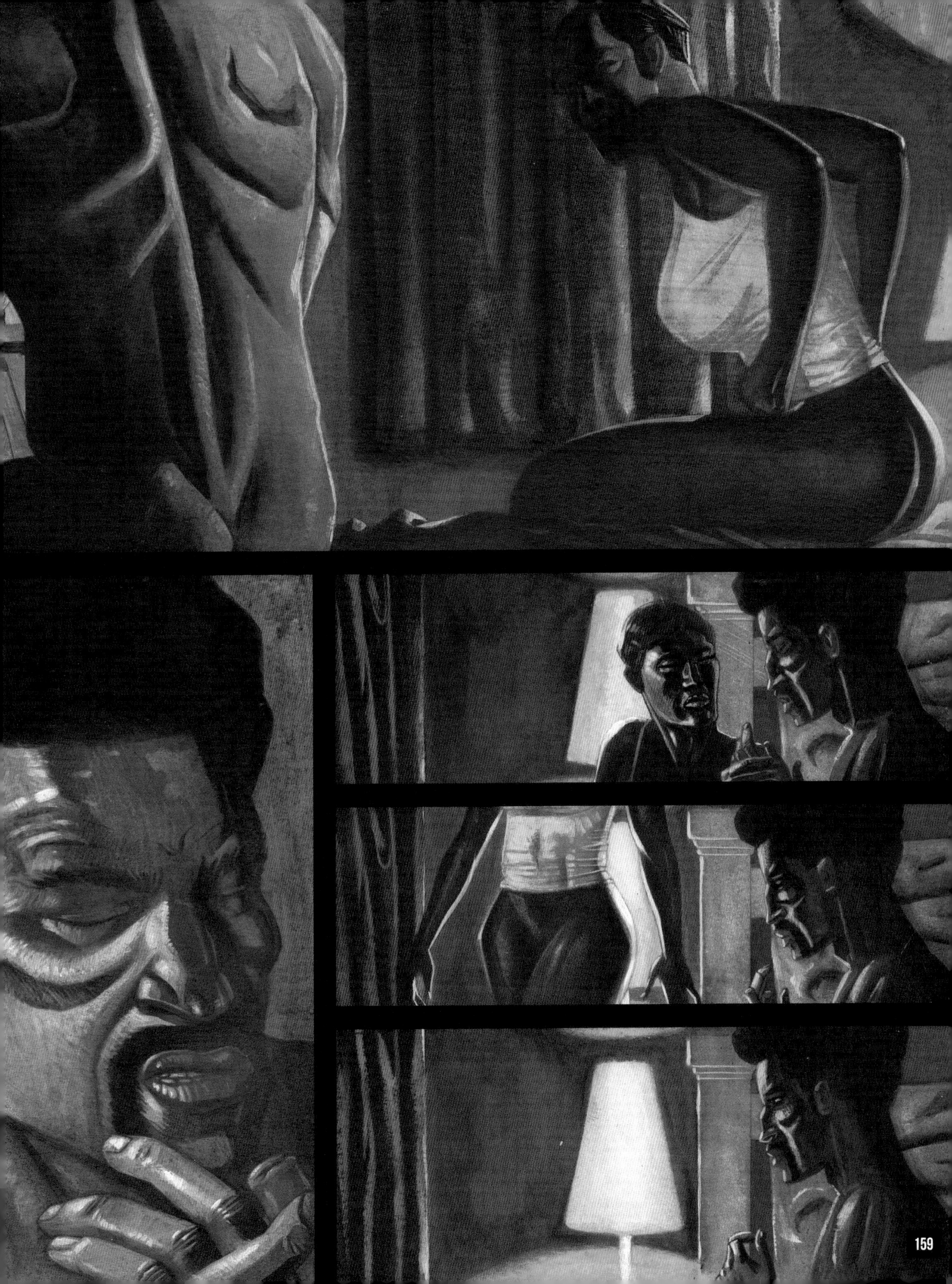

For my Beloved
DYANE KAREN BONCZUK
24 march 1968 ~ 27 june 2017